A CENTENNIAL BOOK

One hundred books
published between 1990 and
1995 bear this special imprint of
the University of California Press.
We have chosen each Centennial Book
as an example of the press's finest
publishing and bookmaking
traditions as we celebrate the
beginning of our second
century

UNIVERSITY OF CALIFORNIA PRESS
Founded in
1893

BLOOD CINEMA

THE RECONSTRUCTION OF NATIONAL IDENTITY IN SPAIN

MARSHA KINDER

UNIVERSITY OF CALIFORNIA PRESS   BERKELEY   LOS ANGELES   LONDON

University of California Press

Berkeley and Los Angeles, California

University of California Press

London, England

Copyright © 1993 by The Regents of the
University of California

Library of Congress Cataloging-in-Publication Data

Kinder, Marsha.

    Blood cinema : the reconstruction of
national identity in Spain / by Marsha Kinder

       p. cm.

    Includes bibliographical references and index.

    ISBN 0-520-08153-6 (alk. paper). — ISBN
0-520-08157-9 (pbk. : alk. paper)

    1. Motion pictures—Spain. 2. National
characteristics, Spanish, in motion pictures. I. Title.

  PN1993.5.S7K5 1993

   791.43′0946—dc20   92-31697

                       CIP

Printed in the United States of America

1 2 3 4 5 6 7 8 9

This book is dedicated
to the memory of my dear
friend and former collaborator,
Katherine Singer Kovács,
who first asked me to write
about Spanish cinema;

to my good friend,
José Luis Borau, whose
fascinating film *Furtivos* first
made me want to write
a book on the subject;

and to my husband,
Nicolás Bautista, and our
children, Gabriela and Victor
Aurelio, whose heritage has
been greatly enriched by
Spanish culture.

▪ CONTENTS

▪ ACKNOWLEDGMENTS

The person to whom I am most deeply indebted is José Luis Borau, who has been a great source of knowledge, encouragement, and assistance throughout the six-year period that I have been working on this book. We first met in Los Angeles in 1982, when he came to show *Furtivos* at the University of Southern California School of Cinema-Television. I began to realize the extraordinary range and depth of his knowledge when I interviewed him at that time, and that realization has been reconfirmed over the years through many intense conversations about cinema and culture. He also has helped me to meet many other key figures in Spanish cinema and to obtain the permissions that made the CD–ROM possible. He was the first person to read an early draft of the manuscript and to offer valuable suggestions on how it might be improved.

I am grateful for the total cooperation and enthusiastic support I have received from the Spanish Ministry of Culture—particularly from Carmelo Romero, who helped me at virtually every stage of my work, and Fernando Méndez-Leite, the former general director of cinema, who first made it possible for me to see many films at the ministry. I am also deeply indebted to the Filmoteca Española where I did a great deal of my research—particularly to its director, José María Prado García, who made it possible for me to see films and to reproduce some of the excerpts on the CD–ROM, and to Dolores Devesa at the library, who was extraordinarily generous and efficient in helping me locate the specific information, journals, and stills that I needed. Unless otherwise indicated, all of the illustrations that appear in the book were obtained from the extensive collection at the Filmoteca.

I also want to express my thanks to three institutions in Spain and the United States that have financially supported this project. In Spain, the U.S.-Spanish Joint Committee for Educational and Cultural Exchange awarded me a grant in 1986-87 which enabled me to start doing the research for the book; at my home institution, the University of Southern California, a grant from the Faculty Innovative Research Fund supported my writing during summer 1989; and in 1992, the Program for Cultural Cooperation between Spain's Ministry of Culture and United States' Universities partially funded both the publication of the book and the production of the related interactive CD–ROM.

Several scholars working on Spanish cinema read earlier versions of various chapters and gave me valuable critical response. First among them is my close friend, the late Katherine Singer Kovács, who collaborated with me on organizing the first scholarly panel on Spanish cinema at the annual meeting of the Society for Cinema Studies in Bozeman, Montana, in 1988 (where we both read selections from the chapters we were working on) and a retrospective in 1989 called Spanish Cinema: The Politics of Family and Gender, which included many of the films we were both writing about at the time. Unfortunately, she did not live long enough to complete her own book on Spanish cinema, which is a great loss to the field. I am also grateful to her husband, Steven Kovács, who made many of her books and journals on Spanish cinema available to me and who, as the producer of *Río abajo*, also provided valuable information for chapter 7.

I want to give special thanks to Marvin D'Lugo for his perceptive reading of my manuscript and his valuable suggestions for improving it and for sharing with me many of his videotapes. He has been an important influence on my work, not only through his wonderful book on Saura and his published essays but also through the many stimulating conversations we have had over the years about Spanish cinema, regionalism, and theory, which helped to clarify many of my own ideas. Kathleen M. Vernon, Agustín Sánchez Vidal, Román Gubern, Victor Fuentes, and Jénaro Talens have also given me supportive readings of parts (or all) of the manuscript as well as useful suggestions.

Several important figures from Spanish cinema (in addition to José Luis Borau) spent time talking to me about their work and its relation to Spanish history and culture—José Luis Alcaine, Pedro Almodóvar, Pablo G. del Amo, Vicente Aranda, Jaime de Armiñán, Carmen Maura, Luis Megino, Marisa Paredes, and Carlos Saura.

I also want to thank Margaret Morse, who suggested a few sources that proved to be very useful, and my students at the USC School of Cinema-Television in a wide range of courses on national cinemas (Spanish, Italian, French, Eastern European), auteurs (Buñuel), international film history, and theory who have listened to earlier versions of these ideas and raised many excellent questions.

At the University of California Press, I want to thank my sponsoring editor, Ed Dimendberg, my copy editor, Sheila Berg, who helped make my text more readable, and the managing editor, Rebecca Frazier, who supervised its production, and Charles Tashiro, who did the index.

Finally, I am grateful to my husband, Nicolás Bautista, for some of the translations he did when I first started my research and for encouraging me to improve my own Spanish, thereby enabling me to say that, unless otherwise indicated, the translations from Spanish to English are my own. I also want to thank him and our son, Victor, for accompanying me to Spain and for their patience and emotional support during the time when I was writing this book. Their presence made me feel a blood relation to Spanish cinema and culture.

Victor Erice's *El espíritu de la colmena* (The Spirit of the Beehive, 1973).

BEYOND THE BOUNDARIES OF A NATIONAL CINEMA

Blood Cinema: a title that is likely to evoke Lorca's *Blood Wedding* and Saura's cinematic adaptation of that work as well as familiar images by Goya—of *Saturn Devouring His Son, Duel with Cudgels,* and *The Third of May*—and the frequent reference to them in Spanish films. And beyond these specific allusions, a national cinema that is frequently described as excessive in its graphic depiction of violence and obsessive in its treatment of incestuous relations. And beyond the cinematic context, a nation whose history is marked by a fratricidal civil war with bloody repercussions, by a long period of Francoism that glamorized death, by a deep immersion in the conventions of the Counter-Reformation that fetishized the bleeding wounds of Christ and other martyrs, and by a "Black Legend" of cruelty and violence dating back to the Inquisition and the Conquest which Spaniards have tried to overcome for the past five hundred years. And beyond this Spanish specificity, the question of whether the cinema of any nation carries distinguishing traces of its own unique history, culture, race, or blood and the correlative issues of how these "fictional" concepts of national identity are constructed through cinema and other forms of popular culture.

Blood Cinema is not another English-language historical survey of filmmaking in Spain. Yet it draws and depends on the existence of such works, especially on Peter Besas's *Behind the Spanish Lens: Spanish Cinema under Fascism and Democracy,* which was one of the first, and John Hopewell's *Out of the Past: Spanish Cinema after Franco,* which is probably the best.[1] Though not organized strictly chronologically, *Blood Cinema* does have a historical trajectory, starting in Part I with a focus on the 1950s and ending in Part IV with an emphasis on the late 1980s and early 1990s but drawing examples from earlier periods and moving freely backward and forward throughout.

Nor is *Blood Cinema* an auteur study focusing exclusively on well-known filmmakers like Saura, Luis Buñuel, and Pedro Almodóvar.[2] Instead, the films are usually chosen to illustrate broader conceptual issues, and they are drawn from the authorized Francoist cinema as well as from the cinema of opposition and of the post-Franco period. The two chapters that do focus on selected works of single auteurs (chapter 6, on Buñuel, and chapter 7, on José Luis Borau) present these figures as case studies for the broader issue of exile and diaspora. As a consequence, several of Spain's most accomplished filmmakers—such as Saura, Almodóvar, Victor Erice, Manuel Gutiérrez Aragón, Vicente Aranda, Jaime de Armiñán, and Luis García Berlanga—and many of their best works receive less attention than some readers might expect or desire.

Nor is *Blood Cinema* a study of a film movement strictly within a national context, like the New Spanish Cinema, which was the focus of a special issue of *Quarterly Review of Film Studies* edited by Katherine S. Kovács in spring 1983 (the first book-length work on Spanish cinema published in the United States). Yet it does stress the importance of that movement in its cultural specificity and expands it beyond its usual location in the 1960s.

Drawing on the historical divisions made by Robin W. Fiddian and Peter W. Evans, I would distinguish among three phases of the New Spanish Cinema. Fiddian and Evans observe,

It is possible to perceive four clearly delimited stages in the country's economic history between 1939 and 1982, with significant points of articulation in the years 1951, 1962, and 1973. Spain's domestic political history as mapped out by the radical reorganisation of government ministries in July 1959 and July 1962, the assassination of Admiral Carrero Blanco and his replacement as Prime Minister by Arias Navarro in December 1973, and the victory of Felipe González's Socialists in the democratic elections of October 1982, illustrates the same trends, as does a particularly important set of relations between the State and the Church which underwent major transformations in 1953 (when the régime signed a new Concordat with the Vatican), 1961–63 (upon the publication of two encyclicals by Pope John XXIII), and 1971 (when the Joint Assembly of Bishops and Priests issued a communiqué which was sternly critical of some of the policies of the Franco régime). This sketchy outline . . . confirms the practical value of the conventional historiographic tool of analysis-by-decade. At the same time, it draws attention . . . to certain crucial dates . . . which may be regarded as turning points in contemporary Spanish affairs . . . allowing us to perceive [the texts discussed here] as events embedded in a highly complex field of historical and cultural forces.[3]

Mapped against this historical grid, my reading of the New Spanish Cinema dates the first phase between 1951 and 1961. Beginning with an Italian film week in Madrid in 1951 (which featured a program of neorealist films that strongly influenced Berlanga and Juan Antonio Bardem) and ending with Buñuel's return to Spain in 1961 to make *Viridiana,* this period includes the founding of Spanish television in 1956 and the Salamanca Congress in 1955, where Spanish filmmakers from diverse ideological backgrounds came together to reject the Francoist cinema and to demand a new kind of cinema that could address contemporary social problems in Spain and achieve international recognition abroad.

The second phase occurs between 1962 and 1972, beginning with Franco's appointment of Manuel Fraga Iribarne as the new minister of information and tourism, a position he held from 1962 to 1969 (the period of *apertura,* or cultural opening, usually associated with the New Spanish Cinema). One of the ways Fraga helped to accelerate the liberalization of cultural production was by appointing cinephile José María García Escudero general director of cinema, a position he had already held from September 1951 to February 1952 (when he promoted the neorealist model) but from which he had been forced to resign. Now that Spain was moving toward greater integration with Europe, he was able to accomplish more tangible goals. He reformed government policies on censorship by making the rules more concrete; he reorganized the Instituto de Investigaciones y Experiencias Cinematográficas (where Berlanga and Bardem had studied), turning it into the influential Escuela Oficial de Cinematografía (EOC), which trained an entire generation of filmmakers; and he considerably expanded the government subvention system, not only increasing the amounts of the grants but also changing the basis of selection from political issues of "National interest" to aesthetic concerns of "Special interest" so as to privilege sophisticated art films. All these measures led to the government's active promotion of what García Escudero called the New Spanish Cinema—a movement that proved to be an effective vehicle for liberalizing Spain's image abroad, especially through innovative, award-winning works like Berlanga's *El verdugo* (The Executioner, 1964), Miguel Picazo's *La Tía Tula* (Aunt Tula, 1964), Basilio Martín Patino's *Nueve cartas a Berta* (Nine Letters to Berta, 1965), Saura's *La caza* (The Hunt, 1965) and *Peppermint frappé* (1967), Buñuel's *Tristana* (1970), and Armiñán's *Mi querida señorita* (My Dearest Lady, 1971).

But in 1969, this period of liberalization was seriously disrupted by the Matesa scandal, which intensified Spain's economic crisis and led to the firing of Fraga. Hopewell (1986:80) reports, "On 10 August 1969 the government admitted that credits of about L80 million granted to the textile firm, Matesa, for the export of machinery had in fact been used for private investment abroad. Fraga was slightly too keen to publish the involvement of three Opus Dei Cabinet Ministers in the affair. Franco sacked him." Fraga was replaced by the extremely reactionary Alfredo Sánchez Bella, who held the post from October 1969 to June 1973. While he was in office, rigorous censorship was restored and government subventions to filmmakers were severely cut. As Hopewell notes, these cuts were particularly devastating since they occurred precisely when the Spanish film industry was just beginning to experience serious competition from television. The sixties ended with a political and economic crisis that went far beyond the Matesa affair. As Fiddian and Evans observe, "Divisive debates about the legalising of political associations took place between 1967 and 1969 against a backcloth of severe economic difficulties, open rebellion by the student population in April 1968, and a state of emergency imposed in January 1969"—conflicts that structure works like Saura's *Stress es tres, tres* (Stress Is Three, Three, 1968) and Elías Querejeta's anthology film, *Los desafíos* (The Challenges, 1969).

The third phase of the New Spanish Cinema occurs between 1973 and 1982 and moves into the post-Franco period. Although by this time many Spaniards perceived the New Spanish Cinema to be over, it was now becoming more widely recognized internationally. Beginning with the assassination of Franco's anointed right-wing successor Admiral Luis Carrero Blanco by Basque terrorists in 1973, which assured that Spain's move toward liberalization would continue after Franco's death in 1975, this period of "soft dictatorship" (or *dictablanda*) includes courageous, ground-breaking films, many of which obtained critical acclaim and distribution abroad, such as Erice's *El espíritu de la colmena* (Spirit of the Beehive) and Saura's *La prima Angélica* (Cousin Angélica) in 1973, Armiñán's *El amor del Capitán Brando* (The Love of Captain Brando) in 1974, and Borau's *Furtivos* (Poachers) and Saura's *Cría cuervos* (Raise Ravens) in 1975. It also includes blatantly subversive films from the period of transition that immediately followed Franco's death, such as Jaime Chávarri's *El desencanto* (Disenchantment, 1976), and *A un dios desconocido* (To an Unknown God, 1977); Vicente Aranda's *Cambio de sexo* (Sex Change), José Luis Garci's *Asignatura pendiente* (Pending Exam), and Gutiérrez Aragón's *Camada negra* (Black Brood), also in 1977; Saura's *Los ojos vendados* (Blindfolded Eyes), José Juan Bigas Luna's *Bilbao,* and Eloy de la Iglesia's *El diputado* (The Deputy) in 1978; and Pilar Miró's *El crimen de Cuenca* (The Crime of Cuenca) in 1979. The terrorist bombing of theaters that were playing *Camada negra* and the temporary banning of *El crimen de Cuenca* because of its attack against the Guardia Civil clearly demonstrated that political censorship was still operative during the transition. As soon as the Socialists were voted into power in 1982, they appointed the controversial Miró as general director of cinema, dramatically demonstrating that censorship was long gone and that a new era was beginning both in politics and cinema. One dimension of this change in the 1980s was the acceleration of Spain's integration into the European community and into the emerging configurations of global mass media. This acceleration was at least a contributing factor to Spain winning its first Oscar (significantly in 1983) for the earnest, yet sentimental *Volver a empezar* (To Begin Again, 1982), and to the stunning international success (even in the daunting North American market) of Saura's dance trilogy and of Almodóvar's outrageous comic melodramas.

Blood Cinema emphasizes the international dimensions of the New Spanish Cinema. Like Homi Bhabha's *Nation and Narration,* it traces a movement "from the problematic unity of the nation to the articulation of cultural difference in the construction of an *international* perspective."[4] It assumes that every national film movement seeks to win legitimation as the "valid" representative of its culture by striving for international recognition—the way revolutionary governments seek to be recognized by other nations. Virtually all film movements attack the dominant cinema within their own nation as nonrepresentative and unrealistic or as too reflective of foreign influences, yet ironically they themselves usually turn to other marginal cinemas within a foreign context for conventions to be adapted to their own cultural specificity. This was true of Italian neorealism, which turned to French poetic realism. It was true of the French *nouvelle vague,* which turned to Hollywood B movies and to outsiders like Rossellini and Lang. And in the 1950s—that first phase of the New Spanish Cinema—it was true of Spanish filmmakers like Bardem and Berlanga, who dialogized the neorealist aesthetic against the conventions of Hollywood melodrama. And at the end of the decade, it was also true of Saura, who tried to signal the break from Bardem and Berlanga and the move toward a second phase by claiming the exiled Buñuel and the French new wave as his models instead of neorealism. And at the beginning of the third phase, it was also true of Erice and Armiñán, who dramatized very concretely in *El espíritu de la colmena* and *El amor del Capitán Brando* how Hollywood films and stars were culturally reinscribed by Spanish spectators living under Francoist repression.

In contrast to the New Spanish Cinema, most of the European film movements that emerged during the post–World War II era, whether in Western or Eastern Europe, were struggling to demonstrate their independence, not only from the dominant cinema at home but also from the hegemonic power (either the U.S. or the USSR) in whose sphere they were placed by the Yalta treaty. Simultaneously in the international sphere, they also tried to distinguish their own national culture from those other countries in a similar position (e.g., Czechs as opposed to Poles or Hungarians and French as opposed to Italians or West Germans). But since Spain had stayed out of the war and was locked in hermetic isolation under the Francoist regime, the New Spanish Cinema could turn to the cultural productions of any other nation as a means of escaping the Francoist hegemony. Within all these national contexts, critics, historians, and participants frequently argued over whether it was really a coherent movement, that is, one with shared goals and aesthetic principles. But this essentialist argument is not really an important issue. What is more significant was the break from the dominant cinema within the nation and the international acknowledgment of that functional difference.

Using Spain as a case study, this book seeks to explore and problematize the concept of a national cinema, claiming that it must be read against the local/global interface, which has become increasingly important in the new world order of the 1980s and 1990s. This interface operates in every national cinema, primarily because the film medium has always been an important vehicle for constructing images of a unified national identity out of regional and ethnic diversity and for transmitting them both within and beyond its national borders and also because from its inception, the history of cinema has always involved a fierce international competition for world markets. This competition has been intensified at certain key historical moments—the coming of sound at the end of the 1920s, the restructuring of the world order at the end of World War II, the globalization of mass culture in the post–cold war era of the late 1980s and early 1990s—moments that will be stressed in this study.

I have chosen Spain for my case study primarily because, despite the richness of its film history and its success at international festivals, with very few exceptions, Spanish cinema is largely unknown or ignored in the English-speaking world. In fact, it is virtually omitted from most of the currently popular English-language one-volume texts of world film history, which necessarily depend on the primary research of others.[5] This dearth of critical and scholarly attention is obviously linked to material conditions of distribution. Except for the works of Buñuel, Saura, and Almodóvar, few Spanish films have been widely distributed in the United States, or, for that matter, anywhere else outside of Spain.

Thus, as a North American scholar trying to help demarginalize Spanish cinema, my own work (like that of Besas, Hopewell, Virginia Higginbotham, Kovács, and D'Lugo) is immediately absorbed as part of the government-sponsored culture industry—a dynamic that Thomas Elsaesser has brilliantly analyzed in the context of Germany.[6] His analysis is also applicable to Spain, where the Socialist Ministry of Culture has been active in financially supporting the promotion of its cinema and auteurs for world consumption—a tradition that was also operative under García Escudero. As Christian Metz observes in *The Imaginary Signifier,* the film historian frequently finds herself becoming an intellectual publicist for the texts she describes: "Often, by unexpected paths, unperceived by those who have quite unintentionally taken them, . . . writings on film become another form of cinema advertising and at the same time a linguistic appendage of the institution itself."[7] I cannot deny this dimension of my own work; in fact, far from being "unperceived," I hope to demonstrate that it is part of the process being described—

the reconstruction of national identity through the production, promotion, and reception of popular culture.

In working toward the demarginalization of Spanish cinema, I choose not to focus exclusively on industrial history or the distribution of Spanish films in foreign markets (in order, for example, to update and globalize Santiago Pozo's valuable 1984 study, *La industria del cine en España: Legislación y aspectos económicos, 1896–1970*) but rather to apply many of the theoretical concepts that have been developed over the past twenty years in film studies, concepts that are not present in the historical surveys by Besas, Hopewell, and Higginbotham but that inform the writings of scholars like Marvin D'Lugo, Kathleen M. Vernon, Robin Fiddian, Peter Evans, Victor Fuentes, and Román Gubern. In this sense, *Blood Cinema* takes a transcultural approach, which leads me to the second reason for focusing on Spain.

I am convinced, and I hope to convince my readers, that a knowledge of Spanish cinema alters and enriches one's understanding of world cinema.[8] I have been convinced not by Spanish film scholars focusing exclusively on the national context but by three works that have nothing to do with Spain: Noel Burch's *To the Distant Observer: Form and Meaning in Japanese Cinema,* which demonstrates that an intensive focus on certain issues within a single national context can substantially alter the way one conceptualizes the history of world cinema and its reception; Elsaesser's *New German Cinema: A History,* which shows how film can be used as a means of ideological reinscription both by filmmakers struggling against a dual hegemony in domestic and international markets and by the government that hopes to change the international image of the nation; and Kay Schaffer's *Women and the Bush: Forces of Desire in the Australian Cultural Tradition,* which illustrates how "master narratives" like the Oedipal plot can be inflected by a specific cultural context and a particular national imaginary. Like those three works, *Blood Cinema* seeks to decenter a national cinema by reading it in relation to several other cultures both within and beyond its own national borders, both in the regional and global contexts.

For this reason, my book addresses at least two different audiences—those who already know Spanish culture and Spanish film history but who are unfamiliar with English-language film studies and those who already know film studies and culture theory but who are basically unfamiliar with Spanish history, culture, and cinema. For the former, my goal is to demonstrate that theoretical approaches currently being used in English-language film studies can lead to new and valuable readings of Spanish texts both in their local and global contexts and that an "outsider" can sometimes perceive patterns that are less visible to those inside the culture. Since I am the only non-Hispanist (at least, the only scholar based in a film school rather than a Spanish department) who is currently writing on Spanish cinema, I hope to turn this factor (which many might see as a limitation) into an advantage. For the latter, I seek to demonstrate that a knowledge of Spanish cinema is as essential to those in film studies as a knowledge of French, Italian, German, or any other national cinema.

In this way, I am trying to bridge the gap between two quite different kinds of discourse with very different assumptions, which leads to certain difficulties concerning accessibility and the choice of language, methodology, and texts. For those unfamiliar with English-language film studies, I have tended to quote at length from theoretical sources and to include definitions and explanations of key assumptions that would probably be unnecessary for other readers. The greater difficulty arises with those unfamiliar with Spanish cinema and culture, for I am writing about films that few of these readers have seen.

Although the main lines of my argument are based on the viewing of hundreds of Spanish films, I have purposely avoided long lists of unfamiliar titles, brief plot summaries, and superficial critiques. Rather, I have chosen to develop my argument through the close textual analysis of a relatively small body of films, the analysis of which should be clear even to readers who have not seen them, especially when supplemented by many still photographs as illustrations. In addition to those works described in great detail, I keep returning to another group of key texts—including, for example, *La aldea maldita* (The Cursed Village, 1929), *Raza* (Race, 1941), and *Marcelino, pan y vino* (Marcelino, Bread and Wine, 1954)—so that I can provide the plot summary and basic description once and then frequently refer to the film without repeating that information. Because of my focus on the local/global interface, I have tended to choose films that have been seen outside of Spain, that have won recognition at international festivals, or that have played a significant role within the film history of the nation or region.

Despite all these strategies, the problem posed by the readers' unfamiliarity with the films still remains. Thus, I arrived at a solution that draws on the current state of interactive technology and that is particularly well suited to this project. *Blood Cinema* is accompanied by a CD–ROM (specially produced for this purpose), which contains brief excerpts from fifteen of the films being discussed, with commentaries that address my dual audiences. I am unaware of any other book in film studies that uses a companion CD–ROM in this way.

The book is organized around four basic issues that problematize the notion of a national cinema: transcultural reinscription, cultural specificity in the representation of violence and in the Oedipal master narrative, exile and diaspora, and micro- and macroregionalism. While all four of these issues can be applied to most cultural contexts, they are particularly central in Spain.

Part I, Transcultural Reinscription, is concerned with the ideological reinscription of conventions that are borrowed from other cultures and set in conflict with each other, a process of hybridization that is capable of carving out a new aesthetic language. More specifically, this section focuses on the 1950s, that crucial period when Francoist Spain began to emerge from its hermetic isolation and to become allied with the West and when Spanish films began to be seen and to win prizes at international festivals. Drawing on the writings of Mikhail Bakhtin, Ernesto Laclau, and Stanley Payne, these chapters explore how Spanish filmmakers, both on the Right and the Left, used a dialectic interplay between conventions borrowed from Italian neorealism and Hollywood classical cinema to structure their own films and to develop a new language that would help characterize the New Spanish Cinema. This process is traced in considerable detail through four of the most influential films from the first phase of that movement: *Surcos* (Furrows, 1950), *Muerte de un ciclista* (Death of a Cyclist, 1955), *Los golfos* (Hooligans, 1959), and *El cochecito* (The Little Wheelchair, 1960). Then it moves ahead to the third phase, to see how transcultural reinscription of similar conventions functions in Erice's internationally acclaimed film, *El espíritu de la colmena* (1973).

Part II, Blood Cinema: The Representation of Violence in the Spanish Oedipal Narrative, explores the cultural specificity of violence and of the Oedipal narrative within which it is frequently dramatized—two forms of representation that, in any given moment of history, are capable both of reproducing and challenging the dominant social order. This section traces these cultural inflections in Spanish cinema from the 1940s to the present but emphasizes the post-Franco period.

Drawing primarily on René Girard's *Violence and the Sacred* and Tzvetan Todorov's *The Conquest of America: The Question of the Other* but also on the images of Goya and the writings of Sade, Bataille, Deleuze, Unamuno, Ortega y Gasset, and Gubern, chapter 4 argues that one of the distinguishing characteristics of the representation of violence in Spanish cinema is the interplay between primitive sacrifice and modern massacre. While this duality was glossed over by the unifying ideology of the official Francoist cinema, the filmmakers of the opposition explored Spain's paradoxical role as a dual signifier of Europe's barbaric past and dehumanized future. This duality is traced, first, briefly through two Francoist epics of the 1940s, *Raza* (1941) and *Los últimos de Filipinas* (Last Stand in the Philippines, 1945); then, with increasing elaboration through four productions from the oppositional cinema of the 1960s, *Llanto por un bandido* (Lament for a Bandit, 1963), *La caza* (1965), *Peppermint frappé* (1967), and *Los desafíos* (1969); and finally, through a detailed comparative analysis of the two most excessive and threatening examples of violence from the post-Franco period, *Pascual Duarte* (1975) and *Tras el cristal* (Behind the Glass, 1986).

Chapter 5 examines the way Oedipal conflicts within the family were used to speak about political issues and historical events that were repressed from filmic representation during the Francoist era and the way they continue to be used with even greater flamboyance in the post-Franco period after censorship and repression were abolished. Drawing on Spanish literature (particularly nineteenth-century novels by Benito Pérez Galdós and Leopoldo Alas) and paintings (especially by José de Ribera and Francisco de Goya) as well as film, it describes the specific cultural inflection of that master narrative, demonstrating how this Spanish version leads us to new readings of the original myth. Then it traces these patterns through a diverse range of filmmakers, genres, periods, and tones, from Florían Rey's silent classic, *La aldea maldita* (1929), to recent romantic melodramas like Aranda's *Amantes* (Lovers, 1990) and Almodóvar's *¡Atame!* (Tie Me Up, Tie Me Down! 1989) and *Tacones lejanos* (High Heels, 1991). The chapter concludes with a detailed reading of Bigas Luna's notorious *Bilbao* (1978), as one of the most extreme and illuminating examples of the Spanish Oedipal narrative in post-Franco cinema, comparing it with other related texts either from the same year (Armiñán's *Al servicio de la mujer española* [At the Service of Spanish Womanhood]) or from earlier decades (Saura's *Peppermint frappé*, 1967, and Buñuel's *El* [This Strange Passion], 1955).

Part III, Exile and Diaspora, examines the ways in which the idealized cultural unity of any nation is challenged and ideologically reinscribed by the exile and émigré. After briefly sketching how the theme of exile has been represented in Spanish cinema and citing a number of examples of different kinds of exile within the Spanish context (including both Spaniards who left and foreigners who emigrated to Spain), this section focuses on two case studies. Chapter 6 deals with the unique case of Buñuel, who during his three quite different periods of exile became widely perceived (however erroneously) as the single embodiment not only of an international historical movement like surrealist filmmaking but also of two national cinemas—the Mexican and the Spanish. Chapter 7 describes the voluntary aesthetic exile of Borau, which was represented in his choice of Spanish film projects and aesthetic style as well as in his critical and scholarly writing and which was pursued through international coproductions that culminated in *Río abajo,* the film that turned his dream of working in Hollywood into a nightmare.

Part IV, Micro- and Macroregionalism, argues that regionalism is an ideological construct like nationality which refers to areas both smaller and larger than a nation. Functioning co-dependently, the terms "microregionalism" and "macroregionalism" fluidly shift meaning according to context and thereby serve as an effective means both of asserting the subversive force of any marginal position and of destabilizing the hegemonic power of any center. Once regional structures and the center are seen as sliding signifiers, then there is a movement toward the proliferation and empowerment of new structural units both at the micro and macro level. This cluster of issues is explored first in the context of European television, arguing that Spain provides a particularly effective model for the local/global nexus and for the refiguration of cinema and nations. Then it turns to cinema, showing how this regional/national/global interface was addressed, first, in the regional cinema of Cataluña, particularly in a sophisticated Catalan film from the 1940s, *Vida en sombras* (Life in Shadows, 1947–48), then in recent European coproductions like *El sueño del mono loco* (Dream of the Mad Monkey, 1989) and *Boom boom* (1990), and finally, in films (whether made in Madrid, Barcelona, or the Basque region) that reinscribe the "marginal" as the center—a dynamic that is particularly strong in the international success of Almodóvar and Erice.

Having been completed in 1992, *Blood Cinema* assumes that the present moment demands a global perspective on Spain, as has been dramatized by the events designed to celebrate the 500-year anniversary of Columbus's voyage: the world exposition in Seville, the Olympic Games in Barcelona, and the "rediscovery" of a new "Europe without borders," in which Spain is at last recast in a starring role. This perspective was also partially responsible for the selection of Madrid as the site for the important October 1991 opening of the international peace talks on the Middle East (with Bush and Gorbachev in attendance), as Spain had once expelled both the Moslems and the Jews from its "holy land" but now had been peacefully converted into a reasonable modern nation fully committed to global diplomacy. From our post–cold war perspective, we can now look back and realize that just as the Spanish Civil War was the dress rehearsal for the ideological conflicts of World War II, which originally put the cold war into place, Spain's miraculously rapid and bloodless transition from Francoism to democracy also prefigured the other miraculous transitions that were soon to erupt throughout Eastern Europe. One could even argue that Spain's conversion to democracy was one of the first steps in constructing the new world order of the 1990s, a reconfiguration that is bound to have a dramatic impact on mass media around the globe and to seriously challenge the concept of blood cinema.

Lest this sound too utopian, one must remember that 1992 is also the hundred year anniversary of the birth of Franco, who, after seventeen years of dormancy, is beginning to arouse new interest in Spain, especially in the wake of recent economic crises and a resurgence of xenophobic racist attacks on foreign emigres, particularly from North Africa. These dynamics are part of the wave of post–cold war nationalism now sweeping Europe, with its disturbing calls for ethnic cleansing and its threats of proliferating civil wars that have already devastated what was once Yugoslavia. This new nationalism threatens to undermine the recent moves toward European unity and global democracy—a conflict that will undoubtedly be played out in the new configurations of regional, national, and global mass media and that may give new resonance to the phrase, blood cinema.

The image from Vittorio
DeSica's *Ladri di biciclette*
(Bicycle Thief, 1948) that
appears in Basilio Martín
Patino's *Canciones para
después de una guerra* (Songs
for after a War, 1971).

BLOOD CINEMA · I

TRANSCULTURAL REINSCRIPTION

1 ▪ THE IDEOLOGICAL REINSCRIPTION OF NEOREALIST AND HOLLYWOOD CONVENTIONS IN SPANISH CINEMA OF THE 1950S

FALANGIST NEOREALISM IN *SURCOS*

In *Canciones para después de una guerra* (Songs for after a War, 1971), a subversive compilation film on the construction of popular memory in postwar Spain, Patino includes the scene from *Ladri di biciclette* (Bicycle Thief, 1948) in which the father is hanging a poster featuring Rita Hayworth in *Gilda*—a glamorous image that distracts both the worker and the movie spectator from the contemporary Italian street scene where his bicycle is soon to be stolen. The choice of film is hardly surprising; *Bicycle Thief* was one of the first neorealist films shown in Madrid in 1951 during that historic Italian film week that was to prove so influential for filmmakers Bardem and Berlanga and that was to help launch the first phase of the New Spanish Cinema in the 1950s.[1]

It is the choice of scene that is particularly telling. Not only does it contrast the neorealist attempt to document and analyze the immediate socioeconomic realities of the working class with Hollywood's lucrative escape into the pleasurable excesses of spectacle, melodrama, and stardom but this international postwar opposition is shown to be analogous to that familiar Spanish contrast between realistic depiction and false idealization that can be traced back to Golden Age writers like Cervantes, Lope de Vega, Calderón de la

Barca, and Quevedo and that was particularly vivid in Francoist Spain in the aftermath of both the Spanish Civil War and World War II. *Canciones* repeatedly underlines this contrast by cutting from authentic documentary footage, photos, and newspaper clippings of harsh realities in the 1940s to escapist images from newspaper ads, TV commercials, historical epics, folkloric melodramas, and comedies of the same period.[2]

Patino's use of this excerpt from *Bicycle Thief* is emblematic of how the opposing conventions of Italian neorealism and Hollywood were perceived by Spaniards as a choice of how to represent Spain as it emerged from its hermetic isolation after World War II. Historian Raymond Carr observes,

The difficulties of the regime in imposing its "culture" and the consequences of its failure to do so are nowhere more apparent than in the cinema. With more cinema seats per capita than any other European country, the Spain of the 40s and 50s was a nation of cinema addicts. A financially weak and artistically impoverished local industry could not produce enough films embodying the puritanical, "heroic" ethos of the regime to satisfy demand. Imported American and Italian films, though mutilated out of recognition by the censorship, were carriers of values incompatible with those of the regime.[3]

Because of their popular appeal and despite their ideological differences, both the Hollywood and neorealist models could be used to challenge the regime's monolithic hold over Spanish culture, especially when they were set in dialectic opposition to each other.

By ideology, I do not mean merely a set of beliefs consciously held and promoted by those in power. Rather, I am using the term in the Althusserian sense, that is, as a system of representations (ideas, images, and actions) through which persons experience the material conditions of existence in which they find themselves. Since ideology in this sense functions at the level of structures rather than at the level of consciously held opinions, it is largely unconscious and is transmitted, perpetuated, and naturalized primarily through nonrepressive ideological state apparatuses (such as popular culture, art, literature, education, religion, and the family) and their respective discursive practices.[4] Even within a hermetically sealed culture such as Francoist Spain, the dominant ideology could never be totally monolithic; its hegemony was always being contested and negotiated by conflicting historical forces and by alternative ideologies. In the context of the 1950s, both neorealism and Hollywood provided Spanish filmmakers with such alternative ideologies. The ideological implications of these two foreign aesthetics were never fixed; the meanings of their discursive practices were surprisingly fluid and even contradictory, partly because they were always contingent on what they were being used to oppose within the Spanish context.

If Spanish filmmakers chose Hollywood as a cinematic model, they faced several risks that were dramatized in the figure of Rita Hayworth: moral corruption ("screens showing Rita Hayworth were pelted with ink bottles by Falangists as a protest against the exhibition of a corroding libertarianism");[5] the loss of their own cultural identity (most Spanish spectators knew that this daughter of a famous Andalusian dancer was Anglicized by Hollywood once she became a star);[6] and the exploitation of Spanish folklore as commercial spectacle for foreign viewers. Diego Galán observes,

In 1951 . . . the Ministry of Information and Tourism was created for a double purpose: on the one hand, to control the expressions of increasing opposition to the regime which could even be found among a good part of the people who contributed to Franco's victory in the civil war, and on the other hand, to offer foreign countries a more open view of Spanish life in order to attract economic aid and tourists. It was an insurmountable contradiction that had a clear repercussion on the world of Spanish cinema which was then directly dependent on that ministry.[7]

This contradiction was brilliantly satirized by Berlanga and Bardem in ¡Bienvenido, Mr. Marshall! (Welcome, Mr. Marshall!, 1952), in which an entire Castilian village dresses up as Andalusians, complete with fake movie sets, to compete with other poor villages in

Even the promotional materials for *¡Bienvenido, Mr. Marshall!* emphasized the political-economic context and demonstrated the two-way process of cultural reinscription.

getting their share of the Marshall Plan. In trying to fulfill both their neorealist needs and their Hollywood-imprinted dreams, the Spanish villagers end up deeper in debt. Their reliance on false facades evokes the well-known historic incident, where Mussolini used cardboard sets to impress Hitler and his entourage when they were visiting Italy, implying some connection between the Fascist and Hollywood approach to spectacle and mise-en-scène. Moreover, the colonizing dimension of the substitution of Andalusia for Spain is multitiered and ancient and has an etymological base. Appearing on bilingual coins as early as 716, the term "Al-Andalus" was the Arab translation of *Spania,* the Latin word for Spain. *Bienvenido* parodies the *españolada,* the popular Spanish film genre that creates a distorted image of an exotic Andalusian Spain because it is so marketable abroad. According to Spanish film historian Román Gubern,

The *españolada* . . . originated in France, born during the period of Romanticism with such works as *Carmen* (1845), by Mérimée, which cultivated the exotic nature and the local color of an underdeveloped part of southern Europe. . . . Spanish film-makers willingly accepted this colonization and exaltation of . . . an agrarian and underdeveloped Spain dominated by religious superstitions, the Spain known for large and feudal landed estates, hunger, the cult of masculinity and for bullfighters. This stereotyped and generally reactionary genre, the pride of the pre-modern Spain, . . . was continuously employed by our directors during the silent era, [and] after the advent of sound motion pictures.[8]

Bienvenido underscores the irony that the Francoist regime was now exploiting this reactionary portrait of Spain to capitalize its modernization.

The satire also revealed the connection between the Marshall Plan and the Hollywood domination of European film markets, which proved to be a significant factor in the demise of the neorealist movement in Italy. In *Passion and Defiance: Film in Italy from 1942 to the Present,* Mira Liehm observes, "By 1949, the Italian film

In Luis García Berlanga's *¡Bienvenido, Mr. Marshall!* (Welcome, Mr. Marshall! 1952) the dreams of the Spanish villagers culturally reinscribe movie images from Hollywood westerns and Soviet Socialist realism.

industry entered a slump, caused primarily by unlimited imports of American films and by the American control of distribution." She quotes Carlo Salinari, a prominent Italian literary critic and historian, who blames "the crisis of neorealism" on the restoration of capitalism in Italy, claiming that "all kinds of administrative measures were used to disrupt a further evolution of neorealism."[9] The Christian Democrats had come to power in 1948 in an election that had involved the first covert action abroad by the CIA, for the United States was determined in this cold war climate to keep Communists out of power in Western Europe. In 1949, Italy joined the NATO alliance, and a few months later the Vatican excommunicated Communist voters and their sympathizers. Peter Bondanella claims, "As a result, films with strong social statements became increasingly risky investments, since government subsidies might be withdrawn from a work that was deemed unacceptable."[10] That same year, DeGasperi's government also passed the Andreotti Law, named after his undersecretary of public entertainment. Though the law was designed primarily to protect the Italian film industry against American imports, it also enabled the government to censor Italian films that showed their country in a negative light. This charge was leveled most vociferously against Vittorio DeSica and Cesare Zavattini's *Umberto D* (1952), which proved to be the last of the undisputed neorealist "classics."

Although Spain was not included in the Marshall Plan and not yet a member of the NATO alliance, the United States still posed a similar threat to its film markets, since Hollywood was the primary supplier of foreign films in this decade (as well as throughout most of Spain's history). Though the number of Italian films authorized for exhibition in Spain rose sharply both after the Italian film week in 1951 and the Salamanca Congress in 1955, it in no way compared with the large number of films coming from Hollywood. (See table 1.)[11]

Paradoxically, while Franco courted American investment and favored the promotion of genres (such as historical spectacle and melodrama) that were also popular in Hollywood, he and his censors realized the subversive potential of American culture. In challenging

Table 1. Italian films authorized for exhibition in Spain, 1950–1960.

Year	USA	Italy	Total Foreign	Spanish (including co-productions)
1950	86	6	173	72
1951	74	5	152	48
1952	109	29	231	43
1953	140	27	291	55
1954	158	16	264	69
1955	127	20	216	94
1956	70	54	240	93
1957	48	41	224	64
1958	51	35	209	80
1959	93	28	214	73
1960	99	21	233	78

the hegemony of the official Francoist ideology, the dominant Hollywood cinema represented a potentially liberalizing force, no matter how exaggerated or corrupted. That is why one hegemony could be so successfully played off against the other, as was demonstrated in the double-edged satire of *Bienvenido.* Although it was Spain's official entry at Cannes, the film attacked not only the imperialist goals of America's Marshall Plan but also Francoist policy with its denial of Spanish socioeconomic realities and its ineptness in negotiating with the United States.[12]

In contrast to Hollywood, Italian neorealism appeared in the 1950s to be a more politically effective model for challenging the escapist cinema of the Francoist regime, one that could appeal both to the Left and the Right. Hopewell observes,

Neo-realism attracted supporters right across the political spectrum of Spanish cinema. It was the perfect rallying call for a reconciliatory policy. Its origins in the aftermath of Italian fascism allowed militants to exploit the international belief that Spaniards, through their cinema, were fighting fascism in Spain.[13]

This position was strongly advocated by *Objetivo,* a left-wing film journal that was founded in May 1953 by Bardem, writer-producer

Ricardo Muñoz Suay, Marxist philosopher Paulino Garagorri, and Eduardo Ducay (who later produced Buñuel's *Tristana*). Assessing *Objetivo*'s influence on Spanish film culture, Spanish critic José Luis Guarner wrote,

It fully immersed itself into the "realist" current of Italian neorealism—whose deep imprint on this generation has already been pointed out. . . . For example, the first number included 18 pages dedicated to Cesare Zavattini. Faithful to the principles of *Cinema Nuovo, Objetivo* exalted the auteurs defended by Aristarco (Visconti) and rejected those dismissed by him (Rossellini), it attacked the American cinema of Hollywood in order to defend the independent Yankee productions of the social or testimonial type.[14]

One of the last issues of *Objetivo* included a long article entitled "Neorealismo: 1955" which covered the latest Italian imports (all released in 1955): Federico Fellini's *Il bidone* (The Swindle), Michelangelo Antonioni's *Le amiche* (The Girlfriends), Francesco Maselli's *Gli sbandati* (The Runaways), Francesco Rosi's *Amici per la pelle* (Friends for Life), and Mario Soldati's *La donna del fiume* (The Woman of the River). By 1955, neorealism may have been nearly dead in Italy, yet this article shows the movement was still very alive as an influence in Spain—particularly as it broadened to include bourgeois protagonists and as its melodramatic elements became more blatant (as in the case of *Le amiche*).[15] Although neorealism was rooted in a subversive melodrama like Luchino Visconti's *Ossessione* (Obsession), and although its greatest commercial successes—Roberto Rossellini's *Roma città aperta* (Open City) and *Paisá,* DeSica's *Bicycle Thief,* Pietro Germi's *La nome della legge* (In the Name of the Law), and Giuseppe DeSantis's *Riso amaro* (Bitter Rice)—all had strong melodramatic elements in plot, music, mise-en-scène, and morality, what had seemed so "new" to critics and spectators were the realistic deviations from conventional melodrama.

One of the primary achievements of *Objetivo* was its role in helping to organize and document the First National Film Congress at

Salamanca in May 1955, an event that helped to establish neorealism as the primary aesthetic model for the first phase of the New Spanish Cinema. As a result of its participation, the journal was suppressed by the government.

Although this four-day congress was partly funded by the government's own liberal Ministry of Education, it was organized primarily by leftists (not only by the editors of *Objetivo* but also by Patino, who then ran the University Cine Club of Salamanca). Yet the participants at the Salamanca Congress represented the full ideological spectrum, including members of the PCE (the Spanish Communist party) on the extreme Left and of the Falange (the Spanish Fascist party) on the extreme Right. All political sides were united in a sweeping condemnation of Francoist cinema, which was most powerfully expressed by Bardem in his frequently quoted statement, "After 60 years of films, Spanish cinema is politically ineffective, socially false, intellectually worthless, aesthetically nonexistent, and industrially crippled."[16]

Most participants still conceptualized a new Spanish cinema almost totally in centralized national terms. They focused on the regime's ambiguous censorship practices, demanding greater clarification of what filmmakers could and could not do without really questioning whether the government should have the right to impose such regulations in the first place. For example, in Bardem's closing speech at the congress, he proclaimed,

We need new laws for our film industry: we need new forms of protection which will not isolate us from our roots: the public. We need a different position for film in relation to the state: Let the state not view us as an enemy, nor restrain us, nor asphyxiate us. We need censorship to show us its face, to show us the way out of this labyrinth, to codify its taboos.[17]

When Bardem turned to a positive description of what a progressive Spanish cinema might be, he clearly had neorealism in mind:

Spanish cinema lives in a state of isolation. It is isolated not only from the world, but from our own reality. While the cinemas of all countries concentrate their interests on the problems that arise from everyday life, . . . Spanish cinema continues to be a cinema of painted dolls. The problem of Spanish cinema is that it has no problems, that it does not bear testimony to our time such as our time demands of all human creation.[18]

Neorealism seemed to provide an effective vehicle for critiquing Franco's false picture of Spain within the national context as well as an ideal means for overcoming Spain's isolation by expressing its unique cultural identity abroad. In fact, Bardem had come to the Salamanca Congress directly from the Cannes Film Festival where he had served on the jury and had won the International Critics Prize for his own film *Muerte de un ciclista* (1955), which used neorealist conventions to rupture a glossy Hollywood-type melodrama and to expose its ideological implications. The recognition he achieved at Cannes protected his film against Spanish censors and gave his statements at Salamanca unique authority.

Shortly after leaving the meetings at Salamanca, Bardem began writing *Calle mayor* (Main Street, 1956), a neorealist melodrama that would win the Critics Prize at the Venice Film Festival the following year. In many ways reminiscent of Fellini's *I vitelloni* (1953) and with a Moraldo-type character named Federico as narrator, this hybrid film about Spanish provincial life contains the following conversation between its handsome protagonist and its victimized spinster.

Isabel: I love movies, especially American ones.

Juan: Because the heroes are more handsome?

Isabel: No, because the houses are so white and clean. Have you noticed how clean and sparkling the kitchens are?

Juan: My friend Federico would say American movies are all lies, absolutely false.

Isabel: It may be so, but it's a pretty lie.

The film's ironic stance as hybrid is enhanced by its casting, for Isabel is played by American actress Betsy Blair, who was highly regarded in Spain for her realistic performance the previous year in Delbert Mann's *Marty* (one of those "Yankee" independent films praised by *Objetivo*) and subsequently in Antonioni's *Il grido* (The Cry, 1957).

If Spanish filmmakers followed the lead of *Objetivo* and the Salamanca Congress and chose neorealism instead of Hollywood as their primary model, those conventions could readily be adapted to Spain's immediate cultural specificity, as the model's importability to many Third World nations would demonstrate throughout the 1950s. Yet what was unique to Spain was how radically those neorealist conventions could be ideologically reinscribed, not only by leftists like Bardem and Patino but also by participants at Salamanca with right-wing backgrounds.

One of those participants was José Antonio Nieves Conde, director of *Surcos* (1951), which is generally considered the first important neorealist film made in Spain, for it shocked moviegoers with the first glimpse of Spanish poverty and slums, images that had been suppressed from the screen. Politically, Nieves Conde had formerly been an *hedillista,* a supporter of Manuel Hedilla, the extremist leader of the Falange whose protest against Franco's forced unification of all right-wing parties eventually led to his imprisonment. The screenwriters of *Surcos,* Gonzalo Torrente Ballester and Natividad Zaro, were also former Falangists.

Another key right-wing participant at the Salamanca Congress was García Escudero, a reformist Catholic of Falangist origin who was the government's moderate general director of cinema from September 1951 to February 1952. García Escudero was fired for granting the "national interest" category to *Surcos,* which was condemned as "seriously dangerous" by the National Board of Classification of Spectacles but which he hailed as a model for a new Falangist cinema, calling it "the first glance at reality in a cinema of papier-mâché."[19] The reason the government found this action so objectionable was that he simultaneously denied the "national interest" category to

The lavish finale of José Luis Sáenz de Heredia's historical film, *Alba de América* (1951), demonstrates the colonizing power of cross-cultural spectacle.

Cifesa's big-budget historical spectacle, *Alba de America,* which had been personally sponsored by Franco and his hand-picked successor, Admiral Luis Carrero Blanco (who was frequently called the "apostle of *continuismo*").[20] Looking back to the 1940s, Franco and Carrero Blanco apparently assumed that the most effective way to popularize Spain's ideological goals was through the use of the historical film, one of the genres that was also popular in Hollywood. This strategy may have failed in *Alba de America,*[21] but it had succeeded both critically and commercially in *Raza* (1941), a film directed by José Luis Sáenz de Heredia which was based on a fictionalized auto-biography written by Franco himself under a pseudonym.

In contrast, García Escudero and Nieves Conde perceived that postwar neorealism, in defining the immediate cultural specificity of Spain, might serve as a more effective vehicle for strengthening the populist appeal of fascism, enabling it to address the actual contemporary problems of "the people." Although the strengthening of fascism was hardly what leftists like Bardem and Patino had in mind, the participants at Salamanca had agreed to set aside their ideological differences during the congress to gain strength from unity—a value that was deeply distrusted by leftists in Italy but which the painful lessons of the Spanish Civil War and the popular success of the Franco regime helped to valorize in Spain. This false unity enabled García Escudero to co-opt the leftist call for a neorealist "social cinema," particularly in his book *Cine social,* which was published in 1958. According to Gubern,

> In appropriating this polemical and uncomfortable theme, . . . García Escudero proposed a . . . valorization of films that fit under this epigraph from his own ideological perspective, . . . the social thinking of the Catholic Church before the Second Vatican Council. With this maneuver of exorcism, the author tried to deactivate the propositions that Marxist critics had expressed combatively in the journals *Objetivo* . . . and *Cinema universitario* (which was edited by the Cineclub of the Spanish University Syndicate of Salamanca and prohibited in 1963, during the mandate of García Escudero as general director of cinema and theater). Since 1961, these propositions have continued being expressed in *Nuestro cine,* a journal that inherited the same ideological postulates.[22]

Like the technocrats from Opus Dei, García Escudero supported the conversion of Spain into a modern European nation. He assumed that for a model of film aesthetics, Spanish filmmakers should look not to Hollywood but to Italy, another Latin country that had already provided Spain with a model for fascism.[23] Thus, these two models could be seen as compatible—especially since Mussolini had created the infrastructure for the postwar Italian cinema, and many of the leading neorealists (including Visconti, Rossellini, and DeSica) had made important neorealist precursors during the Fascist era.

Ironically, this position is consistent with the current revisionist view of neorealism that began to emerge at the Mostra Internazionale el Nuovo Cinema in Pesaro in 1974—one that rejects any essentialist or monolithic definition of the movement and that explores its continuities with popular films made during the Fascist era, most particularly with melodrama. More recently, this revisionist approach has led Marcia Landy to argue persuasively that "although the neo-realists sought to examine the nature of fascism, they obscured their own beginnings in the fascist era . . . and underrated the role of popular cinema in the formation of ideology."[24] This role was never underrated by the Italian Fascists, whose films were strongly influenced by popular Hollywood genres (melodrama, comedy, and the historical film) that continued to exert an influence in Italy both within neorealism and long after its demise.

Neorealism's potential compatibility both with fascism and Hollywood genres was perceived in the early 1950s, not only positively by right-wing supporters of Franco like García Escudero and Nieves Conde but also negatively by Buñuel, a member of "the Other Spain," those hundreds of thousands of left-wing exiles who fled Spain after the Civil War and who saw themselves as surviving representatives of an enlightened Spanish culture. Even though it was the critical success of neorealism that helped establish a favorable climate for the reemergence of Buñuel within the international film scene in the early 1950s, he ultimately rejected the movement because he believed its basic humanism was conformist and its subversive potential a sham.

I am ideologically opposed to the neorealist tendency. Neorealism introduced some enrichments to cinematographic expression, but nothing more. Neorealist reality is partial, official, above all reasonable; but poetry, mystery, are absolutely lacking in it. . . . If it were possible for me, I would make films which, apart from entertaining the audience, would convey to them the absolute certainty that they DO NOT LIVE IN THE BEST OF ALL POSSIBLE WORLDS. . . . Movies today, including the so-called neorealist, are dedicated to tasks contrary to this.[25]

Buñuel demonstrated neorealism's susceptibility to ideological re-inscription in *Los olvidados* (1950) by undermining its aesthetic with surrealist conventions, particularly with subversive dream sequences, an Oedipal subtext, the antihumanist assumption that everyone is potentially evil and capable of murder, and a documentary prologue that becomes parodic when read intertextually against the deeply ironic travelogue sequences in *L'age d'or* and *Tierra sin pan* (Land without Bread).

Buñuel's own experience of reediting and redubbing films at the Museum of Modern Art (MOMA) in the 1940s (even such propagandistic works as Leni Riefenstahl's *Olympia*) must have made him aware that all film traditions could be subtly subverted from within. And if that were the case, then why not subvert the most powerful of all—the Hollywood melodrama. This is a strategy he would master in Mexico, particularly in a film like *El* (1952), and a strategy that would lead him ever after to prefer melodrama over neorealism as the cinematic form with the greatest subversive potential.

Although most Spanish filmmakers in the 1950s had heard about Buñuel's success with *Los olvidados* at Cannes, they were unable to see his films or to know what he was up to at MOMA in the 1940s, but they had another vivid example of Hollywood's susceptibility to ideological reinscription. Beginning in 1941, the Francoist regime required that all foreign films be dubbed into Castilian in Spain by Spaniards. Thus, these filmmakers witnessed how easily the plots, meanings, and values of American films could be altered to suit the official ideology of Spanish censors. The most notorious example of such ideological reinscription is John Ford's *Mogambo* (1953). To purge the film of adultery, Spanish dubbers changed Grace Kelly and her husband into siblings, freeing her to fall in love with Clark Gable but also creating an incestuous subtext.

Partly because of such examples, many Spaniards, particularly on the Right, tended to underestimate the ideological effect of the image in American cinema, thinking that the superficial changes in plot and dialogue imposed by Franco's censors could totally defuse its colonizing power. An example of this attitude can be found as early as 1940 in an often-quoted article published in the Falangist weekly, *Primer plano:*

A people less infantile than the Yanks would have succeeded in imposing their convictions by means of their gigantic film markets on other nations and won the sympathies of the world. But American movies, albeit magnificent in sight and sound, lack any deep proselytizing purpose. . . . If American films with their at times almost pornographic excesses had not aroused the embarrassed repulse of our Catholic moral values, they surely would have Americanized the social mores of Spain and the entire world.[26]

The irony that this writer failed to see (but which was always so apparent to Buñuel) was that it was precisely those pornographic excesses of infantile visual pleasure that masked their ideology and thereby enabled Hollywood to dominate international markets and Americanize the world. And that is why its ideological reinscription had to operate on the level of filmic language. On the contrary, neorealism seemed to offer a new filmic language capable of validating the political reality of any populist movement whether of the Left or the Right—which is one of the reasons Buñuel distrusted it.

For many Spaniards, Italian neorealism presented a model not only of how to develop a national cinema that could challenge Hollywood's domination of world markets but also of how such a movement could change a nation's international image from that of a Fascist supporter of Hitler to a progressive European center of humanism. This goal was very appealing to the Franco regime, particularly in 1953 when Spain was negotiating its military base agreement with the United States and in 1955 when Spain was admitted to the United Nations. This kind of reinscription clearly had been operative in *Open City,* neorealism's first big international success, which presented Nazis as melodramatic monsters without ever mentioning Mussolini and while figuring Italian Fascists as nearly benign. A similar miraculous transformation was later achieved in the 1970s by the New German Cinema (but using Hollywood rather than neorealist conventions as the primary medium of reinscription), making it another viable model for Spanish filmmakers in post-Franco Spain.[27]

According to Payne, the defascistization of Spain began as soon as it became clear that Hitler and Mussolini were going to lose World War II: "Franco had to develop an alternate political theory and tactic, unveiling his new scheme of a corporative *Rechtsstaat* 'organic democracy' based on Catholic doctrine by the time that the war ended in 1945."[28] Skillfully playing each political faction off against the others, Franco was able to construct a monolithic Spanish unity with great popular appeal, particularly when it was promoted not as a radical form of fascism but as a populist return to traditional sacred values centered in the family and the church. In "Spanish Fascism," Payne wrote,

The limitation in the fascistization of the Franco regime lay not only in the fact that the government had been founded by the non-fascist (and increasingly anti-Falangist) military, but equally in the very character of the Civil War itself, which had quickly become a mass mobilized revolutionary-counterrevolutionary conflict. The true popular support culturally and ideologically for the Nationalist forces was thus not to be found among the radical new fascism of the Falange, but in the defense and reaffirmation of Spanish national culture, tradition, and religion. The Nationalist zone became the scene of a neo-Catholic traditionalist revival without precedent or sequel in any other twentieth century European country, one that might bear comparison with the revival of Islamic fundamentalism in the Middle East. (107)

Although this return to an almost feudal orthodoxy might seem incompatible with the drive toward industrialization, the technocrats of Opus Dei (the Catholic lay order that infiltrated and dominated Spain's political, economic, intellectual, and social elite) played a key role in negotiating this contradiction by forging "an amalgam of authoritarianism, traditional Catholicism, and the world of Americanized business efficiency."[29] This articulation of formerly contradictory elements helped to construct a new hegemony in Francoist Spain.

Payne describes three phases of defascistization: the first between 1942 and 1947 (when the Falange Española Tradicionalista was not abolished but "new policy required that the term 'National Movement' replace Falange"); the second between 1945 and 1957 (when the regime would come to occupy "a kind of halfway house between the central European fascist structures of the preceding generation and the resurgent new European democracies"); and the third that resulted "from the tremendous transformation of Spain's society after the great development boom and massive industrialization of the 1960s" ("Spanish Fascism," 101–112). The second stage was greatly facilitated by the cold war climate, which made the United States and its European allies more willing to cooperate with Franco despite his Fascist past. In the third stage, the Franco regime introduced *aperturismo,* that official seven-year policy (1962–1969) of opening Spain to rapid industrial, economic, and cultural growth, which was to be stimulated by outside investment and influence. This policy came with Fraga's appointment as the minister of information and the reappointment of García Escudero (who had earlier been a supporter of neorealism) as general director of cinema.[30]

By the time neorealism arrived in Spain in 1951, the process of defascistization was well under way. Thus neorealism itself could be seen as a vehicle of ideological reinscription, one that was opposed both to fascism and to Hollywood, which were perceived as aligned partly because conventions from popular Hollywood genres had been so effectively absorbed by the commercial films made during the Fascist era both in Italy and Spain. Within all three postwar national film movements of former Fascist nations—Italian neorealism, the New German Cinema, and the New Spanish Cinema—the United States would be figured as a hegemony that was able to replace, perpetuate, or co-opt fascism—primarily through the economic leverage of the Marshall Plan and the cultural imperialism of Hollywood.

Instead of choosing one model over the other, many of the most influential Spanish filmmakers of the 1950s (whether on the Left or the Right) used neorealism and Hollywood as a dialectic opposition within their films. Bakhtin argues that in such intentional hybrids, the crucial activity is not so much the dialogizing of linguistic forms "as it is the collision between differing points of view on the world that are embedded in these forms" and "the carving-out of a living image of another language." He claims this dialogic effect is even more powerful when the linguistic forms are chosen from an alien culture.

Consciousness awakens to independent ideological life precisely in a world of alien discourses surrounding it, and from which it cannot initially separate itself. . . . It is not so much interpreted by us as it is . . . applied to new material. . . . It enters into . . . a *struggle* with other internally persuasive discourses. Our ideological development is just such an intense struggle within us for hegemony among various available verbal and ideological points of view, approaches, directions and values.[31]

This statement precisely describes the process of ideological re-inscription that occurred in the Spanish cinema of the 1950s when it dialogized the "alien" languages of Hollywood and neorealist cinema as a means of destabilizing the mythologized Spanish unity and its "imperial Castilian language," which were imposed by the Francoist regime. This process exposed the ideological operations in *all* cinematic language. Bakhtin claims,

This verbal-ideological decentering will occur only when a national culture loses its sealed off and self-sufficient character, when it becomes conscious of itself as only one among *other* cultures and languages. It is this knowledge that will sap the roots of a mythological feeling for language, based as it is on an absolute fusion of ideological meaning with language. (369–370)

Bakhtin's account helps to explain why the dialogism of Hollywood and neorealist conventions was frequently linked in these films of the 1950s with an exploration of the semic codes of Spanishness—a hybridization that enabled these works to be distinguished from the official Francoist cinema while still remaining readable to an international audience.

In "Rhetoric of the Image," in which Roland Barthes describes a system of semantic signs (or semes) drawn from a cultural code, he defines connoters whose "common domain . . . is ideology" and which, in contrast to a denoted word, are "organized in associative fields, in paradigmatic articulations, even perhaps in oppositions, . . . according to certain semic axes: *Italianicity* belongs to a certain axis of nationalities, alongside Frenchicity, Germanicity or Spanishicity."[32]

What I will be demonstrating in the following textual analyses is how the various connoters of Spanishicity (or *Spanishness,* as I prefer to call it)—including those that were exploited (such as the españo-lada) and those that were repressed (such as the Black Legend stereotype or the Spanish Civil War) in the official Francoist cinema— were ideologically reinscribed by being associated with the neorealist and Hollywood stylistics. That is, I will be exploring how cinematic conventions from these two opposing axes helped determine how Spanishness would be redefined in contrast to Italianness, Americanness, and other national semes, both to Spaniards and to foreigners.

While many of these Spanish filmmakers associated the Hollywood model with the use of folkloric stereotypes as a signifier of Spanishness, they saw neorealism leading to the adoption of the urban collective as an alternative seme. What remained hidden behind both alternatives was the Spanish Civil War, the repressed signifier that *Canciones* had sought to liberate from the archives which was increasingly fetishized by its repression.[33] Except for a flurry of patriotic historical films in the early 1940s such as *Raza* (which presented the Civil War from the victors' point of view), the Civil War remained a taboo subject both for Spanish films and for foreign imports in the 1940s and 1950s because it was perceived as a threat to the monolithic national unity imposed by Franco and to his ongoing process of defascistization.[34]

Yet as the training ground for the ideological struggles of World War II and the cold war, the Civil War proved that Spain was neither as irrelevant nor as backward as it appeared in the Francoist period— even as a subject for Italian neorealism and Hollywood melodrama. Although the specific association with the Republican cause in the Spanish Civil War was suppressed by Italian censors from "lo Spagnolo" (the Spaniard), that enigmatic character in Visconti's *Ossessione,*[35] the Spanish Civil War was the acknowledged site where Manfredi (Rossellini's Communist resistance leader in *Open City*) had first fought the Fascists. Thus, as a signifier, the Spanish Civil War was essential to the ideological foundation of the neorealist movement. In Hollywood, even though its ideological associations were rarely foregrounded, the Spanish Civil War still functioned as a signifier for individual heroism. For example, it is the war in which the Bogart character in *Casablanca* (1942) claims to have fought and in which both Hemingway and his most romantic hero, Robert Jordan, had first tested their "manly" courage, which continued to have such glamorous appeal not only in print but also, with Hollywood's 1943 adaptation of *For Whom the Bell Tolls,* on movie screens worldwide.

The dialectic between neorealism and Hollywood and their respective semes of Spanishness is an important structural principle in at least four of the most influential films of the period: *Surcos* (1951), directed by former Falangist Nieves Conde, the neorealist film that led to the firing of García Escudero; Bardem's *Muerte de un ciclista* (1955), which was released during the year of the Salamanca Congress and was one of the first Spanish films to win a major prize at Cannes and to be widely distributed and critically acclaimed abroad;[36] *Los golfos* (1959), the debut feature of Saura, who was to become a major force in the New Spanish Cinema of the 1960s and 1970s; and *El cochecito* (1960), one of the collaborations between Italian director Marco Ferreri (who made his first three features in Spain) and Spanish screenwriter Rafael Azcona (who also worked frequently with Berlanga and Saura), which demonstrates that distinctively Spanish form of "absurdist neorealism" based on *esperpento* which Almodóvar was to revive in the 1980s.

Since I intend to demonstrate how these dynamics work on the level of stylistics as well as within the broad outlines of narrative and thematic content, close textual analysis is essential. This requirement necessarily limits the number of works that can be examined. I have chosen these four films not because they are "typical" of the 653 Spanish movies produced during the 1950s but for two specific reasons: first, because they have already been singled out by other critics and historians as having been influential; and second, because their use of this dialectic is clearly foregrounded.

In all four of the hybrids from the 1950s, Hollywood conventions are linked with a capitalist promotion of individualism, which proves to be divisive and destructive, while neorealist conventions are associated with the collective (whether family, proletariat, or street gang). Yet all four films imply that the dialectic combination of the two aesthetics (as well as the related thematic opposition between the individual and the collective) is essential to portray the cultural specificity of Spain in the 1950s. Although all four films expose the high costs (both for the nation and the individual) of the capitalist model of individualism, it was nevertheless used to seek international stardom for their own talented young auteurs, who were trying to compete with their European counterparts, particularly from Italy and France.

In the first half of the decade, in *Surcos* and *Muerte,* the dialogized opposition between Hollywood and neorealism was highly polarized, almost Manichaean, whether the ideological background of its director was Falangist (Nieves Conde) or Communist (Bardem). Both used neorealist conventions to document the immediate socioeconomic reality of Spain, and both reinscribed conventions from Hollywood gangster films, psychological thrillers, and noir to construct that "other scene" of fiction onto which the harsher political critique could be displaced and in which the troubling issues of class exploitation and sexual repression could be more safely dramatized.

But by the end of the decade when the second phase of defascistization was already accomplished and Spain had moved closer to the new European democracies, and when neorealism was dead as a movement in Italy and the French New Wave was now leading the European challenge of Hollywood, *Los golfos* and *El cochecito* interrogated and recombined both sides of the opposition, "carving out" the distinctive idiom that would help to characterize the New Spanish Cinema of the 1960s and 1970s—a stylistic that would still carry the trace of that reinscription, as is most powerfully demonstrated in *El espíritu de la colmena.*

FALANGIST NEOREALISM IN SURCOS   Hopewell observes that *Surcos* is "a curious graft of American gangster thriller and neo-realism. It is also a Falangist thesis drama."[37] The two most interesting questions raised by this combination are: How are conventions from a supposedly left-wing discourse like neorealism ideologically reinscribed to serve an ultra right-wing Falangist thesis film such as this, and why are they positioned within a Hollywood genre?

Although it does not specifically address the Spanish context, Laclau's *Politics and Ideology in Marxist Theory: Capitalism-Fascism-Populism* might be useful in answering the first question as it theorizes the process of transforming ideologies. Drawing on Althusser's idea of interpellation ("the basic function of all ideology is to interpellate/constitute individuals as subjects," 100), Laclau argues that fascism is characterized by a highly unified, yet inconsistent ideological discourse in which *one* interpellation, like the family, becomes the main organizer of all others.

When a familial interpellation, for example, *evokes* a political interpellation, a religious interpellation, or an aesthetic interpellation, and when each of these isolated interpellations operates as a *symbol* of the others, we have a relatively unified ideological discourse.[38]

Laclau claims that ideologies are "transformed through class struggle, which is carried out through the production of subjects and the articulation/disarticulation of discourses" (103). He argues that each sector in the struggle tries to create a new ideological unity by using a "system of narration" to disarticulate the ideological discourses of the opposing forces. Thus, each sector "tries to give coherence to its ideological discourse by presenting its class objectives as the consummation of popular objectives" (109).

Although based on a disarticulation of opposing ideological discourses, this Fascist process of reinscription is diametrically opposed to Bakhtinian dialogism, for it seeks to construct and perpetuate (rather than undermine) a monolithic hegemony. Yet the new hegemony it constructs is not restricted to a narrow elite; it is deliberately designed to appeal to a wide range of classes, which is one of the reasons melodrama was the ideal system of narration to express such ideological struggle. As Christine Gledhill explains,

Emerging with capitalist mass entertainment, [melodrama] defines a terrain in which different classes and social groups meet and find an identity. . . . However, if the "popular" is claimed as a point of social cohesion, it is also contested. The "popular" is fraught with tension, struggles and negotiations. In this context the heterogeneity of the melodramatic aesthetic facilitates conflict and negotiation between cultural identities.[39]

This kind of ideological transformation is precisely what happens in *Surcos:* the struggle to define "popular objectives" is played out not in class conflict but in the opposing conventions of neorealism and Hollywood melodrama. At one point in the film, two characters associated with Hollywood gangster movies explicitly critique neorealism. When Don Roque's mistress asks him to take her to the movies, the villainous gangster boss says, "They're showing a neorealist film." What's that? asks the bimbo. "Social problems in the barrio," he replies. After leaving the theater, she complains, "What an idiotic film! Why show such misery? A millionaire's life is so much more fun."

Surcos adopts melodrama as its unifying system of narration to gloss over all logical contradictions and to expand its populist appeal. Although melodrama had been central to both Fascist and Hollywood discourse as well as persistent within neorealism, the film uses the American form, perhaps because its "transposition of class conflicts into country/city oppositions" was so well suited to the film's Falangist perspective and to its theme of urban migration. By displacing all political issues onto the family, this melodramatic system implies that if an individual peasant family can preserve its traditional values, then the state, no matter how severe its socioeconomic problems, will survive. Thus, the moral restoration of the patriarchal family (rather than the political solution of urban problems in the barrio) becomes the primary "popular objective."

In focusing on the urban migration of the peasant farmer, *Surcos* foregrounds one of the major contradictions in Francoism, which drew criticism both from Falangists and Marxists. According to Carr,

In spite of an enthusiasm for the peasant farmer as the "core of the race," insulated from the subversive doctrines that had infected the urban workers after 1931, the regime early saw that . . . migration to the cities was a natural consequence of industrialization. Without it there would have been no industrial take-off—as the regime recognized when it abandoned its efforts to stop the exodus from the land and the agrarian ideology that idealized the peasant farmer. Even so, industrial growth could not absorb the totality of the rural underemployed. . . . The radical Falangist notions of agrarian reform dissolved in a regime dominated by conservative interests.[40]

Instead of analyzing the complexities of this political issue, *Surcos* presents it as a simplistic Manichaean opposition between the corrupt city undergoing industrialization and the innocent rural Spain being ravaged—a contrast that is foregrounded by the juxtaposed images of train and wheat fields that frame the film. Consequently, at the Salamanca Congress, Bardem attacked *Surcos* for not dealing with the underlying causes of urban immigration.[41] While granting that the migrants' desire for old rural values has traditionally been considered reactionary by Marxists, Laclau perceives a potential for radical transformation in this theme, arguing that the migrants' "refusal to accept capitalist legality . . . expresses a more 'advanced' and 'modern' attitude than European-style trade unionism" (158).

We can see both the radical rejection of capitalism and the glossing over of logical inconsistencies most clearly in the villainous figure of Don Roque. He is both a corrupt godfather from Hollywood gangster movies and a Europeanized Francoist politician (with his nickname "The Chamberlain" and with his slim black umbrella that he admittedly carries for "a sophisticated look"). He evokes the typical villain from early American melodrama, which Gledhill describes as "sport[ing] European airs" and "associated with the city, and its growing divisions between rich and poor" (24). Yet in the Spanish context, this condensation also brings to mind the oligarchy created by the black market and Franco's courting of American investment— associations that suggest a more radical critique of capitalism.

Surcos traces the moral disintegration of a peasant family from Salamanca once it migrates to Madrid. Partly because of the father's weakness and the mother's quick adoption of urban values, their daughter, Tonia, loses the family honor in cabaret singing and sexual transgression (which are frequently linked in Fascist melodrama). Their two sons seek alternative patriarchal models: the younger son, Manolo, luckily finds a good puppeteer, whose populist theater positions him on and in the Right, whereas the older son, Pepe, like an antihero from noir, is lured by a bad woman into a world of crime. Thus, these moral struggles of the family are partly expressed through a conflict among three popular forms of entertainment associated with melodrama in Spain: cabaret singing, puppet theater, and *cine negro*.

Though frequently compared to Visconti's *Rocco e i suoi fratelli* (Rocco and His Brothers, 1960), which it precedes by nine years, *Surcos* is actually ideologically closer to Rey's silent classic, *La aldea maldita* (1929).[42] Both Spanish melodramas present a highly unified ideological discourse through the single interpellation of the family, which organizes all others. In contrast, Visconti's melodramas tend to present multiple discourses, whose complex relations can be examined with considerable specificity within the small social unit of the family, which is always positioned within larger contexts of class struggle and historical change.

Unlike *La aldea maldita,* where the intertitles present urban migration as a biblical theme within traditional Christian discourse (another "tragedy of Exodus"), *Surcos* uses neorealist conventions to place this theme within a contemporary political discourse as "the most painful problem of our times." Nevertheless, both Spanish films connect the urban migration of the poor with the corruption of women as a combined threat to the moral rigidity of the Spanish patriarchy. As a supporter of the Falange, Nieves Conde subscribed to the "extreme stress on the masculine principle and male dominance," which Payne includes as a key tenet within his typological description of European fascism. Acknowledging that "all European political forces in the era of fascism were overwhelmingly led by and made up of men, and those that paid lip service to female equality in fact had little interest in it," Payne insists that "only fascists, however, made a perpetual fetish of the 'virility' of their movement and its program and style. . . . No other kind of movement professed such complete horror at the slightest suggestion of androgyny."[43] Similarly, Geoffrey Nowell-Smith includes this fetishization of maleness as an essential characteristic of melodrama and explains how it functions even in those films where the protagonist is a female (which could be claimed for *La aldea maldita*) or an impotent male (as in *Surcos*).

"Masculinity" although rarely attainable, is at least known as an ideal. "Femininity," within the terms of the argument, is not only unknown but unknowable. . . . For both men and women, however, suffering and impotence . . . are seen as forms of a failure to be male—a failure from which patriarchy allows no respite.[44]

Both *La aldea maldita* and *Surcos* stress the thematic opposition between phallic rigidity and female malleability, between the eternal bonds linking fathers and sons versus the supposedly more unreliable relations with mothers, wives, and daughters. In the silent film, the stability of Castilian values is represented visually through static painterly compositions and architectural tableaux, which evoke art forms from Spain's glorious past. In contrast, the forces of change are associated with the uniqueness of cinematic spectacle, with the new film medium's reliance on the theatrical specularization of the woman's body, of clouds and wind moving ominously across a dark sky, and of vehicles and crowds moving dynamically across the frame.

To express a similar contrast, *Surcos* turns to the contrasting styles of neorealism and Hollywood. What *Surcos* seems to offer as the primary seme of Spanishness is not the folkloric spectacles of cabaret singing or puppet shows but a rigid moral adherence to the feudal patriarchal family in the face of historical change. This same seme was dominant not only in *La aldea maldita* but also in Franco's *Raza* (1941), which officially sanctioned the fusion of the compatible discourses of fascism and melodrama.

Surcos focuses on the father's loss of power and the corruption of the children once the mother and the eldest son (who is dominated by his fiancée and who convinced the family to migrate) take charge of the family. When the father fails as a breadwinner, his wife tells him, "You peel potatoes, I'll get the money. I should have left you behind."

The father's failure reaches its climax in a powerful factory sequence where the dynamic montage, slanted camera angles, and omission of dialogue evoke Soviet expressionism. Landy notes that the influence of Soviet montage (though never as dominant as American) also appeared in Italian melodrama of the Fascist era, emanating "most conspicuously from the 'fascists of the left' whose interest was in a vision of fascism as a new and revolutionary movement." She claims, "Soviet montage in the films of the era was not indicative of adherence to Marxist theory and practice but a recognition of the effectiveness of montage in the treatment of 'epic' subjects, of historical events, and of mass action" (15). While this is precisely how it functions in a Spanish epic like *Raza,* in the subversive satire of *¡Bienvenido, Mr. Marshall!* Soviet montage is parodied along with Hollywood and Spanish genres.[45]

In *Surcos,* the status of Soviet montage is more ambiguous, for in this crucial sequence it evokes the celebratory attitude toward industrial progress that is normally found in historic epics but that is here being questioned, partly by foregrounding these Soviet filmic conventions. At its emotional peak, the sequence rapidly intercuts between a steel rod being pounded and bent into shape and the father weakening until he faints. The feudal patriarch identifies with the steel rod, resisting malleability even though it is required by industrialization, fast-cutting, and other forms of technological progress associated with major world powers in the cold war era.

Despite the father's economic failure, he remains morally intact, while the more malleable women and children adapt and succumb to the forces of corruption. The daughter, Tonia, with the encouragement of her mother and with Don Roque's financial backing, tries to become a singing star but is tricked into becoming his mistress. The corrupting cabaret theater of erotic spectacle is set in Manichaean contrast with the moralistic puppet theater of the widowed patriarch who saves young Manolo. His populist performances clearly interpellate their gendered subjects within the discourse of the traditional Castilian family. For example, one puppet waves a big stick and proclaims to his complaining wife, "My father said he had a cure for women like you. . . . This is the best invention for putting women back in their place!" The only woman in *Surcos* who accepts her subordinate place is the puppeteer's daughter, Rosario, whose meek submission to the patriarchy helps restore potency both to Manolo and his father (who is finally able to reassert his authority by striking his wife and daughter). Such blatant misogyny is characteristic of both villains and good guys; only Pepe allows himself to be manipulated and destroyed by the woman he loves. According to Carr, such regressive attitudes toward women in Spain during this period cut across class, party, and gender.

The Women's Sector of the Falange accepted the view of most churchmen that a woman's place was in the home. . . . Workers, increasingly militant and class-conscious, were as conservative as the ideologues of the regime and the more puritanical sectors of the Church as to the role of women in a modern society. (162)

Despite these reactionary sentiments, *Surcos* uses neorealist conventions effectively to depict "social problems in the barrio." There are many wonderful depth-focus long shots documenting Madrid's teeming streets, open markets, subways, employment offices, and tenements where the members of the family are contextualized amid the anonymous poor. The multitiered tenements with their barred railings, small overcrowded rooms, and overlapping voices, entrap their inhabitants no matter whether they are positioned in the foreground or background.

Yet *Surcos* disarticulates the class discourse of neorealism by presenting the crowd primarily in negative terms and in sharp contrast to the family. Although all the main characters of the film belong to the proletariat, they are interpellated, not through class alignment but through their hierarchical position within the patriarchal family. They are set in opposition, not only to the power bloc (which is

José Antonio Nieves Conde's
Surcos (Furrows, 1951) adapts
neorealist conventions to
present a Falangist
perspective on the patriarchal
family.

displaced onto the personal plane in the villainous Don Roque) but also to the unruly mob. This moral distinction between the family and the mob marks a sharp departure from neorealism, where both are presented as valid collectives and both identified in class terms.

In neorealist classics such as *Paisà, Bicycle Thief,* and *Umberto D,* protagonists are frequently introduced within a crowd, from which they are visibly selected for foregrounding during an action that is usually in progress and that is presumably a common occurrence (e.g., the liberation of an Italian village by American soldiers, a daily hiring of workers, an impromptu demonstration by pensioners in postwar Rome). In this way, it is the typicality of the character and his actions that are valued and emphasized throughout the film, not their singularity or uniqueness. Thus, the emphasis is placed on the iterative or frequentive aspect (narrating once what supposedly has happened several times) rather than on the singulative (narrating once what happened only once).[46]

Surcos takes an ambiguous position on this aspect of representation. Even though the Perez family is chosen from the many that daily arrive in Madrid (and from the millions who moved to the cities in the 1950s), and even though its members are frequently positioned against a crowd of which they are presumably representative, the two Manolos (father and son) are clearly singled out by their moral struggle to retain their rural values and the integrity of the traditional patriarchal family. In this way, the emphasis shifts to the singulative, which is more typical of melodrama.

Surcos expresses a deep distrust of the mob, which is always depicted as anarchic, selfish, and hostile. Repeatedly the mob is instantly transformed into a mass audience for the many brawls, robberies, or confrontations with the police that suddenly erupt in the tenements or streets, its greedy members always ready to grab the spoils.[47] The implication is that such an audience needs to be educated by moralizing puppet shows or Falangist films like this one with a clear ideological thesis.

The anarchist impulse of the mob is particularly strong in the many stray youngsters who are seen roaming the streets without parental supervision—an emphasis that helps the film interpellate its spectators as children who need the strong guidance of a benevolent patriarch like Franco. For example, in the film's most Rosselliniesque sequence, a gang of boys steal the wet shirt that the destitute Manolo had left to dry in the rubble of a bombed-out building while waiting in a soup line provided by soldiers. The marching boys turn this white shirt into a flag, as if they are incipient terrorists. But unlike the precocious left-wing resistance fighters at the end of *Open City* who represent hope for the future, these little anarchists forebode nothing but trouble.

One of the most powerful crowd scenes occurs when the senior Manolo first tries to make money as a street vendor. Against a cheerful background of children playing ring games in the park, he is immediately approached by a small boy who has no money; Manolo's generous patriarchal impulse leads him to give the penniless child a piece of candy. The image then dissolves to three more boys asking for candy who doggedly pursue him; now the children's voices in the background begin to grow louder and more demanding. This time when Manolo gives away candy, it is not out of generosity but out of growing desperation; yet instead of making them go away, his action attracts more children who swarm around him like flies. The image dissolves to a crowd of young faces totally filling the frame, chanting, "We want candy." When the camera pulls back, we see Manolo totally encircled by this threatening mob, which not only draws the attention of a policeman (who confiscates Manolo's merchandise since he has no license) but also acts as gawking spectators to his arrest.

The loss of the father's power is compounded when the young Manolo shares a similar failure, losing his job and his merchandise in a crowded amusement park, where he is distracted by *folklorico* (a bullfight puppet show). After telling his family of his failure, he runs out of the flat in humiliation; only his father follows to console him. Outside in the street when the son hides from the father, we are unsure of whether the son is ashamed of his own failure or whether he sees it merely as a reflection of his father's defeat, with which he refuses to identify. It evokes the moving scene in *Bicycle Thief* in which the boy runs from his father after witnessing his humiliation. Both the neorealist-Hollywood opposition and the centrality of the patriarchal issue are underlined when we recognize in the foreground the movie poster on the structure behind which the son is hiding. It is *Father of the Bride*, a Hollywood comedy starring Spencer Tracy as a lovable patriarch who may be financially successful but who is so easily manipulated by wife and daughter that he is totally anti-thetical to the Falangist ideal. With his father's voice still calling out the name they both share, young Manolo walks away from this poster into the neorealist depth of field.

As the antithesis of neorealism, Hollywood provides *Surcos* with an external force of corruption, which substitutes for the analysis of causes and solutions that are missing from the film. More specifically, the film relies on the fast-paced gangster genre, where divisive in-dividualism and social mobility weaken family ties, and on American noir, where a vision of social corruption and the violation of patri-archal law are displaced within a domesticated Oedipal narrative.

The negative influence of Hollywood escapist films is also evoked in the movie star photos on the walls of rooms inhabited by Pepe's jaded fiancée, Pili, and by Don Roque's mistress, whom Tonia will eventually replace. When Tonia's father goes to retrieve his fallen daughter from Don Roque's flat, she is shown in close-up cowering under a glamor photo of Rita Hayworth. When she leaves the room to get her things, the camera moves in on the father as he breaks into tears under the same photo. The film suggests that the desire for silk stockings and other glamorous paraphernalia featured in Hollywood movies leads women to imitate actresses and to become whores (two terms that were almost synonymous in Francoist Spain). This same pattern was also present in neorealist films such as *Open City* (in which the promiscuous actress Marina betrays Manfredi for a fur coat), in *Bellisima* (a Visconti comedy shown during the Italian film week which features Anna Magnani as a proletariat stage mother who prostitutes herself to make her young daughter a star), and in *Bitter Rice* (in which, as in *Surcos,* the glamour shots are pointedly used as a critique of Hollywood). But in these neorealist examples, the emphasis is more on the conditions of poverty that make these women so susceptible to the lure of glamour than on the assumed (and naturalized) malleability of their gender, as in *Surcos.* This glamorous lure is actively promoted by Don Roque, who capitalizes Tonia's debut as a singer, claiming of her talent, "It's like money in the bank." Yet to make her totally dependent on him so that he can more easily exploit her sexually, he arranges for her performance to be heckled. As Elsaesser observes, melodrama frequently presents "the metaphorical interpretation of class conflict as sexual exploitation and rape."[48] The heckling scene also demonstrates how easily the mass audience can be manipulated; it warns Spaniards against relying on corrupt politicians who want to capitalize Spanish folklore as commercial spectacle.

Like the poster for *Father of the Bride,* the gangster boss represents an alternative route to patriarchal force; he is a corrupt godfather who selfishly exploits and destroys his recruited sons and daughters in crime. One of the strongest images in the film is the erect, dark-clad figure of Don Roque standing over the train tracks where he has dropped Pepe's body after ignoring his pleas for help, overseeing his death with the cold detachment of a remote god. As we hear the whistle of the fast-approaching train, we watch him in medium shot as he calmly lights a cigarette. Then there is a cut to a long shot, which dwarfs his figure, and the steam from the passing train totally engulfs him. Despite the beauty of the spectacle and its symbolic meaning as historic destiny, the image of the steam obliterates both victim and killer, inextricably fusing their fates (as the father and son had earlier been linked in failure within the neorealist aesthetic) and morally reinscribing the American gangster genre as demonic.

From here the film dissolves back to a neorealist depiction of the family collective, where the suffering victims are reunited and redeemed. A slow tracking shot moves us into the cemetery where Pepe's coffin is being lowered into the earth and where the senior Manolo decides, over the protests of wife and daughter, that the family must return to the wheat fields of Salamanca. *Surcos* ends with the bipolar images of train and fields that opened the film and with patriarchal power restored—even though Tonia jumps off the train to pursue her inevitable doom in the city.

This shot of Tonia's escape was censored from the film, as if to assure a happy ending and to position this melodrama more solidly within the escapist category. The suppressed ending could be read as a neorealist resistance to narrative closure, a subversive reminder that the social problem of urban migration still persists. Yet within the gender discourse of Hollywood melodrama and Falangist ideology, it could also be read as the eternal lure of glamour and stardom to those who are malleable, immature, or merely female. And even within the neorealist aesthetic, it could be read as a warning to spectators of either gender who are still captivated by the seductive image of Rita Hayworth.

2 · THE SUBVERSIVE REINSCRIPTION OF MELODRAMA IN *MUERTE DE UN CICLISTA*

DEFINING MELODRAMA   Despite their opposing ideological perspectives, both *Surcos* (1951) and *Muerte de un ciclista* (1955) use melodrama, not only as one side of a Manichaean bipolarity (that is to be associated with Hollywood and contrasted with neorealism) but also as the larger generic framework or mode in which this dialectic is positioned. This doubling is more understandable when one considers four paradoxical dualities within which melodrama has recently been conceptualized.

First, within traditional humanist discourse, melodrama is usually a pejorative term for a low form of entertainment drama, characterized by Manichaean morality, one-dimensional characters, histrionic posturing, musical intervals, and emotional manipulation. However, this popular genre has recently been rehabilitated in the contexts of poststructuralism, postmodernism, and feminism where the distinctions between high art and popular culture are no longer valid, where excess, acknowledged simulation, and breaks with realism are highly valued, and where the politics of gender within a domestic Oedipal narrative are a prime object of scrutiny.

Second, in *The Melodramatic Imagination* (1976), Peter Brooks (one of melodrama's most powerful rehabilitators) distinguishes between the noun, *melodrama,* as a definite dramatic genre with a specific history that differs in various national contexts, and the adjective, *melodramatic,* as "an abiding mode in the modern imagination" that is characterized by excess and that cuts across many periods, cultures, and art forms, both of the high and low variety.[1] Third, an analogous duality within cinematic melodrama is posed by Gledhill, who defines it both as "a particular, if mobile and fragmentary, genre, specializing in heterosexual and family relations," and as "a founding mode of Hollywood cinema" cutting across all periods and most genres.[2]

Finally, in terms of ideological function, melodrama can work, on the one hand, as a reactionary escapist genre that naturalizes the dominant ideology by displacing political issues onto the personal plane of the family, as in the case of most popular Hollywood genres and of the popular cinema made under Fascist regimes in Italy, Germany, and Spain. On the other hand, it can function subversively—either through excess and contradictions that are part of the genre itself or through radical innovations by a wide-ranging group of practitioners, including a German émigré like Douglas Sirk, a former neorealist like Luchino Visconti, radical homosexuals like Pier Paolo Pasolini and Rainer Werner Fassbinder, radical feminists like Helma Sanders-Brahms, Chantal Akerman, and Nina Menkes, and Spanish mavericks like Luis Buñuel, Pedro Almodóvar, José Juan Bigas Luna, and Eloy de la Iglesia. By pushing the conventional excessiveness to an even greater extreme, these subversive filmmakers foreground the ideological contradictions that Hollywood melodrama normally glosses over, demonstrating that family and gender are a legitimate site for serious political struggle. As Spanish philosopher Ortega y Gasset observed of Wagner (whose *Tristan and Isolde* frequently provided the subversive *melos* for the deeply ironic melodramas of Buñuel), "In Wagner, melodrama reaches its highest exaltation. And as always happens, when a form attains its maximum its conversion into the opposite at once begins."[3]

Although most Spanish discourse in film criticism uses melodrama only in the pejorative sense, it is the rich interplay among all of these meanings that best accounts for how this mode functions in actual filmic practice within Spain. A notable exception is Gubern, who writes in his "Teoría del melodrama,"

The term *melodrama* . . . today is used in the Castilian language to designate something that in common expression is very much like *dramón* (the expressive suffix *-ón* specifies *overblown, bigwig*—at the same time, an extolled and contemptuous performance), that is to say, a variant of drama that is simultaneously the most exalted and the most abject.[4]

Within these various dualities, we can see melodrama's ambiguous relationship with realism, which is crucial to its usage in the Spanish context of the 1950s. This ambiguity is addressed in Brooks's definition of the melodramatic mode, where the extravagant representations and moral intensity of the form simultaneously place it in opposition to the realistic mode and yet require a realistic context to rupture.

Within an apparent context of "realism" and the ordinary, they seemed in fact to be staging a heightened and hyperbolic drama, making reference to pure and polar concepts of darkness and light, salvation and damnation. (Brooks, ix)

Like Brooks, Gledhill also acknowledges that melodrama is both dependent on realism (against whose shifting meanings melodrama is constantly redefined) and its archrival—as co-founders of popular cinema, as diverging epistemological projects, and as competitive survivors against the onslaught of deconstruction.

While the drive of realism is to possess the world by understanding it, . . . the central drive of melodrama is to force meaning and identity from the inadequacies of language. . . . In the face of the limitations of realism exposed by poststructuralism it operates on the level not so much of "yes, but . . ." than of "So what!" (33)

One of the primary ways that melodrama forces such meaning from inadequate representation is through its excessiveness, which is displayed not only in the histrionic language, gestures, and behavior of its characters but also through lurching ruptures in the narrative and through extravagant expressiveness in the mise-en-scène. In his influential analysis of Hollywood melodramas made between 1940 and 1963, Elsaesser observes,

Considered as an expressive code, melodrama might therefore be de-scribed as a particular form of dramatic mise-en-scène, characterized by a dynamic use of spatial and musical categories, as opposed to intellectual or literary ones. . . . This type of cinema depends on the way "melos" is given to "drama" by means of lighting, montage, visual rhythms, decor, style of acting, music—that is, on the ways the mise-en-scène translates character into action . . . and action into gesture and dynamic space.[5]

In applying this expressive code, Spanish filmmakers using melo-drama in the 1950s could create sudden discontinuities in mise-en-scène by shifting abruptly between Hollywood and neorealist con-ventions—a strategy that is most striking in *Muerte de un ciclista,* where it is used as a class discourse to reveal the Hollywood genre's traditional alignment with the bourgeoisie.

Melodrama's identification with the bourgeoisie is connected both to its historical links with realism and to its departures from tragedy, an earlier genre of excess and Oedipal transgression. British critic Nowell-Smith claims that in contrast to tragedy in which all subject positions (i.e., those of protagonists, author, and spectator) belong to the aristocracy, in melodrama the address is from one bourgeois to another, and the represented "object" is the Oedipal drama within a bourgeois family.[6] This explanation helps account for why the melodramatic elements within neorealism grew stronger as the move-ment increasingly included bourgeois protagonists, as in Antonioni's *Cronaca di un amore* (Chronicle of a Love, 1950), which exerted such a strong influence on *Muerte de un ciclista,* and even in *Umberto D* (which was widely regarded as one of the purest examples of the neorealist aesthetic). Yet in restricting melodrama's class identification solely with the bourgeoisie and its "middling power relations," Nowell-Smith denies a place in the genre for "the exercise of social power"—a key concern both for neorealists and for Spanish filmmakers of the 1950s.

Elsaesser's conception of melodrama (which allows a subject position for the proletariat and which puts greater emphasis on the powerlessness of its characters and their inability to "change the stifling social milieu") seems more compatible with the working-class victims in neorealism and more relevant to the Francoist context. Although this emphasis on powerlessness may increase the populist appeal of melodrama, it leaves little room for political change. Gledhill argues that, even with these limits, melodrama can still serve a valuable political function.

Melodrama addresses us within the limitations of the status quo, of the ideologically permissible. . . . Not having a programmatic analysis for the future, its possibilities lie in this double acknowledgment of how things are in a given historical conjuncture, and of the primary desires and resistances contained within it. (38)

Although many Spanish filmmakers were content to work within the limitations of the status quo, those like Bardem and Nieves Conde who had participated in the Salamanca Congress were eager for social change. For this dimension, they would turn to neorealism. Yet as Marxist critics frequently noted, a pragmatic political agenda was difficult to find even within this discourse. Despite their theoretical claims, instead of offering viable political solutions for the socioeconomic problems they depicted, neorealists (especially DeSica and Zavattini) frequently displaced these issues onto melodramatic conflicts within an individual family, particularly the restoration of an impoverished patriarch's moral authority over his cherished dependents. We find this dynamic in the similar final reconciliations between victimized father and son in *Bicycle Thief* and homeless master and dog in *Umberto D.* According to Besas, when *Bicycle Thief* was shown in Madrid in 1950, Spanish censors added the following narratorial voice-over to the ending, as if to anchor an optimistic reading that would be consistent with escapist melodrama and Francoist discourse: "But Antonio wasn't alone. His little son, Bruno, squeezing his hand, assured him that the future was bright with hope."[7]

Practically everyone writing on melodrama emphasizes the centrality of the family to the genre, which is one of the reasons it had such great appeal both for a popular cinema under fascism and for an oppositional cinema forced to negotiate with Fascist censors and commercial pressures. Unlike tragedy in which the royal family and their power struggles simultaneously involve both the public and private spheres (a condensation that Franco tried to retain in *Raza,* the historical melodrama that idealized his own family against the background of the Civil War), melodrama typically displaces issues of political power onto the domestic register where they are frequently transformed into generational conflicts (as in *Surcos*) or sexual transgression (as in *Muerte*). Landy finds this same pattern of displacement onto generational conflicts and romance to be typical of the Italian melodramas made under fascism;[8] it is also commonplace in the official melodramas supported by the Francoist regime. Nowell-Smith reads this family emphasis in class terms.

The locus of power is the family and individual private property, the two being connected through inheritance. In this world of circumscribed horizons (which corresponds very closely to Marx's definition of "petty bourgeois ideology") patriarchal right is of central importance. The son has to become like his father in order to take over his property and his place within the community (or [if] the father is evil, [then] the son must grow up different from him in order to be able to redistribute the property at the moment of inheritance, etc., etc.). Notably, the question of law or legitimacy, so central to tragedy, is turned inward from "Has this man a right to rule (over us)?" to "Has this man a right to rule a family (like ours)?" (191– 192)

This privileging of the relation between father and son, which was also characteristic of Fascist discourse, was dramatically foregrounded in the Spanish version of film noir (cine negro), one of the most popular new forms of melodrama to emerge in Spain during the early 1950s and to exert a strong influence on *Surcos* and *Muerte*. According to Antonio Lloréns, *cine negro español* (which was launched in 1950 by films like *Apartado de correos 1001* [Post Office Box 1001] and *Brigada criminal* [Criminal Brigade]) served during this decade as one of the most effective forms of political critique for both the Left and the Right.[9] It continued to be tolerated by the Francoist regime through the 1960s and 1970s, partly because these films so blatantly imitated American and French action genres (e.g., gangster, policier, psychological thriller) and thereby appeared to minimize Spanish specificity. Lloréns suggests that their common denominator was crime, or more specifically, the violation of patriarchal law, which enabled them to make allegorical statements about Francoism that slipped past the censors.

Visconti's *Ossessione*, his 1942 adaptation of *The Postman Always Rings Twice*, offered a powerful Italian precedent for using noir in this way; even though it was banned in Spain, the film was widely acknowledged as one of the first examples of neorealism made under the Fascist regime. Yet unlike *Ossessione* and classical Hollywood noir (e.g., *Double Indemnity, The Postman Always Rings Twice, Gilda, Laura,* and *The Lady from Shanghai*), Spanish cine negro does not focus on erotic desire for the woman. It expresses its cultural specificity by operating primarily as a discourse on fathers and sons.[10] Most of the criminals become deviant because there is something wrong with their father: either he is a dead idol impossible to equal (*Crimen de doble filo* [Double-edged Crime], 1964), or too weak (*No dispares contra mi* [Don't Shoot Me], 1961), or too strict (*Los atracadores* [The Robbers], 1961), or, if he is a good father, then he inspires heroic imitation (as in *El ojo de cristal* [The Glass Eye], 1955). In these examples of cine negro, the concern is not with the son's inheritance of private property but with his patrimonial right to wield phallic power and to embody patriarchal law. Thus, by means of political allegory, the melodramatic question, "Has this patriarch the right to rule over a family like ours?" was easily re-translated back into the tragic question, "Has this patriarch the right to rule over Spain?" Despite the different class alignments of melo-drama and tragedy, this slippage weakened the boundary between the two genres—a boundary that always remained permeable in Spain.

By attending to the cultural specificity of melodrama, one can perhaps clarify the issue of the genre's class alignment with the bourgeoisie and the working class. Gledhill reminds us that the meaning of *bourgeoisie* changes according to its contexts.

Melodrama is frequently associated with the bourgeoisie—in the eighteenth century a European bourgeoisie, struggling for ascendancy over a decadent aristocracy, or, two hundred years later, a bourgeoisie "decaying from within" in Eisenhower's America. However, between these two periods of bourgeois "crisis" lies the intervening generaliza-tion of "crisis" and "mode" across social classes and cultural forms which made melodrama both a central nineteenth-century paradigm and a formative influence in twentieth-century mass culture. A cru-cial factor in these shifts is the role played by emergent working-class audiences and "popular" tradition in the early formation of melo-drama. (14)

It is generally assumed that Pixérécourt invented the popular dramatic genre and its name shortly after the French Revolution, in which the bourgeoisie were triumphant.[11] According to Brooks, classic French melodrama was written for "a public that extended from the lower classes, especially artisans and shopkeepers, through all sectors of the middle class, and even embraced members of the aristocracy—including the Empress Josephine herself . . . whereas in England, melodrama seems quickly to have become exclusively en-tertainment for the lower orders" (xii).

Elsaesser claims that another important determinant of the genre's class identification in different national contexts is the choice of artistic forms in which the melodramatic situations were habitually embodied.

> In England, it has mainly been the novel and the literary gothic . . . ; in France, it is the costume drama and historical novel; in Germany, "high" drama and the ballad . . . ; and finally, in Italy the opera. (166)

In Italy, where a successful bourgeois revolution never occurred, Verdi's popular operas linked melodrama to the failures of the *risorgimento,* in which the proletariat and peasantry were betrayed by the bourgeoisie and its alliance with the aristocracy. Thus, in the cinematic melodramas of the aristocratic Visconti (which are so heavily steeped in the operatic traditions of Verdi), the genre's class alignment is very malleable, moving from a conflict between the proletariat and petit bourgeoisie in *Ossessione* to the peasantry in *La terra trema* (The Earth Trembles) to the aristocracy in *Il senso* to the proletariat in *Rocco and His Brothers* and to an analysis of the complex class struggles during the risorgimento in *Il gattopardo* (The Leopard).

While European melodrama allowed for analyses of class conflict, Gledhill observes that the American adaptation of the genre to its "egalitarian" sociopolitical context tended to erase class differences, or to transpose them "into country/city oppositions." She claims that this ideological reinscription produced "an insistently populist address" with an extraordinary international appeal that could easily cut across class lines and national boundaries (24–25).

In redefining what was "popular" and in erasing class oppositions, this form of Hollywood melodrama had considerable appeal to Fascists, whose populist movement suppressed class struggle, and this is precisely how it was used in *Surcos.* Yet it was also possible for leftist filmmakers like Bardem to reinscribe Hollywood melodrama with the class oppositions it had formerly contained in its European context, particularly following the model of Visconti, who had been so highly regarded by *Objetivo.* Thus, melodrama offered Spaniards an effective site for dialogizing Hollywood and Italian conventions.

THE CULTURAL SPECIFICITY OF SPANISH MELODRAMA   As in most other national film histories, melodrama has been an important staple in
virtually all periods of Spanish cinema. From the silent era to the
present, the genre has drawn heavily on Spanish popular traditions
to give it a specific cultural inflection. There was the Golden Age
drama of Lope de Vega and Calderón de la Barca with its hysterical
excesses. There was *Rinconete y Cortadillo* by Cervantes and picaresque fiction like *El Lazarillo de Tormes* that helped spawn the serial
novel, which Gubern claims is "synonymous with melodrama in
Latin countries."[12] There was the ritual art of the bullfight, whose
rigorous aesthetic fusion of tragedy, melodrama, music, violence,
and spectacle was codified in the late eighteenth century. There were
popular theatrical and musical genres that proliferated in the eighteenth century, such as *sainetes* (one-act farces), *jácaras* (ballads and
dances), and *tonadillas* (musical interludes). There was the *zarzuela,*
a form of light comic opera of courtly origin that became increasingly popularized in the eighteenth century; introduced to the silent
cinema by Segundo de Chomón as early as 1910, it was widely
adapted to Spanish talkies in the 1930s, where it competed commercially with the original theatrical versions. There was the popular
puppet theater, which was radicalized by Ramón del Valle-Inclán,
particularly in his "melodramas for puppets." There were the great
nineteenth-century melodramatic novels, such as Leopoldo Alas's
La regenta and many works by Benito Pérez Galdós, which were
frequently adapted to the screen. There was also the colonization
of Spain and gypsy culture as the exotic "Other" in the French
romantic novel, particularly in Mérimée's *Carmen.* And, drawing
on many of these earlier forms, there were the poetic plays of
Federico García Lorca that, in blurring the line between tragedy
and melodrama, reached new heights of emotional excess and stylization.

   As a distinct dramatic genre distinguished from tragedy, Spanish
melodrama must be traced back to the late eighteenth century. As an
admirer of tragedy and realism in the great humanist tradition, I. L.
McClelland takes the pejorative view of melodrama in his two-

volume *Spanish Drama of Pathos,* 1750–1808, in which he is primarily concerned with exploring the transformation of "tragedia pura" into an "emotionally contemporary" popular form of late-eighteenth-century bourgeois drama. Nevertheless, he is very helpful in defining the national specificity of Spanish melodrama and its historic roots. McClelland finds its external sources not in "the lugubrious settings and supernatural horrors popularized in the rest of Europe by Pixérécourt and others" but in Rousseau's *Pygmalion,* a one-act *scène lyrique* for one or two characters with intervals of music, which was known in Spain for some five years before being performed in Paris in 1775; and in Italian opera, which not only contributed to the development of the light comic opera of zarzuela but also modified classical tragedy by introducing the "tragic pause" during which soliloquies were replaced by stilted posturing to music.[13] According to McClelland, by the end of the century, these two influences generated two main streams of Spanish melodrama: the musical monologue or solo recital (adapted from Rousseau) and the full-scale melo-dialogue (modeled on Italian opera) involving several characters and broader emotional situations in a short drama with a generous adornment of mime and music.

In both streams, he claims the primary drive was to create a new "acceptable form of concentrated tragedy." As a mark of Spanish melodrama's national specificity, this drive helps to explain why the fusion of tragedy and melodrama constantly recurs—not only in Spain's Golden Age drama of the past and more recently in the plays of Lorca but also in historical films like *Raza* (1941), *Los ultimos de Filipinas* (1945), *Locura de amor* (Madness of Love, 1948), and even in Saura's *Llanto por un bandido* (1961) and in films featuring matadors and gypsies like *Los golfos* (1959), Mario Camus's *Con el viento solano* (With the East Wind, 1965), and Saura's dance trilogy in the 1980s, *Bodas de sangre* (Blood Wedding, 1981), *Carmen* (1983), and *El amor brujo* (Love, the Magician, 1986). Because of McClelland's emphasis on melodrama's relationship with tragedy, he tends to consider the genre's connections only with bourgeois forms of legitimate theater and to ignore the influence of low popular culture, which, as Gledhill demonstrates, was an equally important source for the forging of this new mode.

Yet McClelland does make the important observation that in the Spanish context, bourgeois melodrama was almost immediately fused with its parodic double, particularly in the form of the farcical sainete popularized in the eighteenth century by Don Ramón de la Cruz.[14] This distinguishing Spanish characteristic can be at least partially explained by the strong tradition of burlesque and satire and the coupling of high and low forms in Golden Age writers like Cervantes and Quevedo—a tradition that was central to Bakhtin's concept of dialogism and that would later draw new energy from *esperpento* in the plays and novels of Valle-Inclán.

In the cinema, we find this same kind of parodic doubling in the sainetes with music that Buñuel made at Filmófono in the 1930s and in his subversive Mexican melodramas of the 1950s, particularly in *El* (1952) and *Ensayo de un crimen/La vida criminal de Archibaldo de la Cruz* (The Criminal Life of Archibaldo de la Cruz, 1955). One also thinks of Almodóvar's parodic adaptations of Cocteau's melodramatic monologues from *The Human Voice* in both *La ley del deseo* (The Law of Desire) and *Mujeres al borde de un ataque de nervios* (Women on the Verge of a Nervous Breakdown) in the 1980s. This tradition of immediate parodic doubling also helps explain why it was so easy for Spanish melodrama to be dialogized and ideologically reinscribed both by the Left and the Right, why it could so readily serve the cinema both of the Francoist regime and the opposition, and why it could so easily cross class lines.

Ortega y Gasset is much more illuminating than McClelland on the popular local sources for Spanish melodrama and its parodic doubling. He helps to explain why the genre has always had such a strong populist appeal in Spain, which cuts across boundaries of class and ideology. He argues that the eighteenth century was marked by a "frenzied" enthusiasm for popular Spanish customs identified with the common folk, which were imitated by all classes, especially by the aristocracy, which, having proved itself incompetent in politics, administration, war, and every other form of cultural leadership in the late seventeenth century, turned to the "humbler" classes to define and stylize what was distinctively Spanish.

> The Spanish people created as it were a second nature which was shaped by aesthetic qualities. And that repertoire of constantly-used lines and rhythms constituted a vocabulary, a precious substance from which the popular arts emerged.[15]

It was this stylization that would survive over the next two centuries and continue to be popularized in the españolada. Ortega y Gasset claims this "wave of plebeianism" found its grandest expression in the bullfight and the popular theater, two forms of indigenous melodrama that emerged and flourished with extraordinary success in the middle of the eighteenth century. He credits the brilliance of this theatrical period not to the writing of the dramatists but to the histrionic performances of the actors, who, like the matadors, were primarily of plebeian birth and whose popularity was comparable to that of Hollywood stars.[16]

Although this passion for Spanish customs and its melodramatic expression could be found in a wide array of genres ranging from tragedy to farce, it became a divisive political issue on which two opposing factions were polarized. As in subsequent periods of crises (such as the Civil War), the nation in the eighteenth century was already divided into two Spains. The vast majority, who wanted to protect Spain's cultural purity and glorify its unique traditions, were opposed by an elite group of noblemen, intellectuals, and statesmen who wanted to modernize Spain by importing the Enlightenment from France and by ridding the country of its "ignoble" local customs (a position that was compromised by Napoleon's invasion of Spain).[17] Yet Ortega y Gasset observes that when these men of learning "denounced plebeian fashions, their prose was saturated with the very idiom used by partisans of the popular in conversation, which shows how deeply and irresistibly plebeianism had penetrated" (117).

Although this struggle was in full swing in 1775, the year that Goya arrived in Madrid, Ortega y Gasset insists that it was not until 1787 (when Goya became committed to the Enlightenment) that this conflict began to affect the representation of Spanish customs in his paintings.

> Then and not before does he begin to paint themes which have been called essentially Spanish, precisely because he . . . had ceased to have a typically Spanish outlook. . . . As that viewpoint is double and contradictory—a liking for the plebeian when contemplated from a superior position, and a rejection of it triggered off by the "idea"—Goya's work in this area is ambivalent and equivocal. Often we do not know if he is exalting or condemning his subjects. (120–121)

Goya's ambivalent parodic stance would provide Spanish filmmakers in the 1950s with a model for how to defamiliarize stylized Spanish customs and their melodramatic excesses, but in their case, the "outsiders'" view would come from the populist perspective of Italian neorealism rather than from the elite vantage point of the French Enlightenment.

Another important characteristic of Spanish melodrama that Mc-Clelland identifies is the representation of mental activity through "posturing silences," which were accompanied by music during the "tragic pause" in the narrative. This strategy was later well suited not only to the silent cinema, where melodrama was to flourish and where it was traditionally accompanied by music, but also to a cinema of repression where many topics could not be spoken. McClelland claims that these late-eighteenth-century plays and their parodic variations moved away from direct narration to a more indirect, intense psychologizing about a limited number of characters, creating an emphasis on memory and interiorization that was essentially modern and that made challenging cognitive demands on the spectator.[18] This suggestive observation helps explain how this genre could become a subversive force in the New Spanish Cinema—how the indirect, highly interiorized narratives of Saura and Erice with their complex hermeneutics owed a great deal to the melodramatic genre in which they were positioned.

McClelland also helps us to see that in Spain, as in Italy, the combination of *melos* and *drama* was taken quite literally, for the varied Spanish musical traditions were a rich resource for the genre's emotional rhythms—not only in musical monologues, zarzuelas, tonadillas, jácaras, bullfights, and operatic versions of *Carmen* but also in the varied "plebeian" traditions of cabaret, music hall, and flamenco. In fact, many of the most popular melodramas in the 1930s and 1940s featured singers, like the celebrated Imperio Argentina.

The most successful melodrama of the 1950s was Cifesa's musical, *El último cuplé* (The Last Song, 1957). Directed by Juan de Orduña, it featured Sara Montiel, who had been working in Mexico and Hollywood. With its extravagant spectacle and lush colors, it competed successfully with Hollywood musicals both at home in Spain and throughout Latin America.[19] According to Diego Galán, the film's popularity derived from the novelty of using the *cuplé* (music hall songs) rather than the clichéd Andalusian numbers usually featured in españoladas, particularly since the lyrics were full of risqué double entendres. Galán claims this explicit eroticism made Montiel "the first woman of Spanish cinema with a sexual capacity"; that is, she was portrayed not just as erotic spectacle for the male gaze but as a sexual subject who actively pursued her own desire.[20] While this dimension was a departure from the dominant ideology, in most other ways, the film was compatible with Fascist discourse.

Set within a flashback structure, the reflexive story of *El último cuplé* traces the rise, fall, and comeback of María Luján, a music hall singer who becomes a great international star but whose three love affairs (especially one with a matador) repeatedly bring her pain. Within this masochistic discourse, it is her capacity to experience and express intense pain that makes her singing so extraordinary and that kills her on stage in midsong. Like the patriotic dramas promoted by the regime, the film refers to specific periods and events, as if it were presenting a history of this musical form, yet it makes several strategic omissions. For example, when in Paris on the eve of World War II, the heroine decides to return to Spain where she claims she can find peace and refuge. Although the film also covers the late 1930s, there

Sara Montiel is constructed as
a folkloric sexual subject in
Juan de Orduña's musical
melodrama, *El último cuplé*
(The Last Song, 1957).

is no mention whatever of the Spanish Civil War, which presumably must have occurred in one of the narrative's many ellipses. Though the flashback structure foregrounds memory, what is emphasized are personal recollections of romantic highs and lows and popular memories of changing styles in fashion and music (precisely the kinds of memories that Patino would repoliticize in *Canciones para después de una guerra*). But in *El último cuplé*, all traces of contemporary Spanish political history are conveniently repressed.

This kind of escapist melodrama (which included musical interludes and drew on Spanish popular forms) provided Cifesa with many of its biggest successes, even in the 1930s. As Gubern explains,

The introduction of talking pictures in North American and European film industries coincided with the birth of the II Republic in Spain (1931). . . . The shaky Spanish film industry which got under way in 1932 . . . almost exactly copied the cultural models established during the silent era under the dictatorship of General Primo de Rivera. . . . Side by side with the production that imitated the cosmopolitan genres colonizing our screens, there persisted a local cinema dominated by ruralism, religious conservatism and aesthetic autarchy. . . . The cosmopolitan directors tempted by Hollywood film-making techniques were relatively few, since most of the production of the Republican period before the civil war was dominated by a mannered or rural provincialism, whose most privileged genres were the *españolada* . . . , the *zarzuela* . . . and clerical cinema.[21]

What is most pertinent here to my argument is the cultural and ideological adaptability of melodrama, which could so readily be absorbed both by the local Spanish genres and by the Hollywood imitations and which could retain its popularity both with Republicans and with Nationalists. Perhaps the best example of this ideological instability is provided by Rey's *Morena Clara* (Clara, the Brunette, 1936), a melodramatic españolada of class-crossed love featuring a poor gypsy girl (played by singer Imperio Argentina) who falls in love with a bourgeois Andalusian prosecutor and who is unjustly accused of stealing. Besas observes,

Even when the Spanish Civil War broke out . . . , the film continued its run in both the Nationalist and Republican camps. It was only after denunciatory pressures due to Florián Rey and Imperio Argentina's activities in Nazi Germany that Republican authorities prohibited the film. . . .[22] The film's enormous popularity with both of the contending sides is perhaps indicative of the Spanish public's total lack of awareness at that time of the ideological capacities of cinema. Films were still regarded as a form of naive entertainment, like seeing a *zarzuela* or an opera. (11–12)

Although Besas claims this "lack of ideological awareness" is a Spanish trait, one could argue conversely that each side was attempting to claim this populist melodrama (and its vision of Spanishness) for its own ideology. Yet to function subversively either for the Right or the Left, melodrama would have to push these local Spanish traditions associated with the españolada and zarzuela to the point of parody where they would reveal their ideological implications. This is precisely what happens with cabaret singing in *Surcos,* flamenco in *Muerte,* bullfighting in *Golfos,* and all three in *¡Bienvenido, Mr. Marshall!*

What is perhaps most significant about the cultural specificity of Spanish melodrama is the way it is inflected with fascism and Catholicism. Melodrama had an immediate appeal to Fascist discourse, partly because the two share so many crucial characteristics. They are both highly contradictory (which may be partly caused by their adoption of a Manichaean morality), both capable of being read as both radical and reactionary, both historical and ahistorical, both rooted in realism yet highly idealized and hyperbolic. Within melodrama, we have already traced these contradictions through a series of paradoxical dualities. And within fascism, Ortega y Gasset defines the contradictions most succinctly:

It asserts authoritarianism and organizes rebellion. It fights against contemporary democracy and, on the other hand, does not believe in the restoration of any past rule. It seems to pose itself as the forge of a strong State, and uses means most conducive to its dissolution, as if it were a destructive faction or a secret society. Whichever way we approach fascism we find that it is simultaneously one thing and the contrary.[23]

Even a filmmaker like Douglas Sirk, whose films were so central in theorizing the radical potential of Hollywood melodrama, had his first encounter with the genre in a Fascist context, while he was still working at Germany's major studio complex, UFA (Universum Film A.G.), shortly after Hitler came to power. Gledhill claims that this early experience "gave him particular understanding of the contradictions hidden in the formal and ideological operations of melodrama" (7).

The most important common trait shared by melodrama and fascism is the privileging of the family as the primary site where ideological issues can be displaced and naturalized. Yet rather than suppress the political plane by focusing entirely on the private sphere as in most classical Hollywood melodrama, Fascist melodrama acknowledges and politicizes the connection between the domestic and public realms. Like subversive melodrama, it proclaims the family as a legitimate site for effective political action, mobilizing "the people" around universal issues of morality, generation, and gender that cut across class lines.

While this convergence of Fascist discourse and melodrama also occurred in Italy and Germany, it assumed special significance in Spain, because only here did the authoritarian ruler increasingly disavow his allegiance to fascism, displacing it (as we have seen) onto Nationalism and a revival of traditional Catholicism. Only in Spain was Fascist ideology subordinated to and rewritten as traditional Catholic doctrine. Hence, Spain was the context that could take the greatest advantage of melodrama's drive to reinvest the secular world of the family with (what Brooks calls) "the moral occult"—to create a "domain of operative spiritual values" that would replace the "Traditional Sacred" that was lost during the Enlightenment. Like the neo-Catholic revival that provided the base for Franco's populist appeal and unifying power, melodrama sought to reverse this historic "desacralisation" in which "the explanatory and cohesive force of sacred myth lost its power, and its political and social representations lost their legitimacy" (Brooks, 15–18).

Another trait shared by the aesthetic discourses of fascism and melodrama is the cultivation of excess or the grand scale, which is expressed not only through the hyperbolic language, gestures, and behavior of characters but also in the extravagance of the mise-en-scène—qualities that can be found in Fascist rallies and architectural monuments as readily as in Hollywood melodrama. While this convergence on excess also occurred in Italy and Germany, only in Spain was it further intensified by the conventions of the Counter-Reformation, which were stronger and longer lived in Spain than in any other European nation and which drew new energies from Franco's neo-Catholic traditionalist revival. As an artistic legacy of the Counter-Reformation, the *baroque* shared with the melodramatic mode and with the Fascist aesthetic that paradoxical combination of wild excessiveness, on the one hand, and moral correctness and rigidity, on the other.[24]

Thus, in Spain, the conventional emotional excesses of melodrama were inflected with a specifically Catholic sadomasochistic discourse, which merged with Fascist rhetoric in fetishizing suffering and death. In contrast to the masochism of Hollywood family melodrama, described by Elsaesser, where suffering victims "emerge as lesser human beings for having . . . acquiesced to the ways of the world" (177), the neo-Catholic Spanish context ensures that such suffering always ennobles the martyred losers, as is powerfully demonstrated in *Muerte de un ciclista*.

MUERTE DE UN CICLISTA   Bardem's *Muerte de un ciclista* (1955), with its stunning visuals and brilliant structure, demonstrates a mastery of both the neorealist and Hollywood styles, which helped it to become an international success. The film adopts the language of the classical Hollywood melodrama, specifically the Hitchcock thriller—its narrative syntax, its strategies of suture, its glossy surface, and its glamorous close-ups that privilege the star. Yet it exaggerates these conventions to such a degree that it exposes their implicit ideological endorsement of the destructive egotism of the haute bourgeoisie. Then it ruptures that style with a neorealist sequence whose deep-focus long shots reduce the size of the protagonist and reposition him within a broader context of class conflict. Since the film devotes most of its screen time to the rich, it is primarily the Hollywood discourse that is disarticulated and reinscribed. The neorealist discourse remains largely intact, for it is the disruptive alternative that helps the spectator and the protagonist Juan see what is wrong with his life.

Both visually and verbally, this rupture is figured as the breaking of a window, which reflexively exposes the naturalized representation implicit in Bazin's notion of the movie screen as window, which is essential to both stylistics. The film goes beyond Bazinian realism to create a reflexive structure in which the aesthetic discourses of Hollywood melodrama and neorealism can be ideologically repositioned. This strategy in some ways anticipates what the Cuban cinema was later to achieve in the late 1960s in *Memorias de subdesarrollo* (Memories of Underdevelopment, 1968) and *Lucia* (1969). It also reflects the influence of Antonioni's first feature (one of the neorealist films shown in Madrid during the Italian film week), *Cronaca di un amore,* 1950, which also starred Lucía Bosé as a bourgeois adulteress suspected of murder in a class-crossed melodrama.[25]

Muerte opens with the iconographic image of a desolate country road. A lone cyclist emerges from the left foreground and rides off into the background, disappearing out of the frame. Then a dark car drives forth from the background, swerving. Since the road is hilly, we do not actually see the collision, which is evoked by overly dramatic nondiegetic music. As in films by Rossellini and Antonioni, we are expected to fill in the ellipses. When the film cuts to a close-up of the bourgeois couple in the car, we are firmly positioned within the narrative vehicle of melodrama. The close-up immediately sutures us into identification with the bourgeois killers, María José and Juan, who are individualized in the singulative, rather than with the anonymous cyclist whose face and corpse we never see and who

Juan (Alberto Closas) and
María José (Lucía Bosé) are
the bourgeois murderers
privileged by the
melodramatic narrative and
its close-ups in Juan Antonio
Bardem's *Muerte de un ciclista*
(Death of a Cyclist, 1955).

always remains representative of the working class in the iterative. When the couple gets out of the car to examine the victim, we see only the wheel of his broken bicycle spinning in the foreground. The man says he is still alive; but the woman, who was driving, summons her companion back to the car. As they drive off and leave the cyclist to die in the road, they evoke the glamorous Daisy and Gatsby in a similar incident from F. Scott Fitzgerald's American novel, *The Great Gatsby*.

This opening introduces a pattern of perpetual slippage between alternative ways of reading any scene, in the singulative or the iterative—a decision that is determined not by an anchoring voice-over but by other narrative and stylistic choices. The highly stylized nature of this sequence calls attention to the choices being made: of what to show and what to omit, of which character to hold on, of whether to use a close-up or a long shot, of what sound will accompany the image (like the monotonous rhythm of the windshield wipers that heightens the tension and accentuates the temporary absence of dialogue). These images do not seem natural or inevitable as in most Hollywood films that erase the marks of their enunciation; rather, they appear to be the result of deliberate choices with specific ideological implications.

This issue of taking responsibility for choices is central to the plot. It is the position Juan reaches at the end of the film and which is imposed onto María José both by her lover, Juan (who wants her to go with him to the police to confess), and by her husband, Miguel (who wants her to go abroad with him to escape). She chooses to murder Juan in precisely the same way she had killed the cyclist in the so-called accident that opened the film.

Though this theme has existential resonance, it is made explicitly Spanish by being connected with the Civil War. Later we learn that Juan and María José had been engaged before the war. When he went off to fight for Franco, she did not wait: she married someone else. The war emptied Juan's life of meaning, leading him to a disillusioned cynicism in which no choice seemed possible. But later he admits the war was only an excuse ("a useful thing . . . you can blame everything on it"). In the final sequence, we discover that the location of the accident was chosen by Bardem because it was a major battlefield in the war and the site of the trenches where Juan had brooded over María José. Thus, this choice forces us to confront the responsibility of their class for the murder of Juan in the singulative melodramatic plot, for the careless destruction of the working-class cyclist in the real-life news event on which the film was based, and for the wanton slaughter of so many Spaniards in the historical events of the Civil War.

The link to Hitchcock is made explicit in the party sequence that follows the opening, where the parasitical art critic Rafa sings a song called "Blackmail" because he has seen María José and Juan together in her husband's car. Later, in an art gallery (which exhibits modernist painters like Klee), Rafa will remark that *blackmail (chantaje)* "is an ugly word that's not even Castilian," evoking Franco's law of allowing only Castilian to be spoken in the Spanish cinema. The word also evokes the title of one of Hitchcock's earliest thrillers, *Blackmail* (1929), the first sound film made in England, which also focused on a couple trying to cover up a murder that the woman had committed and being blackmailed by an odious little man.[26] In its ideological reinscription, *Muerte* reverses the class positions. Whereas Hitchcock's murder victim was an artist, the killer a shopgirl, and the blackmailer a subproletariat criminal, Bardem places the blackmailer in the art world and makes the victim a worker and the killers members of the haute bourgeoisie. More specifically, they are members of the international set who want to modernize Spain and position it with the Western capitalist democracies (whose paintings, novels, and movies are frequently evoked), even if it demands the sacrifice of traditional Catholic values.

The dynamics of the suture are most effectively revealed in a brilliant sequence that intercuts between María José in her brightly lit modernist flat, trying to persuade her husband, Miguel, to take her away from Madrid on a business trip, and Juan smoking alone in his traditional dark bedroom brooding. The Manichaean contrast in lighting, decor, and tone helps to underline the moral difference in the way the two lovers cope with the manslaughter—to escape or to brood, the same respective reactions they had to their separation during the Civil War. Although nothing really happens in this sequence in terms of plot, the visual style is so excessive that it functions as one of those hysterical moments of melodrama described by Nowell-Smith, in which the repressed desire of the characters is displaced onto the mise-en-scène.[27] This hysterical rupture not only expresses the emotions of the characters but also exposes the ideo-logical implications of these melodramatic conventions. After large matching facial close-ups of Juan and María José in separate spaces, she gestures her husband to come to her, and the film cuts to Juan walking forward, then shows him in increasingly larger and longer close-ups, as if substituting him for her husband, Miguel, whom he physically resembles. Even the dialogue calls attention to these visual dynamics, for María José and her husband talk of "missing someone" and "being bored by the same faces." Moreover, in the previous scene, Juan walked out of a movie theater, where he had been disgusted to see María José, his sister, and their friends in a newsreel on screen, and then stared absently into space, drawing our attention to the structure of the gaze, to his resistance to spectator identifi-cation, and to his role as spectator-in-the-text.

These stylistic excesses accentuate the normally invisible chain of substitutions that are conventionally demanded by the shot/reverse shot pattern of suture, where the position of camera and absent enunciator are subtly attributed in the following shot to a character within the diegesis and to the spectator in the theater, who are assumed to belong to the same gender and class as the enunciator. But here the exaggerated pattern of cutting between the matched gazes of the lovers in close-up sutures them together as if they were in the same room, underlining their adulterous relationship in the romantic triangle and their complicity in the manslaughter. It also positions them within the same social-ideological space in terms of class position and the same foregrounded space in terms of narra-tive—a space from which the cyclist and the neorealist aesthetic are barred and whose gaps the language of classical Hollywood melodrama so artfully smooths over. But in this sequence, those tricks of continuity are pushed to the point of parody, particularly when Juan exhales smoke and María José brushes away the smoke from her husband's cigarette in the very next shot. Instead of smoothing over the gaps, this cutting on action helps to accentuate the spatial rupture being denied.

This artificially unified space is dismantled in a series of subsequent sequences featuring depth focus compositions, where the ideological dynamics of foreground and background are demystified and the suturing power of the close-up undermined. The first such sequence immediately follows. While defining Juan's social position as a university lecturer in geometry, it privileges his role as star. Opening with a close-up of a diagram being drawn on a blackboard by a young woman, the scene cuts to a medium shot where Juan is positioned in the foreground next to a male colleague and then to a long shot of the entire classroom where a group of anonymous students function as spectators. After his colleague leaves the room, Juan reads a newspaper, ignoring the test in progress. Privileging his actions and effacing the crowd, the camera moves in to increasingly tighter close-ups as Juan discovers the article he is looking for, "Death of a Cyclist," then closes in on the single word *muerte,* then on details of his face, and finally on his eyes. Visibly shaken, he turns back to the class of spectators (who are more interested in the math than the melodrama) and interrupts the performance of the student, who is also shaken, thinking she has failed. At this point she is still just an anonymous victim like the cyclist, whose actions have accidentally collided with those of a star, who is doubly privileged by class position and by the language of melodrama. But this time, because of the alternating close-ups between Juan and the student, we see the face of the victim registering humiliation and pain.

She becomes a fully individualized character named Matilde Luque in a later scene in which she comes to Juan's office to protest the unjust grade he has given her. Matilde enters the room from deep in the background and gradually reveals Juan reading in the foreground. She keeps moving closer to the camera, challenging his dominance over the frame and over spectator identification. When the film cuts to a reverse shot, Matilde becomes the larger figure in the foreground and Juan is reduced to a small figure in the background. The intercutting between reverse shots clearly reveals the ideological implications of camera positioning. When she finally leaves the room, he is a diminished figure in the background.

Ultimately, Matilde will become the character who redeems Juan and who mediates between the stylistics of Hollywood melodrama and neorealism, between the singulative and the iterative. As the most sentimental and idealized figure in the film (the "good" blondish patriarchal woman contrasted with María José's raven-haired corrupt femme fatale), she also reveals the ideological limitations of the film, particularly concerning the issue of gender. For, although she is represented as a math student seriously pursuing her college degree, she soon becomes more concerned with Juan's fate than with her own academic future; no wonder, then, when Juan wishes her a happy future, he envisions it within the domestic realm of the family rather than within the public realm of science or industry.

The intervening sequence between these two appearances of Matilde opens with dissociative cuts to close-ups of children laughing and eating and of a clown weeping. We wonder who are these anonymous urchins and what do they have to do with our bourgeois lovers! When the camera finally reveals Juan and María José in the back of the circus audience, we realize they have purposely staged their rendezvous in a setting where they will not run into anyone from their own class. The choice of mise-en-scène also offers the spectator the kinds of ironic emotional contrasts and flashy theatrical visuals that are characteristic of thrillers by Hitchcock and Welles (particularly in *Lady from Shanghai*)—though the specific circus images and sounds evoke Fellini's neorealist *La strada* (The Road). When the film cuts to a reverse angle, positioning the couple in the foreground where Juan declares his love for María José, we see the clown show between them deep in the background. Not only does the circus undermine the romance but the blatancy of the contrast between foreground and background weakens the suturing power of the close-up in sustaining sympathetic identification with the bourgeois couple.

The key neorealist sequence wrenches Juan out of the ideological space he has previously shared with María José and their class and accentuates the competitive slippage between the iterative and the singular. As if stressing the contrast, it is intercut with a socialite wedding, during which someone reminds María José about a canasta game to raise money for underprivileged children. The film cuts directly to an illustrative shot (presumably in the iterative) of such children playing in rubble outside a suburban tenement—a jarring contrast between the empty words of the melodrama and the emotional power of the neorealist image in documenting the Spanish collective reality. As in the clown show, Juan is out of place in this setting but this time with a singular purpose that concerns the anonymous crowd as much as the melodrama—to find the family of the dead cyclist. As in the treatment of the cyclist in the opening, the iterative is evoked, for we are denied the individualized image of widow and child. Instead, Juan speaks to a neighbor, representative of the collective, who says, "All the flats are alike. . . . My husband worked with hers. It might have happened to him." When the film cuts from a close-up of Juan on the balcony gazing down at the family of the dead cyclist to what appears to be the object of his gaze—a long shot that evokes the neorealist treatment of the suburban tenement—at first we do not realize that we are again watching rich guests at the socialite wedding, which has previously been depicted with visual codes that evoke the singular. This momentary confusion highlights the class discourse as well as the power of cinematic conventions (such as shot/reverse shot, and close-up versus long shot) in determining how spectators read an image. Then María José and Miguel move into the foreground, reclaiming the space for melodrama.

When she is summoned to a telephone call from Juan, who is calling from a café, the film intercuts between the two stylistics and their contrasting uses of depth composition. At the wedding, María José is dramatically posed on an elegant high-backed chair in the right foreground, while deep in the left background we see in a mirror the artfully arranged reflections of Rafa and Miguel talking, perhaps about her affair with Juan; while contrasting foreground and background evoke dramatic tension, they are both clearly functioning as singulative events in the melodrama. However, in the café, Juan talks on a telephone, evoking the singulative in the foreground while the anonymous waiter and customers pursue their ordinary daily routines in the iterative in the background. When he hangs up, Juan abandons the foreground and walks off into the neorealist depth of field, where he is no longer privileged over the many cyclists passing by who could have ridden right out of *Bicycle Thief.*

Melodrama recaptures the narrative when its various revelations—concerning adultery, blackmail, and manslaughter—climactically converge. Significantly, it occurs in the sequence where the Spanish haute bourgeoisie are entertaining American VIPs. Echoing *¡Bienvenido, Mr. Marshall!* the clichéd Andalusian stereotype is shamelessly exploited as commercial spectacle to attract American capital. As Rafa plays a song, he says, "This is in honor of the U.S.A. . . . something typically Spanish . . . you know, Olé, Olé, toreador!" What is new is the skillfully choreographed convergence of the clichés from the españolada (with all of its gypsy inflections) and the cinematic language of the Hollywood thriller—two forms of melodrama that Spaniards can safely exploit in pandering to international tastes. This reflexive spectatorial moment calls attention to the performative narcissism shared by the gypsies and the Americanized protagonists, which is demanded equally by their respective forms of melodrama. As Ortega y Gasset has observed,

This propensity of the Andalusians to play act and mimic themselves reveals a surprising collective narcissism. The only people who can imitate themselves are those who are capable of becoming spectators of themselves, of contemplating and delighting at their figure and being.[28]

Yet these Andalusian performers are no more to blame than those who promote these false images of Spain. According to D'Lugo,

Spaniards, having come under the spell of the foreign, imposter impressions of Spain, find themselves seduced by this falsification of their own cultural past. The creative artist, bereft of any authentic tradition with which to identify, and situated within an artistic milieu he does not even discern as colonized by a specious foreign mentality toward Spain, only repeats the models of that fraudulent Spanishness in his own works and perceptions.[29]

Muerte breaks from this pattern by calling attention to the double colonization of the Spaniard, both from within Spain and without. In an earlier sequence, where Juan was a spectator of a No-Do newsreel (one of the hated state-controlled Noticias Documentales that held a monopoly in presenting the official version of "the news" in Spanish movie theaters after 1942), he watched María José and other members of their class "performing" at a party very much like this one, yet their narcissistic display clearly brought him no delight.

At a high point of tension when the blackmailer taunts the lovers, the film suddenly cuts to a close-up of hands clapping and other details from the flamenco dancers as they perform for the Americans. When Rafa speaks to María José, with husband Miguel looking on, the flamenco music drowns out their words. We do not have to hear the singulative dialogue because we already know the clichés, and the flamenco provides the right emotional atmosphere and intensifies the suspense. The rest of the sequence works by a dramatic exchange of gazes and glances, fast cutting among close-ups that grow successively larger, almost as if to parody earlier sequences but with an emotional impact that still works with audiences raised on melodramatic conventions. It evokes the tragic pause of opera described by McClelland, in which characters convey their mental activity through posturing gestures set to music, and those hysterical moments of melodrama described by Nowell-Smith, where "music and mise-en-scène do not just heighten the emotionality of an element of the action [but] to some extent . . . substitute for it" (193).

As an alternative to the false Andalusian signifier of Spanishness that would be recognizable to an international audience, *Muerte* earlier had alluded verbally to the taboo topic of the Spanish Civil War and had shown populist images of the Spanish collective—the working-class families in the suburbs, the proletarian children at the clown show, and the student demonstrators at the university. Such class-bound images are usually omitted from folkloric stereotypes or backgrounded in melodrama, but they are powerfully documented in the neorealist aesthetic.

The competition among these signifiers of Spanishness is played out in the pointless dual climax of the sequence—a gypsy mano à mano between Rafa with broken bottle and Juan with broken chair which erupts after the police come looking for Juan (presumably about the death of the cyclist). When Rafa finally reveals what he knows about the adultery, María José is relieved to find he knows nothing about the murder. She demonstrates that adultery (the moral crime that was formerly censored on Spanish movie screens) is nothing compared to the wanton crushing of the working class, a political crime that is a daily occurrence. The sequence ends with the drunken Rafa angrily throwing a bottle through a window, protesting against the class that he both hates and envies because it always protects its own.

This melodramatic act of a selfish opportunist segues into unselfish collective action—the breaking of a window by student demonstrators, who demand Juan's dismissal for his unjust treatment of Matilde Luque. Again, this exaggerated cutting on action calls attention to the spatial and thematic rupture and to the precise moment when the film moves away from its moral attack against the bourgeoisie and finally refers directly to actual political events—the student demonstrations that occurred in the 1950s. This rupture finally enables Juan to see through the egocentricism of melodrama and to accept responsibility within the neorealist discourse for the two injustices he committed unintentionally against workers and students, the prime agents in a coalition that has historically proved important for revolutionary change. Juan regains his belief in meaningful choice, making stilted heroic speeches as he and Matilde are seen in close-up through the shattered window.

Though the dialogue in these conversion scenes is heavy-handed, the demystification of the visual choices continues to be very sophisticated. Juan's next rendezvous with María José takes place in a church. This time the setting separates them both spatially and morally, particularly in the two-shot where we can see the church ritual in the background between them through a circular window. As in the earlier wedding sequence, what is indicted here is not the church but rather the hypocritical distance between outward adherence to religious forms and the secret violation of basic fundamental taboos like murder and adultery. In such sequences the mise-en-scène is quite literally used to reinvest the secular world of melodrama with the "moral occult," which proves to be compatible with "traditional" Christian values. In this particular scene, the religious setting actually contributes to Juan's moral conversion, helping him decide to resign his faculty position and "confess" to the police.

When Juan describes himself as some kind of hero (who begins to win as he renounces his privileged class position), one could see him as a modern antihero. Yet he also functions as an ironic inversion of the left-wing Churruca brother Pedro from Franco's historical melodrama *Raza,* whose last-minute conversion to the Nationalist cause is similarly inspired by an idealistic young woman like Matilde and similarly instrumental in sanctifying his martyrdom. But in *Muerte,* the ideological positions are reversed, for Juan moves from right to left and is martyred, not by the political cause he betrays but (like a noir hero) by the femme fatale he loves and by the class they both represent. Like Pedro, Juan also comes from a "heroic" family whose father and good brothers fought for Franco and were martyred in the war. And he also has a kind, loving mother, who embodies patriarchal law in her husband's absence and who organizes her children's interpellation as loyal Francoist subjects. As she herself acknowledges, she oversees their participation in their First Communion, at school, in politics, in military service, in war, and in death—rites that are documented in family photographs. Nevertheless, like the idealized Churruca matriarch, she fails to understand her complex wayward son.

As in *Raza,* melodrama demands narrative closure, and Juan, who has broken out of its ideological space, becomes its final victim. When

Spanish censors insisted that María José also be punished, Bardem obliged by adding a third fatal car crash, taking one last swipe at the suturing function of the close-up. In the final grotesque shot of María José's inverted face, which is illuminated by the flashlight of the passing cyclist she had tried to avoid hitting, the function of the facial close-up is ironically reversed. Instead of arousing our sympathy or identification, it gives us pleasure by revealing the witch is dead and by punctuating the ironic rhyming reversals of the exaggerated narrative closure. In the final image, our sympathetic identification is carried by the anonymous Spanish cyclist whose face we see this time and who rides off to find help, like the filmmakers at Salamanca, in the neorealist depth of field.

3 · BREAKING NEW GROUND IN *LOS GOLFOS,* *EL COCHECITO,* AND *EL ESPÍRITU DE LA COLMENA*

This chapter traces how the ideological transcription of Hollywood and neorealist conventions helped forge the language of the New Spanish Cinema in three pivotal films—*Los golfos* and *El cochecito,* which were made at the end of the 1950s when the neorealist model was already perceived as passé, and *El espíritu de la colmena,* which was made in 1973 during the *dictablanda* (the period of soft dictatorship), those five or six years preceding Franco's death when Spanish artists were making new inroads against the remaining limits of government censorship and when the New Spanish Cinema enjoyed some of its biggest successes worldwide.

Los golfos (1959) and *El cochecito* (1960) have a great deal in common: both were made at around the same time, with the same director of photography, Juan Julio Baena, and with the same producer, Pere Portabella of the Barcelona-based production company Films 59 (which in 1961 was also a coproducer of Buñuel's *Viridiana*).[1] Both films presented a vision of Spain that displeased Franco's censors, yet they were sent to international festivals: *Los golfos* to Cannes as the official Spanish entry and *El cochecito* to Venice where it won the International Critics' Award for Best Film and to the London Film Festival where it won for Best Picture. Higginbotham helps to explain this contradiction.

In 1960 a new official committee was selected to choose the films that would represent Spain at international festivals. While Falangist José Luis Sáenz de Heredia [the director of *Raza*] headed this commission, it also included Juan Antonio Bardem and other film professionals who represented the industry and not the administration, as did the censors.[2]

As in the far more scandalous case of *Viridiana* the following year, both *Los golfos* and *El cochecito* exposed the contradictions inherent in Franco's ongoing defascistization of his regime. While striving abroad to present a more liberal image of Spain as a modern industrialized nation, at home the government was still censoring any direct criticism of its policies.

Saura claims that *Los golfos* was the most difficult film he ever made, for it was censored and delayed at virtually every stage of its production. He was forced to do four major revisions of the script, on which he collaborated with his former student, Mario Camus (who would later become an important director in his own right) and Daniel Sueiro, the journalist who had written some of the news stories on which the characters in *Los golfos* were based. D'Lugo claims that the net result of the interaction with the censors was actually positive, for it enabled Saura's original idea of a "documentary on slum life in Madrid" to evolve "into a complex narrative structure" and into a more forceful ideological critique. When the censors suggested that the hooligans be given a socially redeeming motive for their crimes, Saura chose bullfighting, one of the most distinctively Spanish sources of melodrama. His protagonists steal to capitalize the debut of one of their members. D'Lugo observes,

The final reworking of *Hooligans* in the form eventually authorized by the censors is the tale of the ideological "usage" of the torero's story . . . as a symptomatic expression of the cultural blockage that besets the Spaniard in coming to grips with his own social and personal plight.[3]

Still, the film was given one of the worst classifications, a 2B rating, which restricted its distribution and limited the percentage of government rebate on production costs to the 25 percent minimum (instead of the 50 percent maximum granted to films with the "national interest" category). Many of the scenes in the final version of the script remained unshot because of a lack of funds. The film's release in Spain was held up until 1962 because, according to Saura, censors told him "dirty clothes should be washed at home."

Although the production and release of *El cochecito* were somewhat smoother, government censors did require some cuts and tried to change the central dramatic outcome of the plot. Moreover, despite its success at Venice, the distribution of the film was limited to second-rate theaters. Hailing the film as a "great discovery" that "deserves to be a classic," British critic Peter Baker wrote in November 1960, "Why then, is *Films and Filming* the first to rave about this remarkable film? Simply because it received no support from the Spanish authorities. The Spanish film export organization has cold shouldered it."[4] Moreover, in 1960, Marco Ferreri's request for a renewal of his residence permit was denied, forcing him to continue his innovative filmmaking in Italy.

Nevertheless, by 1960, these two films were already perceived as taking an important step toward developing an innovative Spanish cinema with international appeal. Each film had an entire issue of *Temas de cine* devoted to it, including the publication of the complete script with commentary by critics and the filmmakers.[5] And that same November 1960 issue of *Films and Filming* that carried Baker's rave also contained an English translation of an article by Juan Cobos (editor of the Spanish monthly *Film Ideal*) hailing both Saura and Ferreri as heroes:

A Spanish picture must obtain at least a 2A classification so as not to lose money. . . . As far as the exterior market is concerned the possibilities are practically nil, because very few movies of medium quality ever obtain a first night outside of Spain. Up to the present, only the films by Bardem and Berlanga have had any success. . . . Does one realize now the difficulties and heroism necessary in order to devote oneself to the making of a movie, which must be made on a low budget, [that is] much less than [that] of any of the "nouvelle vague" [films and] which will have great difficulties with the national censors? . . . Sometimes, however, there comes the unexpected happiness, as happened this year, that the two movies made by Film 59, namely *The Scoundrel (Los golfos)* and *The Wheelchair* were shown in Cannes and in Venice. (9)

THE DISAVOWAL OF NEOREALISM   Before we turn to a close analysis of *Los golfos* and *El cochecito,* it is necessary to explain why these filmmakers and their critics tended to disavow the neorealist influence on these works. The primary reason is that both films were released at the end of the decade, long after the demise of the neorealist movement in Italy and in the first rush of excitement over the French nouvelle vague. Since Spaniards were quite defensive about their cultural backwardness (which they blamed on the government and its censors rather than on Spanish filmmakers), they were eager for their films and criticism to be up-to-date and hence were embarrassed by the association with neorealism, which already seemed anachronistic. For example, in 1962, critic Santiago San Miguel writes,

> *Los golfos*—is it neorealism? It is a reproach that has been made with enormous levity—neorealism is old. If it becomes neorealism in Spain, it will be because the social and cultural situation of the country has that possibility and condition. And if it does not become a cinema like that of Godard, Resnais, and Malle in France and that of Zurlini, Pontecorvo, and Masseli in Italy, the reason is simply that here we have had no Autant-Lara, Allegret, Carne ("tradition of quality") and no DeSica, Rossellini, Germi (neorealism of one or another form), and even less, names like Becker, Bresson, or Antonioni and Visconti. . . . We will not be able to pass judgment on *Los golfos* with fairness if we forget in what country we are living.[6]

If neorealism was widely perceived at the end of the decade as being out-of-date, then why did these filmmakers still use it as a model for their films? Why did they not turn to the French nouvelle vague instead, as some critics would subsequently claim they had? For one reason, it was not until 1959 that the nouvelle vague emerged on the international scene at Cannes, where filmmakers like Truffaut, Resnais, and Camus took some of the most important awards. By then, *Los golfos* was already completed. Yet when Saura took his film to Cannes in 1960, it is hardly surprising that he would want it to be seen as a cutting-edge work, as up-to-date as the nouvelle vague films that were currently generating so much excitement. Yet, unless they crossed over the border to see films in France, most Spanish filmmakers had not yet seen any nouvelle vague works; they merely read articles about them or excerpts from their scripts in Spanish film magazines like *Temas de cine* and *Nuestro cine.*

Another reason for still using the neorealist model is that in 1960 this movement was still widely perceived internationally as having been far more politically engaged than the current nouvelle vague, which (with the exception of Resnais's *Hiroshima, mon amour*) seemed to restrict its subversiveness to stylistics and modes of production. For example, along with ads for Rossellini's *General de la Rovere* and a long article (by Adolfo Muñoz Alonso) lavishing praise on Fellini's *La strada* and *Le notti di Cabiria* (Nights of Cabiria), the March–April 1960 issue of *Temas de cine* contained a transcription of an international colloquium on "New Cinema and the Nouvelle Vague" held at the Venice Film Festival in August 1959 which included the following exchange.

Roberto Rossellini: The revolutionary aspect of the "nouvelle vague" consists precisely in the revolution in the means of production; it has seen that it is possible to make cinema with little money . . . [whereas] the political principle of the official cinema is to make a very expensive cinema. . . . The American cinema is practically a cinema of monopoly. . . . *Andrzej Wajda:* I believe that in a single film by Rossellini there are more things than in all of the "nouvelle vague." For me the cinema is sick, so sick that it is almost dead, dead because of the lack of ideas. . . . *François Truffaut:* Neorealism was built on the common base of a social truth, that did not happen with the "nouvelle vague." . . . In Italy there were historical reasons: it was a reaction against Mussolini's cinema of propaganda and after the Liberation, they made films of the Resistance. In France it is a reaction only against insipid cinema, it is an affirmation of the director.[7]

The disavowal of neorealism was particularly strong in the case of Saura, who had hopes of becoming a Spanish auteur whose international stature might someday equal that of Buñuel. Thus, what was stressed both by him and by his critics was his originality, his arch-Spanishness, and his connections with Buñuel.

Saura's trip to Cannes in 1960 was an important turning point in launching both his own career as an international auteur and the idea of a New Spanish Cinema that could rival other national film movements at international festivals. Though his own film, *Los golfos,* was not widely acclaimed at Cannes, there he met Buñuel and helped convince him to come back to Spain to make *Viridiana.* While protecting his own claims to originality, Saura's statement in the special *Los golfos* issue of *Temas de cine* shows how this conception of a New Spanish Cinema was to draw strength by being aligned with Buñuel and by denying the influence of neorealism, which was not only passé but which had always been harshly criticized by his mentor.

Luis Buñuel used to say that it is absurd to say that *Los golfos* is a neorealist film, considering that, for him, the neorealist cinema usually ends happily, usually contains a final hope which either is projected from the work or is already intrinsic in it. . . . I'm not very concerned whether *Los golfos* is a neorealist or romantic film, or how some critics have pointed out that it resembles *Los olvidados,* which is one of the few Buñuel films that unfortunately I don't know. . . .

The mark that the work of Luis Buñuel has left on me . . . is definitive. It is the first time that I have seen reflected on the screen what seems to me the essence of our future cinema: the humor, but an indirect humor, bitter and bland; the enormous truth which many situations acquire when pushed to the edge, when told with simplicity; a profound love toward those beings whom society usually repudiates; and, above all, the struggle which Luis Buñuel constantly maintains against hypocrisy and lies. (Saura, 6–7)[8]

A similar line of argument (stressing Saura's alignment with Buñuel and other Spanish sources of realism while disavowing the influence of neorealism) was also used in the statement by García Escudero that appeared in the same special issue on *Los golfos*. Though he had earlier championed the neorealist tendencies of *Surcos*, once he was reappointed general director of cinema in 1962, García Escudero would stress the unique cultural heritage of the New Spanish Cinema as its primary international appeal.

Neorealism is only apparent when the film portrays Madrid, which, if to some foreign critic it has appeared "irreconcilable, squalid and sad," it is probably because that critic knows Madrid only through tourist postcards; but that portrait lacks what neorealism (at least, the most characteristic works—those of Zavattini-DeSica) put over everything—a patina of tenderness. Neither is *Los golfos* "esperpentica," like the cinema of Azcona-Ferreri, a grotesque deformation of reality with the finality of denuded satire. Saura is realistic, in the line of the harsh realism that has produced Buñuel in cinema, Goya in painting, and our picaresque in literature. . . . For this reason, we don't have the right to disavow the arch-Spanishness of the line to which Saura belongs in *Los golfos:* an unforgettable film, passionate and harsh like the red wine that sticks to the palate and makes the throat grow hoarse; like the dark thick blood that gushes from the bull agonizing in its final death throes. (24)

What emerges in this statement is a strategic attempt to single out Saura from all other filmmakers working in Spain in this period (including the Italian Ferreri, the Communist Bardem, and the Falangist Nieves Conde) as the one liberal artist whose originality and "arch-Spanishness" make him worthy of the kind of auteurist treatment that only the exiled Buñuel had thus far received outside of Spain. In this way, Saura could be transformed into a cultural commodity that would help sell the liberalized reinscription of *franquismo* in international markets—a strategy similar to the one that Elsaesser has so persuasively theorized in the context of the New German Cinema.[9]

García Escudero's attitude toward Saura is echoed in the recent books by Hopewell and Besas, which both single him out as the only auteur who merits a separate chapter (even though the latter is no Saura fan); and it is elaborated and intensified in D'Lugo's *The Films of Carlos Saura: The Practice of Seeing* (1991), the first book-length study of a Spanish auteur (other than Buñuel) to be written and published in English. For example, in his discussion of *Los golfos* (which I consider to be the most thorough and perceptive reading of the film yet available either in English or Spanish), D'Lugo accepts Saura's denial of the neorealist influence at face value, lamenting,

> The conventional wisdom is that Saura's first feature-length film, *Hooligans,* represents the apotheosis of Spanish neorealist cinema. The use of authentic street locales in Madrid as the principal space of action and the appearance of a nonprofessional cast of actors connect in a seemingly logical way with the social realism of Bardem, Berlanga, and Ferreri. Yet, tellingly, Saura rejects the neorealist label, preferring, instead, to see *Hooligans* as "a search for and the molding of a Spanish reality." . . . One could trace a direct line of precursors to Saura's film beginning as early as José María Nieves Conde's *Surcos* (1951: Furrows) and including sequences in *Muerte de un ciclista* (1955: Death of a Cyclist) and Marco Ferreri's *El pisito* (The Little Flat) in 1959, all of which involved authentic working-class urban locales. But something quite new and startling surfaces in the introduction of urban space in *Hooligans.* (30–31)

While willing to grant the neorealist influence on the other Spanish films I am tracing here, D'Lugo exaggerates the uniqueness of Saura's deviations from the tradition.

In the case of Ferreri, his Italian nationality and his connections with the movement in Italy before he came to Spain led critics to define all of his Spanish films in relation to neorealism. Like Saura, he disavowed the label, yet he granted that neorealism was part of a playful opposition, which interrogated several aesthetics. Though less zealous than Saura in asserting his originality and arch-Spanishness,

Ferreri nevertheless linked himself with Spanish tradition—not with the realism of Buñuel but with the esperpento of Valle-Inclán (1866–1936), the modernist playwright and novelist from the Generation of '98 who claimed his satire derived from Goya and Quevedo.[10]

Despite earlier claims of being a Carlist, Valle-Inclán was greatly admired by leftists for mocking the military, the monarchy, and the church and for opposing the dictator Primo de Rivera, who ruled Spain in the 1920s. His satiric plays were revived in the 1950s by university students who saw him as a key figure in the Spanish avant-garde.[11] Although he was Spanish, Valle-Inclán assumed the image of an outsider so that he could more effectively demythicize Spanish illusions and destabilize the so-called reality within previous realistic conventions. These were strategies with which Ferreri could readily identify, particularly as a foreigner.

I don't want to be a chronicler. Sadoul and the others are mistaken when they speak of neorealism. Neorealism is the fraud of my films. The appearance may be neorealist, but not the substance. In *El cochecito,* for example, there are inventions and annotations that Azcona would not have put in. . . . He used to say that Spanish reality did not exist. And he is Spanish. Later we discovered that some analogous points already existed in Valle-Inclán. Valle-Inclán had seen them many years before and I was returning to find them again, I who am a foreigner. At times, to be a foreigner is important. . . . He has a greater distance, new eyes, a different and more acute sensibility. When certain things are always in front of your eyes, you get used to them. You no longer know how to see them.[12]

Spanish filmmakers and their critics rarely showed the same kind of defensiveness about their American influences that they showed toward neorealism, partly because this influence was rarely stressed and also because Hollywood's domination of world markets made it the inevitable competition that every "foreign" auteur and movement were forced to challenge. Nevertheless, Spaniards tended to exaggerate the gulf between Hollywood and their own newly emerging cinema. For example, in praising *El cochecito* for being "a hundred percent Spanish," Juan Cobos distinguishes it not from neorealism but from "the empty American moviemaking, always based upon 'stars.'"

> Spain's future lies in this kind of picture as made by Ferreri, Saura, Berlanga, Bardem, and many others who confidently are longing for their opportunity. But this so very Spanish moviemaking can be hurt by the great amount of American pictures that monopolize our screens. . . . What would happen if our movie industry should go along the lines of *The Wheelchair?* . . . This would mean a very great setback for the American movie industry, because ours has "life" and Hollywood has none. (41)

Despite these disavowals of neorealism and attacks against Hollywood, the dialogism and ideological reinscription of their conventions in *Los golfos* and *El cochecito* achieved at least three different kinds of results. For Spanish filmmakers, this process helped to construct a creative opposition of distinguished artists who could compete with other international auteurs at international festivals and in global markets. For the Francoist regime, it paradoxically advanced their ideological goal of creating a more liberal, defascistized image of Spain abroad. And for Spanish spectators, it created new signifying practices that demanded new kinds of competence in the reading of cinematic language.

LOS GOLFOS Though diametrically opposed to *Surcos* ideologically, *Los golfos* shares many similar strategies in adapting the neorealist-Hollywood dialectic. Both films use neorealist conventions to document contemporary social problems of poverty in urban Madrid, which the characters (recent immigrants from Salamanca or Andalusia) try to overcome by turning to criminal moves learned from American gangster movies. In each case, there is an attempt to capitalize a young Spaniard's performance as a folkloric star (Tonia's cabaret singing, or Juan's bullfighting) so that this youth can rise above the impov-

In Carlos Saura's *Los golfos*
(Hooligans, 1959) the
working class collective is not
the family, but a gang of
hooligans.

erished masses and bring glory to the collective to which he or she
belongs (the family or the gang of hooligans). But whereas Tonia's
singulative humiliating failure is staged by a melodramatic villain (her
corrupt backer, Don Roque), Juan's defeat is far more devastating.
Within the strict codes of bullfighting and melodrama, it seems to
be based on his own inadequacy as a performer. Yet the larger
sociopolitical analysis in *Los golfos* shows that it was largely deter-

mined by cultural forces and therefore inevitable. His failure is also far more painful because it is shared by his group of friends, whose inflated expectations and painful risks and sacrifices prove to have been in vain. Unlike *Surcos, Los golfos* does not morally condemn its characters but shows how the social conditions and dominant ideology have constructed these subjects and have both fostered and defeated their capitalist dreams of individualism and stardom.

As in *Surcos, Los golfos* contains reflexive allusions to cinema. As a film about young Spaniards with limited options, it cultivates a reflexive analogy with the situation of its own filmmakers (a connection that has been noted by several critics). It introduces a new production company and youthful crew with limited means who are collaborating on a project that breaks the rules of the censors and that launches the career of its aspiring young director.

One of the primary means by which *Los golfos* ideologically reinscribes the conventions shared with *Surcos* is in making the working-class collective (that seme of Spanishness associated with the neorealist aesthetic) not the patriarchal family but a gang of young hooligans whose fathers we never see. They are a slightly older version of the thieving, anarchistic kids who posed such a threat in *Surcos*. As a subversive social unit that has no place in Fascist discourse, the street gang evokes a moral ambiguity that helps to dismantle the more simplistic Manichaean oppositions that were so blatant in *Surcos* (and to a lesser extent in *Muerte*). The ambiguity arises partly from the contrasts among its highly individualized members (each drawn from authentic news stories and played by "ordinary people" rather than actors). They range from the hardworking Juan (who, in preparing for his career as matador, carries the same kinds of heavy sacks that young Manolo had dropped in the marketplace in *Surcos*) to the cynical madrileño Julian (a pimp who dresses like an American gangster and who could easily grow up to be a Don Roque).

Not only is the group associated with both the neorealist and Hollywood models and the respective semes of Spanishness they promote but it also evokes the international genre of films that examine the plight of two or more young delinquents, usually against the dual contexts of the family and of another social institution (such as school or prison), and that present an analysis of contemporary social reality that can be read as political allegory. This delinquency genre includes such works as Jean Vigo's *Zero de conduite* (Zero for Conduct, 1933), DeSica's *Sciuscià* (Shoeshine, 1946), Buñuel's *Los olvidados* (1950), Karel Reisz's short *We Are the Lambeth Boys* (1958), François Truffaut's *Les 400 coups* (The 400 Blows, 1959), Tony Richardson's *The Loneliness of the Long Distance Runner* (1962), Volker Schlöndorff's *Der junge Törless* (Young Torless, 1966), and Lindsay Anderson's *If* (1968). Perhaps because of their thematic focus on rebellious youths struggling against the oppressive status quo, these films frequently help to launch a new national film movement—as in the case of Italian neorealism, French poetic realism and the nouvelle vague, British Free Cinema, the New German Cinema, and, with *Los golfos,* the New Spanish Cinema. Even when Saura questions the link between *Los golfos* and such films, he only strengthens his position in the genre, for all of these works strive for cultural and historical specificity.

I do not understand how some foreign critics confound our golfos with those called *teddy boys.* The Spanish golfo has nothing to do with the *teddy boy* nor with the *blousson noir,* nor barely with the stray youth that proliferate in Europe and in the United States. The essential difference is that the Spanish golfo is delinquent because he has to eat, because he has to live and because no one has taught him anything else.[13]

Saura's presentation of the dual contexts in *Los golfos* emphasizes Spanish specificity. The fact that no fathers appear in the film shows an ideological departure from the Fascist glorification of the patriarchal family and its idealization of the bond between fathers and sons and also speaks to the historical reality of so many Spanish fathers having been killed in the Civil War.

The second social context is not a school or a prison but the distinctively Spanish institution of bullfighting. The examination of its class and economic determinants makes it analogous to boxing in American movies. Within their respective cultures, both activities glorify ritualized violence and machismo and equally foster illusions of social mobility and individual autonomy. Carr sees the promotion of such escapist macho pastimes, including football and bicycle racing (which is represented in *El cochecito*), as a "culture of evasion" that plays a particularly crucial role in "authoritarian systems based on political demobilization."[14]

Within *Los golfos,* bullfighting is implicitly made analogous to prostitution, which is embodied in the young girl Visi who caters to American clients. She is attracted to the aspiring matador Juan partly because she understands they are both selling themselves to become a star. Yet while prostitution is an international institution, bullfighting (with its historical connections to "plebeianism" and melodrama) is far more culturally specific.[15] As D'Lugo persuasively argues,

Certainly, by the time Saura and Camus started to revise the script of *Hooligans,* it was a commonplace that bullfighting was at best a reactionary art that catered to the basest values and instincts of the Spanish lower classes, and, at worst, for its emphasis on virility, sex, blood, and death, a uniquely Spanish expression of fascism. . . . Saura's evocation of the system of exploitation of lower class youth by the greedy impresarios emphatically draws on that strain in Spanish cultural thought that sees bullfighting as connecting all too logically with the reactionary and authoritarian tendencies of Francoism. (34)

Saura manages to recoup and reinscribe the Andalusian stereotype, a project he would resume in the post-Franco era with his dance trilogy. *Los golfos* reveals how it functions as an ideological state apparatus, while still using it as a means of international appeal. He shows its susceptibility to corruption as well as its dramatic power both in the art of bullfighting that is so central to the narrative and in the flamenco guitar that dominates the sound track and in which the loner Manolo, the most traditionally Spanish and most self-contained member of the group, is so deeply absorbed. The fact that Saura himself appears in the audience of aficionados who hiss Juan down in his debut is another indication of this duality—both the conscious immersion in and rigorous critique of the Spanish stereotype. It is a duality that is similar to the one we find in the representation of Spanish popular culture in so many works by Goya.

Through Baena's brilliant cinematography, *Los golfos* dismantles the Manichaean opposition between neorealism and Hollywood, subtly integrating the two stylistics within the same sequence or shot. Before we see any titles, the opening sequence seems to document an ordinary Spanish street theft, yet with stylistic choices and details that evoke the United States. A blind woman selling lottery tickets and tobacco is robbed in broad daylight by a young hooligan (whom we later recognize as Ramón). The opening shot is of the lottery stand, an image that introduces gambling and the wheel of fortune, which later will be identified with the risks of capitalist investment. The camera moves down to the blind woman, who evokes the symbolic blindness of fortune as well as Buñuel's nonsentimental treatment of the stereotypical Spanish maimed as complicitous victims. She is making change for a customer who asks, "You have Chesterfields?"—the first expression of a consumerist desire for the American product. After the customer leaves, we see many close-ups of the woman's hands as she works, accelerating the pace of the cutting and building tension as Ramón watches, waiting to make his move. The robbery and chase that follow are treated with the fast-cutting characteristic of Hollywood action films, establishing the film's rapid rhythm of fairly brief shots.

The main title for the film is superimposed over a jump cut to a young vaquilla charging into a ring, introducing the next sequence which is both expository and lyrical. Immediately confronting us with Spanish semes from the españolada that are recognized world-wide, with the image of bullfighting and the sound of a flamenco guitar, the sequence also introduces the six individualized members of the gang and their dream of capitalizing Juan's career as matador.[16] The rhythms of the scene are unusual, moving from increasingly long takes of Juan doing graceful passes in the ring to brief shots of his friends amid other young, hopeful spectators. As in the opening robbery sequence, spectatorship is shown as an essential step in constructing the subject and in determining his actions (which D'Lugo has persuasively shown to be operative throughout Saura's career and which is also an important dynamic in all of the films from the 1950s discussed above). In foregrounding the dramatic actions of Ramón and Juan, the first two sequences present the limited alternatives (stealing and stardom) available to young Spaniards who want to be individualized from the mass. Despite the Spanish specificity of both sequences, this goal is already associated with the Hollywood model.

The next nine scenes tend to decenter the narrative, establishing the city itself as a primary character and clearly presenting actions within the iterative aspect—tendencies that are characteristic of the neorealist aesthetic. The first of these scenes, which shows the hooligans against the city after having left the little plaza toreo, is transitional. Still focused on individuating the boys, it positions Ramón and Juan in front of the group with Manolo, the Andalusian, lagging slightly behind singing, as if only he hears the nondiegetic flamenco score. As the camera follows the boys moving across an apparently level street, it suddenly comes on a bridge and then a steep stairway leading down to the working class suburbs where they all live in *chabolas*. Although part of the realistic setting (one of the titles even tells us that this film has been totally shot in natural settings), the bridge and stairs recur as important symbolic images of the characters' strong desire to transcend their downtrodden social conditions. As in *Surcos,* we begin to see how their particular story is largely determined by the forces of industrialization and the urban space in which it occurs.

Perhaps even more important, this sequence introduces the recurring stylistic pattern of opening with a medium shot of one or more of the boys positioned very close to the camera in the foreground and then following their movements as they scatter or regroup or move off into the depth of field where they mingle with the anonymous members of their class. Such shots create a tension between the apparent restless, choreographed mobility of the camera and its chosen subjects and the structural limits and unpredictability of the open space through which they move.

The next eight scenes (scenes four to eleven in the screenplay) document a typical morning in the barrio. This iterative segment opens with one of the most impressive shots of the film: a slow languorous pan to the left, which begins with human figures in midground and medium shot and then fluidly transforms into an extreme long shot as it reveals the barrio in the distance at daybreak with smoke rising from the rooftops and workers moving against the muted gray tones of the landscape. Accompanied by a solo flamenco guitar on the sound track and natural sounds of animals braying and cocks crowing, this image is lyrical without being picturesque; it creates a mixture of sadness and beauty that is very moving and that is unparalleled by any other neorealist film (with the possible exception of Visconti's *La terra trema*).

The interior scenes that follow introduce the families of the hooligans and the cramped spaces in which they live, documenting the conditions of poverty with striking formal compositions. In the home of Juan and his brother, Chato, we see on the walls the typical Spanish icons—of a flamenco dancer and of the great matador Manolete positioned next to sacred images of the Virgin and the Last Supper. Within this neorealist and politicized context, they cease to be merely folkloric stereotypes and instead (like the star photos in *Surcos*) become carriers of the dominant ideology that glamorizes sacrificial death.

Similarly oppressive are the posts, door frames, and walls that divide the cramped rooms into even smaller spaces. Outside the individual flats, the dark, narrow, claustrophobic corridors also restrict both the physical and social mobility of the characters. In contrast to a right-wing neorealist film like *Surcos,* in which unruly tenants are restrained by barred railings within the spacious interior courtyards of heavily populated, prisonlike multitiered tenements, here it is the architectural and social structures rather than the lax morals of the crowd that are the root of the problem and that turn these boys into hooligans.

Within virtually all of the subsequent sequences there is a rhythmic alternation between a neorealist focus on the crowd, frequently in long shots and occasionally in long slow takes, versus the American focus on individuals in close-up or medium shot performing spectacular fast-paced actions that distinguish them from the mass. This alternation creates a constant slippage between the iterative and the singulative. D'Lugo argues,

Through the portrayal of the crowd and its antithesis, the strongly individualistic torero, Saura conveys the sense of a cultural dilemma lurking beneath social facades. The youths' struggle for achievement is itself born of a tacit recognition by each gang member that he is merely an inconsequential element in an anonymous mass. (35)

What I am suggesting is that this opposition between the crowd and the illusion of individuality is frequently expressed by a struggle between the two stylistics for dominance over the sequence—a strategy that was also used more blatantly in *Muerte*. For example, in the brilliant sequence set in the open market of Legazpi, Juan is contextualized as one of the workers carrying heavy sacks of produce, carefully rigged with a strap around their foreheads as if they were beasts of burden. Virtually without dialogue, this highly rhythmic sequence opens with a medium shot of Juan with a co-worker close to the camera in the foreground, then cuts to an establishing long shot of hundreds of workers streaming to their jobs, then to a medium shot of the other hooligans emerging from the subway. Though the many close shots of Juan's arduous labor help us understand his determination to become a matador, his actions in this context are no more interesting than those of the anonymous Spaniards being documented by the camera: for example, one man loading another with two more heavy sacks, whose weight grows palpable; a fat man tripping on a nun's habit as they both descend a steep flight of stairs. The camera captures both the poverty of the scene and its bristling energy, which provides a form of neorealist spectacle. The alternating cuts to close shots of the individualized hooligans show them moving through the market, casually stealing both food and the spotlight from the crowd of workers, as if it were their ordinary daily routine, the iterative aspect of Hollywood.

The virtuosity in combining and transforming both stylistics is perhaps best demonstrated in the truck robbery in Calle Taberna and the dance hall sequence. While the actions of the hooligans, film

crew, and camera are carefully plotted and choreographed throughout, the spectator is at first in doubt about what is at stake in these
sequences and what should dominate his or her attention.

Like the opening theft, the truck robbery opens with many un-
contextualized shots of varying lengths that call attention to individualized characters or details. As we gradually recognize the hooligans carefully positioned as spectators in strategic positions both
outside and inside the taberna, we begin to perceive a plot. For
example, as two of the hooligans admire the visual spectacle created
by the languorous walk of a whore, both we and the camera follow
her into the café, but when we see Julian at the door, Manolo seated
alone inside at a table, and Paco outside looking through the window,
we realize she is merely a decoy being used to distract the truckers.
Once the actual robbery is set in motion, the cutting accelerates
among even briefer, closer shots of the carefully coordinated moves
of the thieves performing the caper. The sequence ends with a
surprising jump cut to a medium shot of two women in the street
facing the camera in direct address as they sing a ballad about a
criminal. Much longer than any of the takes in the previous action
sequence, this reflexive shot (which Baena would use again in a
similar way in *El cochecito*) smooths over a temporal ellipsis and
identifies the source of the music that continues in the following
scene where two of the boys sell the stolen loot. The overall effect
is an asynchronous rhythm in pacing and an unpredictability in
narrative—qualities that are not particularly characteristic either of
neorealism or of Hollywood classical cinema but that emerge partly
out of the combination of the two aesthetics.

In the dance hall sequence, the attention to individuals is almost
constantly juxtaposed with a documentation of the crowd—a combination that is shown to be compatible with both stylistics. The
sequence opens with a close-up of a trombonist (prefiguring the
close-up of the trumpeter that will introduce the final climactic
sequence of the bullfight), then a couple of brief shots of other
members of the band, before cutting to an establishing long shot of
the crowded dance hall. The multipurpose nature of the sequence is
demonstrated when the film rhythmically cuts among three of the

In the truck robbery
sequence in Saura's *Los golfos*
the visual spectacle of the
whore serves as a decoy not
only for the truckers being
robbed, but also for the
camera and us spectators,
who follow her into the café.

hooligans seated at a table in the foreground with the anonymous dancers visible in the background; a medium shot of Julian successfully pursuing his seduction of Visi on the dance floor; and a long shot that foregrounds the inexperienced Paco (whose youthful vulnerability is all the more poignant in light of his coming death) as he unsuccessfully tries to get a young girl to dance with him. As in the Legazpi market sequence, the individuals who are foregrounded include the characters we know (like Ramón positioned under a huge Coca-Cola sign) as well as anonymous members of the crowd.

These visual dynamics are most effective in the talky scene at the bar (where Ramón, Cato, and Juan are depressed over not having enough money to bankroll the latter's debut), for here the montage within the long take achieves the kind of visual unpredictability usually associated with Welles (whose synthetic depth focus style had been linked to neorealism by Bazin). The scene opens with a cut to a slightly upward angle medium shot from behind the bar, where an anonymous young girl sits alone facing the camera, waiting for someone to ask her to dance; the three boys arise unpredictably from out of the space in front of the bar, and the bartender enters the frame from the foreground with his back to the camera. This dynamic long take is punctuated by a cut to a side angle, enabling us to see other youths and actions that have nothing to do with the foregrounded conversation of the hooligans. When the film cuts back to another long take of the original frontal angle, Paco enters the shot and shoulders the girl to the side, accentuating the crowding within the frame and capturing the space for the singulative plot. The second cutaway to the side angle reveals a young man coming to ask the girl to dance; but instead of pursuing their story, the film cuts to a close-up of Chato, then pans back and forth among the hooligans, as they decide to make an all-out effort to steal the capital for Juan's debut as a star. D'Lugo says of this scene,

Ramón . . . convinces the other members to help Juan only after he has viewed his friends in a crowded dance hall. Saura seems to be telling us here that the real inducement to action is less a matter of camaraderie with Juan than the oppressive knowledge Ramón achieves of the inconsequential status that they all share. (35)

Although this talky scene advances the plot by moving the boys toward their "American-style" solution, the dynamic long takes decenter the narrative by surrounding it with open-ended encounters between anonymous characters. They demonstrate that to pursue the singulative plot, the film must sacrifice many other stories that may be potentially as interesting.

Even after such a synthesis is achieved, the explicit allusions to the growing influence of the American style increase. Triggered by the capitalist moves of the impresario (who ups the price for Juan's debut) and followed by a fast-paced iterative montage of robberies, the boys stage a singulative job in a new kind of setting proposed by Julian: a bar that caters to American tastes, with Visi as erotic decoy, with American jazz (à la Brubeck and Desmond) replacing the flamenco guitar on the sound track, and with Juan and Ramón as star performers. As soon as they enter (what the screenplay calls) this "decadent atmosphere," the purist Juan asks, "What are we doing here?" Before Ramón can rob one of the Americans, Juan has fled, leaving his accomplice to be rattled by the crowd and by the attentive waiter. This is clearly not Ramón's style of robbery, and we have always known that Juan feels out of place in an American setting. Earlier, when Paco asked him, "Why don't you go fight outside? Like in America, for example," Juan had responded, "No, because where I have to make it first is here."

The Andalusian loner, Manolo, and the blood brothers, Juan and Chato (linked by the family tie), are the most traditionally Spanish and the most closely identified with the folkloric stereotypes of flamenco and bullfighting. Paco (the sacrificial victim) and Ramón and Julian (joined in a competitive struggle over who controls the gang) are all infected by the American dream but in different ways. Paco naively believes America is paradise; he insists to Juan, "I tell you, America is great . . . they have everything, man." Ramón, who executes more fast-paced action than the others, always adopts an American modus operandi, particularly in the singulative garage heist he proposes, which he describes as "a lo Americano!" and which turns out to be the most action-packed, sparsely dialogued sequence in the film. (In fact, footnote 27 in the published screenplay observes that

In the action-packed garage heist in *Los golfos*, Julian is knocked out by the drunken American.

"the garage robbery . . . told with certain humor . . . seemed in part from American gangster films" [109].) The cynical dandy, Julian, perhaps the most complex character, both hates and envies Americans. In one scene, he questions Visi about her American customers, casting them as rivals in his own Oedipal drama and implying that such clients make her even more desirable to him. His passion grows murderous in the garage heist, where the primary victim is not the crippled Spanish attendant but a huge drunken American customer with a crewcut and a new Chevrolet. Julian is knocked out by this Daddy Warbucks, who is then overpowered by the other boys, who finally have to hold Julian down to prevent him from killing the

American. The image of the American giant fighting off six young fatherless Spaniards helps politicize the Oedipal dimensions of Julian's narrative line.

Despite their fast-paced action, the American-style robberies usually are aborted, either by the interruption of the action within the diegesis or by an abrupt jump cut to the next sequence. The film ends with two powerful dramatic climaxes, more closely associated thematically with neorealism and the Spanish aesthetic. Though almost expressionistic with its accelerated montage, overhead angles, converging camera moves, blurred focus, and close-ups of running feet, the chase of Paco that leads to his fatal descent into the sewers evokes the sequence from *Bicycle Thief* in which the crowd chases the protagonist after he has stolen a bicycle in desperation. The crowd is not condemned, as it was in *Surcos,* but is figured with ambivalence, as it was in *Bicycle Thief.* D'Lugo perceptively observes,

All the gang members find themselves unsuspectingly encircled by mobs whose presence carries the ambivalent mark of easy manipulation and of retaliatory ensnarement. . . . These agents of order are themselves the pawns in a more elaborate ideological maneuver when they block from movement other individuals, like themselves, who are struggling to break out of the trap of their collectivized and manipulated existence. (36)

In the climactic scene in which Chato discovers Paco's corpse, the neorealist-style long shots document the impoverished living conditions where the sewer empties into the river. This setting, where women and children habitually till the soil amid stray dogs and pigs, detaches Paco's death from the American genre and contextualizes it with the kind of precise cultural specificity that Visconti had also achieved with his backgrounds in *Ossessione.* The setting also evokes the grim ending of Buñuel's *Los olvidados* in which the corpse of the young protagonist is dumped on the garbage heap. When Chato first sees the police and then a crowd forming around a washed-up body, the recognition strikes a flamenco chord in his heart; he runs, he looks, and the camera slowly pans up the body covered with newspapers, allowing us to recognize an ad for the Hollywood musical *Gigi* (a choice even more bitterly ironic than *Surcos'* allusion to *Father of the Bride*) before stopping at Paco's youthful face frozen in death.

Paco's death stare prefigures the final close-up of the dying bull. These two wasteful deaths reveal that despite their promises of social mobility and stardom, the two melodramatic alternatives of bull-fighting and crime are self-destructive traps; for both inevitably doom the individual and his antagonist as well as the crowd that witnesses their fatal struggle. *Los golfos* suggests that any art form that glorifies the individual hero over the collective while ignoring the underlying ideological forces that determine their relations functions as part of the ideological trap. This accusation applies not only to the Spanish art of bullfighting but also to Hollywood classical cinema, whether the gangster movies that inspire Ramón or escapist musicals like *Gigi* that glamorize the exploitive corruption of youth.

EL COCHECITO   Based on a novel by screenwriter Rafael Azcona, Marco Ferreri's *El cochecito* (1960) is like a cross between Frank Capra's *Arsenic and Old Lace* (1942–1944), a theatrical black comedy about two old lovable killers, and DeSica and Zavattini's *Umberto D* (1951), the purest yet most sentimental of the neorealist classics, which became a primary target of the Andreotti Law and helped mark the demise of the movement. Neither sentimental nor purist, *El cochecito* tells the story of Don Anselmo, a lovable old retired widower who is so determined to buy his own motorized wheelchair to keep up with his physically disabled friends that he poisons his entire family and is arrested by the *guardia civil.*

Like *¡Bienvenido, Mr. Marshall!* it takes a contemporary social problem that would appeal to the neorealists (a conflict between generations over limited economic resources in contemporary urban Spain) and proposes a solution associated with the United States which is shown to be part of the problem. This time it is not a group of villagers harmlessly dressing up as Andalusians to get their share of the Marshall Plan but an individual becoming motorized so as to get his share of the benefits promised by industrialization. The connection between the two films is strengthened by having Don

Anselmo played by José Isbert, the same actor who played the mayor in *Bienvenido*.

Though the salesman will never tell Don Anselmo the cost of the motorized wheelchair, he *is* told that the latest model "was invented by Americans . . . for their disabled veterans" and that "it was made in Spain but under a U.S. license." The motorized wheelchair is repeatedly contrasted to buses, which frequently appear in the background—either carrying foreign tourists (Americans, Germans, or Japanese) whom the Francoist regime was so actively courting or being denounced by Spaniards for their inefficiency and dehumanized rules. The Spaniards' frustration with government management is one reason that the motorized wheelchair is so appealing as a model of American capitalism with its promises of mobility and autonomy. Yet in raising these expectations, it turns Don Anselmo into a self-centered, consumerist killer and ends up costing him his family, freedom, and humanity. Hardly an endorsement for the modern industrialized Spain then being promoted by the technocrats in Franco's regime.[17] No wonder the censors tried to force Ferreri and Azcona to have Don Anselmo warn his family about the poison before it was too late.

The film does not blame the kindly Don Anselmo, who is treated sympathetically, even after he massacres his family. That is part of the corrosiveness of the satire, for, as in Buñuel films, everyone is seen as potentially murderous. Rather, the blame falls on the regime's contradictory policies of importing industrialization from abroad while maintaining authoritarian repression at home. These policies failed to solve the severe economic inequities of Spain's population (which had been crippled and infantilized by years of hermetic isolation), and they also divisively set one group against another in a new form of civil war. Carr explains,

The conflicts inherent in rapid industrial growth set off an internal contradiction between the ideology of the regime and the "conditions" of industrialization. . . . After 1957 . . . the technocrats associated with the Catholic lay order, Opus Dei, introduced the "conditions": the creation in Spain of a market economy where prices would control the allocation of resources and the integration of that market into the capitalist economy of the West. The Stabilization Plan of 1959, a drastic remedy for inflation and a severe deficit in the balance of trade taken from the recipe book of orthodox capitalism, would cure the economy of its inherited impurities so that it would function as a modern, "neo-capitalist" economy. Rapid growth would take care of all problems. . . . The technocrats' faith in private enterprise as the *motor* [italics mine] of growth, it was held, reinforced the hold of a narrow financial oligarchy. . . . The planners' concentration on aggregate growth . . . increased the gap between the rich and the poor provinces. (156–160)

El cochecito departs from *Surcos, Muerte,* and *Golfos* by mocking the conventions from both sides of the neorealist-Hollywood dialectic and their respective Spanish semes, playing them off against each other. The collective is represented by two groups that compete for Don Anselmo's allegiance: his right-wing patriarchal family, which is headed by his authoritarian lawyer son who serves the bourgeoisie and the Catholic church, who tyrannizes over the other members of his household, and who threatens to put his father in an asylum; and the physically handicapped, who at first are associated with the proletariat or the underprivileged but then cut across class lines to include the paralyzed retarded son of a rich marquesa and the able-bodied bourgeois Don Anselmo. While we spectators are led, like Don Anselmo, to condemn the authoritarian family and to sympathize with those who are physically disabled, we are shocked by the poisoning of the family, which can be read either positively as a radical overthrow of the entrenched Francoist regime or negatively as a critique of the illusory dehumanized freedoms offered Spain by consumer capitalism. This ambiguity leads us to keep our emotional distance from Don Anselmo and to reexamine the rival populist collective.

As a product of industrialization, the motorized chair offers the promise of a new community—one based not on feudal class divisions but on a fluidly mobile separation between the "haves" and the "have-nots" (what Eisenstein had perceived as the ideological base behind Griffith's American forms of montage and melodrama). The

In Marco Ferreri's *El cochecito* (The Little Wheelchair, 1960), Don Anselmo (José Isbert) is treated sympathetically, particularly in his relationship with the young handicapped lovers and with their community of motorized "have-not's." (Photo courtesy of Kino International Corporation.)

marker of the group's difference is the fetishized wheelchair that each member of the group possesses as well as that medley of signifiers that includes what each of them lacks (money, power, phallus, arms, legs, eyes, intelligence, or any other ellipsis) and that unifies them as a class of castrated have-nots. In this way, the motorized wheelchair (like any other fetish) is revealed to be a narrative and ideological apparatus that promises mobility, pleasure, and freedom while actually bringing regression, dependence, and impotence.

Thus this so-called new community actually looks very much like a motorized version of the Black Legend stereotype—that cruel and grotesque parade of violent, maimed Spaniards, which Buñuel had used ironically as spectacle in *Tierra sin pan* and which the Francoist cinema had displaced with optimistic images of folklorico and false heroics. Because this Spanish collective is so strongly identified with the American "model" of industrialization, we realize that the Black Legend stereotype is merely the flip side of folkloric spectacle—the seme of Spanishness usually associated with the Hollywood aesthetic.

What *El cochecito* offers instead as a primary seme of Spanishness is esperpento, that specifically Spanish form of absurdist humor frequently associated with Valle-Inclán. Though frequently alleged to be incompatible with realism, esperpento could be used to reveal historical realities that were traditionally denied in other aesthetic discourses. Ricardo Gullón argues,

In Valle-Inclán's case, it was perhaps his awareness of this historical reality, present in him since the twenties, which turned him toward the esperpento. . . . The caricature was to be the starting point for a reconstruction of a reality which, to be sure, would never again seem as solid as it had in the past. . . . If the esperpento is subversive, it is because it degrades myth, the idea of myth and its value or values, upon which the continuity of the bourgeois world, our world, depends.[18]

In the context of cinema, esperpento became the trademark of Azcona (no matter what director he was working with); it was carried back to Italy by Ferreri (where he continued making black comedies like *La grande bouffe*), and it remained central to the Spanish surrealism of Buñuel. Hopewell defines esperpento as

the grotesque, the ridiculous, the absurd. Enrolled in the interests of an essential, historical realism, it points and derides the anomalous abyss between Spain's sublime tradition and her dismal reality. Characters in Valle-Inclán's esperpento grimace, gesture, grunt, performing mechanically like human marionettes. They are swept along by a tide of misunderstandings, imbecility, chaos. They struggle to transcend the crippling biological, social, psychological and accidental banality of life in general, their present predicament in particular. They fail. (59)

The mechanized puppets of Valle-Inclán's esperpento were very well suited to a satire on Spain's industrialization, as was, according to Gullón, his "belief that the most urgent need at the time was to stave off the materialism of a society ruled by the idea of profit" (126). Gullón observes that the "most obvious feature" in Valle-Inclán's aesthetic is mechanization, which "reveals the process by which man in modern society, becomes a mere thing" (127). He also claims that Valle-Inclán turned the technique around, "describing an inanimate object—a piano, a toy car—as if it were animate" (127). These are precisely the techniques that Ferreri and Azcona use with Don Anselmo and his beloved cochecito.

The centrality of esperpento in *El cochecito* was immediately recognized by Spanish critics, whether it was treated pejoratively, as in the passage already cited by García Escudero ("a grotesque deformation of reality with the finality of denuded satire") or positively, as by Manuel Villegas López, whose essay "On the route of Spanish Humor" (included in the special issue of *Temas de cine* devoted to *El cochecito*) first described the film's distinctive combination of neorealism and esperpento.[19] This hybridization later influenced Almodóvar, who claims,

In the 50s and 60s Spain experienced a kind of neo-realism which was far less sentimental than the Italian brand and far more ferocious and amusing. I'm talking about the films of Fernán Gómez (*La vida por delante, El mundo sigue*) and *El cochecito* and *El pisito*. It is a pity that the line has not been continued. (Hopewell, 238–239)

A good example of this combination of neorealism and esperpento occurs in the scene where Don Anselmo first visits the orthopedic shop that caters to the handicapped. It opens with a neorealist-style tracking shot of Don Anselmo walking down a crowded downtown street. When he spots an armless man getting on a cochecito, he is pleased and envious, and we are amused by the ironic distance that keeps him blind to the physical loss and attuned only to the marvelous machine. But when Don Anselmo enters the shop and we see in the foreground a little lame boy being fitted with an orthopedic shoe, we are no longer so amused by the incongruities and may even feel a twinge of guilt for our earlier identification with the old man's absurd point of view. Once it is Don Anselmo's turn to inquire about the cochecito, the tone turns funny again and remains so as long as his obsessive desire holds center stage—even though a one-eyed woman waits in the background and the father of the lame boy returns to change the color of his son's singular shoe. The satire reveals that it is the aura of the fetishized commodity (whether shoes, wheelchair, or any other desirable apparatus) that turns Spaniards into eager consumers and makes them forget the depressing material realities of contemporary Spain and the moral costs of capitalism.

Another good example of how esperpento reveals historical reality occurs at the marquesa's grand feast, which highlights the marquis as both a pampered aristocrat and an infantilized drooling idiot. While dining downstairs in the kitchen with the servants, the marquis tries to adopt a lobster as a pet. When one of the servants tries to retrieve the creature, the marquis has a tantrum and stubbornly holds on until he snaps off one of the lobster's legs, turning him into a fellow have-not. While parodying Don Anselmo's idiotic tantrums over the wheelchair, the marquis's comic business with the lobster is situated within a discourse on manhood and infantilization. His tantrum arises out of the frustration of having been denied not only the pet lobster and the other privileges that normally go with his class position but also a cigar as a signifier of manhood and his mother (to whom he blows kisses when he hears her voice over the intercom giving commands to the servants below). When the marquis insists, "I want to shave like Daddy" (an icon of masculinity and castration that is ubiquitous in Spanish movies from the silent period to the 1990s), he is shaved, not with a phallic straight-edge but with a motorized razor and not by himself but by his attendant, who observes with affection, "He's like a baby."

This scene presents the distinctively Spanish paradox of a strongly patriarchal society in which men from all classes are interpellated as infantilized, impotent subjects and where there is constant Oedipal rivalry between fathers and sons over who should embody the law. This issue is particularly strong in the figure of the lawyer (Don Anselmo's authoritarian son) who uses money to infantilize both his father and his future son-in-law and who evokes the figure of Franco (the ultimate son who functions as patriarch to all of his infantilized subjects). Landy claims that one common characteristic of the Italian comedies made during the Fascist era was the representation of class relations in terms of generational conflict—a strategic means of presenting social and ideological contradictions without directly confronting political issues.[20] In *El cochecito,* Ferreri and Azcona adopt a similar strategy, but the absurd excesses of esperpento help expose the political pointedness of the satire.

Like Bardem's reflexiveness in *Muerte,* the esperpento of Azcona and Ferreri provides *El cochecito* with a conceptual framework in which both the chronicling impulse of neorealism and the escapist drive of Hollywood can be parodically reinscribed. What made this reinscription so brilliant is the camerawork of Baena who, once again as in *Los golfos,* exaggerates the main visual techniques of both aesthetics and comes up with a very different kind of combination that would enrich the distinctive language of the New Spanish Cinema.

As in *Muerte* (as well as in Buñuel's *El*), there is an exaggerated opposition between the close-up and the long shot in long take, but here it is tailored to the satiric dynamics of esperpento. As Gullón perceptively observes, almost as if anticipating the cinematic adaptation of esperpento,

Visual distance is a decisive factor in the process of turning reality into an esperpento. From afar the individual is diminished and dehumanized. This, in turn, lets him be observed ironically, so that the onlooker does not participate in the movements and gestures which seem ridiculous or even senseless. The onlooker cannot participate in what he sees because he is incapable of distinguishing or discerning. . . . He comes to realize that to see things from the inside leads to tolerance, whereas to see them from the outside leads to criticism, distortion and caricature. . . . If an individual who is inside accepts the view as seen by one outside, what occurs is a voluntary transformation of reality into an esperpento. (136)

In his influential essay, "The Dehumanization of Art" (1925), Ortega y Gasset identified this rupture of "customary perspective" as a central characteristic of modernism, which included both the surrealism of Buñuel and the esperpento of Valle-Inclán. He claimed that this rupture could be achieved not only through the emotional excesses of melodrama or through a distancing ironic overview but also through the close scrutiny of an "infra-realism."

Reality can be overcome, not only by soaring to the heights of poetic exaltation but also by paying exaggerated attention to the minutest detail. The best examples of this—of attending, lens in hand, to the microscopic aspects of life—are to be found in Proust, Ramón Gómez de la Serna, and Joyce.[21]

In film, this dehumanizing rupture could easily be obtained through a reflexive foregrounding of extreme close-ups and long shots.

In *El cochecito,* neither the long shot nor the close-up poses as an unmediated documentation of reality; both are blatantly manipulated and distorting. However, the technique that dominates this film is the long take, which not only provides a dynamic montage within the shot and contributes to esperpento by repeatedly exposing new comic absurdities but also reveals the way characters compete for the limited space within the crowded frame. Although this dynamic may have occurred within individual sequences in Italian neorealist films, there it was never a controlling structural principle as it is here in *El cochecito* and even more emphatically in Ferreri's first feature (also co-written by Azcona), *El pisito*. In *El cochecito,* this effect is periodically augmented by overlapping dialogue, as if voices are also competing for the spectator's ear and for the limited space on the audio track—a technique pioneered by Welles in *Citizen Kane.*

These stylistic dynamics are immediately introduced in the opening sequence behind the credits. In a series of three depth-focus long takes, punctuated by two intrasequence dissolves, we watch Don Anselmo walking through the crowded streets of Madrid carrying a bouquet of flowers. We do not yet know who he is, where he is going, or what he intends to do with the flowers—the hermeneutic questions that launch the plot and that help focus our attention on this foregrounded protagonist who is clearly central in the narrative and the frame. yet our attention is distracted by at least four other elements. First, there are the titles—white letters on multishaped black blocks that vie for our attention and for the limited space within the crowded frame, always moving, sometimes breaking into fragments, and occasionally covering a particularly intriguing part of the image (what *are* those dogs doing in the street?) as if functioning as a parodic form of censorship.

Second, on the sound track, there is the bouncy Italian-style music by Miguel Asins Arbo (evocative of Nino Rota's scores for Fellini), which immediately accentuates the rhythm of the movements in the image, turning Don Anselmo's awkward city walk into a comic dance. While here the music is nondiegetic, in a later sequence in which Don Anselmo arranges a romantic reconciliation between two estranged handicapped lovers, the camera cuts directly to a pair of blind street musicians and then pans to the young couple already successfully reunited. As in *Los golfos,* when the music turns diegetic, it becomes another competitor for the space within the frame, both blocking out and suturing over the intermediate actions that have been omitted from the narrative.

The third distraction is the background—all the vehicles, creatures, and construction that Don Anselmo must dodge in the street. Consistent with the neorealist principle of positioning characters within their socioeconomic context, these long takes reveal the old man to be frightened and astonished as he encounters a city undergoing industrialization. They acknowledge the iterative aspect of the image. Yet within the ordinary background of urban traffic, there is the occasional surrealist "jolt" that evokes esperpento and prefigures absurdities to come; for example, the line of quixotic workers carrying long poles and wearing toilets on their heads and a limping cow wearing a brace who is the film's first instance of lameness.

The fourth distraction is the rhythmic quality of the long takes and intrasequence cuts and of the interaction between the moving camera and the moving objects in the frame. All are carefully choreographed to create the kind of aesthetic manipulation that neorealists usually tried to avoid or disavow.

These same stylistic dynamics are continued after the titles when Don Anselmo reaches the first stage of his destination, the house of his disabled friend, Luca, who will accompany him to the graveyard where they will place their bouquets on the graves of their respective dead spouses. Again the sequence is divided into three long takes (this time punctuated by two intrasequence cuts), but once the camera moves indoors, the competition for the limited space is intensified and the contrasts in lighting become more pivotal. As Don Anselmo moves through the house—through a series of variously lit, multipurpose rooms and hallways—the camera never reveals the full contours of any interior but gradually exposes more characters and objects occupying the space, whose presence always surprises us, making us feel we can never predict what lies beyond the range of the camera. This effect is heightened by the sound track. For example, while Don Anselmo is flattering Luca's young niece for her beauty, we hear the offscreen moans of a cow and later the barking of a dog. Like the combination of tinkling cowbell and barking dog that acts as a bathetic reminder of animal desire in Buñuel's *L'age d'or,* these incongruous surrealistic sounds deflate the human discourse and shatter the realist illusion of the visuals.

After the first cut, Don Anselmo encounters Luca, who is positioned at the threshold of an interior patio waiting to be carried to his new motorized wheelchair. The depth focus shot enables us to contrast the two rooms: the interior patio in the background is flooded in a wonderful, natural diffused light, which contrasts with the darker room in the foreground. The patio space is framed on each side, creating the effect of a proscenium. In the left foreground, there is a pile of straw, which, along with the framing and radiant lighting, helps to transform this realistic crowded interior into a parodic image of the holy manger with the cochecito in the fetishized role of savior. When Luca is wheeled out of the patio into the outer room, the camera (still in the same long take) briefly exposes the rear end of a cow. Not only does this bovine allude to the incongruous cow in *L'age d'or* but it also explains the straw and the offscreen mooing and thereby deflates the religious vision. After the second cut, when Luca is wheeled outside in the street for his first ride on the new vehicle, his female relatives prophesy, "This chair will bring us trouble," and he caustically retorts, "Don't worry, I am not going to the United States!"

The interior long takes are most impressive in the long narrow hallways within Don Anselmo's house. Frequently beginning with a static camera, the shot then follows or precedes someone (usually Don Anselmo) either up or down the hall as he moves in and out of adjoining rooms, all crowded with persons, objects, and sounds. The old man constantly closes and opens doors onto the hallway—to get privacy, to conserve space, to alter the lighting, or to provide access or camouflage for the film crew.[22]

The best example occurs during the murder sequence, where the cramped space is a contributing factor and where the camera moves within the two long takes constantly comment on the action. The first shot begins with a rowdy argument between Don Anselmo and the rest of his family, who are led by the bossy son. The camera precedes the noisy group down the dark hallway, pausing just beyond the door where the old man is deposited in his room. Waiting for the rest of the family to recede into the background (though their greedy remarks continue to be audible on the sound track), the camera continues to track ahead of the weeping old man as he reenters the hall and goes to the bathroom, where he takes his eyedrops and spies and grasps the bottle of poison clearly visible in the foreground. As if activated by the idea of murder, Don Anselmo now leads the camera back up the hall to the threshold of the kitchen, where he pauses and where the camera catches up with him to show him entering the room and pouring the poison into the soup, while the maid, busily humming and working in the same crowded frame, tells him not to rummage around but never gives him a glance. The camera continues to precede Don Anselmo down the hall and then, after the first intrasequence cut, follows him into his son's office, where he steals the money for the wheelchair, weeping more heavily all the time, as if he were the primary victim of his crime. Throughout the sequence, we continue to hear the sounds of street traffic, singing, and the family, signaling that the rest of the world proceeds with their ordinary activities in the iterative, oblivious to his singulative deed. When Don Anselmo opens the cash box, the camera moves in closer to a medium shot, pointedly associating these closer moves with the crime and with the blind self-centeredness that inspired it.

In contrast to the long takes and long shots that dominate the film, *El cochecito* contains only one close-up whose very singularity intensifies its impact. It occurs in the scene in which Don Anselmo discovers his family is dead. Opening with the traditional ironic distance of esperpento, a long shot of the bodies being carried into the ambulance with the surviving son-in-law scampering back and forth, the scene begins to shift tone when Don Anselmo rides into the right foreground from behind the camera. Then there is a reverse angle medium shot of Don Anselmo as he looks directly at the morbid scene, followed by a zoom into a closer shot of the object of his gaze. Following the Hollywood suturing pattern of shot/reverse shot, there is a cut to a facial close-up of Don Anselmo that is held for a very long time as he registers awareness of what he has done, creating that unexpected moment, which Gullón describes as so characteristic of Valle-Inclán.

Now and then buffoonery comes to a halt, and in the sudden stillness of the moment, brought about by the intrusion of something unexpected and tragic . . . , there is a change of atmosphere. And the reader, like the characters in the story, suddenly discovers he is in the presence of true drama. The puppets take on a human aspect. (133)

Suddenly the comic distance of esperpento is suspended, but as in the case of the neorealist long take, the normal functions of this Hollywood technique are reversed: instead of easily suturing us into sympathetic identification with the old man, this facial close-up (like the final close-up of María José in *Muerte*) marks the moment when we most want to distance ourselves from the killer and his crime. But as if to achieve that infra-realism described by Ortega y Gasset, the camera keeps moving in even closer on his face, which becomes almost painful to watch, and we hear the exaggerated sound of his panicky breathing, first overlapping the sound of the ambulance siren and then drowning it out, as if his painful subjectivity takes over and makes the outer reality recede. Like Don Anselmo, we spectators are forced to confront the cost of Hollywood's suturing techniques (the close-up, shot/reverse shot, and subjective sound) that reveal its intoxication with the singulative and glamorize the destructive self-ishness of American-style individualism.

This exaggerated contrast between the close-up and long shots in long take is analogous to the high-contrast photography, yet both are carefully positioned within a realistic "look" that has been carefully cultivated by Ferreri and Baena.[23] The competition is also played out in the lighting, where different styles (associated with different characters) struggle for control of the scene. Baena claims,

The lighting also helped to create character. For example, . . . I saw [the son of Don Anselmo] as a type of monolith, like a marble statue. Consequently, the light that we used for him had to distance the hardness of his facets. In contrast, I saw Don Anselmo more sympathetically and therefore I tried in most of the film to use lights that favored his point of view. The problem emerged when both characters were together. (13–14)

The fierce Oedipal rivalry between father and son—and their respective lighting styles, spatial positions, and voices—is most effective in the hilarious scene in which, between angry shouts and accusations, Don Anselmo (garbed in soft gray pajamas and bedding) lies in bed having a tantrum in the well-lit foreground while his son (dressed in high-contrast white shirt and black trousers and tie with light reflecting off his bald pate) stands erect, wheezing and having a coughing fit in the dark shadows of the background. They fiercely compete for the sympathy, attention, and allegiance of the rest of the family who move in and out of the room as roving spectators.[24]

All of these contrasts contribute to the power of the stylistic and narrative closure of the final sequence-shot, capturing Don Anselmo's arrest in one dazzling long take. It opens with a neorealist-type long shot of a desolate country road and loud offscreen cries of an animal, perhaps the braying of a donkey—a surreal expression of the bestial panic the old man feels at the prospect of being arrested. These animal cries evoke both the subjective sound of Don Anselmo's exaggerated breathing when he saw the corpses of his family and the earlier series of absurd Buñuelian animal images (of cows, dogs, and lobster) that intermittently shatter the realist illusion. Trying to make his getaway in his beloved wheelchair and continuing the journey that he launched in the film's opening sequence, Don Anselmo quixotically sallies forth into the frame riding toward the foreground past the camera on the sidelines, which pivots to watch from behind as the old man is stopped by two members of the guardia civil on bicycles. Directed by the arresting officers, Don Anselmo is forced to make a U-turn and ride back in the reverse direction. As soon as they begin to move, we hear the bouncy Italian music from the opening sequence, which now sounds grimly ironic. When they ride past the camera, Don Anselmo demonstrates that he still will not renounce his consumerist illusions of freedom, asking, "Will I be able to take my cochecito to prison?" As if parodying the final shot of *Muerte,* the camera watches from behind as the two anonymous cyclists ride off with the killer into the neorealist depth of field, enabling us to see a bus (that rival vehicle of official public conveyance) slowly moving forward from the background and, on the right, a line of utility towers that testify to Spain's ongoing process of industrialization. Within this extraordinary long take with its strong graphics and abstract minimalism, the camera literally turns full circle, to show Anselmo retracing his steps on that long, desolate road, which in the context of Spanish cinema typically functions as an icon for the transition between the feudal past and the industrialized future. The ending shows, through the choice of camera moves as well as the choice of what is in the image, that motorization leads to no progress whatsoever.

Thus, at the brink of the 1960s, we find a Spanish cinema that had absorbed the dialogized conventions of neorealism and Hollywood and successfully demonstrated (as Buñuel had done independently in Mexico) that both stylistics could be ingeniously subverted and ideologically reinscribed from within. The New Spanish Cinema that began to emerge in the 1950s, partly through the experimentation with this dialectic opposition I have been tracing, was to become official in the 1960s—part of Franco's "National Movement." In 1962, when García Escudero was reappointed general director of cinema, he deliberately reformulated the neorealist side of the dialectic in broader terms. He now referred to it as an intellectual European cinema that could include both the then highly successful French nouvelle vague and their own distinctive New Spanish Cinema, which despite its continuing struggles against Francoist censorship, would help pave the way for Spain's reentry into the mainstream of Western European culture. García Escudero wrote, "A film is a flag. . . . We must have that flag unfurled. . . . If you can't beat Hollywood on its own ground (a commercial cinema), you can, and Europe has actually done this, on Europe's home ground: intelligence."[25]

EL ESPÍRITU DE LA COLMENA   Nowhere were these two "grounds" dialogized with greater intelligence and subtlety than in Victor Erice's feature debut, *El espíritu de la colmena* (The Spirit of the Beehive, 1973), which was produced by Elías Querejeta (the Spanish producer most frequently associated with the New Spanish Cinema) and which won First Prize at the San Sebastián Film Festival and the Silver Hugo at the Chicago Film Festival. Although born in the Basque region like Querejeta, Erice, as Hopewell points out, "is loosely associated with the Madrid Independent Cinema, but his early career was more shaped by the zealous critical war sustained at the EOC [the Escuela Oficial de Cinematografía that García Escudero had reorganized in the 1960s], and carried over into the magazines *Nuestro cine* and *Film ideal,* between the advocates of neo-realism and the admirers of Hollywood cinema" (203). In fact, Erice was one of the founders of *Nuestro cine,* the journal (as Gubern observed) that carried on the ideological legacy of *Objectivo* and that frequently published Erice's reviews of both Spanish and foreign films.

Hopewell claims that "Victor Erice is one of Spain's few main-stream directors who invites a detailed study of style" (203), and, indeed, it is difficult to think of other Spanish films, besides those by Buñuel, Saura, and Almodóvar, that have gathered more critical acclaim abroad than *El espíritu de la colmena.* Yet despite his aesthetic rigor, the sparsity of Erice's output—one episode in the anthology film *Los desafíos* (The Challenges, 1969) and only two other features, *El sur* (The South, 1983) and *El sol del membrillo* (The Sun of the Quince, 1992)—has prevented him from being treated at length as an auteur. In the textual analysis that follows, the emphasis will not be on the uniqueness of Erice's style but on how the mature language of the New Spanish Cinema from the dictablanda continued to reinscribe the Hollywood and neorealist aesthetics.

El espíritu de la colmena focuses on a child's imaginative recon-struction of images she has seen in a Hollywood movie. It shows how she uses the myth to deal with the painful experiences in her own Spanish context (a small rural village in Castile shortly after the end of the Civil War), especially her interactions with a Republican fugitive who is captured and murdered by local authorities and with her father who is suffering from a state of inner exile. Thus, like *Muerte de un ciclista,* it emphasizes the legacy of Hollywood cinema over that of any other film tradition because of its cultural dominance worldwide. Yet in this instance, the genre chosen for reinscription is not a Hitchcock thriller or noir but rather the horror film, specifically, James Whale's 1931 version of *Frankenstein.*

This choice is significant, for Whale's film is also a reinscription of a work from another culture (England), art form (the gothic novel), period (the late eighteenth century), and gender (female writer Mary Shelley).[26] Moreover, this Hollywood classic is the perfect choice for adaptation to the Francoist context because it is of the right vintage (1931) and because, of all the versions of the Frankenstein myth, it places the greatest emphasis on the dramatic contrast between the monster's infantile emotions and his adult, giantlike body and also on the patriarchal nature of the powers that pervert and destroy him. By transforming the monster into a Republican fugitive fleeing from the Fascist authorities after the Civil War, Erice's narrative appropriates the myth for a political discourse that was still suppressed from representation in Spain. It demonstrates that under the pressures of a war that divided the nation, the family, and the individual, an entire generation of impressionable children felt a mixture of love and fear for repressive patriarchs—a combination that generated distorted fantasies of heroic allegiance and rebellious patricide and that led them to identify with both the victim and the monster.

Erice's young protagonist Ana (brilliantly played by Ana Torrent) is most deeply moved by the sequence from *Frankenstein* in which the monster seems to befriend the little girl Maria but then inexplicably kills her offscreen (a death that was cut out of the movie by Spanish censors). The inset sequence begins with the little girl asking her father to play with her and ends with him carrying her dead body through the village square while a wedding is being celebrated. Absorbing both monster and victim as her own doubles, and the primal associations of the love and violence between them as the deep structure for her own fantasies about the father figures in her life, Ana reinscribes the Gothic myth to suit her own Spanish melodrama, just as it had earlier been reinscribed by Whale to suit the Hollywood horror genre. Only she as a child and Erice as a filmmaker (working under repressive censorship practices rather than commercial pressures) foreground nonverbal images and concrete sounds and their impact on the personal plane while the narrative resolutions and political implications regarding Francoist Spain remain implicit and oblique. Yet the film implies that the children of Franco would turn out to be the children of Frankenstein. Thus, in *El espíritu de la colmena,* it is the *process* of cultural reinscription that is emphasized more than the conventions being reinscribed.

Although Erice's film also reinscribes neorealist elements, this process is much more subtle. The neorealist legacy is reduced primarily to the iterative mode in which the dailiness of the small Spanish village is represented and to the reliance on "image facts" set in a highly elliptical narrative—qualities that Bazin had so much admired in the early work of Rossellini and that here become integrated with the cryptic symbolic language associated with the Querejeta style.[27] As in the neorealist aesthetic, intertextuality also takes on an iterative dimension, for it at least partially decenters the personal journey into the past and identifies the paradigm to which this particular instance belongs. Thus, what is emphasized is a constant slippage between the singulative and the iterative, which Gerard Genette identifies with "the pseudo iterative" mode found in Proust's *À la recherche du temps perdu* and which he defines as "scenes presented, particularly by their wording in the imperfect, as iterative, whereas their richness and precision of detail ensure that no reader can seriously believe they occur and reoccur in that manner, several times, without any variation."[28]

In the opening of *El espíritu,* we see behind the titles typical children's drawings, visual adaptations of their daily experience that prefigure primary images from the drama to come. A printed title introduces the story as fable, "Once upon a time . . . ," and partially disavows its cultural and historical specificity, telling us it takes place "*somewhere* in Castile, Spain, *around* 1940."

Like many Spanish films of the 1950s that used the iterative subversively (such as *¡Bienvenido, Mr. Marshall!, Muerte de un ciclista,* and *Calle mayor*), *El espíritu* opens with the image of a desolate country road, an iconographic representation of the continuity between Spain's feudal past and current modernization. The narrative vehicle is figured as a truck bringing a Hollywood movie from the outside world to a typical isolated village. This iterative opening details, with an almost ethnographic interest, the cultural specificity of the distribution and exhibition of a Hollywood film in rural Spain during this period. As soon as the truck enters the village, it is chased by a group of children who are eager to know the film's genre and hungry for any images from the outside. The movie is promoted by a town crier in the village square and touted by the truck driver who claims, "It's the most beautiful film in the world . . . it's tremendous, olé!"

Ana is singled out from the other spectators at the movie by the intensity of her response and by her insistent questioning of her older sister, Isabel, as to why the monster killed the little girl and why the people killed the monster. Finding that it does no good to tell Ana that "nothing is for real in the movies," Isabel claims that she knows the monster is still alive because she has actually seen this spirit around the village. When the girls try to invoke this spirit, they hear only their father pacing overhead. Later, when Ana again tries to call forth the monster, this time by herself, there is a dissolve from a close-up of her face to the image of an approaching train, an "image fact" that can be read in several ways: as an ambiguous subjective memory or an objective repetition of an earlier sequence, as an iterative image of a daily occurrence or the next crucial singulative event in the narrative (for the train brings to the village the Republican fugitive who will play "monster" to Ana's Maria).

In addition to the intertextuality with Frankenstein, *El espíritu* also uses purely visual devices to evoke the iterative. The strongest germinal images in the film are not Ana's visions of the monster but the close shots of the beehive and the desolate long shots of landscapes, night skies, train tracks, and village exteriors. When treated with painterly compositions, long takes, and the brilliant elliptical editing rhythms of Spain's foremost film editor, Pablo G. del Amo, these images of ordinary objects become detached from the spare narrative line and achieve a powerful resonance—a resonance whose aestheticism (like the morning barrio shot in *Los golfos*) goes beyond the boundaries of neorealism.

For example, the morning following the *Frankenstein* screening is presented in a very unusual way, which paradoxically suggests the resumption of normal routines. Following a fade to black, we see an angular exterior long shot of the typical one-room village school-house, with children approaching from all sides. Then there is a series of jump cuts to the same shot but each with a slightly different arrangement of children, creating brief ellipses of indeterminate length. In the last image, the surrounding streets are empty. Since this series of shots is unified by a jaunty tune on the sound track and since it is followed by a cut to the interior of the school (where children sing songs that help them memorize their sums and perform exercises in anatomy), we assume that the series is contained within a single day. In no way motivated by narrative, the jump cuts merely signal the dailiness of this routine and setting and thereby place the sequence firmly in the iterative.

Yet in the following sequence, in which the two sisters first visit the site where Ana will later encounter the fugitive, the very same technique is used for precisely the opposite effect: to underscore the singularity of the event and to imbue the setting with a deep sense of mystery. The sequence begins with a long shot of an expansive field, whose brightness sharply contrasts with the dark cinematography that dominates most of the film (and for which cinematographer Luis Cuadrado is so well known). Deep in the background we can see a barn and well and in the foreground, the two sisters. Isabel tells Ana that this is the place where she has seen the monster/spirit. As the two girls run toward the barn deep in the background, there is a series of jump cuts that reposition them closer to the building until they disappear from view. Then there is a cut to a closer shot of the dwelling, where the two girls face the gaping black doorways, which look like eyes. A little later, there is a dissolve to the same shot, but now Ana has come there alone, and, unlike the previous jump cuts of the field, this time we have no way of knowing the duration of the ellipsis, that is, whether or not it is confined within the same day. In both sequences, these jump cuts create a rupture from conventional modes of realistic representation; in the latter instance, they also help prepare us for Ana's subjective visions. As Elsaesser has observed, in melodrama sudden changes, reversals, and excess in the mise-en-scène "lend a symbolic plausibility . . . to a reality of the psyche."[29]

Despite their differences, both sequences make us more aware of the impact of the specific setting in which the actions—the personal adaptations of movies, myths, and history—take place. These sequences seem to embalm moments in time, as a reconstruction, a memory, an imaginative speculation, or merely an iterative account of what happened many times.

These dynamics evoke what Genette calls in Proust an "intoxication with the iterative." Yet (as I have written elsewhere) within the neorealist aesthetic, the spectator is immersed "not in the emotional intensity of personal memory as in Proust but rather in the ideological relations between individual and collective experience."[30] Not only does the New Spanish Cinema emphasize the slippage between the singulative and the iterative but it also expands the iterative by combining these two forms of intoxication; it is as if despite the protagonists' intoxication with the presumed uniqueness of their own personal experience, the texts are intoxicated with how that experience is related to cultural production and history.

While this combination can be found in all of the films discussed thus far, it reaches its most intense synthesis in the oppositional films made during the dictablanda. This synthesis is vividly apparent not only in El espíritu de la colmena but also in Saura's La prima Angélica (Cousin Angélica), which was released the same year (1973) and which was the first Spanish film to treat the losing side of the Civil War sympathetically and to blatantly mock the Falangists. Both of these films probe the memories and fantasies of individuals who were emotionally stunted as children and interpellated as permanently infantilized subjects by the traumatic events of the Spanish Civil War. To get their political critiques past the censors, they both use melodrama, a genre that effectively plays at the border between evasion and subversion. More specifically, they both foreground what appears to be the immersion in singular personal memories and thereby create a subversive form of *pseudo singulative,* which functions not to naturalize dominant ideology (as in Hollywood classical cinema) but to expose its contradictions. For example, once he becomes totally immersed in painful childhood memories from 1936, Saura's protagonist Luis explicitly identifies his exploration of the past with the tradition of Proustian narrative, as if to disavow its political meaning: "One day Proust dipped a madeleine in his tea and his mouth was full of the smell of his grandmother's garden."

Though triggered by powerful germinal images whose vivid sensory details suggest the singulative, the historic traumatic memories in the melodramas of Erice and Saura are deeply embedded in a rich intertextuality with other movies, myths, and texts, which decenters the personal journey into the past. Both films isolate these powerful images from the flow of their respective elliptical narratives—images whose referents remain ambiguous (despite their richly detailed sensory qualities) and closely connected to the historic trauma (though they do not depict it directly). This disarticulation from the narrative heightens the uncertainty about whether such images evoke a unique event in a particular individual's life or are representative of collective experience, whether they accurately represent the past or are mediated by present desire and fear, whether they reside only in this film or adapt and allude to images from other texts, whether they are specifically rooted in this historic moment and location or are universal in scope. These resonant images seldom answer the narrative questions that define the singularity of the plot. Rather, they redirect our attention to the cultural background—to the associative links and mnemonic traces of a personality immersed in painful events from the past and to the iterative traces of collective history and dominant ideology.

Francisco de Goya's *Saturno devorando su hijo* (Saturn devouring his son). Museo del Prado, Madrid.

BLOOD CINEMA · **II**

THE REPRESENTATION OF VIOLENCE
IN THE SPANISH OEDIPAL NARRATIVE

· SACRIFICE AND MASSACRE

ON THE CULTURAL SPECIFICITY OF VIOLENCE

In Ricardo Franco's *Pascual Duarte* (1975), a peasant relentlessly hacks his mule to death with a knife both in close-up and in long shot in an agonizingly long sequence; in a later scene, in deep focus and long take, he fatally shoots his mother at point blank. In Borau's *Furtivos* (1975), after literally being thrown out of her incestuous bed by her emotionally stunted son, who has replaced her with a young runaway, the devouring mother, in long shot, brutally beats a chained she-wolf to death with a big stick. In Manuel Gutiérrez Aragón's *Camada negra* (1977), a slow zoom reveals a teenage Fascist repeatedly crushing the head of his lover with a stone as he chants, "¡España, España!" In Saura's *Los ojos vendados* (1978), a blindfolded actress recites the detailed testimony of a torture victim in Argentina, as the performers and spectators in the theater are gunned down by terrorists. In Miró's *El crimen de Cuenca* (1979), a guardia civil drives a spike through a prisoner's tongue in a fetishized close-up; in a later scene, the camera pulls back from a large inverted facial close-up of the same prisoner to reveal him hanging by his chained hands and bloody feet, and then a close-up exposes a rope tied to his penis, implying that if his hands or feet should slip, his penis will be torn off. In Imanol Uribe's *La muerte de Mikel* (1984), a repressed homosexual Basque terrorist bites through his wife's clitoris in a long slow-motion sequence as she screams in agony and counterattacks with a bottle. In Almodóvar's *Matador* (1986), a former bullfighter, with a VCR positioned between his spread legs, masturbates to images of women being impaled, drowned, and decapitated, violent acts he will imitate in his own serial murders; later, after watching the "lust in the dust" climax of *Duel in the Sun,* he will become obsessed with reenacting that death scene with his new lady love, another serial killer obsessed with bullfighting. In Agustín Villaronga's *Tras el cristal* (1985), a young man ritualistically slits the throat of a choir boy under the erotic gaze of his beloved former torturer, a former concentration camp doctor now imprisoned in an iron lung.

These are some of the most disturbing images of violence in the Spanish cinema—*not* from cheap exploitation films but from works by highly respected auteurs which were partly financed by the ministry of culture, critically acclaimed, and (in most cases) commercially successful. Anyone attempting to describe the distinctive characteristics of Spanish cinema usually begins with its excessive violence. For example, Hopewell observes, "Film-makers return time and again to the brutality of Spaniards, their residual animality of conduct, with an insistence even on the same broad metaphor—human relations as a hunt."[1] Even Gutiérrez Aragón, co-writer of *Furtivos* and director of *Camada negra*, observes, "Indeed, our films are violent—because this is a violent country."[2] Yet I doubt whether Spanish cinema is really *more* violent than the cinema of other nations (say, the United States or Japan). Rather, I would argue it is the modes of violent representation and their cultural implications, determinants, and reception that are different. This subject, which has thus far received little attention, is the focus of this chapter.[3]

We can already note certain patterns emerging in the violent images just described: the eroticization of violence, by targeting the genitals and by using fetishizing close-ups, ellipses, and long takes; the specularization of violence for spectators both within the film and in the movie theater; the displacement of violence onto surrogate victims, especially animals, children, and women; and the displacement of violence from one sphere of power to another, between sex and politics, between private and public space, and between the body, the family, and the state.

Not all Spanish cinema is violent. The most violent excesses occur in the opposition cinema of the dictablanda and in the post-Franco cinema when all censorship was suspended. In fact, all the examples cited above derive from this period. Within the Spanish context, the graphic depiction of violence is primarily associated with an anti-Francoist perspective, which may surprise foreign spectators, particularly Americans who are used to linking it with right-wing sentiment (as in the personal vengeance genre starring reactionary superheroes played by Charles Bronson, Chuck Norris, Clint Eastwood, and Sylvester Stallone or in the backlash horror films of the 1970s and 1980s). During the Francoist era, the depiction of violence was repressed, as was the depiction of sex, sacrilege, and politics; this repression helps explain why eroticized violence could be used so effectively by the anti-Francoist opposition to speak a political discourse, that is, to expose the legacy of brutality and torture that lay hidden behind the surface beauty of the Fascist and neo-Catholic aesthetics. Moreover, this graphic violence had commercial appeal, especially in the post-Franco era when foreign pornography began to flood Spanish screens and Spanish spectators were drawn to the violent excesses of foreign cinemas. Thus, this oppositional system of violent representation developed against a double hegemony: domestically, it had to be distinguished from the conventions of the Counter-Reformation (particularly as remolded by the Fascist aesthetic), where violence was eroticized as ritual sacrifice; globally and commercially, it had to be distinguished from Hollywood's valorization of violence as a dramatic agent of moral change.

From their own cultural heritage, Spanish filmmakers had the powerful example of Goya, whose pictorial representations of violence as a means of political critique exerted a strong influence on the cinema of opposition. Goya's work provided two useful models.[4] The first was a form of subtle social critique within well-established genres, such as the court portrait and the rustic scenes of Spanish folklore for paintings and tapestries, where the potential for violence is sometimes only implied. As a figure of the Enlightenment who contributed to the desacralization of Spain with his satires of religious corruption and as a supporter of liberalism who had to contend with King Fernando VII's betrayal of Spain's liberal constitution, Goya, the court painter, developed strategies that enabled him to mock these generic conventions in works that sometimes were considered the best examples of the very conventions they parodied. In describing Goya's famous painting, *Duelo a garrotazos* (Duel with Cudgels), which represents violent combat between two peasants, noted art historian Fred Light observes,

> It is precisely this vision of mortal humanity as a moral arena in which the results are hardly decided, which also distinguishes the genre scenes painted by Goya from other equivalent works painted in the 18th century by French artists and also by Spaniards. . . . Goya didn't accept that vision in which all social and moral values were so obvious and valid to the painter as they were for his models or his public. In many of these genre scenes by Goya, so lively in appearance, we cannot be sure that anyone is really enjoying himself.[5]

Some of these strategies (partially learned from Velázquez, whom Goya greatly admired) would later be adapted in the oblique, nonlinear films of the opposition during the Franco regime.

The second model, far more radical and direct, is found in paintings like *Saturno devorando a un hijo* (Saturn Devouring His Son), *El 3 de Mayo de 1808* (The Third of May, 1808), *Caprichos* (Caprices), and especially in his *Desastres de la guerra* (Disasters of War), where he responded to the atrocities committed during the Napoleonic invasion (which may have equaled those committed later during the Civil War). Here, his depictions are so graphic and brutal that they call into question any attempt to glorify heroics or to rationalize violence.[6] It was this frontal attack on cruelty performed in the name of any form of orthodoxy that became a primary model for the depiction of violence in the post-Franco era. Partly for this reason, in 1987, when the Spanish ministry of culture under the

Socialist government of Felipe González founded the Spanish equivalent of the Academy Awards, they named their Oscar the Goya.

SACRIFICE AND MASSACRE   In *Violence and the Sacred* (1972), René Girard argues that the sole purpose of all sacrificial violence (whether in art, myth, ritual, or religion) is the prevention of recurrent reciprocal violence—a theory that makes violence essential to social order and thereby implies it never can or will be eradicated from civilization. Although his theory attempts to reveal the violence and illusions that underlie religion, Girard's purpose is not to weaken their force but to justify their perpetuation.

> Religion, then, is far from "useless." It humanizes violence; it protects man from his own violence by taking it out of his hands, transforming it into a transcendent and ever-present danger to be kept in check by the appropriate rites appropriately observed and by a modest and prudent demeanor.[7]

Girard claims that all sacrificial violence imitates an original generative event, which he regards as "an absolute beginning, signifying the passage from nonhuman to human, as well as a relative beginning for the societies in question" (309). Even if the nature of the original generative event "can be deduced logically from myths and rituals once their real structures have been perceived," he insists that

> in order to retain its structuring influence, the generative violence must remain hidden: misapprehension is indispensable to all religious or postreligious structuring. . . . It is natural to assume that the best concealed aspect of the generative mechanism will be the most crucial element, the one most likely to render the sacrificial system nonfunctional if it becomes known. This aspect will be the arbitrary selection of the victim, its essential insignificance, which contradicts the meaning accumulated upon its head by the scapegoat projections. (309–311)

Unlike Georges Bataille who argues that "violence is silent" because "language is by definition the expression of civilized man,"[8] Girard suggests violence is a performative language that speaks through an elaborate series of conventions that are codified by the social order it seeks to uphold. The key question for us, then, is what kind of social order specific conventions are designed to defend—a question that makes the representation of violence a crucial issue for exploring cultural specificity.

It can perhaps best be answered by looking at moments in history when such codes underwent a dramatic transformation, such as the Counter-Reformation in the sixteenth century when new modes of representing Christ's Passion and other Christian martyrdoms were consciously designed by the church to uphold Catholicism against the onslaught of the Protestant Reformation. While Luther and his followers used the vernacular to interpellate faithful spectators into religious dogma as individuals, the Catholic clergy turned to a pictorial language of violent sensuality, spectacle, theatricality, and excess, so that they could continue to interpellate the faithful as members of a mass audience. Within these new conventions, Catholic spectators were encouraged to identify emotionally with the eroticized martyrs, whom they were trained to admire and adore. Gubern observes,

During this period and specifically in 1622, . . . Urbano VIII also coined the word *propaganda* (from the Latin, *propagare*) in order to found the Congregation of Faith Propaganda [which was] oriented toward the colonial-missionary activity. . . . In this capital phase of defensive transformation, the iconography of Catholic art was renewed, fixed and schematized according to some new canonical models. . . . The *cult* (the rite, the spectacle) displaces the subjective *faith* before the Protestant threat; the external and public is reinforced against the primacy of Lutheran interiority. The baroque, with its hyperdramatic effectiveness, with the theatricality of its martyrdoms for impressing the faithful, aspires to bring about a renewed emotionality in the spectator.[9]

The church authorized a system of representation to be promulgated both by its missionaries and its artists—a visual and theatrical iconography that could be read by people across vast differences in language and culture. Functioning as an effective ideological state apparatus, this unifying aesthetic helped to eradicate difference, as the church had done earlier with violence in the Inquisition and Crusades and in the expulsion of Jews and Moors from Spain. According to Gubern, the baroque legacy of the Counter-Reformation radiated from two political poles: the Vatican clergy and their secular retainers in Rome, who were served primarily by Bernini; and absolute monarchs, who used baroque splendor "to uphold their magnificence and power" (24–25). I am suggesting that during Spain's neo-Catholic revival in the 1940s, an analogous situation occurs, where the baroque fetishization of sacrificial death in the popular arts helps to empower both the religious orthodoxy of the church and the absolute power of Franco.

Although Girard draws most of his examples of sacrificial violence from myths and rituals in primitive societies, he extends his analysis to modern nations, arguing that we too can be plagued by a sacrificial crisis "when the difference between impure and purifying violence has been effaced . . . and the very viability of human society is put in question" (49). It is difficult to imagine a modern nation to which Girard's theory can be more readily applied than Spain, where sacrificial violence has been institutionalized through the national art of bullfighting, the neo-Catholic revival, and the Fascist aesthetic, all of which glamorize blood and death. In an essay entitled "The Spanish Christ," Unamuno observes, "When you see a bullfight, . . . you will understand . . . these drooping, livid, bloody, wounded Christs . . . that have been called savage. . . . The poor bull is also a kind of irrational Christ. . . . The public . . . applauds when it smells blood in the bullring. Blood of the body or blood of the soul, what is the difference?"[10] Or, as Lorca puts it, "In the liturgy of the bulls, that authentic religious drama, . . . just as in the mass a God is worshiped and sacrificed. . . . Spain is the only country in the world where death is a national spectacle."[11] Spain is also the nation where the fear of rampant reciprocal violence was most recently revived by the fierce atrocities of the Civil War and the bloody reprisals in its aftermath that left over one million dead. Arguing that "the ultimate referent for much of the violence in Spanish cinema is the internecine savagery of the Civil War," Hopewell notes,

From July 1936 to the end of mass executions in 1944, Gabriel Jackson claims, the Nationalists shot 300,000 to 400,000 fellow Spaniards. . . . The war produced "a breakdown of restraint such as had not been seen in Europe since the Thirty Years War," Hugh Thomas observes in *The Spanish Civil War.* (27)

Even earlier in Spanish history, there were the Holy Wars against Moors and Jews, the Inquisition, and the conquest of America, which were pivotal to the creation of the Black Legend, which can be traced back at least to the sixteenth century, at the beginning of the Counter-Reformation. As Besas observes,

The Black Legend is the persistent idea that Spaniards are backward, cruel, humorless, and violent, the Spain of the Inquisition, of poverty and ignorance, a "legend" begun, some authors have it . . . by Protestants in northern Europe to counteract the religious, military, and political power of Spain under the Catholic Monarchs and Philip II in the sixteenth century. (9)

In his brilliant work, *The Conquest of America,* Tzvetan Todorov cites many of the historical particulars on which this so-called legend was based, rejecting its use merely as a cultural stereotype limited to Spain and identifying it instead with the early stages of colonialism when Spain was a leading European power at the cutting edge of modern massacre.

In 1500 . . . 80 million inhabit the Americas. By the middle of the sixteenth century, . . . there remain ten. . . . None of the great massacres of the twentieth century can be compared to this hecatomb.[12]

Todorov distinguishes between two rival models of violence: the "primitive" violence of "sacrifice-societies" like the Aztecs (which conforms to Girard's model of sacrificial violence) versus the "modern" violence of "massacre-societies" like Spain and other European colonial powers (which has no place in Girard's theory except to evoke a perpetual state of "sacrificial crisis" when social order and all of its distinctions break down and recurrent reciprocal violence is imminent). Todorov argues,

Sacrifice . . . is a religious murder . . . performed in the name of the official ideology . . . in public places, in sight of all. . . . The victim's identity is determined by strict rules . . . , his personal qualities [count]. . . . The sacrifice . . . testifies to the power of the social fabric, to its mastery over the individual.

Massacre, on the other hand, reveals the weakness of this same social fabric . . . ; hence it should be performed in some remote place where the law is only vaguely acknowledged. . . . The victims . . . are exterminated without remorse, more or less identified with animals. The individual identity of the massacre victim is by definition irrelevant (otherwise his death would be a murder). . . . Unlike sacrifices, massacres are . . . kept secret and denied. (143–145)

Claiming that "Spaniards appear to have invented (or rediscovered . . .)" massacre, Todorov concludes, "The 'barbarity' of the Spaniards has nothing atavistic or bestial about it; it is quite human and heralds the advent of modern times" (145).

While Todorov acknowledges that both modes were operative during Spain's Golden Age (sacrificial violence in the Inquisition and modern genocide in the conquest of America), he does not observe that it was this very duality, of simultaneously functioning as a signifier of both primitivism and modernism, that helped make Spain so powerful in that particular historic moment and that was to become so crippling yet definitive in Spain's subsequent history, keeping the "two Spains" perpetually in conflict.[13] As one of the most violent eruptions of that conflict, the Civil War not only foreshadowed the modern horrors of world war to come but also hermetically sealed Spain into at least a decade of feudal under-development.

One can find an acknowledgment of this paradoxical duality in Lope de Vega's curious Golden Age drama, *Fuenteovejuna*. Far ahead of its time, this play demonstrates how the meaning of several acts in a chain of escalating violence—war, rape, corporal punishment, murder, torture, and execution—is fluidly transformed by how that violent behavior is represented verbally and in what political context. For example, a brutal massacre in Ciudad Real is eroticized in a highly fetishized description of the handsome commandant and his beautiful horse, an account designed to seduce a young peasant girl who is later raped by the commander and who, in an incendiary speech, provokes the town to take revenge against the rapist. Although this collective act of revenge is described to the Spanish monarchs as a regression to primitive savagery, the villagers consider it a brave act of rebellion that prefigures revolutions to come—long after the play was written. Not surprisingly, *Fuenteovejuna* took on new meaning in the Soviet Union where it was frequently revived, and it became a popular favorite in Spain under the Republic and during the Civil War. In fact, French director Jean Renoir had planned to make a film adaptation in Spain during the 1930s, but the project was cancelled when the Republicans began to lose the war.

The promise to retain (what Buñuel calls) an "exquisite" medieval spirituality while moving forward with progressive social change was one of the features that made Francoism so appealing to the Spanish populace.[14] As we have seen, Payne argues that Spain's neo-Catholic revival has no precedent or sequel in the twentieth century, other than "the revival of Islamic fundamentalism in the Middle East."[15] And as in the Islamic Revolution, in fascism, this fierce idealism was accompanied by violence. But whereas in Germany, Fascist violence was the kind of modern massacre described by Todorov (a purgative use of genocide to "purify" the nation), in Spain (which stayed out of World War II and which underwent progressive stages of defascistization), there was a denial of complicity with such massacre, along with the Black Legend with which it was associated, and in its place a substitution of sacrificial death, which was more compatible with the masochism of traditional Catholic ritual (as well as with Girard's theory). One reason the Counter-Reformation survived longer in Spain than in any other European nation is that there it served to counteract the Black Legend.

One of the most distinguishing characteristics of the representation of violence in Spanish cinema is the interplay between these two models of primitive sacrifice and modern massacre. While this duality is glossed over by the unifying ideology of the official Francoist cinema, the filmmakers of the opposition sought to explore Spain's paradoxical role as a dual signifier of Europe's barbaric past and dehumanized future. Thus they had to expose the aesthetic mechanisms that allowed modern massacre to be transformed into a purifying sacrificial ritual and thereby justified. That is one of the reasons the representation had to be so brutal, graphic, and ugly, so highly fetishized and specularized. Yet it still does not explain why it had to be eroticized.

Todorov gives no explanation for this eroticization. Although Girard acknowledges that "violence is always mingled with desire," that "thwarted sexuality leads naturally to violence," and that "at the very height of the [sacrificial] crisis violence becomes simultaneously the instrument, object and all-inclusive subject of desire," he nevertheless sees violence as the sole active agent in structuring social order. Desire remains merely a subordinate side effect because it is openly revealed rather than hidden and because it is limited to individual acts as opposed to being collective (35–36).

It was the Marquis de Sade and his followers who reversed this relation, arguing that sacrificial violence is activated by desire. In his essay on Sade, Bataille observes, "Sacrifice is passive, it is based on an elementary fear. Desire alone is active, and desire alone makes us live in the present."[16] Emphasizing the political implications of this reversal, Gilles Deleuze argues that in addressing history and challenging the dominant ideology, Sade's writings demonstrated the radical potential of eroticized violence.

It is as though Sade were holding up a perverse mirror in which the whole course of nature and history were reflected, from the beginning of time to the Revolution of 1789. In the isolation of their remote châteaux, Sade's heroes claim to reconstruct the world and rewrite the "history of the heart." They muster the forces of nature and tradition, from everywhere—Africa, Asia, the ancient world—to arrive at their tangible reality and the pure sensual principle underlying them. Ironically, they even strive towards a "republicanism" of which the French are not yet capable.[17]

Similarly, Allan Stoekl observes that Bataille sees "a kind of Nietzschean, parodic counter-history running parallel to but subverting or perverting the official Hegelian-Marxist history; this second history is one of excess, sacrifice, death and art."[18]

It was precisely this radical potential that made Sade so appealing to Buñuel and the other surrealists, who used "l'amour fou" to drive their subversive politics. But what Buñuel, as an anti-Francoist Spaniard, seems to have appreciated most in Sade's writings was its sacrilegious parody of Catholic ritual. Claiming that all other masterpieces pale when compared with *The 120 Days of Sodom*—this "magistral exploration of society, this proposal for such a sweeping annihilation of culture"—Buñuel insists it should have been assigned reading for him instead of the Bible, *The Divine Comedy,* and other Christian epics (*My Last Sigh,* 218). In the final sequence of Buñuel's *L'age d'or,* the libertine torturer espousing lines from *The 120 Days of Sodom* is played by "Lionel Salem, the Christ-role specialist . . . as an homage to de Sade" (117), and Sade appears as an important character in *The Milky Way,* which catalogs the most important heresies against Catholic doctrine.

Sade challenged the masochistic aesthetic of the church by transforming the original sacrificial crisis into an idealized Pure Negation, to which both the sadistic hero (and subsequently Freud's Death Instinct) aspire.

Pure negation needs no foundation and is beyond all foundation, a primal delirium, an original and timeless chaos solely composed of wild and lacerating molecules. (Deleuze, 25)

As we have seen, Girard argued that the mystification of the original generative violence was essential to its structuring function and further required that the arbitrarily chosen scapegoat "appear" to be carefully determined. But in Sade's sadistic model, the inaccessibility of Pure Negation leads to the methodical demonstration of its abstract principles—in countless acts of repetitive violence against interchangeable anonymous victims. His writings reaffirm the modernist model (as described by Todorov) where all social order is destroyed and everything is permissible to the will and imagination of the speculative individual.

It is Girard's theory of violence rather than Sade's that is compatible with fascism and its aesthetic (particularly in the Spanish context), for it shares many key assumptions: the essential role of violence in perpetuating rather than destroying the existing social order; the valuable role of religion in the modern state;[19] the privileging of the sacred mimetic bond between father and son over the son's Oedipal desire for the mother;[20] the justification of the male fear of female sexuality and the disavowal of female desire;[21] and the denial of women's importance in culture, except as a key sacrificial category for the surrogate victim and as the primary scapegoat who is blamed for all violence.[22]

In substituting for the masochistic aesthetic of Catholicism (which was later to be emulated by fascism), Sade's sadistic aesthetic provided an important model not only for Buñuel and the surrealists but also for the post-Franco cinema, whose representation of violence would play dialectically between modern massacre and religious sacrifice (as defined by Todorov) and between the aesthetic languages and structures of sadism and masochism (as theorized by Deleuze).

Challenging Freud's single entity model of sadomasochism, Deleuze's *Masochism: An Interpretation of Coldness and Cruelty* (1971) conceptualizes masochism and sadism as two separate sexual perversions as well as two distinct aesthetic discourses with quite different formal languages. While he credits the Marquis de Sade and Sacher von Masoch as patients and clinicians who meticulously described and distinguished the symptoms and signs of their respective perversions, he also sees them as "great artists" who "discovered . . . an entirely original language" and as "great anthropologists . . . whose work succeeds in embracing a whole conception of man, culture and nature" (16). Deleuze claims that their respective aesthetic discourses rearrange the power dynamics of the Oedipal family in two opposing ways.

The masochist's experience is grounded in an alliance between the son and the oral mother; the sadist's in the alliance of father and daughter. . . . Sadism stands for the active negation of the mother and the inflation of the father (who is placed above the law); masochism proceeds by a twofold disavowal, a positive, idealizing disavowal of the mother (who is identified with the law) and an invalidating disavowal of the father (who is expelled from the symbolic order). (59–60)

What is most curious about Deleuze's analysis is that although he claims that Sade and Masoch "muster the forces of nature and tradition from everywhere," he never fully acknowledges Christianity as one of their primary sources. Bataille, however, insists that Sade helped to reveal the sadism that already existed in traditional religious sacrifice.[23] Indeed, Sade's atheistic writings not only grotesquely parody the Old Testament sadistic God who is above the law but also totally reject the New Testament's masochistic fetishization of the suffering mother and son. Yet such a reading implies that masochism and sadism were already operating as oppositional aesthetics in the myth, ritual, and artistic representations of Judeo-Christian tradition long before they were "discovered" by Sade and Masoch and theorized by Deleuze.[24]

In contrast to Masoch's model, the masochistic aesthetic in post-Franco Spanish cinema is always associated with Catholicism and/or fascism, and its language and formal conventions (especially primary fetishization, suspension, and disavowal) are always used to disguise acts of violence that would otherwise seem more readily assigned to the sadistic aesthetic. In this way, sacrificial ritual is used to justify modern massacre. Indeed, the opposition between sadism and masochism might be conceptualized as another way of representing the conversion of the institutionalized sadistic massacre with its anonymous victims, cruel and obscene acts, and relentless repetitions, designed and performed in secret by an apathetic despot in the name of Reason and Pure Negation, into a highly fetishized, contractual sacrificial killing, featuring a carefully chosen scapegoat who becomes the most celebrated victim in history, one who is capable of absorbing all past and future acts of violence into this well-publicized masochistic ritual. Within this conception, Christ's Passion becomes the ultimate "built-in . . . breaking mechanism" for the final stage of sacrificial crisis so admiringly described by Girard—"that mechanism which in a single decisive movement, curtails reciprocal violence and imposes structure on the community" (Girard, 317).

THE REPRESENTATION OF VIOLENCE IN THE OFFICIAL FRANCOIST CINEMA OF THE 1940S AND IN THE OPPOSITIONAL CINEMA OF THE 1960S   In the authorized films of the 1940s, particularly the historical epics that are most jingoistic in glorifying the national culture and its unification under the Francoist regime, what we see dramatized is the conversion of the historical massacre into religious sacrifice. What is stressed is not violence against Spain's enemies (who are frequently massacred anonymously offscreen or in montage sequences that smooth over temporal ellipses within the main narrative) but the glamorized deaths of individualized Fascist heroes who, like Jesus, sacrifice themselves for God, Church, and State.

Raza   The best example is *Raza* (1941), the prototypical Fascist narrative, directed by Sáenz de Heredia, which was based on an autobiographical novel written by Franco under a pseudonym. When the Churruca patriarch Don Pedro solemnly tells his children, "When death calls, one must go proudly, . . . such was your fore-

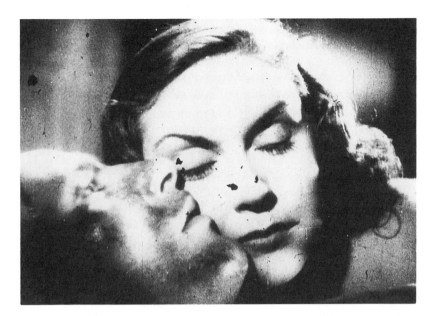

In the nationalist epic *Raza* (Race, 1941), the long shots of violence and victory parades are contrasted with carefully composed close-ups of the fanatical hero José (Alfredo Mayo), whether he is being miraculously brought back to life by his virginal fiancée or persuading his brother-in-law not to desert Franco's holy cause.

fathers' beautiful death," his eldest son asks, "How can any death be beautiful?" The rest of the film is rhythmically punctuated with a series of aesthetic answers to this question. We see the father's heroic death in a battle at sea while defending Spain's interests in Cuba as well as the martyrdom of the youngest son, Jaime, a priest who is shot by Republican soldiers on a romantic moonlit beach in a rhythmic montage of trees, waves, and footprints in the sand accompanied by the spiritual strains of choral music. With the lurching reversals of melodrama, the eldest son, Pedro, betrays and denounces his fellow Communists at the end, just in time to be martyred like a true Churruca and to have the image of his death superimposed over the Victory March of the Nationalists. Labeled an "extremist" by Pedro and a "Fascist" by his Republican captors, the middle son, José (the fictionalized Franco figure), strides toward death with a fanatical bravado. He seems to walk directly through the camera as if transcending materialist limits—a rupture of a film convention that foreshadows his miraculous resurrection after having been gunned down by an entire firing squad (a scene that exaggerates a real-life incident in Morocco, in which Franco allegedly survived a bullet through the abdomen).

All of these deaths are replayed (along with the patriarchal speech on noble sacrifice) in the final historic montage that harmoniously combines individuals and the collective, family and state, archival footage and fiction, past, present, and future into the unifying Fascist discourse of the victory parade. With its goose-stepping troops, tanks, and cheering crowds, this spectacle signifies (we are told) *not* the threat of modern massacre but "the spirit of the race."

Los últimos de Filipinas   A similar pattern can be found in Antonio Román's *Los últimos de Filipinas* (1945), which was made during Spain's first phase of defascistization. An enormous commercial success in Spain, it was called by Emilio Sanz deSoto "without a doubt our best historic film and our best patriotic film."[25] The story is based on a well-known historical incident in which a Captain Las Moreras took over the Baler garrison in the Philippines after his commander had died of the bubonic plague and, with his small band

In Antonio Román's *Los últimos de Filipinas* (Last Stand in the Phillipines, 1945), there is not the slightest interest in the waves of native "Tagalogs" who are needlessly massacred so that Spaniards can quixotically display their courage in noble profile.

of soldiers, successfully defended a church against enemy attacks for almost a year after Spain had renounced its colonialist claims in the islands.

Though offering ample opportunity for violence and political analysis, the film focuses instead on the fetishization of virility and sacrifice. Antoni Rigal and Jordi Sebastián point out that the film contains no expressions of hostility toward the United States, even though Spain lost the Philippines while fighting against this country, for in the post–World War II context in which the film was made, Franco hoped the United States would help Spain break out of its political isolation with dignity.[26] Nor is there much attention devoted to the Filipino enemies. The battle scenes are almost perfunctory: either they appear in marginal montages that cover temporal ellipses or they provide periodic action in the main narrative. There is not the slightest interest in the waves of native "Tagalogs" who are needlessly massacred so that Spaniards can quixotically display their courage in ennobling close shots.

In both of these historical films, the modern massacre that actually took place (the Civil War in *Raza* and the colonization of the

Philippines in *Los últimos*) is symbolically reinscribed as a religious sacrifice performed by glamorous heroes. This dynamic was later ridiculed by Buñuel in *El ángel exterminador* (Exterminating Angel, 1962), when, after describing a train wreck in which "the third-class compartment, full of common people, had been squashed like a huge accordion," a bourgeois woman remarks, "The suffering of those poor people didn't move me at all." But then she reports how she fainted away with grief "before the grandeur of the death . . . of that admirable prince, who . . . [had] such a noble profile!" As in works by Buñuel, Goya, and Sade, the violent excesses in the cinema of opposition are designed partially to jolt the bourgeoisie out of their complacent participation in a corrupt social order.

The Oppositional Cinema of the 1960s As Spain moved into its second and third phases of defascistization, the Franco regime continued to suppress the Black Legend and to restrict the graphic depiction of violence on screen, particularly since it was a sign that could distinguish the conservative Nationalists from the Falangists and the more radical right.[27] Still, we have already seen instances of both in the films we examined from the 1950s: the brutal murder of Pepe in *Surcos* and the brutal beatings of robbery victims in *Los golfos;* and the mocking of the black Spain stereotype in *Muerte de un ciclista, Los golfos,* and *El cochecito.* Yet such representations were still fairly moderate.

In the 1960s, when Franco's government was welcoming foreign tourists and capital and making moves toward the Western democracies and García Escudero was officially sponsoring a New Spanish Cinema that could help modernize Spain's image abroad, there was still censorship to contend with at home. As César Santos Fontela notes, García Escudero's new explicit censorship codes, which in 1963 were joyfully received by Spanish filmmakers, still gave "a wide scope of subjective action to the censors," yet they specifically prohibited, among other things, "images and scenes of brutality and cruelty towards people and animals, and those of terror presented in a [morbid] or unjustified way in relation to the characteristics of the plot or of the corresponding cinematographic genre, and, in general, those which offend the dignity of a person."[28] Thus the nonlinear, allegorical style that was developed to make subtle political commentary possible under these codes also used the representation of violence for political ends.

Usually depicted as the consequence of a repressive society beset by poverty, violence was included in adaptations of well-known classic novels, as in Angelino Fons's adaptation of Pio Baroja's *La busca* (The Search, 1966); in genres that justified its presence, such as a gypsy outlaw movie like Mario Camus's *Con el viento solano* (With the East Wind, 1963), Vicente Aranda's science fiction film *Fata morgana* (1966) and his equally bizarre psychological thriller *Las crueles* (The Cruel Women, 1969); in cine negro español, which grew more popular and sophisticated in the 1960s, with films like *Los atracadores* (The Robbers, 1961), *No dispares contra mi* (Don't Shoot Me, 1961), *A tiro limpio* (A Clean Shot, 1963), *Rueda de sospechosos* (Lineup of Suspects, 1963), and Borau's *Crimen de doble filo* (1964); and in esperpento, where violence was combined with black humor, as in Ferreri's *El cochecito* (1960), Berlanga's *El verdugo* (The Executioner, 1963), and Fernán Gómez's *El extraño viaje* (The Strange Journey, 1964). Yet most of the violence in these films was still suggested rather than explicitly represented on screen.

The filmmaker who pushed hardest against the official censorship in the 1960s was Saura, partly because his growing international reputation gave him and his producer, Elías Querejeta, the leverage they needed.[29] Saura used this leverage to expand the language of cinematic violence and its effectiveness for political ends. In his first feature, *Los golfos,* as we have seen, the modern random brutality of the American-style robberies is made analogous to the ritualized violence of the Spanish bullfight, as two artistic forms of self-destruction within a repressive, dead-end society. In the 1960s, he experimented with new strategies for representing violence that would be pushed much farther in the increasing liberalization of the 1970s.

Llanto por un bandido In *Llanto por un bandido* (Lament for a Bandit, 1963), an Italian-Spanish co-production, Saura turns the story of a nineteenth-century bandit into a perceptive analysis of Spain's formative political history. The film belongs to the genre of political outlaw films that were then drawing attention in Italy (e.g., Francesco Rosi's *Salvatore Giuliano,* 1961, and Vittorio DeSeta's *Banditi a Orgosolo* [Bandits of Orgosolo], 1961)[30] and that would become popular in the post-Franco cinema (with films like *Pascual Duarte, El crimen de Cuenca, El corazón del bosque* [The Heart of the Forest], *La luna de los lobos* [The Moon of the Wolves], and *El Lute*). This genre depicts essentially three kinds of violence: lawless acts of brutal individuals preying on others as poor and powerless as themselves to achieve an illusion of potency; paramilitary actions by a guerilla force that makes political alliances with other groups opposing the government in power; official acts of repression, torture, and murder designed to eliminate criminals and insurrectionists who threaten the social order. By exploring the connections among these three categories, the genre challenges the distinction between the "impure" violence committed by outlaws and the so-called purifying violence imposed by the state.

In *Llanto,* Saura explicitly evokes violent images from Goya. The opening scene (which censors cut out of the movie) depicts an execution of seven bandits (played by well-known members of the opposition, with Buñuel as executioner).[31] The means of death was garroting, a medieval form of execution that had been depicted by Goya and recently used by Franco. According to Saura,

At that time Franco executed—killed—a Spaniard named Julián Grimau, . . . a Communist; they . . . killed him with *garrote vil,* [which] . . . was how they killed bandits in medieval times. They placed them, like in Goya's drawings, so that they were sitting down and with a collar of steel around their necks. They put a screw (pointing to the back of the neck) and when they tightened the screw . . . they killed them. There was an international campaign against Franco stemming from the execution . . . done with this method which was totally primitive, and which had already disappeared from Spain. . . . Because my film had that same type of execution, a parallel was immediately drawn between the film and the assassination.[32]

The film's most violent sequence quotes Goya more directly, which may have saved it from the censors. Depicting brutal combat between the bandit leader El Lutos (Lino Ventura) and the protagonist José María (Francisco Rabal), who are buried in dirt to their knees, the sequence evokes Goya's famous painting *Duelo a garrotazos* (Duel with Cudgels), which has frequently been used to represent the Civil War and which Bigas Luna would later parody with ham bones in *Jamón Jamón* (1992). Despite Goya's realistic depiction of the peasants, their positioning in the foreground against a barren landscape makes them loom like giants; in fact, the contorted posture of the combatant on the right brings to mind the frightening figure from his black painting, *El Coloso o El Pánico* (The Colossus, or Panic).

In Saura's version, the blatant interplay between close shots and extreme long shots enables the spectator to contrast the emotional effects of these aesthetic choices in the representation of violence. This nearly wordless sequence starts with close shots of hands digging a pit. A cut to a long shot establishes the power relations: the leader standing on the left, the challenger seated on the right. The two combatants are led to their respective pits and buried up to their knees, locked into a deadly face-off. A series of close shots reveal the steps in this process, as if objectively documenting the conventions with an ethnographic interest (establishing the kind of emotional detachment that Buñuel achieved in *Tierra sin pan* and in the opening scenes of *L'age d'or*). A cut to an extreme long shot as the two men receive their cudgels allows us to register the iconographic connection with the well-known Goya image. Once the violence begins, a close shot establishes what is at stake for the combatants. This emotional engagement is quickly withdrawn in the next extreme long shot, which shows the spectators retreating to a nearby hill to watch the action and play the guitar; the combatants are reduced to tiny figures who are barely distinguishable. The camera moves back in for close shots of the kill, where now the elliptical chords on the guitar and the rhythmic pace of the cutting underline the strokes of the cudgels. The turning point comes when José María throws sand in his opponent's eyes, breaking the mutuality of their face-off and taking control of the gaze. Then the spectators-in-the-text enter the

In Carlos Saura's *Llanto por un bandido* (Lament for a Bandit, 1963), the dueling thieves are carefully positioned to evoke Goya's famous painting, *Duelo a garrotazos* (Duel with Cudgels). Museo del Prado, Madrid.

close shot to examine the corpse and to dig out the winner. This specularized sequence ends with the burial of the loser (providing narrative closure), yet the men abandon the winner, which renders the duel absurd.

Agustín Sánchez Vidal has noted that although the film was severely criticized for being too "mannered," Saura thought the representation of violence should have been even more stylized than it was.

When two persons from the same town didn't get along, they were buried in the earth and left to kill each other. So, it is not a fabrication by Goya. But, at any rate, that scene was not done well . . . , it

In *Llanto por un bandido* the turning point in this specularized combat is the moment when José María (Francisco Rabal) throws sand in his opponent's eyes and takes control of the gaze.

lacks design and rhythm, it doesn't have the violence that would be desired. Finally, . . . it doesn't work, . . . it should have been done in a nonrealistic key, to make it more stylized. (37)

In his next film Saura would find the key to that stylization.

La caza In *La caza* (The Hunt, 1965), Saura orchestrates the violence not merely within the individual sequence but in the stylistic and narrative design of the whole film. The hunt, which is a common vehicle in many cultures for narrativizing violence allegorically, took on special meaning in Spain where it was a favorite pastime for Franco and his cohorts and where the Civil War was a forbidden topic.[33] But here the ritualized violence of the hunt that substitutes for the Civil War and its reciprocal savagery is suddenly transformed back into an image of modern massacre. Everything in the film—its claustrophobic narrative, its spare landscapes, its emotional rhythms in dialogue and mise-en-scène, its percussive music and montage, its oppressive silences and ellipses, its interplay between extreme close-ups and long shots, and its blatant specularization of the violent gaze—move inexorably toward that explosive shootout and heighten its intensity once it comes.

In *La caza,* three former Civil War buddies (José, Luis, and Paco) who had fought on the Nationalist side and one of their young relatives (Paco's brother-in-law, Enrique) go hunting for rabbits on a game reserve that was formerly a bloody battlefield. Although Saura was not allowed to mention the Civil War directly, the hunt and its setting lead the three veterans to reminisce about their wartime experience and the spectator to decipher the analogy. According to Saura, the censors helped to intensify the atmosphere of repressed violence.

"Civil War" is not mentioned at any point in the film because it was absolutely prohibited by the censors. Only the phrase "the war" is used, and it winds up taking on a strange meaning. Such indirection gives one the feeling that this is an oppressive environment, that there is a sense of violence, not only in the characters but in the setting itself, because everyone understands that there's been a war; there are trenches, a dead soldier's bones, and all the elements that give the presence of "the war" an abstract meaning.[34]

The opening image behind the titles immediately creates an atmosphere of repressed violence. We see a pair of caged ferrets restlessly pacing back and forth in a cramped space and hear a loud, pounding, percussive music, which makes their entrapment seem all the more oppressive. The camera relentlessly moves in closer to a tighter shot that intensifies their desperation, links the close-up with entrapment, and marks the ferrets as surrogate victims for the violence to come.

Later, a montage of close-ups fetishizes the rifles as they are being cleaned, loaded, and handled by the hunters. The juxtaposition of an extreme close-up of Juan (the lame gamekeeper) through an iris that supposedly represents the gunsight with an extreme long shot where he is reduced to an insignificant creature on the desolate plain accentuates the artificial powers of the cinematic apparatus, which can magnify or diminish the characters. The close-up also specularizes the violence by marking the victim as the object of the look—not only the ferrets but the targeted rabbit who is first seen in extreme close-up and Juan's young niece Carmen who is the object of Enrique's erotic gaze. Although Enrique is less experienced with a gun than the older men, he still controls the gaze through his camera and binoculars, which (D'Lugo argues) help establish him as a spectator-in-the-text and the key witness to the final shootout.

In the first hunting sequence, the relentless rhythm of the percussive music and of the fast-paced montage evokes the same feeling of desperation as in the opening images of the caged ferrets. The human violence first erupts between José and Luis, after the latter, in a drunken stupor, sadistically impales a bug, pins it against a dressmaker's dummy, and then blows it away in target practice, establishing the sacrificial slaughter of animals as a prelude to human combat. The displacement is extended to females when Luis puts the dummy in the fire that Enrique has set to burn pinups from a girlie magazine. Like the violence, the fire gets out of hand. The fire-fighting is handled with the same accelerating pace of music and montage as the hunt, both of which increasingly appear to be part of the trap. This montage includes a brief close-up insert of the ferrets (also compared with women), who have been brought in by Juan for the final stage of the hunt and who alert us that we are approaching narrative closure.

The final hunt sequence is divided into three acts, each punctuated by a dramatic pause, as in the bullfight ritual. The first act of the hunt is a highly complex ensemble of dialectic montage: between the animals scurrying in the dark underground burrows and the men restlessly waiting aboveground in the white glare of the plain and Juan, whose inferior social class places him in a submissive mediating position between them, with his ear to the ground; between the exterior action and dialogue in the present and the interior mono-logues of the three veteran hunters who reflect back on their wartime experience; between extreme close-ups of the deadly struggle between ferrets and rabbits and extreme long shots of the men against the landscape, reduced to the size of insects; between the immobility of the hunters as they wait and the fluid movements of the camera as it glides among them; between the relentless pounding of the drums and the desperate squealing of the animals. When the first dazed rabbit slowly crawls out of the burrow, it is shot by the inexperienced Enrique. The second rabbit runs at great speed, followed by one of the ferrets. Paco shoots the rabbit and pauses; José shouts, "Don't shoot"; then Paco deliberately fires at the ferret, and the pounding music comes to an abrupt halt. The first violent act is over, and we are left with the consequences—the twitching bodies of the dying animal opponents lying side by side; the contemptuous looks directed at Paco by Juan and José; the regrouping of the hunters; the departure of Juan with his ferrets and of Luis in the jeep; and the angry brooding of José, who sits apart with his rifle.

The second act begins with the resumption of the music and with a close-up of José, who now seems ready to act out his revenge. As

In Saura's *La caza* (The Hunt, 1965), the violence in the final shootout is intensified by the alternation between close-ups and extreme long shots.

he loads and aims his rifle with a slow deliberation, the camera pans down the weapon as it turns toward its target, which is identified in a quick cut to a close-up of Paco. The intercutting between the two opponents is doubly specularized, for Paco is not only the object of José's violent gaze but he is also narcissistically studying his own image in a mirror. The camera moves in on him for an even closer shot, marking him as the next victim. The visual signs make us expect a shooting, but the music gradually slows down and softens as José suppresses his violent impulse. Then it stops. This murder inter-ruptus heightens the tension and increases the buildup for what is to come.

The pause between the second and third act seems designed to reassemble the four hunters though each remains apart: Paco sitting by the stream; José still sitting alone partly hidden by the reeds; Luis returning with the jeep; and Enrique walking to meet him. As the jeep drives into the foreground, a rabbit unexpectedly races by and Enrique pops up into the foreground to take a quick shot. The music resumes with the cut to a close-up of Enrique, who fires at the rabbit and unleashes the final act of violence. What is so strange is that though we have been expecting the climax all along, when it finally comes, its suddenness takes us by surprise. There is rapid intercutting between Paco shooting at a rabbit, José aiming in the other direction, then Paco turning around smiling in close-up before being blown away by José, and then looking back at his killer, as if they are mirror images of each other in this suicidal shootout. Then come the reactions of others: Enrique crossing himself in disbelief and running to retrieve Paco's body from the stream, Luis jumping into the jeep and screaming for José to finish him off as he drives toward him as if to run him down, and José warning Luis to stop. Again the two combatants are locked in a deadly face-off, doubly specularized. When José finally shoots Luis, the victim grabs his head but does not relinquish the gaze. Instead he grabs his gun and José runs. As soon as José turns his back on Luis and relinquishes the gaze, we know he is to be the next victim. When José is dead, the music stops and Luis curls up in the fetal position to die in silence. Then there is a downward angle extreme long shot of Enrique running on the plain; as he nears the camera, his image is captured in a freeze shot and we continue to hear his desperate panting, which evokes the ferrets and the rabbits caught in the same trap of reciprocal violence.

This powerful orchestration of violence—with its varied rhythms, dramatic pauses, and orgasmic climax—had a major impact on Sam Peckinpah, who reportedly told Saura that seeing *La caza* had changed his life. Indeed, he would adapt these same strategies in films like *The Wild Bunch* and *Straw Dogs* but with totally different political implications.[35]

Peppermint frappé *Peppermint frappé* (1967), a psychological thriller co-written with Rafael Azcona and Angelino Fons, may be Saura's most resonant film of the 1960s in the way it represents violence. Sánchez Vidal describes its "evolution" beyond the earlier films as "the passage from an exterior violence, 'a la Americana,' to an internal violence, psychological and more elaborated" (48).

Like many of the most violent films to come in the post-Franco era, *Peppermint frappé* portrays Francoism as a Fascist ideology that successfully draws on Spain's glorious heritage of institutionalized repression in order to transform dehumanized modern massacre into sacrificial ritual. But, as in the Spanish nationalist films of the 1940s, we actually see very little violence on screen. What dominates is the carefully controlled fetishization of objects in the dual contexts of traditional orthodox Catholicism and postmodern consumer capitalism—a combination that drives both Spain and its repressed protagonist Julian to psychopathic excesses. Like Azcona's *El cochecito,* this film suggests that when a Spaniard is passionately committed both to the Black Legend of Spain's feudal past and to the current Francoist drive toward the miracles of modernization, he is bound to become a killer. While the film's fetishistic structure and ironic Freudian dynamics owe a great deal to Buñuel's subversive melodramas (especially to *El,* 1952,[36] and *La vida criminal de Archibaldo de la Cruz,* 1955, and to his first glossy Parisian color film, *Belle de jour,* 1966), the gorgeous visual surface of *Peppermint frappé* is also reminiscent of the perversely beautiful films noir in color that Chabrol made in the 1960s in homage to Hitchcock. Like the poisonous drink named in the title and the modern image of Spain then being promoted by the Francoist regime, the surface of this lushly colored melodrama is pleasurable to the gaze, but its deep structure ultimately proves deadly.

Peppermint frappé tells the story of Julian, a repressed, middle-aged radiologist from Cuenca, who is smitten with the beautiful young bride of his childhood friend Pablo because she is the living embodiment of the idealized postmodern woman, whose images are fetishized in the fashion magazines he avidly collects. He is also convinced (and tries to convince her) that she is the mysterious woman he met and fell in love with last year at Calanda. Unlike Marienbad, Calanda is the site not of a fashionable European spa but of "the Drums of Good Friday," an ancient Aragonese ritual practiced during Holy Week that is rapturously described by its most famous native son, Luis Buñuel, to whom Saura's film is dedicated.

A powerful and strangely moving communal ceremony . . . in recognition of the shadows that covered the earth at the moment Christ died, as well as the earthquakes, the falling rocks, and the rending of the temple veil . . . which . . . provokes a real physical shiver that defies the rational mind . . . and which I heard for the first time in my cradle. (*My Last Sigh*, 20)

According to Saura,

It was in Calanda with Buñuel that I got the idea for the film. You know the story of the drums of Calanda. The year I saw it a beautiful young woman, she was one of Buñuel's relatives, was beating the drum with all her might. I kept that extraordinary image as a persistent memory. This young woman belonged to another world; while all around her thousands of people were playing, she also beat the drum. It was all the more impressive since it is usually the men who do so.[37]

Though Julian secretly declares his love to the despotic Elena when she and her husband spend the weekend at his family's decaying country estate, like a conscientious masochist he simultaneously tries to transform his mousy, repressed nurse Ana into an exact replica of his idealized object of desire. Conveniently, both women are played by Geraldine Chaplin, who was collaborating with Saura for the first time and who was the new woman in his life. This doubling of the female victim follows a pattern that Girard claims is essential to ritual sacrifice:

Ritual sacrifice is founded on a double substitution. The first, which passes unperceived, is the substitution of one member of the community for all, brought about through the operation of the surrogate victim. The second, the only true "ritualistic" substitution, is superimposed on the first. It is the substitution of a victim belonging to a predetermined sacrificial category for the original victim. The surrogate victim comes from inside the community, and the ritual victim must come from outside; otherwise the community might find it difficult to unite against it.[38]

Julian's substitution of the insider Ana for the desired but hated outsider Elena performs a curious reversal of what Girard describes (perhaps implying that the corrupting transformation of Ana is another form of mutilation as violent as the murder). Nevertheless, as in the Holy Week rituals and glamour magazine photos, this dizzying series of "scapegoat projections" successfully disguises the arbitrariness of the choice of victim—in this case, from the sacrificial category, *women*. This mystification, which Girard claims is essential to the religious structuring of violence, is revealed to be crucial as well to the structuring of erotic desire—an insight that is also central to many films by Buñuel.

When Elena betrays his trust to her husband Pablo and both mock his passion, Julian poisons them with his peppermint frappés, puts their bodies in their flashy red Corvette, and pushes it off a cliff. Then he rushes back to his country hideaway where Ana has miraculously eradicated all signs of the couple's presence and now awaits Julian with blond wig and drum ready to star as Elena's postmodern simulacrum in the ecstatic reenactment of the ritual of Calanda.

The film's stunning opening immediately introduces the mechanisms of fetishization in the dual contexts of religion and postmodern consumerism with their clashing discourses of repression and liberation. As we hear the strains of religious choral music, we see large fragmenting close-ups from a glossy fashion magazine of glamorous women, including British model Twiggy (who epitomized the "pop" modern woman of the 1960s). A man's hands turn the pages, reframing these images as if he were looking at them through a camera lens and selecting certain fetishistic details (e.g., legs, knees, feet, eyelashes, lips) to be reconstructed in his own album. The ritualistic manipulation of these erotic images—with sharp knife, scissors, and ruler—appear to offer him more pleasure than the voyeuristic contemplation of their signifieds.

This action is interrupted by the titles, which appear over stills of the selected fragments, now further fetishized in even larger glossy close-ups. The visual series ends with a parodic image of an old woman in gogglelike glasses with an American flag stuck in the frames—a female who stares back at the repressed male voyeur and mocks his idolatry of the "modern" woman. This visual series appears to extend into the next sequence, which opens with an x-ray image of a rib cage and then pans across sophisticated radiological equipment to introduce Julian and his mousy nurse working in the lab, establishing that his whole life is dedicated to the scopic regime. The choral music resumes in the following scene, as if to mark the fetishistic behavior of this man as he performs his ablutions and dressing rituals and selects an old childhood photo of himself and his friend Pablo before going to meet the woman who will change his life. This woman's power resides precisely in her ability to fuse the two contradictory discourses of Spanish orthodox Catholicism and Anglo postmodern consumerism that hold him enthralled. Consistent with the conventions of melodrama, the repressed conflicts of this impotent protagonist are expressed in the extravagant excesses of

In Saura's *Peppermint frappé* (1967), the protagonist is obsessed with childhood memories of repressive rituals.

mise-en-scène and music before hardly a deed is performed or a word spoken in the narrative.

The fetishistic manipulation of images and sounds grows more explicitly violent and more blatantly Oedipal in a later sequence in which, after having listened to the couple making love and having been coldly rejected by Elena as if he were a naughty child, Julian develops photographs of the couple, methodically slicing off strips of the image with his paper cutter, until his rival Pablo is totally cut out of the picture. As a specialist in X rays, an amateur photographer, a devout Catholic, and an ardent masochist, the emotionally stunted Julian is obsessed with frozen images and other fetishes that embalm the past, partly because they are more easily controlled than unpredictable living creatures in a rapidly changing present-tense narrative. This dynamic is also developed in the sepia flashbacks to his reconstructed childhood memories and to the cherished image of Elena at Calanda and in a religious legend he tells her about a chaste young

Although in the climax of *Peppermint frappé* Julian (José Luis López Vázquez) is shown carrying the limp corpse of Elena (Geraldine Chaplin), his greatest violence is committed against fetishized objects—tearing off her false eyelashes, smashing Pablo's flashy Corvette, and burning his incriminating shoe.

princess who resisted the Devil's seduction but was turned into a stone cross when he laid his hand on her heart (a legend he reenacts with Elena).

Although we see the exhumed skull of a favorite dog that Julian (a hater of hunting) had poisoned when he was a child and although we watch Elena and Pablo succumb to the poison on screen, the film's surface still remains beautiful; the Fascist aesthetic is never violated. The greatest violence is committed against images and other fetishistic paraphernalia rather than against people, a ritualized dynamic of displacement, like the drumming of Calanda. Steven Kovács's description of the violence in Buñuel's *L'age d'or* could apply equally well to *Peppermint frappé:*

The man's fury at seeing his mistress stolen is transformed into the physical pain of being knocked on the head, which is expressed by the loud, rhythmic beating of a drum. . . . The frenetic scene of violence . . . directed against objects rather than people is the sign of a sexuality turned inward . . . , suggest[ing] masturbation.[39]

The most violent images in Saura's murder sequence are the crushing of the ice for the fatal frappés, the symbolic rape when Julian rips off Elena's false eyelashes and roughly smears her eye makeup before placing her limp body in the car, the spectacular smashing of the expensive high-powered Corvette as it bounces down the precipice, and the burning of Pablo's incriminating shoe that was left lying in the road. The film ends with the frenzied beating of the drum in the final repetition of the "good Friday" ritual, where the camera is drawn into the dizzying circle dance of the ecstatic killers.

Los desafíos The 1960s ended with another boldly original Quere-jeta production, a three-part anthology film entitled *Los desafíos* (1969), co-written by Rafael Azcona, in collaboration with the three directors: Claudio Guerin, José Luis Egea, and Victor Erice. All three episodes focus on violence as political commentary, reflexively comparing the Spanish mode of representation with its American counterpart and positioning both within cultural variations on the Oedipal narrative. Set in Spain in the late 1960s, when there was an influx of American capital, tourists, soldiers, and cultural imperialism, all three stories pit a Spaniard against an American in an Oedipal rivalry over two women, a competition that ends in a sudden eruption of violence and death.

Though the Spaniards in each story vary considerably both in their character and casting, the American male in all three is played by the same actor, Dean Selmier, who helped finance the movie.[40] This triple casting of Selmier helps to establish the American as the symbolic Other, the outside catalyst (like the black monolith in Kubrick's *2001: A Space Odyssey,* so popular the year before) that provokes the Spanish responses to modernization. In interviews at the time, Querejeta stressed the film's critical analysis of "the American problematic, and the repercussion that it has on the rest of the world" (Hernández Les, 63).

Nevertheless, the film's implicit political critique of Spain is equally harsh, particularly in the first two episodes where Azcona's contribution was stronger.[41] As in *El cochecito* and *Peppermint frappé* (also co-written by Azcona), despite the outward facade of modern-ization (in the first story) and the intensity of the attraction to the liberties it promises (in the second), Spaniards prove to be still deeply committed to their feudal past and to the black tones of the *duende* celebrated by Lorca, that Andalusian conception of creative power that "loves the abyss and the wound."

Spanish art is always governed by a keen duende that gives it a qual-ity of distinctiveness and invention. . . . Spain is a land of death, a country open to death. . . . In Spain the dead are more alive dead than in any other place in the world; their profile is as sharp as the cutting edge of a barber's knife. . . . A duende inflicts a wound. And in the cure of this wound, which never heals, lies the uncommon, the inventive quality of a man's work.[42]

The first two stories pit the incestuous coupling of father and daughter (which is associated with Spain's patriarchal traditions and with the sadistic aesthetic) against the incestuous pairing of mother and son (which is linked to the neurotic rebelliousness of the Amer-ican counterculture and to masochism as theorized by Deleuze). In both instances, it is the Old World Spanish patriarch who murders the New World American youth to defend his family honor, which has been compromised by the young man's attempt to seduce his wife. The Spaniard considers his own seduction of the younger woman (whether incestuous or adulterous) to be justified, since he sees it merely as part of his feudal privilege as lord of the manor. Thus, despite their brutality, these murders can easily be aestheticized—either within the postmodernist decor of Guerin's mise-en-scène (which juxtaposes classical statuary, Renaissance religious paintings, and pop art cutouts of Twiggy) or in the traditional iconography of the españolada and the Black Legend in Egea's tale.

In the first story (directed by Guerin), a young American soldier named Bill comes to the luxurious, ultramodern home of Carlos, a middle-aged Spanish film star (Francisco Rabal), to see his daughter Cuqui. Lusting after his own daughter (who hopes to flee to America with Bill) and ignoring the sexual advances of his wife, Fernanda (who had formerly been a star), the actor feels threatened by this American soldier. When Carlos sees Bill embracing his wife, he half jokingly challenges him to a duel.

The violence is triggered by the wife's theatrical postmodern cue. Donning a catcher's mask and holding a baseball bat and mitt, she breaks into a stylized Japanese dance, as if transforming the male rivalry into a mortal battle between samurai. When the American youth bests her husband, she erupts into laughter, which unleashes her husband's rage. The camera pans down the baseball bat to a close-up of the Spaniard's gaze as he takes the bat, then cuts to a close-up of its object, the head of the American, which is the target for his blow. Here, as in *Muerte, El cochecito, La caza,* and *Peppermint frappé,* the classical Hollywood conventions of suture (shot/reverse shot) are implicated in the violence. The mortal blow is aesthetically displaced onto a classical statue, which falls from its pedestal and crashes on the ground, creating a witty series of decapitation images that is extended surrealistically in a carefully composed exterior shot of oversized beach ball and luminous moon. The daughter draws the curtains on this murderous melodrama, and, despite all of their previous bickering and pretensions to modernity, all members of the Spanish family silently collaborate in disposing of the corpse.

In the second story (directed by Egea), two young American hippies (on their way to India in pursuit of the Beatles and spiritual bliss) are caught making love in a bull pasture by the owner of the ranch and his servant. When the young American, Alan, sees the Spaniard ogling his girlfriend, Bonnie, he offers her to him for fifty dollars. The patrón (played by Alfredo Mayo, who was the Franco figure in *Raza* and the hateful Paco in *La caza*) takes her to the house of his servant, Benito (played by Fernando Sánchez Polack, who was the exploited gamekeeper in *La caza*), where they can make love. Meanwhile, Alan tries to seduce the Spaniard's wife, Lola, telling her what her husband is doing and giving her the same fifty dollars. When Bonnie finds out about the exchange of money, she laughs at the Spaniard for not understanding "free love" and tells Alan how much

In the first episode of *Los desafíos* (The Challenges, 1969), directed by Claudio Guerin, Cuqui holds the postmodern murder weapons—the baseball equipment—that hardly seem dangerous.

she loves him for his shrewd wit. When the Spaniard discovers that his wife has been with the American and has earned back the fifty dollars, he slaps her.

As the Spaniard and his servant sally forth on the plain to defend their Lady's honor against the decadent modern hippies, they evoke the comic image of Don Quixote and Sancho Panza. But when we see them riding at full gallop with their picas at full tilt and hear a

The killing of the hippies in the second episode of *Los desafíos* (directed by José Luis Egea) evokes Goya's grim drawing of "Unos à otros," from *Caprichos*, 77 (1st edition, 1799). (This reproduction has been made in the photographic laboratory of the Biblioteca Nacional in Madrid.)

militaristic drum roll on the sound track, we know they are out for a kill. They become picadors from the second act of the bullfight ritual, evoking Goya's grim image of *Unos à otros,* from *Caprichos,* 77, which parodies his brother-in-law Ramon Bayeu's idyllic tapestry design, *Chicos jugando a toro* (Children Playing at Bullfighting). Goya's version depicts two deathlike figures riding two others as if they were horses, pushing their picas deep into a traveler who carries a bundle that has a bull's horns. The title evokes the saying, "So goes the world, some make fun of others and bullfight. He who played the bull yesterday, today may be the gentleman of the plaza. Fortune directs the party and distributes the roles according to its inconstancy and its caprices."

This homily is perfectly suited both to the brutal ironies in the parodic ending of this second story and to the sardonic reversals that

will occur in Erice's third episode. Although the violence of the Spaniards is designed to undo the deflating role reversals in the previous international exchange of sex and money, Egea's spectacular ending subjects both Spaniards and Americans to parodic montages that expose the gap between high-flown idealism and brutal historic realities. While we see a distorting wide-angle image of Alan and Bonnie playfully imitating mechanical windup dolls and the Statue of Liberty in the foreground, we hear them singing their parodic rendition of "America, the Beautiful" and the deadly sounds of machine gun fire, exploding bombs, and fighter planes that evoke the war in Vietnam. This grimly parodic play is interrupted by a cut to the Spaniards approaching at full gallop, who gore the frolicking Americans and capture the sound track with their militaristic drum role that evokes the Nationalist heroics of the Spanish Civil War—a strategy that Querejeta's creative team also used with similar music in *La caza*. As the *patrón* rides off with his honor restored, his servant, Benito, is left with the dirty work—disposing of the bodies and torching their van, on which the words Civil Rights are scrawled.[43] Once all of the humans have disappeared from the frame, we are left with a spectacular montage of the apocalyptic fire and of the billowing black smoke that, in extreme long shot, merges into the beautiful, serene Spanish landscape. The continuation of the drum roll on the sound track helps remind us that this aestheticization of violence is a primary convention of Fascist Spain.

Reversing the premise of the first two stories, the third (directed by Erice) casts the American as the seasoned killer and the young Spaniards as his victims. Although the Americans were certainly not idealized in the first two episodes, only in the third does his licentiousness turn nihilistic and his decadence deadly. The story opens with a station wagon driving into a deserted pueblo on a desolate plain, which, as one character remarks, looks like it could be the moon. The vehicle contains an American G.I. named Charlie, who is traveling with two young Spanish women, María and Floridita, a young Spanish doctor named Julian, and a pet chimp named Pinky. Despite his championing of free love, Charlie grows jealous when he discovers that María and Julian are lovers. Sublimating his anger, Charlie breaks down the door of one of the deserted dwellings, providing the kind of spectacular action that is admired by Hollywood movie fans worldwide. In the midst of their game playing with its dramatic swings in music and mood, Charlie challenges Julian to a contest: stomping out his lit cigar with his bare foot. After meeting the challenge, Julian paints "Charlie go home" in big black letters on a building across from their dwelling, under the watchful gaze of the chimp, who is reading F. Scott Fitzgerald's *The Beautiful and the Damned*. Later, Charlie liberates Pinky and dynamites the dwelling with all four characters inside.

Like the Spaniards from the earlier episodes, Charlie's liberalism ultimately proves to be a facade, for underneath he is merely another patriarchal killer who is fascinated with the duende and enamored

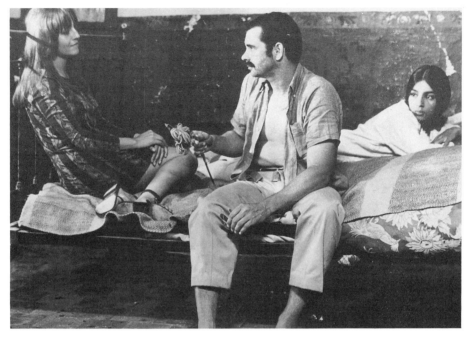

In the third episode of *Los desafíos* (directed by Victor Erice), the nihilistic American Charlie tries to dominate both Spanish women.

with death. But in contrast to the Spaniards in the earlier stories whose crimes of passion are expressed in the language of ritual sacrifice, this American's senseless suicidal gesture evokes the detached absurdity of modern genocide and the insanity of nuclear annihilation, forms of violence that are far more destructive than any Spanish variety (an insight that was already prefigured in Egea's parodic finale). Thus, *Los desafíos* ends with a grim vision of the Spanish/American encounter and with a profound skepticism about the effects of modernization on both cultures. As if reversing the framing images of Kubrick's Anglo celebration of technological progress in his sci-fi masterwork *2001*, Erice's final ironic close-up of the surviving chimp leads us not into the future with a new crossbreed or starchild but back to the relative innocence of our primitive simian past.

It is possible to stress only the lines of continuity among the three episodes of *Los desafíos,* as Juan Carlos Frugone does in his book on Azcona:

They are three stories of cultural confrontations, three stories of couples who don't work, three stories of violence contained and later unleashed.[44]

But the strong similarities in the basic plots of the first two stories help to foreground and dialogize the different languages in which they are told and the false images of Spain with which those languages are associated: the postmodern facade versus the more traditional clichés from the españolada and Black Legend. With its dramatic reversals, Erice's episode makes a sharp break with the others and seems to parody the language of American action films, yet its ending harks back to Egea's climax. The final explosion is another version of the fiery apocalypse, and the close-up of the monkey evokes the earlier final close-up of the inarticulate peasant Benito, as if he is an ironic simian substitute for the peasantry in America's classless discourse. This connection is strengthened in Erice's ending by intercutting between shots of the lone chimp and images crowded with the silent weathered faces of Spanish peasants—perhaps those who fled deserted pueblos like this one to serve and profit from American tourists in the cities.

The three episodes have a cumulative effect in intensifying the specularization of violence by linking it to the scopic dimension of sadism. In all three stories, it is the patriarchal killer who controls the gaze, and his victims are figured as the object of his scopic drive—a pattern that we also found in *Muerte, El cochecito,* and *La caza.* Since the scopic structure has been so profoundly eroticized in classical Hollywood cinema and so frequently cut to the measure of patriarchal desire, as Laura Mulvey has argued, the extension of the classical suture (shot/reverse shot) to the representation of murder is an easy way of eroticizing violence—a strategy, as we have seen, that was also extensively used in the earlier Querejeta production *Peppermint frappé.*[45]

In the first episode of *Los desafíos,* the specularized murder is prefigured by an earlier rivalry in reflexive spectatorship between the two men. Anxious over his waning powers, the Spanish actor spies on his daughter and her scenes with the young American and even secretly looks at the film that his daughter has forbidden him to see. Confident of his future and eager to co-opt the past, the young American leafs through the wife's scrapbooks that document her glorious triumphs in the Spanish theater.

In the second episode, a double voyeurism is constructed around issues of eroticism, violence, and money, in which only males are empowered with control over the gaze. As the Spanish patrón watches Bonnie stroking a horse, his erotic voyeurism in turn becomes the object of Alan's mercenary gaze. Although Bonnie considers herself "free" and identifies with Alan in his triumph over the Spaniard, the woman is figured as a domesticated animal and object of exchange by the films and men of both cultures. Similarly, in the climactic murder, though the two killers control the gaze, the peasant, Benito, also stares at his master (as he gores Alan and rides away from the scene of the crime). Though painfully aware of his own subservience and of his master's complicity in the exchange of women and dollars (the payment of the fifty dollars to Alan and the adultery with Bonnie were both blatantly specularized as objects of the peasant's studied gaze), Benito still identifies (against his own class interests) with his master's victory, as he undoubtedly did in the Civil War. Thus, significantly, the female victim is left for the servant to kill, for both women and peasants are interpellated by the powerful male contenders on the issue of nationalism, while the issues of gender and class exploitation remain suppressed in both cultures.

In the third story, the double voyeurism is constructed along gender and species lines, for within this more apparently Americanized aesthetic, class has been eradicated along with the family and replaced by the domesticated pet chimp, who is a convenient con-

In the second episode of *Los desafíos*, the peasant Benito (center) witnesses his master's complicity in the exchange of money and women.

densation for all those without power. His name, Pinky, might also evoke a racial discourse to those familiar with American film history (and to those who recall the evocation of "civil rights" on the hippies' van in the second story).

Charlie's discovery of the erotic encounter between María and Julian is also constructed as a double voyeurism. As he scans the pueblo with his telescope from an elevated position, his point of view dominates the screen. A series of iris shots encircle María in her bath (as Bonnie had been encircled by a circular pan when the patrón made his first sexual move). Then the image is reversed and Charlie's blue eye appears in the iris (as Carlos's eye had been specularized when he spied on his daughter and her film). Once Julian enters the iris, Charlie pans to find the other girl, Floridita, watching the couple and meeting his own gaze. Yet the woman looking is still being looked at; her gaze remains silent and impotent like those of Pinky and the peasants because only Charlie controls the high-powered apparatus—the telescope, the iris, the dynamite, and the narrative. When the spectacle is over, the apparatus, along with the narrative and its characters, is destroyed, leaving only the powerless spectators—the lone chimp and the mass audience of Spanish peasants.

By the end of the 1960s, a new language was emerging for the representation of violence, one increasingly associated with the independent productions of Querejeta.[46] Within the understatement of his films, the sudden outbreaks of violence were all the more striking, yet the brutality showed on screen was still fairly restrained. It was not until 1975, with *Pascual Duarte,* that a Querejeta production unleashed the violence full force.

A COMPARISON OF TWO POST-FRANCO FILMS: *PASCUAL DUARTE* AND *TRAS EL CRISTAL*   I now want to return to the post-Franco films from which I drew violent images at the opening of this chapter. I do not mean to imply that all post-Franco films depict violence in the same way. One could easily treat *Pascual Duarte* and *Furtivos* together as films made during the dictablanda in the year of Franco's death, both displacing the repressed patricidal rage onto rural matricide and animal sacrifice. Or one could discuss *Camada negra* (1977), *Los ojos vendados* (1978), and *El crimen de Cuenca* (1979), all made during the transition, as three explicitly political, reflexive films about torture and terrorism. Or one could compare *La muerte de Mikel* (1984), *Matador* (1986), and *Tras el cristal* (1986) as three outrageous melodramas from the Socialist era that blatantly eroticize violence within a homoerotic narrative and that challenge (with varying degrees of force) the genre's traditional privileging of heterosexuality, family, and motherhood.

Instead, I have chosen to compare *Pascual Duarte* and *Tras el cristal* because their representations of violence are the most excessive and threatening and also because these two films appear to be so different. Whereas *Pascual Duarte* was made in 1975, the year of Franco's death, and not approved by the censors or released until 1976, *Tras el cristal* was made ten years later, in 1985, well into the flagrantly permissive Socialist era. Whereas *Pascual Duarte* was directed by a young madrileño, Ricardo Franco, and produced by oppositional veteran Querejeta, *Tras el cristal* was the feature debut of young Majorcan filmmaker Agustín Villaronga. Partially funded by subventions from the ministries of culture both of Spain and of the regional Catalán government, it was distributed by Barcelona-based Lauren Films.

Pascual Duarte is a fairly faithful adaptation of what many critics have called "the first important novel of postwar Spain" (which Sam Peckinpah had wanted to make into a movie). *La Familia de Pascual Duarte* (1942), by Nobel Prize winner Camilo José Cela, is a harrowing, realistic first-person narrative of an inarticulate peasant in pre–Civil War Spain, who kills his dog, his mare, his sister's pimp, his mother, and the local patrician landowner, and then is executed by garroting.[47] *Tras el cristal* is loosely based on a perverse foreign source, Bataille's *The Trial of Gilles de Rais* (1965), featuring a fifteenth-century sadist (a precursor of Sade) who began as a follower of Joan of Arc but who, after her execution, allegedly tortured, murdered, and mutilated hundreds of young boys. Along with extensive commentary by Bataille, it contains transcripts of the ecclesiastical trial, translated from the Latin by Pierre Klossowski (who has been described as a "renegade Nietzschean monk" and who, like Bataille, was a member of the College of Sociology, 1937–1939, a group of writers devoted to Nietzsche and Hegel).[48]

Whereas *Pascual Duarte* focuses exclusively on Spanish history (the repressive forces that intensify the violence in the Civil War) and makes the political reverberations far more explicit than in the novel,

Tras el cristal updates the medieval setting to the Holocaust and turns the homosexual child killer into a German doctor named Klaus who performed sadistic experiments in the death camps. Now living in exile in Spain with his wife, Griselda, and their daughter, Rena, he unsuccessfully attempts suicide and consequently is confined to an iron lung. The transcripts of Rais's trial are replaced by the diary accounts of Klaus's murders, which are fetishistically read and re-enacted by one of his young surviving victims, the protagonist Angelo, who has come to murder and replace him. Villaronga's foreign sources and references have led some Spaniards to dismiss the film as "not Spanish." It is frequently compared with two Italian works, Liliana Cavani's *Il portiere di notte* (The Night Porter, 1974) and Pasolini's *Salò o le 120 giornate di Sodoma* (1975). But whereas *The Night Porter* lies totally within the masochistic aesthetic, reuniting torturer and torturee from the Holocaust (who play incestuous lovers locked in a secret room) with little actual violence (particularly in contrast to *Salò* and *Tras*), *Salò* conversely displays the highly organized architectronics of the sadistic aesthetic—its distancing humor, scatological obscenity, and elaborate paradigms (of decadent masters, anonymous victims, and humiliating tortures). Consistent with the Spanish cultural context, only *Tras el cristal* uses the masochistic aesthetic to eroticize sadistic acts (showing homoerotic lovers in a secret room sadistically killing anonymous victims), and the violence is far more threatening as a consequence.[49]

What I want to show here is how, despite these considerable differences, *Pascual Duarte* and *Tras el cristal* share many striking similarities in the way they represent violence—conventions that are also shared by other post-Franco films. In both films, the contemporary historical massacre (the Civil War or the Holocaust) is a structuring absence that helps to generate the escalating acts of primitive sacrificial murder that control the narrative, for, as Girard claims, "in order to retain its structuring influence, the generative violence must remain hidden" (309). As in *La caza,* the sparseness of dialogue and the elliptical nature of the plot help intensify the violence once it erupts. Moreover, the aesthetic rigor of the visual styles with their formalist, painterly compositions and muted colors; the claustrophobic narratives with their flashbacks, condensations, and repetition compulsions; the emotional restraint of the acting performances, particularly of the protagonists; and the minimalist, percussive sound tracks (the obsessive repetitive music that accompanies Pascual's murders and Klaus's rhythmic breathing amplified by the iron lung) all help to ritualize the most excessive acts of savagery. Despite, or rather precisely because of its power, this stylistic rigor implicates these aesthetic conventions for the glamorization of violence and death that are historically associated with fascism, futurism, and Catholicism.

The structure of both films is highly claustrophobic. *Pascual Duarte* begins with a wordless scene in which the protagonist is being taken to prison. This action is interrupted by a series of flashbacks that grow successively longer and more violent. After we see him kill his first human victim (his sister's pimp), ironically the next scene shows Pascual being released from prison, which we at first assume is in the present (or frame) but which turns out to be another flashback to a period of amnesty under the Republic. Like the double entrapment in Buñuel's *Exterminating Angel,* this confusion intensifies the feeling of structural entrapment. This brief respite of illusory freedom in the narrative becomes analogous to that brief period of freedom under the Republic, which was followed by a bloody war and a long entombment under Franco. For Pascual, what follows is escalating violence, culminating in his execution, which, like the explosive shootout in *La caza,* is the hysterical rupture toward which the whole film is inexorably moving. It is the only time in the film when anyone rages against death and struggles to live. According to director Ricardo Franco,

The whole film was born out of some images I had, one was the execution. . . . The historical accuracy didn't interest me. . . . I was interested formally in carrying the execution to a closed space where the spectator could not easily escape. . . . My intention was to make the death extremely expressive. Even today, this shot, which I have seen as many as seventy times, still gives me shivers.[50]

In Ricardo Franco's *Pascual Duarte* (1975) the protagonist's first human victim is his sister's pimp, whom he shoots at point blank range in a composition that evokes their romantic triangle.

The narrative of *Tras el cristal* is framed by two rites—a primal scene of murder and attempted suicide—and a triple transmogrification (where the transformation of an elegant country manor into a primitive, smoky charnel house is completed, where Angelo finally replaces the dead Klaus in the iron lung, and where Rena changes her gender to occupy Angelo's former place atop the machine). The diegetic space progressively becomes narrower and more interior—from the house to the invalid's room to the iron lung. At the end, the film freezes on Rena removing the military jacket she is wearing, just as Angelo had done before he killed her father. Then there is a dissolve to an image of the whole room encased in a glass bell jar, encapsulating the whole text within an interior erotic fantasy but also evoking an ironic reversal of the opening Rosebud image from *Citizen Kane.*

In both films, violence functions as a language, an alternative form of expression for the inarticulate killers. That is why its visual stylization and emotional rhythms are so important. In one of his interviews, Franco observed that in *Pascual Duarte* "violence has been converted into the unique language viable for a class who have been deprived of any identity. Pascual only takes charge of his own life when he exercises that violence; he has no other medium for expressing his frustration."[51] In the novel, this substitution is explicitly reversed, for when Pascual goes to Madrid he is astonished to see how city folk use language to substitute for violence, "how, in view of the volley of insults they spat out, how they did not so much as raise their fists in a fighting pose, let alone actually come to blows."[52] Thus, the writing of his memoirs serves to exorcise and control the violent impulses that drive him. In the film, the memoirs are replaced by cinematic stylization, which calls attention to the issue of language and its paradoxical relation to violence.

In both films, the blatant interplay between eroticizing fetishized close-ups and extreme distancing long shots helps to specularize the violence. As in *Peeping Tom,* control over the gaze is not restricted to the sadistic killer, for the victims are forced to watch their own deaths, demonstrating the chain of brutality and the reversibility of the two subject positions, of killer and victim. Pascual patiently waits for his faithful hunting dog to look directly at him before he fatally shoots her, and in the novel, he claims that it was the bitch's accusative "fixed stare" (which reminds him of "a priest listening to confession") that "roused the blood in [his] veins" and made him pull the trigger (Cela, 20). The same dynamic is repeated with his human victims, particularly with his mother ("Oh, if only she hadn't stared at me! . . . Man . . . simply cannot stand . . . the look that will stare into him . . . without a shade of comprehension" [78, 81]). Whereas the aggressiveness of the victim's stare arouses Pascual's anger, in *Tras el cristal,* the passivity and helplessness of the victim's gaze inflame the killer's desire. Klaus's diary describes in great detail the intense pleasure he derived from watching one of his young victims looking back at him. Moreover, in both films, the reversibility of the matched gaze forces us spectators to confront our own emotional susceptibility to the eroticizing of the most hideous murders—animal slaughter, child murder, matricide, and patricide. We see how murderers are constructed and recruited through spectatorship, by having witnessed or read the same violent representations that we are now watching.

This dynamic is most explicit in *Tras el cristal,* in the primal scene of the pretitles teaser, where first the detached yet eroticized kino eye is associated with the killer and then the hand-held subjective camera represents an unknown, heavy-breathing voyeur (later identified as Angelo) with whom we are sutured into identification. The erotic spectacle he is watching is a ritualistic whipping and murder of a young boy suspended on a rope before the voyeuristic Klaus, who photographs the victim before brutally clubbing him to death. Then the subjective point of view switches back to Klaus, as he leaps from the tower, which puts him in the iron lung, where he is infantilized and passive like his young victims and like the cinematic spectator. Thus, we are immediately positioned, like Angelo, to identify both with the killer and victim, performer and spectator, father and son. Clearly, this Oedipal narrative will favor not Freud's interpretation but Girard's and Devereux's, where the son's central desire is not to possess his mother but to imitate and replace his murderous father and where the originating crime is not the patricide or incest committed by Oedipus but the homoerotic rape and murder committed by his father, Laius.

In both films, the violent behavior of the characters is undermotivated, which creates a different kind of identificatory suture. As spectators, we are baffled by the contradictions in our own emotional reactions to the films—by the emotional distance from the protagonists, yet the intensity of response to the violent excesses, in which they figure both as killer and victim; by the strong desire to close our eyes or leave the theater, yet the compulsion to stay and search for the causes of their murderous deeds. Because nothing in these films is explained, because everything except the violence is so spare, and because everything in the flashbacks has been filtered through memory, the films force us to assume every detail is rich in implications and therefore, despite our lack of emotional identification with the protagonists, to construct an interpretation that might help explain not only these baffling characters and the social forces that created them but also our own baffling response and the cultural and psychic forces that intensify and control it. Although Bataille's analysis of Rais also omits motivation, Hopewell (1986:28) sees this lack as part of the "psychic legacy" that the Civil War left on the Spanish cinema:

Actions in many Spanish films seem undermotivated. The apparent cause of violence in particular seems hardly to justify the result. . . . Behind the Civil War killings were reservoirs of sullen rancor unlocked by any petty incident which could justify public retribution. Motivation in Spanish films seems equally petty at times, the driving force of conduct lying outside the film in Spanish history itself. Hence the extreme importance of background detail and secondary characters in Spanish films. They often establish the protagonist's experience as just one example of a collective condition within the fiction of the film; they inscribe that condition within a broader and enlightening historical framework.

In both films, there is a flashback to the childhood of the killer, where he is enlisted into ritual violence by corrupt patriarchs. We see the young Pascual in his village school, asked by the priest to recite the story of Abraham and Isaac, which he will reenact both in his murders (where he plays Abraham) and in his execution (where he is cast as Isaac). Although this incident does not exist in the novel, there his wife, Lola, tells him, "Blood seems a kind of fertilizer in your life" (Cela, 98). Especially when combined with Spanish Catholicism, this biblical text of violent sacrifice leads one to convert brute savagery into heroism. As Unamuno observes in "The Spanish Christ,"

Are you not mindful of that terrible paradox that bids one hate his parents, his wife, and his children and take the cross, the bloody cross, and follow the Redeemer? While this hate for ourselves passes unnoticed, ill defined, purely instinctive, almost brutish, it engenders egoism; but as soon as we see it as it is, well defined and rational, then it can engender heroism. (79)

We see a homoerotic version of this sacrificial narrative in *Tras el cristal,* where Klaus pays the young Angelo for oral sex, a flashback evoked by a fetishized photo of the pair posed as father and son. This still is first seen at the end of the opening teaser, as a lead-in to the opening credits—a position that accentuates its seminal power. The flashback is intercut with a ritual reenactment, which reverses their roles and serves as prelude to Angelo's sacrificial murder of Klaus.

In both films, there is a fusion of sex and violence, not only in *Tras el cristal* where most of the murders are clearly motivated by erotic desire but also in *Pascual Duarte* where Pascual proposes marriage by brutally raping Lola, an act of violence that leads to a brief period of pleasure for the couple, and where his relentless stabbing of his mule is pursued with a sexual energy that evokes bestiality. This association is made explicit in the novel.

I hurled myself against her, and stabbed her . . . at least twenty times. . . . I was covered with blood up to my elbow. The mare hadn't made a sound. She only breathed deeper and faster, like when we put her to the stud. (Cela, 66)

In both films, violence is further eroticized by being linked with forbidden desire—Pascual's incestuous desire for his sister (only implicit in the novel) or Angelo's homoerotic desire for his patriarchal seducer. In both, violence is positioned within the family, where the murder of the mother (who challenges her husband's authority) precedes the killing of the surrogate father. Both films rely on the kind of double substitution (both for violence and eroticism) that Girard claims is typical of the "purifying" ritual—the choice of an outsider (carefully chosen by category) to stand in for the communal scapegoat. Pascual chooses his dog, mule, and rival to substitute for his sister (Franco claims that *all* of Pascual's victims are surrogates for Rosario); Angelo carefully selects the choir boy and other stray waifs to stand in for himself, who eventually will replace the patriarchal Klaus. Both films show an awareness that such substitutions are eroticized by the symbolic order to protect the patriarchy, yet ultimately these texts trace the responsibility for the violence back to the crimes of the father—whether eroticized (as in *Tras el cristal,* where he is a Fascist pederast, who, like Laius, rapes and murders young boys) or politicized (as in *Pascual Duarte,* where he is the local patrón who represents the forces that destroyed the Spanish Republic). In both cases, the patricide is justified.

In both films, humor is acknowledged as an alternative to violence, another way of discharging the aggression and lust that have been repressed by the Francoist culture. In both texts, this alternative discourse of laughter is linked with the expression of female desire (which is always repressed under patriarchy). In the sequence immediately following Pascual's killing of the dog, he and his sister go to see Buster Keaton's *Seven Chances,* the scene where a frightened Buster (another brutalized inexpressive young man) is chased through the streets by scores of women who want to marry him. After leaving the movie theater, Pascual and Rosario run through the empty streets at full speed, as if discharging the erotic energy that has been aroused by cinema spectatorship. The laughter that erupts in the theater is a displacement both for the incestuous desire of the siblings and for the greater violence to come. It is also an eruption

Director Ricardo Franco claims that *all* of Pascual Duarte's victims are surrogates for his sister Rosario, who is the object of his incestuous desire and his only source of comfort in an otherwise emotionally and materially impoverished life.

of the misogynist fear of female sexuality, which reverberates with the matricide—an excess meaning that is not explained by the political context but is echoed in many other Spanish films. Although this moviegoing incident does not exist in the novel, Cela makes Pascual's misogyny quite explicit, for Pascual admits that he "feared women— mothers . . . more than the plague," and he accuses his mother, sister, and wife of embittering his life (Cela, 87, 73). Pascual's hatred of women is intensified by their laughter, especially in response to violence, as when his wife laughs after the mare kicks an old woman and when his mother laughs at his father's corpse. Similarly, Bataille found Rais's laughter at his dying victims the most horrific detail of his crimes.

In *Tras el cristal,* the humor is introduced by the prattling maid, who stands in the hall with her panties around her ankles after she has been injected by Angelo, who has been posing as a male nurse and heterosexual male—a scene that parodically prefigures the most gruesome murder committed by injecting gasoline into a boy's heart. The maid threatens to deflate the erotic fantasy with her bathos, to carnivalize the masochistic discourse, to expose its sadistic underbelly. She is dismissed shortly after her mistress, the impatient Griselda, is murdered, purging this homoerotic hothouse of all adult women and all heterosexual desire and stripping the master-servant relations of their class discourse. The maid's appearances in the film are framed by a pristine image of an obelisk, the most direct glorification of phallic rigidity in a film full of transsexual identifications. The maid is also the one who explicitly comments on the reflexive analogy between the iron lung and cinema, a remark that positions her as spectator, the Spanish mass audience that will be turned off by this movie and that must therefore be banished from the theater. As she watches Klaus lying passively in the iron lung, looking into the mirror that reflects his facial close-up in a narcissistic matched gaze, she exclaims, "That machine makes me nervous, it's like being at the cinema!" Indeed, throughout the film, both the camera and the iron lung function as fetishized hardware, machines of desire that amplify the eyes for voyeuristic pleasure and the lungs for the heavy breathing of sex and death that also arouses pleasure in the sadistic killer. In both films, the reflexive scenes evoking cinema spectatorship stress

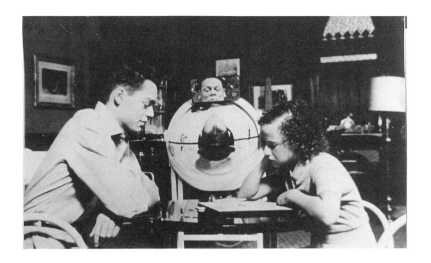

In Agustín Villaronga's *Tras el cristal* (Behind the Glass, 1986), when Klaus lies passively in the iron lung, looking into the mirror which reflects his facial close-up in a narcissistic matched gaze, the iron lung is explicitly compared to the cinematic apparatus. (Photo courtesy of Teresa Enrich, TEM Productores Asociados.)

the passivity or physical immobility imposed on the viewer, a condition like political repression that only heightens the intensity of the violence and eroticism held in check.

In contrast to the reflexive scenes of passivity, both films contain hunting sequences that narrativize male violence and that emphasize the transformative potential of the hunt. *Pascual Duarte*'s first hunting scene contains one of the film's few moments of joy as well as its first act of killing; Pascual's sister helps his dog retrieve a dead bird, and he embraces her while teaching her how to shoot. Once she leaves him, the reenactment of the hunt becomes the painful setting for Pascual's first sacrificial murder—the killing of his faithful dog as surrogate for his unfaithful sister.

In *Tras el cristal,* the hunt (like double voyeurism) demonstrates the reversibility of subject positions: Angelo, once the innocent prey, now becomes the murderous hunter in a nightly quest for young victims. In the most explicit hunt scene, he chases Klaus's daughter through the woods, as she is pulled between split loyalties to her father and his surrogate, whom she will replace in this chain of seductive conquests and betrayals.

Both films are framed by images of official "purifying" violence whose perversion is exposed. In the opening scene of *Tras el cristal,* the hanged boy evokes images of Jesus and of suspended martyred saints, particularly as painted by Ribera. As in the opening cathedral scene in Buñuel's *El,* we watch how "l'amour fou" is perverted by Catholic ritual. In *Pascual Duarte,* the final garroting of Pascual unleashes the screams of protest that have been repressed throughout the rest of the film, evoking images from Goya as well as recent executions by Franco's regime. The director claims, "I began writing the script when they executed Puig Antich and just finished shooting the film after the October executions" (Franco interview, 15).

Thus, the murderous Pascual and Angelo are presented not as deviant individuals but as violent subjects who have been constructed by a perverted culture. Even more important, both films eradicate the distinction between the categories of impure and purifying violence on which all social order is allegedly based. They lend credence to Bataille's claim that the extreme violence of Rais's crimes helps us understand Christianity and its "pressing demand for the horror that . . . it needs in order to forgive" (12–13). And they answer Buñuel's call for a cinema without sentimentality—a radical cinema of cruelty based on Sade's *120 Days of Sodom* that lets us know we do not live in the best of all possible worlds, a cinema that attacks the complacency of the bourgeoisie and makes us face our own complicity, a cinema that remains terribly threatening even in an era supposedly devoid of taboos. That is why these violent films are so deeply embedded in Spanish culture and in what Almodóvar calls its post-Franco mentality.

INTRODUCTION   From a poststructuralist perspective, the story of Oedipus is one of the most powerful master narratives in Western Civilization because, through its successful proliferation and compulsive repetition, it helps the dominant patriarchal culture reproduce itself. Freud and his poststructuralist followers argue that the Oedipal drama is reenacted in every generation because it is the primary means of transforming the small animal into a human gendered subject, that is, one who accepts either the male or female role and everything that goes with that sexual identity, including heterosexual tastes, which are essential to the reproduction of the species and the nuclear family. Given this ideological function, the Oedipal narrative also has the potential to function subversively as a vehicle for cultural change. While this issue has been addressed in many new readings of the Oedipal myth within gender studies, little attention has thus far been paid to cross-cultural variations where changes are linked to cultural specificity, which is precisely the focus of this chapter.[1]

One of the first things that made me want to write about Spanish cinema was its distinctive cultural reinscription of the Oedipal narrative, that is, the way Oedipal conflicts within the family were used to speak about political issues and historical events that were repressed from filmic representation during the Francoist era and the way they continue to be used with even greater flamboyance in the post-Franco period after censorship and repression had been abolished.[2]

In the Spanish Oedipal narrative, the father is usually absent, which enables him to be idealized and sometimes replaced by an ineffectual surrogate, on whom the son's patricidal impulses are displaced. If patricide is attempted, the deed is usually performed by a daughter, which occurs symbolically in post-Franco films as diverse as Saura's *Cría cuervos* (1975), Armiñán's *El nido* (The Nest, 1980), Chávarri's *Dedicatoria* (1980), and Almodóvar's *Laberinto de pasiones* (Labyrinth of Passions, 1982) and quite literally in Uribe's *Adios pequeña* (Farewell, Little Girl, 1986) and Almodóvar's *Tacones lejanos* (High Heels, 1991). As in the myth of Electra, in most of these films the rebellious daughter is assisted by a young man, whose androgyny, class, politics, or outlaw status makes him eager to collaborate with her against the patriarchy, for his own fate and phallic empowerment are already in jeopardy. In most other Spanish Oedipal narratives, it is not that the son fails to see the father's violence or corruption but rather that his own desire to imitate and replace the patriarch leads him either to disavow the patricidal impulse entirely or to redirect that murderous drive toward a rival surrogate.

Nowhere is the absent father more idealized than in *Raza,* the 1941 historical melodrama based on a mythified autobiographical novel written by Franco, which totally absolved his real-life philandering father of his sins. Even though Franco was the nation's ruling patriarch, in his own scenario he curiously appears not as the courageous father (who is quickly killed off in battle) but as the heroic son who replaces him. *Raza* used the Oedipal narrative to support the official version of the Spanish Civil War as a Holy Crusade. It displaces patricide onto fratricide and (consistent with Laclau's theorization of Fascist discourse) glosses over all ideological contradictions, unifying them within the single organizing narrative of the patriarchal family.[3]

In the Spanish Oedipal narrative, mothers frequently stand in for the missing father as the embodiment of patriarchal law and thereby become an obstacle both to the erotic desire of the daughter and to the mimetic desire of the son (a pattern we observed in both *Pascual Duarte* and *Tras el cristal*). This pattern is fairly commonplace in Spanish literature, where the "maternal" is frequently represented as a force that obsesses both mother and child—as a woman's ardent desire to have a child or to dominate the one she possesses and as a child's passionate yearning to be reunited with the lost mother or to defy the one who is present. The patriarchal mother is powerfully represented in the title character both of Federico García Lorca's well-known tragedy *La casa de Bernarda Alba* (1936; adapted to film by Mario Camus in 1987) and of Benito Pérez Galdós's satiric novel *Doña Perfecta* (1876). In both works, a desirable suitor named Pepe is driven off by a provincial iron-willed widow whose feudal sensibility is offended by his erotic appeal to her daughter and by his historic potential for modernizing (and thereby corrupting) Spain. Even though their repressive actions lead to madness and death, these patriarchal mothers feel morally justified.

A more complex example of the repressive mother occurs in Leopoldo Alas's brilliant novel *La regenta* (The Judge's Wife, 1884–85), which is hardly known outside of Spain. Here a tyrannical single mother named Doña Paula deliberately infantilizes and "unmans" her son, Don Fermín, by forcing him to become a successful priest and by either controlling or threatening to kill all female rivals for his love. This strategy enables her to use him to gain the money and power that were denied her as a victimized woman under patriarchal law. As a Christian Jocasta, Doña Paula moves between the contradictory prototypes of the orthodox patriarchal Madonna who upholds God's symbolic order and the subversive phallic mother who challenges the patriarchy; she also usurps the roles both of the father and the son and appropriates the iconography both of Oedipus and Jesus. When her son defies her by defending his love for the protagonist, Ana, insisting, "I am not a little boy," Doña Paula responds with histrionics:

Your mother gives you her blood, gouges out her eyes for you, damns herself to hell for you—but no, you aren't a little boy, and you go and give your blood and your eyes and your chances of salvation, for a hussy.[4]

For the Spanish son, the patriarchal mother is frequently both an object of desire and the instrument of its repression—contradictory functions that are sometimes embodied in one woman and other times split between two.

In *Raza,* the patriarchal mother is idealized and explicitly linked to the Virgin Mary as the embodiment of sacred law. While the emotional and ideological bonding between the holy mother and her Christlike son supports family patriarchs, it also challenges the corrupt materialist patriarchs who were ruling the Republic (a rebellion that evokes Jesus's attack on the moneylenders in the Temple). Soon after the heroic son comes of age, the mother conveniently dies so that *he* can replace the father and purge the family and the nation of the corrupting "foreign" influences on the bad brother. After her death, she is replaced by an equally virginal fiancée. This version of the Oedipal narrative denies all erotic rivalries, for sexuality is totally repressed, its energies displaced to a patriotic fanaticism.

The latent eroticism of this Oedipal narrative with all of its fanaticism and paradoxical rivalries is blatantly exposed in two early post-Franco films that can both be read as parodies of *Raza* and which are consistent with the satiric vision of *La regenta*—Jaime Chávarri's *El desencanto* (Disenchantment, 1976) and Manuel Gutiérrez Aragón's *Camada negra* (Black Brood, 1977).

El desencanto   Opening with a black and white photograph of a mother and her sons, *El desencanto* is a brilliant documentary on the surviving family of a dead Fascist patriarch, the official Francoist poet, Leopoldo Panero, who died on August 28, 1962, and to whom a commemorative statue was dedicated in 1974. Although images of the statue frame the film, it is never unveiled. The "disenchantment" in the title refers to the gap between the idealized image of the Fascist family that is displayed at the ceremonies (and that conforms to the model in *Raza*) and the tangle of mutual

With its fascinating portait of the Panero family, Jaime Chávarri's *El desencanto* (Disenchantment, 1976) deconstructs the idealized image of the fascist family that was fetishized in *Raza*.

recriminations, bitter rivalries, and painful memories that lie hidden behind the facade and that are the primary focus of the film. Shot in 1975 just before Franco's death and released in 1976, the film is masterful in the way it transforms a detailed exploration of one specific family into a complex symbolic portrait of Francoist Spain at a crucial moment of transition. It is difficult to believe that fiction could ever duplicate the rich complexity of these characters and their relations, and yet the distinctively Spanish inflection of their Oedipal narrative has the same deep structure that underlies many fictional works of the period.

Portrayed as a beautiful, cold, rejecting mother who is "always preparing for death," Felicidad inherits her strength and cruelty from her own father (with whom she is still obsessed), a right-wing doctor who, during the Civil War, forced her to assist him in surgery and ordered her not to faint at the sight of blood. Partly because of her subordinate position as a woman under patriarchy, she is jealous and resentful of her husband and his friends (claiming she should have married a doctor rather than a poet). As a repressive patriarchal mother, she displaces her anger and frustration onto her male brood. The youngest son, Michi (who calls himself "the lap dog that watches everything"), recounts a traumatic childhood incident in which she drowned their puppies and forced the boys ("or maybe just me") to watch and then blamed it on her husband who gave the orders. Puzzled by her sadism, Michi cannot understand why she made air holes in the bag before killing them (she claims it was "a kindness") or why she kept the ugly little black runt, with whom he clearly identifies.

Like the siblings in *Raza,* the three Panero brothers bitterly compete over who is the family's primary victim. Wearing a stetson and shooting a pistol, the eldest son, Juan Luis, postures as a western hero. An alcoholic, suicidal poet, he also identifies with "decadent" foreign writers like F. Scott Fitzgerald and Albert Camus. Incapable of equaling his father, he parodies him instead and fetishizes his mementos, permanently entrapping himself in this Oedipal rivalry. While his mother brags that when her husband died, Juan Luis took his place and "became my husband," he reports, with comic self-loathing, that a waiter mistook him for a gigolo: "Imagine being taken as a gigolo to your own mother, it excited me sexually." Insisting that he cannot accept his father's death, he quotes a line from Hemingway that reveals the displacement of his patricidal anger onto himself and his mother: "He who is nobody's son is a son of a bitch."

As in *Raza,* the middle son, Leopoldo, is the colorful star who outdoes the others in excess, madness, creativity, and suffering. Once he enters the film, he displaces Juan Luis, who virtually disappears. His younger brother, Michi, looks up to him with the same combination of adoration and bitter jealousy that Juan Luis feels for their father. In his opening monologue, Michi tells us that the story should start *not* with his father's death but with his fights (about sex, politics, and poetry) with Leopoldo, whom he clearly sees as the main character and the target of his own Oedipal rivalry.

Like his brothers, Michi is another dilettante poet who never succeeded at anything; yet he is the only one who believes that it does not matter whether his father lived or died and the only one who wants to perpetuate "la raza" (the race). Also a friend of Chávarri, the filmmaker, Michi is keenly aware that his performance in this documentary is his one chance at fame. Like the subjects of documentaries by the Maysles brothers (particularly *Gray Gardens*), Michi is victimized even by the film, but he still cannot outdo Leopoldo as scapegoat.

Because Leopoldo is the most talented and politically rebellious of the brothers, the squandering of his talent is the most painful and tragic. Though he has a cultivated taste for masochism ("Any pleasure starts in self destruction"), he accuses his mother of being responsible for his "disaster":

It starts with a brutal father, followed by your cowardice. When I was about to commit suicide, a nosy Andalusian woman told me I was acting like Marilyn Monroe and you stuck me in a clinic where I was miserable. The worst is that the reason they locked me up was not because of the suicide attempt. Because I smoked some harmless pot, my mother stuck me in a series of clinics fearing I was a drug addict.

He also claims that his mother was ashamed when he fell madly in love with a gypsy, implying that (like Alas's Doña Paula) she locked him up to repress his sexuality. But Felicidad blames it on the times, claiming, "The doctors wanted her money, people feared drugs, they weren't open-minded like today." Glibly applying Freud and Lacan to his family legend with black humor ("Perhaps schizophrenics aren't Oedipal. I'd like to sleep with my fa—mother. Oedipus is repressive"), Leopoldo diagnoses the three brothers.

Michi is schizophrenic, Juan Luis is paranoid, . . . full of fears. I've been my family's scapegoat, what they hated most in themselves. I've been more deranged than them. . . . It isn't until my father had the good idea of dying that humor emerged in our family.

Leopoldo emerges as the quintessenial stunted child. When his mother describes his childhood poems (which he started writing at age three), he claims they were the best he ever wrote and then quotes the line, "In childhood we live, afterward we survive."

Camada negra   In *Camada negra,* the ideological and sexual development of a budding young Fascist named Tatin is shaped by two competing Madonnas—his tyrannical mother, Blanca, and his lover, Rosa, a young single mother who initiates him sexually. The film also makes explicit Tatin's bitter rivalry with his older stepbrothers and his own randy father, who is an inadequate substitute for Blanca's first heroic husband martyred in war. Like the cold oral mother theorized by Deleuze and dramatized by Alas and Chávarri, Mother Blanca replaces the "abolished" father as the embodiment of patriarchal law and also appropriates the functions of all other female figures.[5] But this time the Falangist principles of the maternal ideologue dictate the brutal sacrifice of her young sexual rival—the kind of murder that

Manuel Gutiérrez Aragón's *Camada negra* (Black Brood, 1977) presents a satirical portrait of falangist brothers who are choirboys by day and terrorists by night. (Photos courtesy of El Imán.)

Alas's Doña Paula only fantasized. Though the representation of the murder is quite graphic, the violence is never fetishized through close-ups but is kept at a distance. This ironic detachment exposes the ugliness of the rite, which remains idealized *only* for the Fascist killer in the text, *not* for the spectator. We also are led to realize that as an object both of incestuous desire and matricide, Rosa merely functions as a surrogate for Blanca.

Camada negra also exposes the mother's rivalry with her sons who try to replace her as the prime surrogate for the missing father. Like the Panero widow, she is both loved and resented, respected and mocked, by the brotherhood she mothers, whether by blood or by political choice. She is also blatantly identified with a bitch suckling her black brood, which sits atop the cache of weapons, like some matriarchal monster in an ancient myth. To maintain her power, she bonds with her sons against other potential patriarchs (including her second husband) and the new post-Franco government; yet like Alas's Doña Paula and the Panero matriarch, she tries to prevent (or at least delay) her sons from fulfilling their own patriarchal destiny. This pattern helps to explain why Blanca infantilizes Tatin and treats the adult sons like the seven dwarves. Combining the powers of both the oral and the phallic mother, Blanca reigns over her brood both as Snow White and Wicked Queen.

Amantes   Vicente Aranda's *Amantes* (Lovers, 1990) also portrays a mortal struggle between a strong phallic widow and a younger patriarchal woman for the love of a young man—a romantic triangle that results in the former demanding that he murder her young rival. Yet in contrast to *Camada negra,* here the older woman derives her power from an intense sexuality rather than from fanaticism or maternity, and the religious idealism belongs to the young victim. Set in the 1950s and, like *Surcos,* in the genre of noir, this story (which was based on an actual incident) depicts the young man Paco not as the master over these two women who love him but (like Tatin) as the malleable object of their competing scenarios. Despite the physical beauty of the two women, who are brilliantly played by Victoria

Abril (who won the Silver Bear at the 1991 Berlin Film Festival for Best Actress)[6] and Maribel Verdú, it is the handsome young man (Jorge Sanz) who is treated as the primary object of desire. Narratively, he is the one who is seduced by both women; visually, he is the object of the camera's erotic gaze; generically, he is the noir hero who is coerced into committing murder; and allegorically, he is the 1950s generation torn between "two Spains," the feudal vision of a Holy Spain represented by his young virginal fiancée, Trini (Verdú), a maid who faithfully serves in the provincial household of Paco's avuncular military commander, versus the modern vision of a newly emerging industrialized Spain with its technocracy and graft, represented by his ambitious urban landlady, Luisa (Abril).

In contrast to traditional noir, the Oedipal hero murders not a good or bad patriarch (his military commander or Luisa's racketeer boss) but his own provincial fiancée, who becomes suicidal when she learns he no longer loves her. Moreover, this former farm boy is turned into a phallic killer, not by the Francoist army that trained him (which is featured in the church ritual in the film's opening sequence) or by the macho urban swindlers Luisa betrays but by the two women who love him.

Despite being positioned as the opposing stereotypes of virgin and whore, Trini and Luisa are equally passionate and strong willed. Both are frequently robed in blue, a color featured in traditional pictorial representations of the Virgin (as in the painting of the Immaculate Conception that Trini hangs in the hotel room just before her death). While Luisa directs her violent passions outward (confessing to Paco that she murdered her husband), Trini turns them inward on herself, following in the footsteps of her lame mother who threw herself in front of a cart after learning of her husband's infidelity.

Like the phallic mother in *Camada negra,* the victorious Luisa commands Paco to commit the violent sacrifice to prove he is truly a romantic hero, and the victimized Trini masochistically implores him to put her out of her misery and save her from sin. Just as Luisa forced Paco to take hold of his own penis in their pursuit of pleasure, Trini coerces him to wield the razor that will release her from pain.

The minimalist representation of violence in Vicente Aranda's *Amantes* (Lovers, 1990) is limited to a fetishized close-up of the victim's bare feet and a few drops of bright red blood falling on the pure white snow. (Print courtesy Vicente Aranda.)

Staged on a bench in front of a cathedral in the small town of Aranda de Duero, the murder retains the aura of Christian ritual, especially since the minimalist representation of violence is limited to a fetishized close-up of the victim's bare feet and a few drops of bright red blood falling on the pure white snow. Earlier, Paco had sat on the same bench praying, observed by a beautiful young mother who was carrying a bright blue umbrella and tying the shoelace of her young son, a symbolic Madonna who seems to foresee the murder.

In the final scene, Paco goes to the train station to find Luisa. Pressing his bloody hands against a window, he draws her off the train

for a final murderous embrace, a shot that is held, then blurs, and finally freezes. This shot brings to mind both the union of the ecstatic killers at the end of *Peppermint frappé* and the final image of the fallen woman jumping off the train to pursue her corruption in Madrid that was censored from *Surcos* in the 1950s. While in *Amantes* this fetishized image of the embracing lovers represents the triumph of their passion, a printed epilogue delivers the ironic moralizing punch line to the narrative. Three days later, Paco and Luisa were arrested in Valladolid (a city well known for its right-wing sentiments), and they never saw each other again. Though condemned to thirty years in prison, they served between ten and twelve, for Franco commuted their sentence. While Paco now lives in Zaragoza and has a considerable fortune, Luisa is dead. This ironic juxtaposition underlines the gap not only between the respective fates of the man and woman who collaborated in the crime but also between the familiar noir plot and the subversive visual representation of female sexuality that lies at the genre's core.

What most distinguishes *Amantes* from the other films discussed in this chapter and what positions it in the 1990s is the forceful way it depicts the subversive power of Luisa's sexuality—a dimension that was totally suppressed in *Raza* and *El desencanto,* that was only suggested of the corrupt femme fatale in *Surcos,* and that proved less potent than the maternal in *Camada negra.* From the moment she opens the door to Paco, wearing a colorful dark blue robe and draped with glittering streamers that she is using to trim a Christmas tree, Luisa appears as a profane alternative to the Madonna. Her body substitutes for the Christmas tree and all of its religious symbolism, offering eroticism in place of religious ecstasy. Not only is she the sexual subject who actively pursues her own desire and who first seduces Paco but she continues to control the lovemaking—determining how and when they make love. In some extraordinarily graphic sex scenes we see her penetrating his anus with a scarf and then withdrawing it, we see her standing over him with spread legs singing about perfuming her cunt and then squatting over his face when she wants him to perform cunnilingus, and we see her literally manipulating his penis and then deciding when to hand it over to him, as if granting him phallic empowerment. Despite this display of phallic power, she remains loving and emotionally vulnerable. I cannot think of any other film from any culture that represents female sexuality in this way. And what is equally subversive is Paco's responsiveness to this kind of aggressive female sexuality, which comes to obsess him. It not only makes him reject the more traditional passive sexuality of his fiancée but it also makes him willing to rob Trini of her life savings to save Luisa and ultimately to commit murder. Yet, although this *amour fou* wins Paco away from the

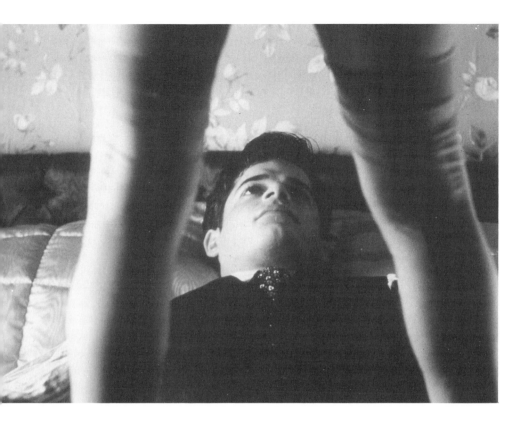

In *Amantes*, Luisa (Victoria Abril) sexually dominates her young lover Paco (Jorge Sanz). (Photo courtesy of Aries Film Releasing.)

Francoist patriarchy and makes him capable of violating its taboos, his patricidal drive is still displaced onto the patriarchal woman, and the phallic woman is ultimately punished more severely than her male accomplice—as in most other Spanish Oedipal narratives.

The woman's challenge to patriarchal order within the Oedipal narrative can be traced back to Sophocles' play *Oedipus Rex,* where it is figured as a conflation of female sexuality and the maternal. In the absence of the dead King Laius, Jocasta and Oedipus rule as equals and thereby keep her brother, Creon, subordinate. Before discovering their blood tie, they share the illusion that a son can successfully evade his patriarchal destiny. In fact, Jocasta expresses her resistance to patriarchal order most explicitly by advising Oedipus to ignore its prophecies, which function as symbolic law. Even before she learns the truth about their crime, she seems to intuit their incestuous bond, yet reassures him,

> As to your mother's marriage bed, don't fear it.
> Before this, in dreams too, as well as oracles,
> many a man has lain with his own mother.
> But he to whom such things are nothing bears
> his life most easily.[7]

Here she asserts the power of female sexuality over her young consort even at the risk of incest, for their incestuous union echoes earlier Greek myths in which the Earth goddess Gaeia formed a rebellious alliance with her sons to protect them against murderous Titan patriarchs. It also evokes Deleuze's description of the masochistic aesthetic that "is grounded in an alliance between the son and the oral mother . . . (who is identified with the law) and an invalidating disavowal of the father (who is expelled from the symbolic order)" (59–60).

To rival his mother's power, the Spanish Oedipal son first escapes from their incestuous bond either by transferring his desire to a younger woman or through matricide. But if the mother is too strongly entrenched as the embodiment of patriarchal law or too phallic, then he murders the young woman instead, as occurs in *Camada negra* and *Amantes.* In either case, the patricidal impulse is displaced onto the woman.

In at least two distinguished post-Franco films, the powerful mother is converted into a positive figure who, like Doña Perfecta and the widow in *Raza,* still must be read against the recurring historic confrontations between the "two Spains."

Mater amatísima   In *Mater amatísima* (Mother, Most Beloved, 1980), by Catalán filmmaker Josep A. Salgot, a stunning film whose painfulness is balanced by its aesthetic rigor, the matriarch is a successful modern career woman (also played by Victoria Abril) who is a single mother with an autistic son. The excessive maternal love, which is so crippling to the son in most other Spanish narratives, is here desperately demanded by the stunted child. The "maternal" draws *her* back into a total fusion with her son and his atavistic world of the imaginary, which forces her to renounce the world of language, science, and symbolic order. Empowered by the total immersion in this masochistic *folie à deux,* she becomes a moon goddess who must decide the moment of her son's ascension. She becomes the awesome oral mother as theorized by Deleuze, who is the source both of nurturing and death.

La mitad del cielo   Although associated with the old provincial Spain like the bourgeois Doña Perfecta and Bernarda Alba, the matriarch in Gutiérrez Aragón's *La mitad del cielo* (Half of Heaven, 1986) is a plebeian, cigar-smoking phallic mother who draws her strength from nature, food, and the body, not the church. Instead of repressing her daughters, she passes on her subversive magic and clairvoyance to her great-granddaughter Olvido, so she can carry on the resistance against corrupt patriarchs. Yet in order for Olvido's mother, Rosa (the film's protagonist), to continue her rise to success within a newly industrialized Spain, the old matriarch (and her ghost) must withdraw. At the end of the film, rather than jeopardize their future in the new Spain, she leaves her strong female brood and returns to the mountains. Yet like the precocious Olvido, we lament her loss.

Gutiérrez Aragón's *La mitad
del cielo* (Half of Heaven,
1986) features three
generations of strong women.

In the Spanish Oedipal narrative, the children are frequently
precocious yet emotionally stunted, for they have been traumatized
by personal and collective history. These children grow up to be
infantilized adults who are powerless and sometimes murderous as
a consequence (like Olvido and the other patricidal daughters mentioned earlier and like Tatin and his brother terrorists in *Camada
negra*). Though their infantilization is imposed on them by their

parents and by history, it fails to protect them against complicity with the crimes of their devouring mothers and murderous fathers. It also positions them as spectators-in-the-text—obsessed with the historical primal scene from the past and restricted to voyeurism and fantasy in the present. They are the children of Franco, who bear the crippling legacy of Francoist cultural and political repression.

We find this family configuration surviving in many powerful post-Franco films, perhaps most blatantly in Borau's *Furtivos*, Franco's *Pascual Duarte*, Chávarri's *El desencanto* and *A un dios descono-cido*, Saura's *Cría cuervos*, *Mama cumple cien años* (Mama Turns a Hundred), and *Dulces horas* (Sweet Hours), Armiñán's *Al servicio de la mujer española*, Bigas Luna's *Bilbao*, Gutiérrez Aragón's *Camada negra* and *Demonios en el jardín* (Demons in the Garden), Uribe's *La muerte de Mikel* and *Adios, pequeña*, Almodóvar's *Matador*, *La ley del deseo* (The Law of Desire), and *Tacones lejanos*, Villaronga's *Tras el cristal*, and Trueba's *El sueño del mono loco*.

These observations made me return to the Oedipal myth to reread it in the light of Spanish cinema. Thus, the rest of this chapter is divided into three sections. In the first, I make some general obser-vations about the Oedipal myth from this Spanish perspective. In the second, I focus on the Spanish version, citing concrete examples from various periods of Spanish film and literary history and concluding with close readings of the Francoist popular success *Marcelino, pan y vino* and Almodóvar's latest international hit, *Tacones lejanos*. In the third, I present an even more detailed analysis of *Bilbao*, one of the most extreme and illuminating examples of a subversive Oedipal narrative in the post-Franco cinema.

OEDIPUS AND THE DOUBLE-STRIKING CURSE   Because the Oedipal narrative is so powerful in Western culture, groups on the margins, who have traditionally lacked power, like women and homosexuals, have striven to alter the myth as a means of changing the social order and its process of subject formation. Feminists like Nancy Chodorow, Luce Irigaray, Jane Gallop, Teresa DeLauretis, Laura Mulvey, Kaja

Silverman, and Susan Suleiman have called for new versions in which the woman is no longer merely a forbidden territory or monstrous obstacle to be conquered like the Sphinx or an object of exchange between fathers and sons like Queen Jocasta but rather the central protagonist whose erotic bonds with the mother are far more complex than Freud suggested. Mulvey claims that "the idea of a founding moment of civilization, repeated in consciousness, suggested that it might be possible to . . . challenge the origins of patriarchal power through psychoanalytic politics and theory."[8]

George Devereux (1953) was one of the first to emphasize the homosexual back story of the Oedipal myth (which was omitted from the well-known versions by Sophocles and Freud) and to link its suppression to Freud's abandonment of his seduction theory (a connection on which Marie Balmary has elaborated).[9] Devereux cites other Greek sources that reveal that Laius and his family were cursed as a punishment for his having abducted, raped, and caused the death of Chrysippus, the son of Pelops, who was not only Laius's host but also his collaborator in introducing pederasty into Greek culture and who himself had been "homosexually raped by the father-figure Poseidon." Arguing that the myth is *not* primarily about the patricidal and incestuous crimes of the son, Devereux insists that "Oedipus' own impulses were stimulated by the behavior of his father" and even claims that in some versions Laius and Oedipus fought over Chrysippus as sexual rivals. He concludes,

Chrysippus is, in a sense, the representative of Oedipus' own passive homosexual characteristics, which were brought into being, or were at least aroused, by Laius' aggressive and homosexual impulses towards his son. (140)

This pre-Oedipal back story actually strengthens the focus on fathers and sons, for even here women are excluded and vengeful and their sexual power deemed inferior to the homosexual alternative. In some versions, Chrysippus's mother is the one who kills her son (a scenario that evokes *La muerte de Mikel*) and Hera (the jealous wife of Zeus) is the one who punishes Laius by sending the Sphinx to block the gates of Thebes.

As in many Spanish versions, the Oedipus story can be read as a myth about the son's struggle against his patriarchal destiny, that is, against replacing the murderous father, who is the structuring absence in Sophocles's play and protagonist in the homosexual back story. As a result of his absence, the blame for the violence is partly displaced onto the patriarchal (or phallic) mother as surrogate.

This displacement of the blame onto women is addressed by Girard in *Violence and the Sacred,* a book that is problematic because of its essentialism (among other things) but very illuminating in the Spanish context. In a reading that is compatible with Devereux's, Girard insists that what is central to the myth is mimeticism—the son's desire to imitate his father—rather than his erotic attraction to the mother, which Freud has overemphasized. Girard claims, "By making one man's desire into a replica of another man's desire, it invariably leads to rivalry; and rivalry in turn transforms desire into violence."[10] He argues that the brutal crime of the devouring patriarch (so vivid in Goya's *Saturn Devouring His Son*) is the central generating violence behind the pre-Socratic myths of internecine struggles between fathers and sons[11] and that it must remain hidden if the myths are to retain their structuring power.

Those desires that the world at large, and the father in particular, regard as emanating from the son's own patricide-incest drive actually derive from the father himself in his role as model. (190)

In reading against the Freudian grain, Girard realizes that this interpretation "may well seem like sheer perversity." Thus, he seeks support not only from Sophocles' *Oedipus the King* and from his less familiar play, *The Women of Trachis* (where Heracles explicitly authorizes his son to kill him and to marry his young widow), but also, much more significantly for my purposes, from two Spanish sources: Calderón de la Barca's Golden Age play *La vida es sueño* (Life Is a Dream) and Cesareo Bandera's "highly original study *Mimesis conflictiva* (Madrid: Gredos, 1975) . . . [which] reveals Calderón as an author who goes one step beyond Freud in dealing with the question of desire and the obstacle that masquerades as the 'law'" (192).

Thus, Girard's theory may have been partially influenced by the Spanish Oedipal narrative, which helps explain why it is so illuminating in the Spanish context. For example, it helps to explain why in those rare instances in Spanish cinema where a young man *does* act out his patricidal impulse against a symbolic father, such as *Tras el cristal* and Gutiérrez Aragón's *El corazón del bosque,* the act is clearly authorized by the murderous patriarch. And it also helps explain why classic cine negro español is primarily a discourse on fathers and sons, which usually emphasizes not the hero's erotic attraction to a femme fatale as in classical Hollywood noir (or in *Amantes*) but his violation of patriarchal law.[12] Girard claims the son's mimetic bond with the father creates a double bind around rivalry (making "an obstacle of the model and a model of the obstacle"), which helps explain why even those sons who love and idolize the father (like Angelo in *Tras el cristal*) still must kill him to take his place. Subordinating desire for the mother as merely one component of the mimetic rivalry, Girard argues that the revival of the Oedipal narrative has more to do with the waning power of the father than with the arousal of incestuous desire.

In Western society, the father had already become the model by the patriarchal era. In order for the double bind to operate, he had also to become the obstacle. And the father can only become an obstacle when the diminution of his paternal authority has brought him into a direct confrontation with his son, obliging him to occupy the same sphere. The Oedipus complex appears most plausible in a society in which the father's authority has been greatly weakened but not completely destroyed; that is, in Western society during the course of recent centuries. Here the father has functioned as the original model and the original obstacle in a world where the dissolution of differences encourages the proliferation of the double bind. (188)

This weakening of the father occurred not only during the Francoist era when Spaniards were infantilized but also in the post-Franco era when the last model patriarch was deposed.

In many of the Spanish Oedipal texts discussed here, the homo-erotic dimension is either latent or explicit. The son has a choice between two competing objects of desire—the mother or the father. Yet, because of the father's absence, the latter choice is both obscured and intensified. While Girard links the displacement of patricide onto the mother with a loss of sexual differentiation ("One of the effects of the sacrificial crisis is a certain feminization of men, ac-companied by a masculinization of the women," 141), he does not directly address the homoerotic implications of his argument. Al-though Mulvey never mentions Girard, she echoes his emphasis on the mimetic relation between fathers and sons but follows Devereux in stressing the erotic dimension of this bond:

Looking at the Oedipal myth in detail it is remarkable to what ex-tent it is about father/son relations and how marginal the feminine is to the story . . . [and how] desire for the mother is more significant as a symptom of father/son rivalry. . . . Perhaps desire for and fear of a powerful mother and the misogyny it generates conceals something even more disturbing, desire for and fear of a violent father. Perhaps it is the "unspeakable" ghost of Laius that haunts relations between men, generating homophobic anxieties and an attraction bonded by physical violence. (199)

In the Spanish Oedipal narrative, the son has a choice between replacing the murderous seductive father or bonding with the pow-erful mother against the patriarchy. Although these choices seem to be set in opposition, they both prove to be equally entrapping, except in idealized Fascist texts like *Raza* which gloss over all contradictions. If the son chooses to bond with the mother, even in extreme instances of obsessive devotion (as in *La regenta* or Saura's *Dulces horas* or *Mamá cumple cien años*), he ultimately rebels against her as well. The case of Spanish cinema supports Suleiman's suspicion that "the son's rebellion, whether 'straight' or 'perverse' and no matter how outra-geously innovative on the level of artistic practice, is always, in the last analysis, phallocentric—and to that extent in alliance with the father and repudiating the mother."[13]

Nevertheless, this choice, in all its varied formulations, is frequently foregrounded in Spanish Oedipal narratives. For example, we have already seen that before the homosexual protagonist of *Tras el cristal* can replace the sadistic child killer who earlier seduced and tortured him, he must first purge the house of women, murdering the tyrannical mother, firing the maid, and recruiting the young androgynous daughter as an accomplice in his crimes. Thus, in Spanish narratives, not only does the "negative" (homoerotic) Oedipus complex frequently replace the "positive" (heterosexual) version but also, in some Spanish movies, like Querejeta's anthology film *Los desafíos,* Almodóvar's *Laberinto de pasiones,* Chávarri's *Dedicatoria,* and Bigas Luna's *Lola,* incestuous relations between fathers and daughters are pitted against incestuous couplings of mothers and sons—an opposition that frequently reveals the collusion of class and gender. For, whereas the father's lusting after his daughter was associated with feudal privilege (*Los desafíos*) and even sons of a certain class were traditionally allowed and sometimes encouraged to have sexual relations with their maternal nannies (*Al servicio de la mujer española*), the mother's lust for her son (*Furtivos*) or the daughter's desire for her father (*El nido*) was severely punished or ridiculed, along with all other expressions of female desire. Yet, from another perspective, this apparent opposition is merely another version of the endless mimetic chain, in which one reproduces one's father in one's son and one's mother in one's daughter.

The doubleness of Oedipus's entrapment is made explicit in Sophocles' play when the blind hermaphrodite Tiresias warns Oedipus against focusing exclusively on his relationship with the father, reminding him, "A deadly footed, double-striking curse, from father and mother both, shall drive you forth out of this land, with darkness on your eyes."

Like the syntax of Tiresias's sentence, the life of Oedipus is framed by two castrating wounds derived from the "double-striking curse" of his parents: the "deadly footed" wound inflicted on him in infancy by his father (which gives him the swollen foot that names him); and the blinding "darkness on his eyes," which he inflicts on himself with the pair of brooches he takes from his mother's corpse. The blinding is doubly linked with the mother, for their erotic union also temporarily blinded him to his violent destiny under patriarchy.

THE SPANISH OEDIPAL NARRATIVE   In the Spanish Oedipal narrative, the primary act of symbolic castration associated with the woman is not blinding but the cutting of hair. Both acts are combined in the biblical myth of Samson (Judges 13–16), which has been read as a variant of the Oedipal narrative. In this myth, the hero is a riddle maker rather than a riddle solver, and incest is replaced by exogamy (Samson is erotically attracted to two foreign women who betray him to their own Philistine patriarchs, his wife and the prostitute Delilah). Moreover, Samson's castrating blindness is not self-imposed as in the case of Oedipus but inflicted on him by foreign patriarchs.

The Museo de Lerma in Toledo also contains an important representation of Samson and Delilah by Caravaggio, who was a seminal influence on Ribera during the Spaniard's long residence in Naples. In Caravaggio's painting, the bulging breasts of Delilah dangle over the bald head of the sleeping Samson, whose hands are in chains and who is guarded by two men, but she holds the knife and presumably has done the cutting. The emphasis is on her abundant sexuality and its castrating power. In Ribera's drawing of the same subject (*Sansón y Dalila,* 1626, housed in the Museo Provincial de Bellas Arte, Córdoba), the emphasis is on Delilah's dramatic performance, which appropriates Christian iconography to control the men in the composition. A bearded Samson lies asleep in the lap of a courtly Delilah in a parodic Pietà; in her left hand this false Madonna clutches a bag of gold, suggesting that she is really a Judas in disguise. Huddled under her right arm, a servant shaves Samson's head, while another servant on her left is about to bind his limbs. As if directing the performance, Delilah gestures theatrically with her extended right arm to halt a soldier who is just emerging from behind a curtain with extended sword, while she turns to speak to two more soldiers on her left who lead an advancing onslaught of swords. Samson's power re-emerges in Bigas Luna's incestuous melodrama *Jamón Jamón* (1992), where a giant billboard for men's sexy briefs features a huge detached crotch shot with the slogan, "You've a Samson inside!"

I do not mean to suggest that the adaptation of this Samson myth in painting or cinema is restricted to Spain. In fact, its most blatant use as a variant Oedipal narrative can be found in Peter Greenaway's film, *Drowning by Numbers*. Yet only in Spain is the use of shaving or the cutting of hair as a trope for castration so pervasive.

In the Spanish version, the emphasis is on the cutting of his hair rather than on his blinding, perhaps because this symbolic castration is overseen by the woman, the treacherous whore Delilah who is usually depicted cradling the sleeping Samson in her lap the way a mother nurtures a child. Unlike blinding, the cutting of hair is reversible and therefore conducive to compulsive repetition and revenge. Yet the attack on the beard and the eyes sometimes occurs together in Spanish narratives, especially as a means for women to overpower men, as in this passage from Galdós's masterpiece, *Fortunata and Jacinta:*

Rafaela says that at that moment she thought of a foolproof plan to defend themselves against the monster in case he should attack them. The moment she saw him make a hostile gesture, she'd pull his beard. If at the very same moment . . . her mistress had enough skill to grab a spit very near her hand and stick it in his eyes, they would be saved.[14]

The pulling or cutting of the beard as a form of humiliation also occurs in *El Cid* and in the common Spanish expressions, *tomarle el pelo* ("to pull someone's hair," which is equivalent to the English idiom, "to pull someone's leg"), *subirse a las barbas* ("to get into the beard," which means "to be disrespectful"), and *en las barbas* ("in one's beard," which means "right to one's face"). The attack on the paternal beard implies that the patriarch is being unmanned, overpowered, or replaced, usually by a younger man or woman. The use of shaving as a form of symbolic cuckolding or castration is also central to Rossini's comic opera, *The Barber of Seville* (which was very popular in Spain and frequently mentioned in nineteenth-century Spanish novels), particularly the scene in which the conniving barber Figaro shaves the lecherous old Bartolo while helping a friend rob him of his young ward and intended bride. The cutting of hair is also frequently represented as a substitute for death, as in Zurbarán's seventeenth-century painting *Martirio de Santiago,* where the executioner holds the saint by the hair, so that it is ambiguous as to whether he is about to be decapitated or shorn. Similarly, in Ribera's painting *David* (1630), the beardless, rosy-cheeked youth holds the huge bearded head of the giant by the hair with his left hand, while in his right hand he holds a sword, presumably used for the decapitation, which may now serve to cut the dark locks and beard of the defeated colossus.

In Spanish Oedipal narratives, the shaving scene becomes the quintessential denouement, which helps explain why it is so pervasive throughout Spanish cinema from the silent period to the post-Franco era. For example, it is prominently featured both in Segundo de Chomón's early modernist trick film, *El hotel eléctrico* (Hotel Electric, 1905), where a man is automatically shaved (and his wife's hair combed) in a totally motorized hotel, whose dehumanizing mechanisms eventually run amok, and in Florían Rey's silent masterpiece *La aldea maldita,* where the hero (a foreman) retrieves his four loafing workers who are all being shaved at the same time by one masterful barber. At times, this trope can be comical, as in Eloy de la Iglesia's *El pico* (The Shoot), where a guardia civil tries to shed the image of castrating father by giving his son a fake mustache and restyling his hair before sending him to a whore. At other times, it is chilling, as in *El crimen de Cuenca,* where a prisoner is shaved by his torturer, a guardia civil who threatens to cut off his tongue with the razor, or in *Tras el cristal,* where Angelo draws the first blood from Klaus while shaving him as he lies in the iron lung—a rite that serves as a prelude to rape and murder. In Bigas Luna's graphically erotic *Las edades de Lulú* (The Ages of Lulu, 1990), the ritualistic shaving of pubic hair is the sexual initiation for the steamy heroine—an act that not only restores her pudendum to its infantile state of powdered perfection (which was fetishized in slow motion images behind the opening credits) but also soon leads to masturbation with a shaving brush (once her seducer is gone) and to a taste for heavy bondage that ultimately threatens her life. In Almodóvar's *¡Atame!* (Tie Me Up, Tie

(Above): In Pedro Almodóvar's ¡Atame! (Tie Me Up! Tie Me Down! 1989), the captive porn queen (Victoria Abril) is finally turned on by the Christlike wounds of her amorous orphaned kidnapper (Antonio Banderas). (Photo: Mimmo Cattarinich; print courtesy of Miramax Films Release.)

(Opposite): In Florián Rey's silent classic, La aldea maldita (The Cursed Village, 1929), the fallen woman who abandoned her child is hounded by the shadow of the patriarchy.

Me Down! 1989), shaving is explicitly used as a "perverted" primal scene; when the resistant captive porn queen is finally turned on by the Christlike wounds of her amorous orphaned kidnapper, he looks directly into the camera and confides, "The only image I remember of my parents is my mother shaving my father."

The Spanish Oedipal narrative is marked by a series of perverse displacements between the mother and the father, which accentuate the choice between the two sides of the Oedipal curse and frequently foreground the homoerotic back story. Sometimes fathers usurp the nurturing functions of the mother, as in the silent melodrama, *La aldea maldita*. Once the fallen mother is exiled and forbidden to touch or look at the child she abandoned, the boy is raised by his nurturing father and blind grandfather, who are both pictorially represented as the Madonna.

José de Ribera's painting *La
mujer barbuda (Magdalena
Ventura, con su marido)* (The
Bearded Woman [Magdalena

Ventura, with Her Husband],
1631), Palacio Lerma, Toledo.
(Courtesy, Fundación Casa
Ducal de Medinaceli.)

Francisco José de Goya y Lucientes, *Esta muger fue retratada en Napoles por José Ribera o el Espanoleto, por los anos de 1640* (This woman was painted in Naples by José Ribera or the Spaniard, in the 1640s, album E, p. 22), about 1814–17. Gift of Frances and Philip Hofer in Honor of Eleanor A. Sayre. (Courtesy, Museum of Fine Arts, Boston.)

The most powerful representation of this gender reversal of the Madonna is Ribera's famous painting, *La mujer barbuda* or *Magdalena Ventura, con su marido* (The Bearded Wife [Magdalena Ventura, with Her Husband, 1631]). Despite the title of the painting, Ribera clearly presents a patriarch with a breast, not a bearded woman. In fact, Ribera used the same male model for his "mujer barbuda" that he had used the previous year for his smiling *Demócrito*. As if to disavow the radical nature of this disturbing visual representation, the right side of Ribera's painting displays a verbal text, seemingly engraved in stone, that narrates the historical circumstances of the portrait, confirming that la mujer barbuda was actually a 52-year-old woman from Naples named Magdalena Ventura.[15] Yet in the painting, it is as if the paternal beard makes the sex change so total that even the nourishing breast (to which the beard clearly points) is physically transformed into the phallus—singular, erect, and repositioned slightly off center, like the stern patriarch himself. Moreover, the alleged husband in black (also bearded and more elderly) appears sinister in the background, doubling the patriarchal usurpation of the child; pink fingers curl out of his garments at his groin, like multiple naked penises that offset the singular breast. On top of the stone (on which the inscription is written) are placed a spindle and a conch, detachable icons of the female labor and sexuality that have been so perversely displaced. In this painting, the father (rather than the mother) is literally cast as the object of desire, precisely because he is so stern and co-optive and because she has been exiled from representation. This is no bearded matriarch who threatens patriarchal order—like Pascual Duarte's mustached mother, who, in the novel, inspires her son to quote the proverb, "A mustached woman who's slow to bear . . . (I don't give the second part, out of respect for the high person [a patriarch] to whom these pages are addressed)" (25). Nor is this a Silvia Pinal with false beard, impersonating the devil as a woman, as in Buñuel's satiric *Simón of the Desert* (1965). Nor is it like Almodóvar's androgynous hero in *Tacones lejanos* who wears a false beard when impersonating a patriarchal lawman and falsies when impersonating the transvestite Femme Lethal, a performer who impersonates the mother of his beloved. Rather, *The Bearded Wife* is more likely to evoke the wolf in "Little Red Riding Hood" who impersonates the grandmother he has devoured.

Goya's parody, entitled *Esta mujer fue retrada en Napoles por José Ribera o el Españoleto, por los años de 1640* (This Woman Was Painted in Naples by José Ribera or the Spaniard, in the 1640s, 1814–1817), also presents a man rather than a bearded woman co-opting the maternal role, though his rounded form, softened, smiling countenance, and feminine robes imply a more androgynous mix. While suckling the breast, the infant even reaches up to play with the beard (which is much more ample, like a woman's head of hair) or to remove what may be merely a patriarchal mask on the mother's face. In either case, the little one seems to be in on the joke. Not only do these perverse Spanish images play both with the beard and the breast as fetishized markers of sexual difference within traditional religious painting but they also reveal that the phallic mother and maternal father are patriarchal constructs used to strengthen man's domination over women and children.[16] Yet, as Suleiman points out, instead of being "a way out of the classic Oedipal scenario," perversion may be "merely a more roundabout way into it" or even a more radical way to repudiate the mother (150).[17]

Ribera's *La mujer barbuda* was prominently featured as a vehicle of patriarchal repression in Vicente Escrivá's popular comedy *Lo verde empieza en los Pirineos* (Sex Starts at the Pyrenees, 1973). The protagonist, played by José Luis López Vázquez (in a comic version of his role in *Peppermint frappé*), is a repressed restorer of old paintings, a man who was traumatized at age seven when his father caught him spying on a little girl squatting to pee. Calling him a "degenerate sinner," his father drags the boy to behold Ribera's *La mujer barbuda* (a crude facsimile rather than the original), shouting, "This is how you must always see women!" As a consequence, he sees all beautiful women bearded ever after and now, as a middle-aged bachelor, is still a virgin.

While a psychiatrist advises the protagonist to solve his problem by chanting "She is an inferior being" whenever he sees a bearded woman (a solution that is as misogynist as the father's curse), two of his married buddies take him across the French border to Biarritz. In the early 1970s, legions of repressed Spanish men followed the same path, for here they could see X-rated foreign movies (like *Last Tango in Paris, A Clockwork Orange,* and *La grande bouffe*), ogle women in bikinis, dance at discos, patronize sex shops, proposition scantily dressed women, and be fooled by drag queens (who really *do* have beards). Although these so-called liberated practices also turn out to be sexist, a young Spanish woman working in Biarritz succeeds

The patriarchy's attempt to appropriate the Madonna's breast is also represented in Alonso Cano's *San Bernardo y la Virgen* (above) and Bartolomé Esteban Murillo's *Aparición de la Virgin a San Bernardo* (opposite), which are described in note 16. (Museo del Prado, Madrid.)

in breaking the patriarchal curse, for her face remains "as soft as an angel" even after he kisses her and generates new images of liberation for both genders. The comic fairy tale ends with the happy couple headed toward marriage, which may possibly turn out to be another trap.

In a parodic pretitles prologue, this Spanish tendency to define sexual desire as a "terrible defect" is positioned in history where it is associated with the Black Legend and the conquest when Spaniards were notorious for raping and dehumanizing foreign women (who are represented as comical animated figures). In the main narrative,

Lola Gaos (left) and María Luisa Ponte (right) play the murderous devouring mother in *Furtivos* (Poachers, 1975) and *Camada Negra* (Black Brood, 1977), respectively, both co-written by José Luis Borau and Manuel Gutiérrez Aragón. (Photos courtesy of El Imán.)

the patriarchal solution of repressing the son's desire (by similarly distorting how woman is represented and perceived) is presented as typical of Spanish culture, a solution that was extended to cinema by Francoist censors. Although this comedy explores the cultural resonance of the Ribera painting, the film never confronts the more disturbing implications of the image—its perverse displacements between mother and father and its hints of matricide—implications that would soon be developed in other texts.

In the Spanish Oedipal narrative, the patricidal impulse is frequently redirected toward the mother. No other national cinema contains so many matricides. For example, in 1975, the year of Franco's death, two of the most powerful films, *Pascual Duarte* and *Furtivos,* portray matricide as revenge against the patriarchal order.

Furtivos

Like *Camada negra, Furtivos* was co-written by Borau and Gutiérrez Aragón. In Borau's next film, *La sabina* (1979), the title character is the primitive, hetaeric uterine mother described by Deleuze
and Kristeva—a legendary monster in a cave who devours the latent
homosexual male rivals who dare to enter her realm. According to
Borau, when he went to Gutiérrez Aragón's wedding, the mother of
the groom approached him and asked, "What do you and my son
have against mothers?"

In *Furtivos,* one of the most crucial films of the dictablanda, the
stunted son tries to escape from his devouring mother, who is an
agent of the patriarchal power she despises and who murders his
delinquent young bride. Finally, he resorts to matricide to break their
incestuous bond, which she has used to infantilize him. In describing

the genesis of the film, director Borau claims the germinal idea was
Lola Gaos, the actress who had played Saturna in Buñuel's *Tristana:*
"Like Saturn devouring his son in the painting by Goya, . . . Saturna
is devouring her son in a forest. That was the origin."[18] In *Tristana*
(which was adapted from a novel by Galdós), Saturna is also a single
mother with a stunted son (a deaf mute named Saturno who masturbates instead of working). Within the class discourse, this grotesque pair of servants is matched against the more traditional incestuous union between the bourgeois libertine freethinker, Don
Lope (who also avoids work to pursue his erotic pleasure), and his
young ward, Tristana (who eventually gains control over the lecherous patriarch but who is crippled both morally and physically in
the process). Thus, both of the couples in *Tristana* belong to the
black Spain stereotype. *Furtivos* conflates the two pairs and reposi-
tions them in a "peaceful forest" (Franco's bogus metaphor for
Spain), where the incest is transferred to Saturna and her son and the
stunted child's patricidal revenge is diplaced onto the murderous,
seductive mother.

In *Furtivos,* both the source and the target of the violence are
literally displaced from father to mother. The father is never mentioned. Instead, there is an infantilized governor (played by Borau
himself) who evokes Franco. Like a series of "scapegoat projections,"
the devouring mother, the incest, the matricide, and the hunt all
function metaphorically for the patricidal impulse and the original
generative violence that aroused it. In this deeply subversive film, the
maternal (like the monster in *La sabina*) is a role imposed on women
by weak men; as in Ribera's painting, *La mujer barbuda,* it is merely
a projection of the patriarchy, whose crimes remain hidden.

Thus, in the Spanish Oedipal narrative, matricide frequently functions to deny the father's responsibility for violence against mothers
and children and the son's responsibility for desiring to be like the
father. As Girard observes,

Like the animal and the infant, . . . the woman qualifies for sacrificial status by reasons of her weakness and relatively marginal social
status. That is why she can be viewed as a quasi-sacred figure, both
desired and disdained, alternately elevated and abused. (142)

There are many historical reasons for these patterns of displacement. In the Civil War, over one million persons were killed, and over 250,000 were sent into exile, many of them fathers; mothers frequently had to take over in the father's absence. Most families were fractured by fratricidal conflict, and most children who lived through it were traumatized.

We can also go farther back to the nineteenth century, to the first Carlist War (1833–1839) and to the earlier struggles between the "two Spains." Here, a key question was who would replace the dead Bourbon king (Fernando VII), his brother Carlos or his widowed Queen María Cristina (and her progeny). This rivalry evokes the latent tension between Creon and Jocasta in the Oedipal myth.

We can also go even farther back, to the fifteenth century, when the original myth of a unified Spain was built on the 1469 marriage and co-rule of Queen Isabel of Castile and King Ferdinand of Aragón. Within this national myth, it was the strong phallic queen who empowered rebellious sons like Columbus and Cortés, sending them to foreign lands where they (like Oedipus and Samson) could act out their patriarchal legacy of conquest and rape without restraint. Meanwhile, at home, like a Doña Perfecta, she also helped unleash the Inquisition as the ultimate repressive apparatus that purged Holy Spain of Moors, Jews, and other "corrupting" foreign influences.[19]

As a key source both for the Golden Age and the Black Legend, this duality of the omnipotent queen can easily be mapped over the psychoanalytic construct of the powerful pre-Oedipal mother, particularly as theorized by Melanie Klein, who has extended Freud's work on the pre-Oedipal formation of the subject in infancy. In the infantilized Spaniard who tries to escape patriarchal destiny, we can see a regression to a pre-Oedipal state where what is all-important is the mother/infant dyad and object relations formed in infancy. Thus, the infant's concept of the good and bad breast is used to divide the world into a Manichaean opposition, which is highly compatible both with Fascist and Catholic discourse and with the recurring historical struggles between the two Spains.[20] The child experiences both extreme love and hate for the mother, on whom he or she is so dependent and would love to control; she becomes the object both

The powerful matriarch is frequently represented seated, as if on a throne, evoking the Spanish trope of the phallic queen, as in this triptych of images from Mario Camus's *La casa de Bernarda Alba* (The House of Bernarda Alba, 1986, left, top), Carlos Saura's *Mamá cumple cien años* (Mama Turns a Hundred, 1979, left, bottom), and Manuel Gutiérrez Aragón's *La mitad del cielo* (Half of Heaven, 1986, right).

of the idealization and of the sadistic violent fantasies that are so prevalent in Spanish cinema.

This psychoanalytic construct would also appeal to the French and Spanish surrealists, who would associate it with the radical writings of the Marquis de Sade, whose outrageous attacks against all bourgeois values made him a hero to most members of the movement. Buñuel and the other surrealists were particularly drawn to Sade's attacks on patriarchal mothers as the embodiment of bourgeois order. In their "vitriolic" document, "Hands off Love!" (1927), the surrealists defended free love against the "petit bourgeois mentality" of patriarchal mothers like Mrs. Charlie Chaplin (who was suing her husband for divorce)—"those bitches who become, in every country, the *good* mothers, *good* sisters, *good* wives, those plagues, those parasites of every sentiment and every love."[21] Paradoxically, while the subversive incestuous bond with the pre-Oedipal mother could heighten the intensity of the surrealists' favorite passion, "l'amour fou," the repressive patriarchal mother was to be despised and destroyed. Both passions were perceived as highly political.

While the displacement of political issues onto the domestic realm of the family can be found in most nations (particularly within the international genre of melodrama), it receives special emphasis in Spain, where melodrama served as the official organizing narrative both for Catholicism and fascism. As we have seen in chapter 2, the conventional emotional excesses of Spanish domestic melodrama were inflected with a specifically Catholic sadomasochistic discourse. Thus, when a Spanish son rebelled against his father, he was also rebelling against Franco and against God. No wonder it was far less threatening to rebel against the mother.

Even before the rise of fascism, we can see the rich ironic interplay between Catholicism and theatrical melodrama in some of the best nineteenth-century novels, where it is frequently set against the ongoing battle between the two Spains—between the opposing desires for enlightenment and orthodoxy, for anarchy and authoritarianism, and between the "alternate fevers of total liberty and absolute peace." For example, in *Doña Perfecta,* the young hero's enlightened critique of the melodramatic qualities of a rural cathedral (e.g., the garish "theatrical costumes" in which the holy images are dressed and the inclusion of music from *La Traviata* during High Mass) is what begins his estrangement from his pious aunt, which (as in a melodramatic opera) ultimately destroys the young lovers. In *La regenta,* three men compete for the love of the passionate, sexually repressed heroine by trying to cast her in three competing melodramatic discourses: her paternal husband casts her as adulterous wife in his beloved Calderónian tragedies of honor, her libertine lover casts her as Don Juan's greatest conquest in his own operatic intrigues, and her tortured confessor uses church rituals and sacred texts to cast her in the dual roles of Holy Virgin and Saint Teresa. With her hysterical swings in mood, the heroine alternates among all of these parts, as well as others of her own design, but reaches her greatest melodramatic extremes under the influence of religion. One of the most excessive moments in the novel is when she parades through the streets as a penitent, exposing her naked shoulders and bare feet to the erotic gaze of the public and making a religious spectacle of herself in the mystical role assigned by the amorous canon theologian—a fanatical performance as "Our Lady of Sorrows" which she later deeply regrets.

In contrast to the Judaic myth of the Old Testament, which presents a lone patriarchal God who (like later Protestant reformers) forbids elaborate aesthetic representations and demands total identification from his children whom he repeatedly subjects to sadistic punishments, the New Testament introduces a masochistic countermyth. Here, the tyrannical castrating father is replaced by a masochistic son, who is sensuously and spiritually attended by his virginal mother (whose sexuality is totally denied). Mother and son are far less threatening than God, the remote father, who is never humanized like Mary and Jesus. Together they costar in a ritual sacrifice that, despite the violence at its core, is artistically represented with a sensual beauty that masks all brutality and ugliness. This idealization of violence and death was sanctioned by the Counter-Reformation in the sixteenth century and later adopted by Fascist discourse.

In Ladislao Vajda's *Marcelino, pan y vino* (Marcelino, Bread and Wine, 1954), the abandoned infant is raised by twelve "mothering" monks, most of whom are bearded.

Marcelino, pan y vino   One of the most fascinating examples of these baroque dynamics can be found in *Marcelino, pan y vino* (1954), directed by Hungarian émigré Ladislao Vajda, which was Spain's official entry at Cannes in 1955 and a big hit not only in Spain but throughout Europe and Latin America as well. Calling it "the most successful priest film among the Spanish public," Galán credits *Marcelino* with launching its own subgenre of folkloric sentimental comedy (which features a child songbird modeled after the talented seven-year-old Pablito Calvo who made his screen debut in the title role).[22] Since this film is a product of the 1950s when Spain's process of defascistization was more advanced, its blatant masochism is no longer directly identified with Fascist ideology (as it was in *Raza*) but connected with Spanish nationalism (as in *Los últimos de Filipinas*) and firmly grounded in Catholicism.[23] Set after the Napoleonic war in a monastery that was built on the last hiding place of the French soldiers, the film is designed to prove the moral superiority of Catholic Spain's masochistic fetishization of suffering and death (here linked with the bonding between mother and son) over the sadistic violence of the invading foreign patriarch.

The film opens with a narrative frame in which a priest tells the story of a local saint to a child who is seriously ill and to her anxious parents, as if to reconcile them to the possibility of her death. The story is about Saint Marcelino, who was abandoned as an infant at a monastery and raised by twelve "mothering" monks, whose nicknames evoke Snow White's Seven Dwarves (the same fairy tale parodied in *Camada negra*). Later, his miraculous death made the monastery famous, converting even the corrupt mayor who earlier tried to drive the friars from the land.

At the Oedipal age of five, Marcelino sees a woman for the first time, who tells him he reminds her of her son Miguel. Immediately, Marcelino becomes obsessed with his dead mother and begins to exhibit fetishistic behavior, hiding secret objects and talking to an imaginary friend whom he calls Miguel. Like the heroine of *La regenta,* the motherless child is portrayed as ripe for eroticized mysticism, which the church easily converts into an ecstatic longing for death. When the monks forbid Marcelino to go upstairs to the attic because "there's a huge man up there," he violates the taboo and finds

At the Oedipal age of five, immediately begins
Marcelino sees a woman to yearn
for the first time and for his lost mother.

not a threatening patriarch but the ultimate institutionalized fetish
for his missing mother—a statue of Jesus on the cross.

Although most of the story is comic in tone and even contains
musical interludes, the miraculous encounters with the statue of Jesus
are eroticized with high seriousness and with all the lush excesses of
baroque pictorial conventions. As Gubern perceptively observes,

The "catalepsia convulsiva" of the baroque images, in which a great
part of their dramatic potential and impact reside, was annihilated by
the moving image of the cinema, which would have to find, as we
say, new expressive strategies. As a result, the "barroquismo" from
seventeenth-century religious painting was degraded in twentieth-
century religious cinema into "kitsch."[24]

Marcelino is forbidden to go upstairs.

In *Marcelino*, the filmmakers rely on a fetishistic use of luminous lighting, accelerated cutting, and extremely large close-ups, a stylistic rupture that shifts the tone. Such sequences strive to convince us that despite its materialist nature, cinema is a miraculous medium capable of animating still images and replicating divine light. Yet despite the supposed spirituality of Marcelino's encounters with the statue, they are rendered very concretely. For example, we see in extreme close-up the statue's hand first leaving the cross to grasp the bread from Marcelino's little fist with its dirty fingernails—a "kitsch" version of Michelangelo's divine rendition of the touch between God and his creation Adam in the Sistine Chapel.

Despite comic deflation, these representations of the statue cultivate an eroticism, which may be kitsch in the context of a film like *Marcelino* but which still evoke the tradition of Bernini's famous baroque statue of Santa Teresa, whose facial expression of religious ecstasy graces both the cover of Bataille's *Erotism: Death and Sensuality* and the pages of Gubern's *La imagen pornográfica y otras perversiones ópticas.* According to Bataille, "Communication is always possible between sensuality and mysticism, obedient as they are to the same motive force," spiritual ecstasy.[25]

In *Marcelino,* the naked body of Jesus is fetishized with the same fragmenting close-ups that are conventionally used to eroticize the female body for the male gaze in Hollywood classical cinema. Despite the rigid material form of the statue, the successively larger close-ups animate his androgynous body, allowing us to savor the sensuality of its rippling lines and fleshlike texture. Though the spectacle is somewhat desexualized by being presented to the gaze of an innocent child, the context creates pederastic overtones. One thinks of the original patriarchal sin suppressed from the Oedipal myth—Laius's seduction of a young boy, which leads (depending on which version of the myth you are reading) either to his conversion to homosexuality or to his death. In this case, Marcelino and Jesus are united in an erotic exchange: the boy lures the beautiful young man off the cross with tempting food and drink, and the boy is lured to his death with the divine pleasures of original plenitude.[26]

The eroticization of Marcelino's masochistic encounter with Jesus is intensified by being positioned within a contradictory discourse on gender, which ends up glorifying the mother. When Father Thomas finds the abandoned infant, he opens the blanket to determine its sex, joyfully announcing, "It's a boy!" (though the English subtitle discreetly substitutes, "It's a baby!"). This gendering is also extended to the story itself; when the holy father narrating the story asks the father of the sick child, "Didn't your father or grandfather ever tell you this legend?" he clearly implies that the legend of Marcelino belongs to the patriarchy. In fact, the author of the original story on which the

The monks voyeuristically
watch the eroticized
spectacle of Marcelino's
miraculous death.

film was based, José María Sánchez Silva, claims, "I wrote the story for fathers to tell to their sons."[27] Moreover, the child is granted twelve fathers rather than one, yet they are really "brothers" who are trying to be "both mothers and fathers," and their masculinity is explicitly called into question by the patriarchal mayor who mocks them for wearing skirts like women. In fact, the only character in the main narrative who is unambiguously presented as a father is the villain—the arrogant blacksmith who physically abuses his children and tyrannizes his wife and who becomes the corrupt mayor. He seeks revenge against the friars because they refuse to let him adopt Marcelino and because they allow the child to challenge the patriarchy. Thus, the film actually disavows the power of the father, replacing it instead with the force of the primal bond between mother and son.

The most formidable power in the film is Jesus, who is introduced verbally in patriarchal terms as a castrating threat ("a huge man up there") that justifies a taboo. The first time Marcelino enters the forbidden attic, he makes his way through threatening phallic tools (scythes, pitchforks, and swords) before penetrating the inner sanctuary where he briefly glimpses the statue of a naked Jesus on the cross. Gradually Jesus is revealed to be a son who draws his strength from the mother, a union that is central to the masochistic aesthetic as theorized by Deleuze and to the vision of Spanish Catholicism as described by Unamuno: "With us the devotion is not so much to the Son lying dead in the lap of His mother as to the Mother herself, the Virgin Mother, who agonizes in sorrow with her Son in her arms. It is the cult of the Mother in agony."[28]

In their secret, closeted encounters, these two masochistic sons are figured as Mama's boys. While discussing their beautiful, giving mothers who are together in heaven, Jesus grants the boy a wish.[29] Marcelino says he wants to be with his mother, and this masochistic desire requires his immediate death. The martyr's desire to be like Jesus (or in Reik's terms, "to die for him in order to be united with him") merges with the desire for original plenitude. Thus, as in the post-Franco *Mater amatísima*, Marcelino's ascension in innocence sanctifies both the sacrificial death of the stunted child and the bonding of mother and son against the patriarchy.

The homoerotic subtext of the Oedipal myth, which is only implicit in *Marcelino,* becomes a blatant political discourse in the post-Franco cinema, where it frequently exposes the lingering legacy of Fascist repression. Here, pederasty is associated with the murderous father, Laius, while transvestism, castration, and transsexualism are associated with the hermaphrodite, Tiresias, and the hybrid Sphinx who oppose the patriarchy and identify with the queen. This pattern is vividly illustrated not only in *Tras el cristal* but also in Almodóvar's most subversive Oedipal narratives, *La ley del deseo* and *Tacones lejanos.*

La ley del deseo   In *La ley del deseo* (The Law of Desire, 1986), both the erotic and murderous impulses of the son are directed toward the father, whose crimes are foregrounded both in the opening inset film (where a middle-aged director/dubber/john dictates the sexual moves of a young hustler who has been paid to masturbate in front of the camera) and in the back story to the main plot (where the father abducts, seduces, and abandons one of his two sons). The elder son chooses pederasty; writer/director Pablo imitates his father and Laius by becoming a charismatic seducer of younger men. The younger son, Tino (brilliantly played by actress Carmen Maura), replaces the victimized mother through transvestism, castration, and transsexuality. As Tina, she plays the nurturing adoptive mother both with her brother Pablo and with the young girl Ada who has been abandoned.

All of these complex erotic relations seem designed to parody the Oedipal triangle and to rupture its reproductive chain. For example, Ada not only rejects her bisexual mother (who is played by real-life transsexual Bibi Andersen) both as an object of desire and as a model of identification but she also falls in love with the homosexual Pablo and yearns to adopt both him and his transsexual brother Tina as idyllic parents—a familial fantasy that restores her faith in the Virgin.

The two brothers are both sexually drawn to Antonio, who is

Above: In Pedro Almodóvar's
La ley del deseo (The Law of
Desire, 1986), Pablo (Eusebio
Poncela, right) seduces
Antonio (Antonio Banderas,
left).

Right: In *La ley del deso* the
transsexual son Tina is
brilliantly played by Carmen
Maura.

Opposite: Tina plays the
nurturing adoptive mother to
Ada.

dominated by his beautiful German mother and whose absent father is a Spanish politician. Originally one of Pablo's young conquests, Antonio eventually usurps the role of the seductive father by murdering his rival and by capturing his patriarchal seducer. By sacrificing himself to that tragic love, Antonio arouses erotic envy not only in transsexual Tina and her female protégé but also in the father/son detectives on the case who are immersed in close Oedipal encounters of the ordinary kind.

In the final love tryst, after Pablo throws away his typewriter and breaks his identification with the patriarchal symbolic order, he appropriates the role of the Madonna for his homosexual romance. He stops trying to manipulate the plot and concentrates instead on the mise-en-scène. For the tragic climax with his martyred lover, he appropriates Tina's postmodernist shrine—a chora that previously enveloped her and her adopted daughter in the Virgin's maternal mysteries. Pablo transforms it into an ornamental backdrop for Antonio's suicide and their final embrace in a homoerotic Pietà.

Tacones lejanos When asked in a 1987 interview why in Spanish Oedipal narratives the erotic desire for the mother is frequently redirected toward the father and the patricidal impulse displaced onto the mother, Almodóvar first claimed he did not know and then went on to describe a forthcoming film project called *Tacones lejanos*. He said it was about two sisters from the south of Spain, who run away from home because their "Bernarda Alba"–type mother frightens them by prophesying they will be guilty of destroying the world. Once they flee to Madrid, their parents perish in a fire. And once they become women, whenever either of them has sex, their mother's ghost appears, which drives the sisters crazy. Finally, they have a duel with their mother's ghost and, after killing her, discover that she was really alive and only pretending to be a ghost. So they inadvertently commit matricide. But, consistent with the surrealists' hatred of the patriarchal mother, Almodóvar claimed that "the mother's behavior is actually more murderous than that of the girls." He explained,

The idea of motherhood is very important in Spain. The father was frequently absent in Spain. It's as if the mother represents the law, the police. . . . When you kill the mother, you kill precisely everything you hate, all of those burdens that hang over you. In this film, I'm killing all of my education and all of the intolerance that is sick in Spain. . . . It's like killing the power.[30]

Four years later at a screening at the Directors Guild in Los Angeles, when asked how an outrageous story of matricide had been converted into an equally outrageous melodrama about mother love, Almodóvar claimed that he had only "borrowed" the title from that other project, which still remained undone.

Yet clearly there was more to it than that, for he had also turned that inverted Oedipal narrative inside out.[31] The subversive goal was no longer to destroy the maternal but to marshal melodrama's full arsenal of emotional excess to eroticize and empower it for those traditionally marginalized under patriarchy—or, in other words, to liberate the maternal from the dreaded image of the repressive patriarchal mother, which so frequently haunts Almodóvar movies.

Tacones lejanos (literally Distant Heels but retitled *High Heels* in English) is still a story about a passionate daughter (now a TV news broadcaster named Rebecca, brilliantly played by Victoria Abril) who is haunted by a powerful mother (played equally brilliantly by Marisa Paredes). The matriarch is no longer a repressive Bernarda Alba, but an aging, promiscuous pop singer named Becky Del Paramo, with whom the neurotic daughter is erotically obsessed and for whose love she jealously kills two patriarchs—both her stepfather and her own husband, Manuel (the owner of a TV network and her mother's former lover). As if working her way toward phallic empowerment, Rebecca uses sleeping pills in the first murder (a weapon frequently associated with women) and her husband's little snub-nosed gun in the second. As in the original matricidal story of *Tacones lejanos,* the murderous daughter (a conflation of the two sisters) is sympathetic, but this time, so is the mother—despite her narcissism and adultery. When Becky learns that her daughter has committed these two murders, she comically advises her in a warm motherly tone, "You need to find another way of solving your problems with men," and then adds, as if to counter any lingering phallocentric assumption, "You need to choose your weapons more carefully." Finally, like Mildred Pierce, she is willing to take the rap. But neither of these crimes is punished or condemned.

The fact that Becky sleeps with her daughter's husband hardly raises an eyebrow, especially since the daughter has purposely chosen to marry Manuel precisely because he had been her mother's lover. This marriage enables her to finally best her mother in their traditional female rivalry and also to replay the murderous Oedipal drama that is represented in the film's prologue (where a freckled little Rebecca kills her stepfather after he tried to sell her into white slavery to swarthy natives in the islands).

Apparently, Girard's thesis (which foregrounds the homoerotic backstory of the Oedipus myth) also applies to the Oedipal heroine, namely, that it is the homoerotic desire to love/imitate/become the parent of the same sex (in this case, the mother) rather than the

In Pedro Almodóvar's *Tacones lejanos* (High Heels, 1991), the hero (Miguel Bosé) substitutes for Rebecca's mother (Marisa Paredes) as the object of her desire. (Photos courtesy of Miramax Films Release.)

heterosexual desire for the other (in this case, the father) that really drives the Oedipal narrative. In *The Acoustic Mirror: The Female Voice in Psychoanalysis and Cinema,* Silverman argues that this "negative Oedipus complex" is essential to feminism because it "make[s] it possible to speak for the first time about a genuinely oppositional desire which challenges dominance from within representation and meaning, rather than from the place of a mutely resistant biology or sexual 'essence.'"[32] In other words, it allows the daughter to *voice* her love for the mother, as is clearly the case in powerful feminist Oedipal narratives like Helma Sanders-Brahms's *Deutschland, bleiche Mutter* (Germany Pale Mother, 1980) and Chantal Akerman's *Le rendezvous d'Anna* (The Meetings of Anna, 1979). In contrast to Almodóvar's previous homoerotic variations on the Oedipal narrative (such as *La ley del deseo*), *Tacones lejanos* (like many subversive feminist texts) boldly proclaims that mother love lies at the heart of all melodrama and its erotic excesses, for it is a passion with primal appeal to all genders and sexual persuasions. Therefore, the rebellious patricidal impulse must be redirected back toward the father, who remains merely a pawn or minor obstacle in the women's game. As Almodóvar quipped in the 1987 interview, "Fathers are not very present in my films. I don't know why. . . . This is something I just feel. When I'm writing about relatives, I just put in mothers" (Kinder, "A Conversation with Pedro Almodóvar," 43).

As in other Almodóvar films, although the patriarchs are soon dispatched, the police endure to the bittersweet end. *Tacones lejanos* also adopts the mother/police dyad that Almodóvar mentioned in the 1987 interview. But, instead of making the police a patriarchal mother like Bernarda Alba, Almodóvar creates a maternal police detective who is frequently called Judge and who doubles as a female impersonator named Femme Lethal. With this false persona, he specializes in impersonating Rebecca's mother on stage and also succeeds in impregnating Rebecca in his dressing room. As if that were not sufficiently confusing, this protean figure also masquerades as a drug addict and other informants fabricated for his various police investigations. Given this endless chain of impersonations, even his role of detective becomes suspect, especially since he wears a false beard and appears to be a mild-mannered young bachelor named Eduardo living with his bedridden mother, an ineffectual repressive matriarch who imagines she has AIDS (as if she believes it is the modern version of the Theban plague), and with no father in sight. His perpetual slippage of identity is heightened by the casting of Miguel Bosé, a well-known Spanish pop singer and sexual icon. Clearly, Bosé's symbolic function in the Oedipal narrative is not to be a seductive or castrating patriarch like Laius or Creon but rather an androgynous hybrid like the mysterious Sphinx and the protean seer Tiresias who both poses and solves the narrative enigmas. Yet instead of being an obstacle to the Oedipal hero or testifying to his guilt, this investigator falls in love with the Oedipal heroine and insists on her innocence under patriarchy, even when he discovers that she deliberately murdered her husband and father.

After tracing Almodóvar's representations of policemen from the odious villain in his debut feature, *Pepi, Luci, Bom y otras chicas del montón* (Pepi, Luci, Bom and Other Girls on the Heap, 1980), to the sympathetic spectators in the closing scene of *La ley del deseo,* D'Lugo concludes that he positions the law to "valorize murder, gay love," and other acts that defy the old Spain. He claims, "The characterization of the police begins to undergo a transformation in *What Have I Done?* where Polo, an impotent police detective who keeps crossing Gloria's path, turns out to be the on-screen witness and authenticator of the heroine's actions."[33] It obviously reaches a new stage of inversion in *Tacones lejanos* where the glamorous androgynous hero is a cop and where virtually all policemen are tenderhearted souls who identify with those marginalized under patriarchy. In this way, Almodóvar subverts dominant ideology by realigning the center with the marginal.

Along with the title, the film version of *Tacones lejanos* also retains the central importance of the audio fetish, which is grafted over the traditional visual fetish of the woman's shoe. Even though its reverberations are somewhat diminished in the translation from the Spanish title *Distant Heels* to the English *High Heels,* the audio fetish dominates the primal scene. In 1987, Almodóvar said,

I remember when I was a child, it was a symbol of freedom for young girls to wear high heels, to smoke and to wear trousers. And these two girls are wearing heels all the time. After running away, the two sisters live together, and the older remembers that she couldn't sleep until the moment that she heard the sound of distant heels coming from the corridor. (Kinder, "A Conversation with Pedro Almodóvar," 43)

In the film, this memory is eroticized and attributed to Rebecca. It is also paired with a primal tale of poverty (evocative of vintage maternal melodramas like *Stella Dallas*) told by her mother, Becky, who replaces the missing sister. As an impoverished child of janitors, Becky watched the well-heeled feet of bourgeois passersby, which could be seen through the window of her humble basement flat, a space that she nostalgically reappropriates, redecorates, and reoccupies (just as her daughter compulsively replays the murderous Oedipal narrative). In the passionate scene in the family basement where Rebecca describes her aural memory to her mother (like a lover confessing her love), we actually witness how the daughter's primal story appropriates the fetishized visual images from her mother's earlier memories, which are still visible through the basement window in the background but which now acquire new erotic associations with mother love.

The power of the audio fetish is also strengthened by giving both daughter and mother oracular professions that rely on their voice and by implying that their speech is connected with their status as sexual subjects pursuing their own desire. Both use the airwaves, ordinarily controlled by the patriarchy, to address their passion to a privileged female listener. In one hilarious scene, Rebecca nervously flubs the news, giggling at disasters because she thinks her mother may be listening; clearly, it is her mother who is both Model and Other, the privileged spectator for whose loving gaze and sympathetic ear she always yearns. Yet the TV network and its hardware are owned by her husband, Manuel, who has hired both her and his current "bimbo" Luisa to do the evening news. Rebecca succeeds in dismantling his power over the airwaves by murdering him and by using his medium to broadcast her "live" confession nationwide. Conversely, her more conventional rival, Luisa, who had sex with Manuel shortly before he was murdered, is forced into silence: she stands by Rebecca, signing the news for deaf viewers, fearful that her impersonation of a deaf mute will be misread as the real thing and that the murder confession will be taken as her own.

Almodóvar claims that Rebecca's TV confession was the germinal idea for (what he calls) this "tough melodrama," as well as its "emotional high point."

Television is a medium I hate, but what Rebecca does on the news program is something I've dreamed about a lot: after reading the news of a death, the presenter confesses that she is the culprit and gives all the details with complete naturalness. But the real key to the scene was what follows. . . . She goes on to show the news audience an envelope of ordinary-looking photos, explaining that after the murder she photographed all the objects she shared in common with the victim, punishing herself with the terrible awareness that, from now on, their only meaning would be as memories. (press kit)

She turns these frozen photographic images into fetishistic substitutes for her dead husband (a strategy of the masochistic aesthetic, at least, according to Deleuze), who proves to be merely a secondary fetish for mother love.

The voice of sexuality is strongest in Becky, whose masochistic torch songs (actually performed by Luz Casal) are primarily addressed to her tormented daughter. This is particularly true when she dedicates the heart-wrenching "Think of Me" to Rebecca, who is temporarily in prison for the murder of her husband. Rebecca is so disturbed by this song that she tries to buy the radio (the patriarchal apparatus on which it is being transmitted) so that she can turn off its erotic force. Not only are these musical numbers particularly appropriate to the romantic excesses of *melo*-drama but they are also resonant in the context of the new feminist theorization of sound, particularly in the work of Silverman and Amy Lawrence, who have emphasized the importance of the maternal voice in subject forma-tion.[34] Thus, the women's subversion of the patriarchy (what Al-modóvar calls in the press kit, "act[ing] behind the back of the law of man and that of God") is achieved primarily by fetishizing the maternal voice, which is amplified through media transmission and hardware as well as through dubbing and impersonation. In this way, it succeeds in replacing the unspoken Name-of-the-Father and the hollow voice of God.

The subversive potential of the maternal voice under patriarchy becomes most compelling in two brilliant comic scenes in which the gender of the maternal performer is most ironically compromised through a dazzling chain of masquerades. In one scene, sexy trans-sexual actress Bibi Andersen leads an extravagant musical dance number in the women's prison yard. This statuesque beauty plays an authentic "idealized" mother, who has broken into prison (by nearly killing a cop with a brick) so that she can protect her beloved daughter. Thus (like Bosé) Bibi performs a triple impersonation—of a woman, a mother, and a criminal. It is a performance that mocks the symbolic order of the patriarchy and dissolves the boundaries between allegedly incompatible genders and genres (the women's prison picture and the musical). It also implies that the opposition between outlaw/lawman is as arbitrarily constructed and gendered as that between female/male and that the boundaries between both sets need to be transgressed as thoroughly as those between genres.

Although the genres hybridized in *Tacones lejanos* are limited primarily to the maternal realm of melodrama, the film's intertex-tuality is pointedly international. There is an explicit reference to *Autumn Sonata* when Rebecca tells her mother how much they resemble (Ingmar/Ingrid) Bergman's talented mother who is an artist and her mediocre daughter. There are also parallels to Hollywood's celebrity versions of that genre like *Mommie Dearest* and *Postcards from the Edge* and many implicit allusions to classical mother/daugh-ter weepies like *Mildred Pierce, Imitation of Life,* and *Stella Dallas* and to Hitchcock's latent lesbian thrillers, *Marnie* and *Rebecca* (partic-ularly through the doubling of the name for mother and daughter). There are even a few allusions to Spanish classics, like Juan de

Orduña's popular musical melodrama, *El último cuplé* (The Last Song, 1957), where an aging popular singer makes a comeback and collapses on stage in midsong, and Edgar Neville's *El crimen de la calle de Bordadores* (Crime on Bordadores Street, 1946), where the mother similarly saves the daughter she once abandoned by falsely confessing to a murder on her deathbed. And, of course, there are echoes of earlier Almodóvar hits, like *Entre tinieblas* (Dark Habits, 1983), where extravagant Mexican boleros are similarly used to fetishize an erotic passion between two women, a torch singer doing Gilda and a smitten Mother Superior, or *¿Que he hecho yo para merecer esto?* (What Have I Done to Deserve This? 1984), where another woman who kills her husband is united in the end with an androgynous love (in this case, her homosexual son rather than the impotent cop whom she tries to fuck in the opening comic sex scene), or even *La ley del deseo,* where Bibi Andersen plays not a "real" model mother (as in this musical interlude) but a real bad mother model who (like Becky) runs off to a foreign country with a lover, leaving her daughter behind.

The other comic musical performance in *Tacones lejanos* is the most brilliant sequence in the film. It is the scene in which Rebecca takes her mother and husband to the Club Villa Rosa to see Femme Lethal do an impersonation of Becky. The chain of simulations is dazzling, for the impersonator is really a male pop star (Miguel Bosé) doing an impersonation of an ordinary man (Eduardo) doing an impersonation of a detective (Judge) doing an impersonation of a female impersonator (Lethal) doing an impersonation of a female pop singer (Becky), who is there in the audience with her daughter Rebecca, who has been impersonating her mother all her life. When the camera cuts to a reverse shot of the spectators, we see that Becky watches the performance with narcissistic fascination, Rebecca with erotic desire, and Manuel with hostility and contempt. Meanwhile, three other anonymous female spectators sing along with Lethal, imitating his every gesture and taking great pleasure in impersonating the impersonator.

Whenever we cut back to the transvestite, we notice that he is performing against a painted backdrop decorated with images of

Flanked by her secretary (Ana
Lizaran) on her right and her
daughter (Victoria Abril) on
her left, Becky the pop star
(Marisa Paredes) confronts
the image of her
impersonator, Femme Lethal
(Miguel Bosé) in *Tacones
lejanos*. (Photo courtesy of
Miramax Films Release.)

gypsies and matadors—the old españolada stereotype of Spain promoted for foreign consumption, which Almodóvar's postmodernist
transsexuals have come to replace in the post-Franco era. This image
takes on even greater irony when we recall that Bosé is the offspring
of the famous union between Italian actress Lucia Bosé (the beautiful
star of *Muerte de un ciclista,* which mocked that bullfighting stereotype) and Spanish matador Luis Miguel Dominguin, who embodied
it, as well as the godson of Pablo Picasso, who helped popularize it
worldwide. As in a palimpsest, one national stereotype (or generation
or genre) is grafted over the other—just as the sound fetish is mapped
over the visual fetish. This constant slippage of meaning evokes both
the endless chain of simulations that characterizes postmodernism
and the endless chain of substitutions and fetishization that characterizes primary process thinking.

After this dazzling performance, when Lethal finally meets Becky,
he proposes that they exchange mementos—her earrings (like the
earrings made of horn that she had earlier given little Rebecca in the
primal scene from the pretitles prologue) in exchange for one of his
falsies. This exchange of fetishes reveals that their referents come from
the mother's body, which is the point of origin for all fetishes (a
revelation that contradicts the co-optive phallocentric theories of
Freud and Lacan). Consistent with Bataille's emphasis on exchange
as fundamental to eroticism, this act empowers the extraordinary
nonphallic sex scene between Femme Lethal and Rebecca that immediately follows in his dressing room. It begins with a wild gym-
nastic form of cunnilingus (a sex act that could just as easily occur
between two women) and ends with impregnation and a proper
proposal of marriage (even though the petitioner is still partially in
drag and the petitionee is already married). What is most remarkable
about the encounter is that it is simultaneously very erotic and
hysterically funny, a combination that is very difficult to achieve but
that Almodóvar consistently masters.

It is this eroticized exchange, not only between two bodies but also
between opposing genders and sexual orientations, conflicting tones
and genres (screwball comedy, maternal melodrama, and soft-core

In *Tacones lejanos* the sex
scene between Femme Lethal
and Rebecca is both erotic
and funny. (Photo courtesy of
Miramax Films Release.)

porn), that finally fulfills Rebecca's subversive dream of maternal
plenitude, of becoming the powerful sexual mother she so ardently
desires. By celebrating the love between mothers and daughters and
giving new meaning to the epithet "Mommie Dearest," *Tacones
lejanos* provides a new erotic fantasy for empowering a strategic
alliance among straight women, lesbians, gay men, transvestites,
transsexuals, and all other forms of nonpatriarchal androgynes. And
it adds new maternal resonance to Almodóvar's ongoing project of

making the "marginal" central to mainstream cinema, not only in Spain but worldwide.

In these subversive Almodóvar Oedipal narratives, where the tone slides fluidly between grand passion and parody, all boundaries are called into question—not only between genders and genres but also between religion and pop culture, holy communion and crime. We are no longer so sure what the Oedipal myth is reproducing, for the symbolic order teeters on the verge of an ideological breakdown.

READING *BILBAO* AS A POST-FRANCO STORY OF OEDIPAL LOVE   Finally we come to *Bilbao, a Story of Love* by Catalán filmmaker Bigas Luna, which carries us over the brink. Here, the stunted protagonist Leo is trapped in an Oedipal drama with his uncle and with his middle-aged mistress Maria, who has been hired by his family to replace his dead mother. Like a matriarchal trinity, she services Leo as mother, nanny, and whore. As in *Furtivos,* the kind of incest they practice is tolerated by the patriarchy because it keeps the son infantilized. Not only has his uncle stolen his inheritance (like Creon) but his sausage factory vividly reminds Leo that his patrimonial legacy is butchery and murder. To escape his family and his patriarchal destiny, Leo fantasizes about kidnapping a prostitute named Bilbao and making her float like Jesus but "accidentally" kills her in the process.

You might wonder why a feminist would devote so much attention to a film that depicts such obscene crimes against women. On the one hand, *Bilbao* exploits the sexual freedom of the post-Franco era by portraying this perverse sexuality in graphic detail. It could easily be called soft core and even includes an excerpt from hard core pornography. Indeed, in the post-Franco period, Spain was immediately inundated with pornography once censorship bans were lifted. On the other hand, *Bilbao* uses such representations to demonstrate that the post-Franco era is not really so free, that even in the superliberated city of Barcelona, Spaniards still retain an internalized repression that cultivates a taste for perverse sexuality.

This aspect is in marked contrast to the films of Almodóvar, which seem optimistic and almost innocent by contrast. The contrast is most apparent in Almodóvar's X-rated *¡Atame!* which is an erotic captivity narrative like *Bilbao* and which also reworks William Wyler's *The Collector* (1965), one of the most seminal films in the genre. While Almodóvar's comical happy ending celebrates the transformative power of l'amour fou (even between the kidnapper and his captive), Bigas Luna focuses on adapting Wyler's class discourse and the repressed infantile sexuality of its death-loving captor, reversing the class positions of kidnapper and victim and politicizing their perverse sexuality so as to comment on the legacy of Fascist repression in post-Franco Spain.

Beyond the Spanish context, what may be of particular interest to feminists is the way *Bilbao* reveals the inherent misogyny and perversion in the so-called normal resolution of the Oedipal conflict. We watch the son transfer the incestuous erotic desire he feels for the mother figure onto a younger woman, whom he can call his own and whom he can manipulate with pleasure within his own private space. Like a colonized new world, this space is apart from yet subject to the patriarchal family; it is a privileged site for the projection of home rule. The woman's body is used to negotiate the terrifying gap between self and other and the paradoxical taboos against the violation of both domestic and foreign territories. Yet, as both the myths of Oedipus and Samson demonstrate, exogamy offers only an illusory escape from incestuous desire. Moreover, like the reflexive thriller *Peeping Tom* (1960; a film with which *Bilbao* has frequently been compared), "it deploys the film-within-a film trope . . . for dramatizing the displacement of lack from the male to the female subject."[35]

To fully understand its treatment of the Spanish Oedipal narrative, *Bilbao* must be read intertextually against three other contexts. First, it can be contrasted with other erotic captivity narratives from other cultures, such as William Wyler's *The Collector* (1965), based on the John Fowles novel, which has the victim die off screen but only after a bloody struggle against her sexually repressed captor; Yasuro Masumura's *Blind Beast* (1969), which ends with the blind kidnapper and his captive model killing his mother and then hacking each other to pieces in a frenzy of violent eroticism performed on a rubber sculpture of the mother's body; and Ingmar Bergman's *From the Life of the Marionettes* (1980), which, though not strictly a captivity narrative, shares many striking similarities with *Bilbao* (the same chain of erotic/murderous displacements from mother to wife to whore; the same obsession with control; an equally claustrophobic narrative structure; a victim who looks amazingly like the actress who plays Bilbao; and the use of the same Donna Summers song, "I Love the Way She Moves," in the erotic dance sequences); yet the representation of violence could not be more different, for Bergman's film opens with a graphic depiction of murder and sodomy in lurid color before draining to black and white. What distinguishes *Bilbao* most dramatically from these other films is its near-suppression of physical violence, which is surprising given that post-Franco Spanish cinema is so notorious for its graphic depiction of brutality in fetishized close-ups.

To understand this aesthetic choice, *Bilbao* must also be read intertextually against two key films by Spanish filmmakers from earlier decades—Buñuel's *El,* a film made in Mexico in 1955, and Saura's *Peppermint frappé* (already discussed in chap. 4), which was made in 1967 and dedicated to Buñuel. In all three of these films, we find an infantilized, impotent man who becomes erotically obsessed with a young "modern" woman, who is associated with a foreign place—Argentina, England, or Bilbao. Though she represents the Other, he casts her in the maternal role and uses her as a site of projection for his own feelings of castration and his Oedipal fantasies of empowerment. In all three films, we never see the protagonist engage in genital sex; his erotic passion is displaced onto other obsessive specular activities, like taking photos, making scrapbooks, or watching pornography.

In all three texts, his erotic obsession has a strong religious cast and veers toward or ends in the woman's sacrificial murder. He tries to turn her into a dehumanized object he can manipulate—like an icon, a fetish, or a rubber doll (an impulse Buñuel had parodied in *Exterminating Angel* with his "washable rubber virgin"). Whereas in *El* and *Peppermint frappé,* the selection of the sacrificial victim is put in the religious context of Holy Week, in *Bilbao,* it is contextualized within consumer capitalism, which creates the illusion of freedom while actually increasing dependency on the system. *Bilbao* foregrounds the problem that was articulated by the surrealists in their pamphlet that accompanied the first Paris screenings of *L'age d'or:* "The problem of the failure of sentiment, intimately connected to that of capitalism, has not yet been resolved." Leo chooses Bilbao as if he were selecting merchandise in a department store, confessing, "I can't get her by mail order, I can't buy her. I would for sure. She's the best object. I want to have everything that's hers." In all three films, the erotic obsession is linked with inheritance of property (his family legacy) and with a rivalry with other men whom he casts as surrogates for his dead father. In all three texts, the violence against the woman is masked by the baroque structure or surface beauty of the film, which reflexively foregrounds eroticized close-ups.

Bilbao can also be read intertextually with Armiñán's *Al servicio de la mujer española* (At the Service of Spanish Womanhood), released the same year, in 1978, a film that also used the new post-Franco freedom to portray the Francoist legacy of repression. Missing that first phase of the political transition when many Spanish productions with a new daring perspective enjoyed considerable box office success, both films were part of the second phase when it was already harder to attract Spanish spectators. Explicitly mentioning *Bilbao* as an example, filmmaker Miró (who would later, in 1982, be appointed general director of cinema by the newly elected Socialist government) explains it this way:

In a second phase, once censorship had disappeared completely, the screens were invaded by foreign films that had been prohibited in the past years. Being bombarded with these productions, all the more attractive because of the forbidden element, the Spanish public forgot about national film altogether. Thus national products that some months earlier would have had a good reception were practically ignored.[36]

Thus, in 1978, Spanish filmmakers had good reason to try to outdo these foreign imports in outrageousness.

In both *Bilbao* and *Al servicio de la mujer española,* a stunted male character of ambiguous sexuality has an incestuous relationship with a maternal nanny and flirts with transvestism. As if to get revenge against his family and culture for the psychic damage they have done him, he picks a younger woman (either a prude or a whore, but in both instances a public performer) to star as sacrificial victim in his own perverse scenario. In both cases, the family legacy is embodied in a factory that manufactures a consumerist product—sausage or fish—commonly associated with sex. In both cases, the most intense moment of his revenge is carried out in a ritualistic shaving scene, which evokes a historical primal scene and stands in for sex, castration, and murder. This scene reveals that the female scapegoat being shaved substitutes both for the mother who aroused and repressed his desire and for the castrating patriarch whom he is too weak to confront.

What distinguishes *Bilbao* from these other Spanish and foreign texts is the way it is presented so totally from Leo's point of view, and yet we spectators remain as emotionally detached from *him* as he is from Bilbao. Leo's voice-overs totally dominate the film, making it claustrophobic. His voice is hushed, confiding, with little or no affect, as if he were addressing a single voyeuristic male spectator like himself who shares his erotic tastes rather than a mass audience who is judging him. Sometimes he uses direct address, as if interpellating us against our will. Yet, because the stylization is so rigorous and Leo's character so extreme, regardless of our gender, we resist being drawn into identification with him—even though we are forced to recognize the power of the erotic pull. As Linda Williams has argued about Buñuel's subversive melodramas, we observe the voyeuristic dynamics without experiencing the perverse pleasures they are "normally" designed to generate.[37]

The film is also unique in the way it is totally dominated by extreme close-ups, which evoke two contradictory traditions: the detail from the fine art of painting (which highlights artistic technique) and the insert shot from pornography (which both objectifies and eroticizes the body). In fact, the two artistic representations that Leo tries to replicate and synthesize in his ritual are Ribera's baroque

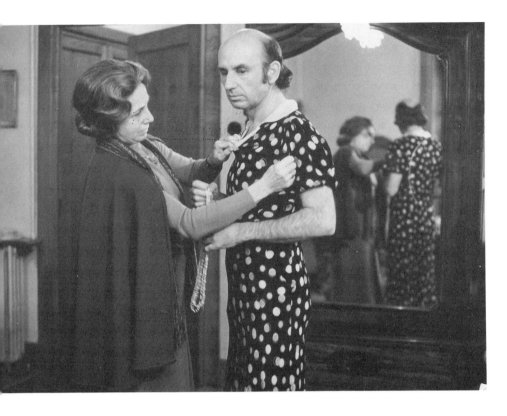

In Jaime de Armiñán's *Al servicio de la mujer española* (At the Service of Spanish Womanhood, 1978), the stunted male of ambiguous sexuality has an incestuous relationship with a maternal nanny and flirts with transvestism.

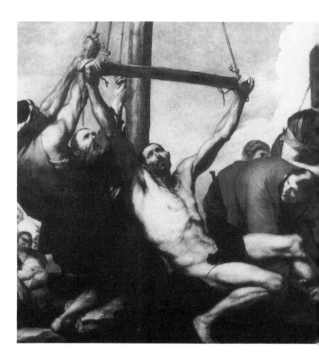

In Bigas Luna's *Bilbao*, 1978, Leo's fantasy of making his captive "float like Jesus" is based on Ribera's baroque painting, *Martirio de San Felipe* (The Martyrdom of San Felipe, formerly known as The Martyrdom of San Bartolomé, 1639), which hangs on the wall of the warehouse where he holds Bilbao prisoner. Museo del Prado, Madrid.

painting, *Martirio de San Felipe* (1639), formerly known as *The Martyrdom of San Bartolomé*, which hangs on the wall of the warehouse where Bilbao is held captive, and the pornographic film that he watches with her at his side. In both traditions, the close-up achieves that magnified "infra-realism" that Ortega y Gasset claimed was as effective a means of modernist dehumanization as the distancing overview.

The narrowness of this tunnel vision intensifies and eroticizes whatever is seen, but it also omits a great deal. The unanswered questions about plot and historical context force us to be more active as spectators in figuring out what is happening. The tunnel vision also makes us wonder whether many sequences are subjective daydreams, for Leo's point of view expresses primary process thinking, in which there is no real distinction between fantasy and reality.

We first begin to suspect this story is fantasy when the uncle comes to visit and Leo claims he does not mind that he is sleeping with Maria. As Leo lies on his bed, we see his face in close-up, and then the camera cuts directly to Bilbao fucking a john in a car, with her fetishistic spiked heel prominent in the foreground. The cut suggests Leo's associative displacements; the reason he fantasizes about capturing Bilbao all for himself is so that he can escape (or win) the Oedipal conflict with his uncle and Maria, which reproduces the triangle he earlier experienced with his father and mother. From this sex scene (the only genital sex in the film), we cut back to the facial close-up of Leo in bed, and (as in Buñuel's *Belle de jour*) the linear narrative unravels.

In the scene where Leo is waiting for Bilbao in her apartment, the fantasy element is even more blatant, for we get two versions of the abduction—one violent and the other less so. Yet, apart from the repetition, there is nothing in the film to mark the first version as a fantasy. As in Buñuel's *Exterminating Angel,* such repetition forces us to see how the narrative drive tempts us to ignore perceptual discontinuities.

This repetition makes us reconsider the opening, where we see first a large facial close-up of Bilbao and then her name flashing strobically and growing larger with each beat and then hear the obsessive romantic theme from the opening movement of Ravel's "Rhapsodie español." The repetition compulsion is introduced and immediately fetishized on all three registers—image, word, and music. Then there is an ambiguous scene in a hotel, shot in a different, more detached style with sparse dialogue, where a man (possibly Leo) photographs a woman (possibly Bilbao or another prostitute), who keeps saying, "Mira! Mira!" (Look! Look!). Though the room is dark, the flash on the man's camera provides strobic lighting that syncopates the scene with a percussive rhythm. Thus, cinematic representation is linked with voyeurism even before the narrative is focalized exclusively on Leo's narrative through voice-overs.

Leo first appears on screen in a subway station in the following sequence, moving anonymously among the crowd. The film cuts directly to his destination—bright neon in an urban night and a nightclub interior where Bilbao dances in the nude to Donna Summers's "I Love the Way She Moves." The dance is punctuated not only by the music and strobe lights but also by inserts of male spectators and of a cash register, which link voyeurism to commodification. As the camera pans down Bilbao's body and reaches her groin, the sound of an electric razor fades in from the following scene—a connection that introduces Leo's morning rituals (which are the site of his fantasy) and prefigures the climactic scene where he will shave her pubic hair. Like aural close-ups, the sounds are carefully selected and intensified—not only the buzz of the razor but also the water gurgling down the drain and Leo slurping his yogurt, sounds that will also recur in the final ritual when he washes off the blood and performs cunnilingus. Thus, the juxtapositions of sound and image actually help to generate the erotic fantasy.

These morning rituals are also the point of origin for Leo's voice-overs, which immediately introduce his orality and his obsession with cleanliness: "It's Monday. . . . I have to brush my teeth, it's a long process, but I have to do it, I have to keep my mouth clean, very clean. . . . I've had my yogurt, I love to lick it." We wonder whether the previous images of Bilbao are the erotic fantasies he sees as he shaves and eats his yogurt. Perhaps the only "real" settings in the film are the symbolic spaces: the home, where he makes the albums, blueprints, and photographs that provide a realistic mise-en-scène for his erotic scenarios; the subway train, which, as an underground medium, is particularly conducive to perverse fantasy; and the department store, which caters to consumerist desire.[38] This reading is supported by the ending, where he says, "She's dead. My whole world is destroyed. I'm in reality again" and then resumes his morning rituals, which he describes in the iterative.

We are forced to reconceptualize the narrative as a double time structure that is more characteristic of the whodunit and of Sophocles' version of Oedipus. Freud observed that this play "consists of nothing other than the process of revealing, with cunning delays and ever mounting excitement—a process that can be likened to the work of psychoanalysis."[39] This shift also makes us reconceptualize the spectator position—from an accomplice to an analyst—as we try to solve the riddle of whether the captivity plot is erotic fantasy or symbolic history. In either event, we want to know what it implies about the cultural and historical context in which it was generated. Thus, the film retains the conflation of cultural history and development of individual consciousness that is so central to the Oedipal myth.

If it *is* only fantasy, then how does the plot serve Leo? The fantasy satisfies his infantile urge to kill Maria and yet still keep her because he desperately needs her. The fantasy proves that she is not the controlling bitch or bad breast but the nurturing mother who cleans up his mess, reassuring him that nothing matters except little Leo's safety. When Leo sees the two women together for the first time (while Maria is helping him dispose of Bilbao's corpse), he realizes they have the same body. Bilbao is like a rubber fetish for the mother's body, which, in turn, is a fetishistic substitute for the missing father and for the phallus that Leo has never possessed. The chain of violent displacements from mother/father/uncle/Maria to Bilbao retraces the chain of fetishistic substitutes for the lost object of desire—from mother's body to phallus to Maria's body to Bilbao's corpse.

Leo is attracted to Bilbao as a voice and a space, which both evoke maternal plenitude. He loves her voice with its Andalusian accent but hates her talk, because it pulls him out of the imaginary into the symbolic. He says, "Her words are the real world outside." The semic code of Bilbao is documented in the album, which maps her as a space, identifying her with the colonized Basque city with all of its political reverberations, as an important industrial center, and as a center of resistance in the Civil War and ever after. The semic code is extended internationally by Lotte Lenya's recording of *Bilbao* from Kurt Weil's *Happy End* (1929), which gives Bilbao's voice historical reverberations and intensifies her identification as a site of exotic pleasure and nostalgia.

In the nightclub scenes where Leo watches Bilbao perform, her red glossy lips, grotesque smile, and bobbing breasts make her look plastic. This look evokes the masquerade of femininity, which not only creates some distance between her and her image (as Mary Ann Doane has argued) but also simultaneously arouses the perverse infantile pleasure that many male spectators take in the woman's objectification—a pleasure that is gratified in most Oedipal narratives.[40] Leo picks a simulacrum of Maria so that he can compulsively repeat the same pre-Oedipal rituals of oral narcissism, like pouring milk on her body, which evokes the lifeline connection between mother and child. But now *he* controls the flow, reversing the awesome dependency he once experienced in relation to the mother.

This doubling of the female victim follows the pattern of double substitution that Girard claims is essential to ritual sacrifice. Maria is chosen as surrogate victim from *inside* the community to represent the repressive family on whom Leo is so dependent. Bilbao is chosen as ritual victim from *outside* his family and class to substitute for Maria. She belongs to the sacrificial category, whore, which is determined by her subordinate gender, class, and region (Andalusia) within Spanish patriarchal capitalism. Paradoxically, Leo selects a common prostitute controlled by a pimp as the unique woman to call his own because part of the pleasure is in taking her away from another man. Ironically, her murder succeeds in reuniting the family, for (as in the first episode of *Los desafíos*) the Oedipal triad collaborates in disposing of the corpse.

While Girard acknowledges that this kind of double substitution occurs both in ritual violence and in the choice of erotic object, what he fails to make explicit is that this double substitution is precisely what occurs in the so-called normal resolution of the Oedipal complex where exogamy displaces incest. Yet this dynamic *is* made vividly clear in *Bilbao*.

The most threatening part of the film is the scene in which Leo obsessively shaves Bilbao's pubic hair with an electric razor. It is so disturbing not only because it is an image of castration but also because it goes on so long and because it is shot in such huge close-ups. It gives us plenty of time to realize that we are watching a castrated male displacing his castration onto a woman. Like a child

When Leo pours milk on María's buttocks in *Bilbao*, he evokes the life-line connection between mother and child but now he controls the flow.

in the process of being gendered as male, he fears that the woman's body (with its lack of phallus) represents the threat of his own castration (a dynamic theorized by Freud).

The shaving scene shows the infantilized male trying to fathom the "mystery" of female sexuality—to reclaim that lost territory that he has tried to map and possess. It is hard to imagine a more blatant confirmation of Teresa DeLauretis's argument that within the sadistic drive of the Oedipal narrative, woman functions as a space to be conquered.[41] The shaving is also a prelude to cunnilingus—a means of transforming the pudendum into a breast and of avoiding the son's patriarchal destiny of genital sex and murder.

As in the biblical story of Samson and Delilah, he is cutting her hair to steal her power. Earlier, when he said he planned to cut her hair, we assumed he meant the hair on her head, to make her look more like Maria, but now it evokes the iconography of shaving as symbolic castration and murder that is so prevalent in Spanish films.

In contrast to erotic captivity narratives from other cultures, what is strangest about *Bilbao* is the way it disavows all physical violence against its female victim—not only by literally censoring it from the abduction scene but also by disavowing the murder. The representation of Bilbao's death is extraordinary because Leo does not notice when it happens and neither do we, so he has to replay the scene to find the moment when she hit her head. But even in repetition, the murderous moment remains elusive. This is a radical narrative strategy that evokes the suppression of violence in Fascist discourse. Moreover, her death appears almost incidental because he has already been treating her as if she were dead, as an object without consciousness. This kind of psychic and representational violence against women is characteristic of most Oedipal narratives.

The disavowal of her murder also demonstrates that this is Leo's narrative, where *he* is the victim because he has been deprived of his toy and has lost control of his game of *fort/da*. When her body is ground up in the factory, she literally becomes a sausage, the missing phallus that speaks *his* castration, not *hers*. In this primary process fantasy, the boundaries between Leo and Bilbao are erased—like the boundaries between Bilbao and Maria, or between mother and infant. Leo says he possesses *her* ticket stub, but it is really *his;* he claims he is putting it in *her* album, but it is really *his* album; the movie is called *Bilbao,* but it really belongs to Leo and to the Name-of-the-Father. The film has nothing to do with real women but is merely the fantasy projection of men. The same is true of the Oedipal myth, which so effectively reproduces patriarchal order. And that, I would argue, is precisely what this film, as an extreme example of a subversive Spanish Oedipal narrative, so brilliantly dramatizes.

José Luis Borau's *Río abajo*
(On the Line, 1984) opens
with a group of Latinos
illegally crossing the border
between Mexico and the
United States. (Photo
courtesy of El Imán.)

BLOOD CINEMA · III

EXILE AND DIASPORA

6 · EXILE AND IDEOLOGICAL REINSCRIPTION

THE UNIQUE CASE OF LUIS BUÑUEL

Rockwell Gray's incisive essay, "Spanish Diaspora: A Culture in Exile," opens with a statement that gets to the heart of what was uniquely paradoxical about the Spanish experience of exile connected with the Civil War—that national trauma that severed the two Spains and "scattered abroad hundreds of thousands of the Iberian Peninsula's citizens and snuffed out the lives of perhaps a million others."[1] Not only did this mass hegira prefigure in the international context "many political cataclysms that have bequeathed to the world a legacy of wandering souls—refugees, exiles, émigrés, emigrants, displaced persons" (Gray, 53) but it also echoed many other earlier periods of exile specifically within Spain, a connection that has been most powerfully described by Jorge Campos (whom Gray quotes at length):

With the political exile of 1939 there occurred again something which had been repeating itself in Spanish history like the recidivist form of an endemic disease. No country in the world exhibits a chain of persecutions and exiles like ours . . . [for example,] the expulsion of the Jews, the Moors, the Jesuits in the eighteenth century, the liberals during Fernando VII's absolutist periods, the three Carlist, Progressive and Republican emigrations, up to the current century under the government of Miguel Primo de Rivera, and even a brief spurt in 1934.[2]

Thus, Gray presents Spanish exile both as a unique experience that helps distinguish Spain from other nations and as a global paradigm that gives Spain a central position within a unified international field—the same kind of paradoxical dynamic that was operative, as we have seen in chapter 4, in Spain's relationship to modern massacre.

Although Campos claims that this unique history of exile gave Spaniards an inordinate "intolerance, the incapacity for living together," one could argue that it also engendered in Spanish artists and intellectuals (both those in exile abroad and those who suffered an inner exile at home) a propensity toward dialogism and double vision. While Gray emphasizes this capacity for heteroglossia and double vision in his analysis of Spanish diaspora, at the end of his essay, he tries to bring those dispersed Spanish exiles back into the fold, a move that inadvertently evokes the monolithic unity Franco had imposed during his reign.

The bearers of the exiled culture, whether dead or alive, have now in some degree been rescued from the oblivion that threatened them. Their words and deeds can be seen once again as part of Spain's cultural history. The meaning of their diaspora can now be understood, and the threads of modern Spanish history can again all be woven on a single loom. (83)

In this chapter, I hope to unravel this unity (or at least tangle its threads) because I want to emphasize the dialogic legacy of Spanish exile and diaspora both to Spanish and to world cinema. I agree with Hamid Naficy that exile breeds a "hybridity" that "involves an ambivalence about both the original and the host cultures, thereby leading to the creation of a slipzone of indeterminacy, . . . a state of unbelonging, in effect a condition of freedom, nomadism, homelessness, or vagrancy—even opportunism."[3] This dialogic discourse of exile resists the cultural "melting pot" both in the old and new lands; it retains its Otherness in both contexts, which enhances its cross-cultural appeal.

Although there are several productive ways of approaching these issues,[4] I have decided to focus on two specific case studies—Luis Buñuel (in chap. 6) and José Luis Borau (in chap. 7)—because they so fully illuminate the ironies involved in the national-international interface of exile. Yet before turning to these cases, I think it might be useful to briefly sketch how exile itself was represented in Spanish cinema.

THE REPRESENTATION OF EXILE   Although the representation of exile was suppressed from the Spanish cinema in the 1940s and 1950s, it began to emerge in the 1960s, during which time it frequently was connected with other discourses of Otherness, especially of gender. One of the first Spanish films to present a Republican exile on screen was Bardem's Spanish/French coproduction, *Nunca pasa nada* (Nothing Ever Happens, 1963). Near the end of this story about a French ballerina who is stuck in a small Spanish town (a role played by French new wave actress Corrine Marchand),[5] there is a brief scene in which she goes to a bar and meets a Republican exile, who has just returned home from France after having spent time in a concentration camp. This nameless minor character challenges the narrative's primary assumption, namely, that the French generation of liberated youth (immortalized by the French new wave) are more liberated politically than those Spanish exiles (at home or abroad) who still suffer the consequences of the Civil War, for he becomes contemptuous of her when he discovers she has never heard of Laval. Perhaps equally important, this incident suggests that the image of foreigners in Spain could function as an indirect means of talking about the taboo topic of exile as well as of exaggerating their otherness on issues like sexuality. This entanglement of exile with a discourse on gender and sexuality could be traced all the way back to the silent version of *La aldea maldita* (1929), where, as we have seen in chapter 1, the urban migration from a Castilian village to Segovia was linked with a woman's flight from the rigid Castilian patriarchy, a juxta-position that evoked the historic conflict between the two Spains.

Looking forward, one could see the theme of the Spanish exile developed much further in Alain Resnais's *La guerre est finie* (The War Is Over, 1966). Written by Spanish exile Jorge Semprún in France, it (like Bardem's film) also explores an exiled Spaniard's generational and cultural conflicts with young French radicals, es-pecially with a young woman. Moreover, Bardem's positioning of the Republican exile within a discourse on a female émigré anticipated other Spanish films of the 1960s and 1970s that would use the xenophobic reaction against foreigners as a means of talking about the suppression of "that Other lost Spain." For example, in some of Saura's films from this period (*Peppermint frappé*, 1967, *Ana y los lobos* [Ana and the Wolves], 1972, and *Los ojos vendados,* 1978), the émigré is a foreign woman who (like Bardem's ballerina) elicits "inordinate intolerance" in the Spanish men she arouses and eventually becomes the object of their murderous rage. Even in Armiñán's *El amor del Capitán Brando* (The Love of Captain Brando, 1974), where the returning Republican exile is finally one of the main characters, he becomes an important symbolic figure of sexual liberation (capable of displacing even a romantic Hollywood idol like Marlon Brando) both for the rebellious fatherless teenager, Juan, and his sexually awakened young teacher, Aurora. Yet the middle-aged exile is not so easily recuperated into his home village and fails to satisfy the ro-mantic yearnings of the younger generation, whose fantasies of Oth-erness go far beyond his lived experience. These two young figures (Juan and Aurora) are conflated into the formidable thirteen-year-old Goyita in Armiñán's *El nido* (The Nest, 1980), where this rebellious young girl seduces a middle-aged former Republican exile, Don Alejandro, into a deviant romance, which may liberate her from her weak father and his tyrannical boss (both members of the repressive guardia civil) but which costs her quixotic lover his life.

The coupling of the middle-aged exile with a rebellious young girl also occurs in the films of Erice, both in *El espíritu de la colmena* (1973) from the period of transition and *El sur* (The South, 1983) from the post-Franco era. In both texts, the brooding father is locked in an "inner exile" that roots him in the past and that becomes a site of imaginative projection for his perceptive young daughter. As bold and free-spirited as the foreign female émigrés in the films of Saura and Bardem, these Spanish daughters seek inspiration in foreign territories (either within or outside Spain), particularly as represented in movies, postcards, or reconstructed memories of inner exile. By positioning this discourse of Otherness within intimate family relations, both works question whether its most resonant sources come from without or within. They bring to mind Homi Bhabha's statement that "the 'other' is never outside or beyond us, it emerges forcefully, within cultural discourse, when we *think* we speak most intimately and indigenously 'between ourselves.'"[6]

Even in Gutiérrez Aragón's *El corazón del bosque* (The Heart of the Forest, 1978), where a Communist exile returns from France to convince El Andarín, the leader of a group of maquis still waging anti-Francoist resistance, to cease their rebellion or to kill him if he refuses, the exile's complex interactions with his sister and with a young girl (who help and betray him) lead both to his prey and to his own entrapment. In this loose adaptation of Conrad's *Heart of Darkness,* the returning Spaniard eventually *becomes* El Andarín, collapsing the boundary between the exile and the one who stayed home to fight. The recuperation of the exile proves as painful as the death of the maquis (whose skin disease makes his Otherness grotesquely mythic and beyond all recuperation).

The recuperation of the Spanish exile from oblivion is represented as least problematic in José Luis Garci's *Volver a empezar* (To Begin Again, 1982), the most sentimental and most patriarchal treatment of the theme. Here the exile, a Nobel Prize–winning poet, returns from the United States to his hometown with an incurable disease and stoically settles his affairs with his former fiancée. Since this was the first Spanish film to win an Oscar for best foreign film—significantly, right after the Socialist party was peacefully voted into power—some observers concluded that the figure of the Republican exile had lost its subversive power and could now safely rest in peace.[7]

Yet the power of the exile has been partially resuscitated in the late 1980s and early 1990s, by being displaced onto young women or foreigners. For example, in Fernando Fernán-Gómez's *El mar y el tiempo* (The Sea and Time, 1989), a middle-aged exile returns home from Buenos Aires in 1968 to find that the significant political work is now being done by his young niece and her generation of student activists. Similarly, in Antón Eceiza's *Dias de humo* (Days of Smoke, 1990), a Basque exile (played by Mexican actor Pedro Armendariz, Jr.) returns home to find that he and his generation have been replaced in the political struggle for regional autonomy by his young daughter, who is now the symbolic figure of resistance. In Patino's *Los paraísos perdidos* (The Lost Paradises, 1985), the daughter actually becomes the returning exile, leaving the home her Republican parents made in Germany to explore her roots in Salamanca. Even in those instances where the exile is a foreign male—like the German documentary filmmaker in Patino's *Madrid* (1986), or the African illegal alien in Montxo Armendáriz's *Las cartas de Alou* (The Letters of Alou, 1990), or the Irish exiles from John Ford's native village in José Luis Guerin's intriguing documentary *Innisfree* (1990)—their émigré experience is linked to that of a young woman struggling to assert her identity in her homeland.[8]

The resurgence of interest in the representation of the exile can be partly explained by the recent influx of foreigners into post-Franco Spain. With borders that were closed to foreigners for centuries, Spain is now drawing immigrants like a magnet with its peaceful conversion to democracy, its economic boom, its liberal atmosphere, and its prominence in the European Community, all proudly promoted by its Socialist regime. In 1991, over 130,000 illegal immigrants regularized their status within the Community of Madrid under a special amnesty program.[9] According to *El País,* half of those foreigners came from the Third World—especially from Morocco and Black Africa, and to a lesser degree from Latin America and the Philippines. Thus, while other members of the European Community are primarily concerned with stabilizing Eastern Europe, Spain would like the organization to put more effort into the economic

In a diverse range of
post-Franco films, the exile is
associated with a rebellious
young woman, whether she is
the Spanish daughter of an
"inner" exile, as in Victor
Erice's *El sur* (The South,
1983, opposite, top); the
Spanish girl friend of a foreign
émigré, as in Montxo
Armendáriz's *Las cartas de
Alou* (Letters from Alou,
1990, opposite, bottom); or
the returning exile herself, as
in José Luis Guerin's *Innisfree*
(1990, above).

development of the Maghreb region. Although Spain is earnestly trying to cope with the social problems raised by these new immigrants (such as racism, cultural integration, and social welfare), it has little prior experience. There is a desperate need for the central government and the Community of Madrid (as one spokesman put it) "to design a global policy on immigration that is directed not only toward foreigners but also toward the indigenous population,"[10] who are once again sensitized to the issues of exile and diaspora. These issues are addressed most directly in *Las cartas de Alou.*

Although Spanish films about exile from different decades and regions focus on different aspects of the problem, it is hardly surprising that virtually all of them present a movement between personal and collective history (the traditional territory of melodrama) and a fixation on a particular moment frozen in memory—a historical primal scene that obsesses the exile both at home and abroad. What is far more surprising in this discourse on exile is the emphasis on the rebellious young woman as an agent of subversion for both cultural contexts, a connection, as we will see, that also occurs in the works of Buñuel and Borau.

THE UNIQUE CASE OF BUÑUEL   In previous chapters, I have included many references to Buñuel, weaving him in as an outside voice and comparing the subversive strategies he developed in exile with those that other Spanish filmmakers were using at home. In other words, he has been positioned in that "slipzone of indeterminacy" where he could "question, subvert, modify, or adopt . . . the structural force fields of both social systems."[11] Although he is one of the most well-known exiles in world cinema, many of the most interesting dimensions of his case have not been fully explored.

Like Spain, Buñuel is both the paradigmatic case of exile and its unique exception. His case is unique primarily for two reasons. First, although he was born in the small village of Calanda where (he reports in his autobiography) "few outsiders ever came,"[12] he himself was always an outsider who experienced many successive periods of exile extending over several decades and involving several different cultures: Paris as an international center of modernism in the late 1920s, when surrealism was a major movement; Hollywood as the center of hegemonic practice in 1930, when the conventions for the international sound film were being standardized; Paris in 1936 and then New York in 1938 as political sites for left-wing activism, where he could work on political documentaries or reedit others until being ousted by repressive right-wing forces (the German occupation of France and blacklisting in the United States); Mexico as a political and economic refuge for Spanish exiles in the mid-1940s and 1950s, where he could make commercial films in his own language; and France as the center of the European art film in the 1960s and early 1970s, where he could make films with bigger budgets, better actors, and more artistic freedom. These various periods of exile were motivated by virtually all of the reasons for which filmmakers have historically left home: to satisfy curiosity, fame, or hunger; to find a more stimulating artistic environment or better economic opportunities; to escape oblivion, censorship, harassment, political persecution, or death. His individual experience of exile represents the whole paradigm.

Such an emphasis on exile necessarily problematizes the nationality of the émigré artist and his films, particularly amid the growing complexities of international coproductions and multinational capitalism. For it makes us question what factors determine a film's nationality—the country where the production company is based or where the film is shot; the nationality of the director, producer, writer, cinematographer, stars, or other key personnel; the source of its funding; the cultural source of its subject matter and thematics; or unpredictable events in its reception. Since the nationality of virtually all of Buñuel's films is hybridized, his exile status helps to demonstrate that nationality is an ideological construct. Perhaps the most instructive case is *Viridiana* (1961). Although it is one of the few films Buñuel made in Spain (with a Spanish subject, partial Spanish financing, and a primarily Spanish cast and crew), when it was denounced by the Vatican and banned in Spain, the film's nationality changed from Spanish to Mexican—the way its director's had in 1949.

The second reason that Buñuel's case is unique is that despite his perception of himself as an outsider, he is the only filmmaker in the world who has been described (however incorrectly) as the singular embodiment not only of a major film movement like surrealism but also of two national cinemas, the Spanish and the Mexican. This is a unique situation not only with respect to cinema but also with respect to other arts such as music or painting. Although Spanish exiles like Pablo Picasso, Salvador Dali, and Pablo Casals may have been as celebrated internationally as Buñuel, none was ever seen as the single embodiment of a national art form or movement. In fact, it is much more common for exile to diminish rather than inflate an artist's prominence, as was the case with the seventeenth-century painter José de Ribera (1591–1652), who did most of his major work in Italy where he was called "el spagnoletto" and whose exile status prevented him from receiving the recognition he deserved in either country—a situation that is only now (in 1992) being rectified by a major retrospective of his work in Madrid, Naples, and New York.[13] But Buñuel was another matter.

As far as surrealism is concerned, Buñuel reports in his autobiography that his "entry into the surrealist group took place very naturally" and that his "connection with the surrealists in many ways determined the course of [his] life" (105–106). Yet he never totally overcame his initial contradictory perception of Paris—as the international "capital of the artistic world" and as the place where he most deeply experienced "the abyss between Spain and France" (79). Breton and the other surrealists loved *Un chien andalou* and immediately made him and his Spanish collaborator Dali members of their movement, but they also turned on Buñuel when that film achieved commercial success. Ironically, this is the precise moment when he says he felt his love for them and their acceptance of him most strongly, a feeling that he claims was capable of compromising his freedom as an individual (109). This dynamic helped inspire him not only to make the scandalous *L'age d'or* (The Golden Age, 1930) in

Paris but also to Hispanicize his surrealist perspective in *Tierra sin pan* (Land without Bread, aka *Las hurdes,* 1932), a unique documentary that combines surrealist conventions with the cultural specificity of Spain and with the distinctive Spanish tradition of esperpento.

Although other filmmakers were connected with the surrealist movement (e.g., Man Ray, Antonin Artaud, Germaine Dulac, and René Clair), none of them other than Buñuel continued making films in this mode throughout their entire career. And while there were later surrealist filmmakers in different cultural contexts (e.g., Jean Cocteau, Slavko Vorkapich, Alejandro Jodorowsky, and Bruce Conner), none of them was a member of the historic movement that flourished in Paris between 1923 and 1930. Thus, many film historians—even those scholars who present diametrically opposed readings of the movement (e.g., Linda Williams, who explores its connections with psychoanalytic theory, and Steven Kovács, who emphasizes its increasing political militancy)—claim that Buñuel is perhaps the "only true" surrealist filmmaker.[14]

Even though he made most of his films in exile, for many people in the English-speaking world, Buñuel is also *the* Spanish cinema. This situation is due primarily to the limited distribution and coverage of Spanish cinema, for most of the popular one-volume world history texts in English virtually omit Spanish cinema except for Buñuel and claim (or at least imply) that he is the only world-class filmmaker to come out of Spain. For example, in his influential text, *A History of Narrative Film,* David Cook devotes his one chapter on Spanish film to Buñuel, relegating the rest of that nation's cinema to a footnote, which opens, "With the exception of the work of Buñuel, that cinema has been almost uniformly undistinguished due to the repressive nature of the Franco regime."[15] Buñuel's Spanish biographer, Francisco Aranda, also supports this position in his chapter on *Viridiana,* in which he claims that even before making this film, "Buñuel's Spanish production was our only cinema worthy of the name." Insisting that "the key to Buñuel remained his *Spanishness* in the sight of the world," Aranda argues that "his return would be of special significance for those inside Spain who were struggling to give the cinema a national character," for Spanish cinema "had not yet found a national personality."[16]

Yet even Saura and Borau, those fellow Aragonese filmmakers who most enthusiastically embraced Buñuel as the model world-class Spanish auteur, displayed ambivalence when he was cited as an influence on their work. For example, as we saw in chapter 3, Saura denied he had seen *Los olvidados* before making his own first feature, *Los golfos,* and Borau rejected the term "buñuelesque" (along with "quixotic" and "goyesque") as words used by foreigners "to mask an incredible lack of knowledge of and interest in Hispanic culture."[17] Besas correctly points out that within Spain,

> opinions are split about Buñuel's influence on Spanish filmmakers and indeed whether he should even be considered a part of the national cinema. Some . . . aver that Buñuel is the most Spanish of all, . . . but the predominating opinion in Spain is that, though greatly admired, he was basically a foreign director, since he made virtually all of his films abroad and lived outside of Spain most of his life. Moreover, since most of his films were not shown in Spain, their influence was minimal on filmmakers in that country. . . . Though Buñuel maintained personal contacts with friends in Spain, he never lived there for any length of time after 1925. . . . The feeling is that he is not Spanish but universal like Pablo Picasso. (*Behind the Spanish Lens,* 50–51)

Given these Spanish attitudes, it is no wonder that the misrecognition abroad of Buñuel as the singular source of Spanish cinema aroused resentment at home. It put Buñuel in a unique position in film history, comparable only, perhaps, to that of Ingmar Bergman, who is also frequently considered to be the sole embodiment of Swedish cinema and is resented for this misperception but without the complication of long-term exile, which added a further irony to Buñuel's situation.

Even more extraordinary, a similar situation also developed in the Mexican context, where Buñuel worked in a commercial film industry (which was ordinarily difficult for foreigners to enter). In his history of Mexican cinema, Carl Mora explains that although the United States is an important foreign market for Mexican films, they have been restricted to the Spanish-language theater circuits where they are shown without English subtitles and therefore rarely reach English-speaking spectators. He concludes, "Mexican cinema, with the exception of Luis Buñuel's work, remains all but unknown in the United States."[18] That means that for most English-speaking spectators, Buñuel is also *the* Mexican cinema.

Buñuel's career of exile dialogizes the auteurist and national contexts, revealing that neither perspective is sufficient by itself.[19] His exile status has led some critics to grossly exaggerate his powers, to see him not only as the singular embodiment of a movement or national cinema but, along with Picasso and Casals, as a one-man resistance who "fought the Franco regime from afar, as did other exiles in Paris, London, Mexico and New York, gradually creating in their minds the myth of a country in which no changes ever occurred, one that remained frozen in time in 1939, eternally Fascist."[20] The problem with this vision is that it also turns Buñuel into a frozen image; it ignores the fact that although he was always subversive, he was also a powerful shifter whose meaning changed according to which particular hegemony he was working against—Francoism, Catholicism, or Hollywood. His effectiveness as an international seme of Spanishness was also recognized by the Francoist government, which both repressed and promoted this image (especially in the case of *Viridiana*). Yet it was a seme that Buñuel took great delight in contradicting. Borau cites the times "when the divine Aragonese dedicated one of his best films [*Nazarin*] to celebrating the brotherly love of a village priest and won a prize for it from the office for Catholic Cinema . . . , or when he broke his exile of so many years and returned to shoot a film under Franco, or when he burnt—so to speak—his surrealist founder membership card, or when he let himself be photographed with the cream of the Hollywood film industry, his mortal enemy, before winning an Oscar and then later claiming that he had bought it."[21]

To fully appreciate these ironies, Buñuel's career as an exiled artist must be read against an international grid, within which this array of national and auteurist discourses can be dialogized. The rest of this chapter will focus on three key issues that augment rather than repeat what others have written on Buñuel: the formative experience of his relationship to sound, the cultural continuity within his narrative experimentation in Mexico and Spain, and the way in which the French/Spanish dialectic is interwoven with other rivalries to structure his films made in France.

THE SOUND OF EXILE Buñuel's life and career have always been deeply affected by sound and its ability (like Proust's madeleine) to bring memories of alternative realities to mind, along with the feelings with which they are associated. In his autobiography, we learn that one of his earliest passions was music (he sang, played the violin, was "very enamored of Wagner" [35], and dreamed of becoming a composer). This passion distanced him from the other surrealists, most of whom, he claims, "detested music, particularly the opera" (113), and it was intensified by loss when he started going deaf in the 1950s. We also learn that some of his strongest memories were linked to the distinctive ritual sounds of his native Calanda—the daily bells of the Church of Pilar, which he associated with the village's immersion in the Middle Ages, and the communal drum ceremonies of Good Friday, which he claims affected the speaking rhythms of the villagers as well as the sound tracks of many of his own movies and to which Saura pays tribute in *Peppermint frappé* (as we have seen in chap. 4).[22]

Perhaps even more significant, Buñuel started his filmmaking career in 1928 at the precise moment when cinema was converting to sound and made his first trip to Hollywood in 1930, when the conventions of the classical sound film were being codified. These conventions would increasingly nationalize cinema and strengthen Hollywood's domination worldwide. As Buñuel observed,

When talkies first appeared in 1927, the movies instantly lost their international character; in a silent film all you had to do was change the titles, but with talkies you had to shoot the same scenes with the same lighting, but in different languages and with actors from different countries. (*My Last Sigh,* 128)

This nationalization of film had tremendous personal consequences for Buñuel, for the conversion to sound helped to destroy the French infrastructure for international modernist cinema, which had made *Un chien andalou* and *L'age d'or* possible. As Cook succinctly puts it,

> The coming of sound spelled the end for the French avant-garde cinema. The French mode of production during the twenties had been one in which a large number of small studios leased their facilities to independent companies formed to produce single films, and this method had lent itself readily to experimentation. But production costs soared with the introduction of sound because France, unlike the United States and Germany, possessed no patents for the new process. . . . But the success of American and German sound films in France . . . [made] financiers . . . eager to invest in the foreign patent rights. . . . They were able to group most existing studios into two large combines around the old trade names Gaumont and Pathé, thereby replicating the monopolistic structure of the American film industry. Hollywood and Tobis attempted to further plunder the French industry by establishing huge production facilities in the suburbs of Paris. Paramount built a vast plant at Joinville, but the quality of its mass-produced multi-lingual films fell to such a low level that the facility eventually became a dubbing studio for American-made films.[23]

Buñuel quickly responded as a modernist to the challenge posed by sound—by adding a musical track with tangos and Wagner's *Tristan und Isolde* to his silent film *Un chien andalou,* by experimenting with contrapuntal sound/image relations in *L'age d'or* (one of the earliest sound films made in France and perhaps one of the most innovative),[24] and by adding a brilliant ironic voice-over (co-written with Pierre Unik) to his Spanish surrealist documentary, *Tierra sin pan*. Nevertheless, he soon was employed in American dubbing facilities, working for Paramount in Paris at Joinville in 1933–34 (where he learned English), for Warner Brothers in Madrid in 1934–35 (where he supervised the dubbing operation), for the Museum of Modern Art in New York between 1939 and 1945 (where he both dubbed and reedited Spanish versions of documentaries), and for Warner Brothers again in Hollywood (as producer and administrative head of the Spanish dubbing department) in 1944–45. In fact, he spent most of that fifteen-year period (from 1930 to 1945, the mysterious gap in his canon) mastering the conventions of the sound film (particularly within the flexible international genre of melodrama), which enabled him to subvert them more effectively once he returned to directing. This was particularly important since from the 1940s through the 1960s he would be making most of his films in Mexico and Spain, where sound technology was technically inferior to that of Hollywood and where conceptual experimentation in sound was therefore all the more essential.[25] A similar conceptual compensation helps explain why, after he had gone completely deaf, he credited himself for "sound effects" in *The Discreet Charm of the Bourgeoisie* and *The Phantom of Liberty*.

Describing his first trip to Hollywood in 1930, Buñuel claims he was paid $250 a month by MGM to "stay six months . . . and learn how to make a movie, . . . [to] learn some good American technical skills" (128). What he actually studied were the narrative conventions of melodrama, performing a structuralist analysis that seems worthy of Lévi-Strauss.

I devoted myself to a bizarre document—a synoptic table of the American cinema. There were several movable columns set up on a large piece of pasteboard; the first for "ambience" (Parisian, western, gangster, . . . etc.), the second for "epochs," the third for "main characters," and so on. Altogether there were four or five categories, each with a tab for easy maneuverability. What I wanted to do was show that the American cinema was composed along such precise and standardized lines that, thanks to my system, anyone could predict the basic plot of a film simply by lining up a given setting with a particular era, ambience, and character. . . . It became such an obsession that Ugarte, who lived upstairs, knew every combination by heart. (132)

Buñuel tested his theory one night after seeing a sneak preview of Josef von Sternberg's *Dishonored* with the film's producer. Insisting that Sternberg was "notorious for basing his movies on cheap melodramas," Buñuel told the producer that "five minutes into it, I knew [Dietrich would] be shot" (132). To prove his claim, he summoned his friend Ugarte, told him only that the ambience was Viennese, the epoch World War I, and the main character a whore, and Ugarte responded, "Don't bother with any more. . . . They shoot her at the end" (133). Buñuel realized that whether he ended up working in Hollywood or Europe, the way to subvert those conventions of the classical sound film was to reinscribe them ideologically for a different cultural context.

For a brief period (starting in 1935 when he was dubbing films for Warner Brothers in Madrid and ending in 1936 with the outbreak of the Civil War), Buñuel worked for Ricardo María de Urgoiti at Filmófono (a Spanish company originally founded as an importer and distributor of foreign art films), where he produced and at least partially directed four early Spanish sound films: *Don Quintín el amargao* (Embittered Don Quintín, 1935), *La hija de Juan Simón* (The Daughter of Juan Simón, 1935), *¿Quién me quiere a mí?* (Who Loves Me? 1936), and *¡Centinela alerta!* (Look out, Sentry! 1936).[26] He accepted this position only on the condition that his name would not appear in the credits. Although Roger Mortimore ascribes political motives to this provision of anonymity, Urgoiti claims Buñuel merely wanted to protect "his *avant-garde* reputation."[27] Clearly, it gave him the freedom to make a crucial experiment, to see whether he could integrate some of the subversive strategies of his avant-garde works into a new form of commercial cinema with broad popular appeal and whether he could adapt the new sound conventions of Hollywood melodrama that he had been studying at close hand to

Luis Buñuel's early sound films at Filmófono included the melodrama, *Don Quintín el amargo* (The Embittered Don Quintín, 1935).

Spain's newly emerging sound cinema and home market. Sound facilities were not built in Spain until 1932, with the first sound film being made in 1933, which meant that Buñuel came in practically at ground zero.

From the standpoint of melodrama, the most noteworthy film of this period is *La hija de Juan Simón,* an adaptation of a play by Nemesio M. Sobrevila, which was based on a song that had been popularized in Spain by flamenco singer Angelillo. In *My Last Sigh,* Buñuel dismissively calls it "a horrendous musical melodrama" but also duly notes that it was "a big commercial success" (144). Yet Enrique Herreros, who was Filmófono's publicity director at the time, claims, "Even if filmgoers don't recognize it, the Surrealist spirit and Buñuel's own black humour are everywhere in the film."[28] Although the directorial credit is given to Sáenz de Heredia (who also fronted as director for Franco's *Raza*), he acknowledges that the real director was Buñuel.

> I went to the Roptence Studios and had the position explained to me by one of the composers, Remacha. He said that I would be in charge of shooting on the set but that the real director would be Buñuel. I said that I would be pleased to do this because I wanted to learn how to direct. . . . The first scene I shot was a dance by Carmen Amaya. . . . Every day before shooting I would see Buñuel and he would tell me exactly how he wanted each scene shot. I supervised the shooting on the set. In the evening Buñuel saw the takes, and he did all the editing. He also had a hand in the script. Although he didn't interfere in the actual shooting, it was he who made the film.[29]

Mortimore reports that the film "opened simultaneously in fourteen cinemas in Madrid, a move which appalled orthodox distributors: for the first time a new film could be seen the same day in a smart cinema and in a cinema in a working class area. The film was extremely popular, the sales of the music alone paying for its making" (182). According to Aranda, the film was also successful in Latin

America and continued to be shown in Spain after the Civil War and was even remade in 1958 by Gonzalo Delgras (113). Thus, Buñuel clearly demonstrated that he could please a mass audience, but the question was, could he still retain his surrealist edge (as Herreros claims) within this new commercial sound format.

One way the film experiments with sound is by using it to introduce subjective inserts (such as the sounds of a fair that initiate one of the heroine's flashbacks), a technique that Buñuel had earlier used more radically in *L'age d'or* (where interior monologues obstruct the physical consummation of the lovers and where disjunctive animal sounds—a tinkling cowbell and a barking dog—bathetically rekindle the heroine's animal drives) and that he would later exploit more fully in *El angel exterminador* (1962), and *Belle de jour* (1966).

Though its plot is very similar to that of *La aldea maldita*, *La hija de Juan Simón* features the flamenco stereotypes of the españolada in place of the social context of urban migration.[30] Buñuel's male lead was Angelillo, whom he describes as "the most popular flamenco singer in Spain." He also claimed that "the female star was a novice named Carmen Amaya, a young gypsy who went on to become a famous flamenco dancer" (144). Actually, Amaya plays only a minor role as a seductress, yet she is the film's primary agent of subversion. The sequence in which she uses her seductive dancing to frame the hero for the murder of her oppressive pimp is clearly the best in the film and the one that most fully displays Buñuel's controlling hand in integrating sound and image (particularly since the relatively inexperienced Sáenz de Heredia reports this was the first scene he shot).

This long sequence opens with an interior long shot of an Andalusian café, displaying the exaggerated sensuality of its mise-en-scène, a vaginal composition of a double-arched cavelike opening. Designed by playwright Sobrevila (who was also a distinguished architect), the sets are as excessive as those in *El* and (according to Aranda) were considered "outstanding among Spanish film design of the period."[31] The camera slowly glides into the room, as if drawn in by the sexuality of Amaya, who dances while Angel drinks at a table. In one key shot, we see a fragmented detail of the room's adjacent double arches, which look like a woman's cleavage. Thus, it is not only Angel who is captivated by her body in motion and drawn into song by her fiery dance but also the camera, mise-en-scène and montage. Her body is fragmented by shots of the top half of her torso, which are rhythmically punctuated by fetishized close-ups of her feet.

Although these cinematic choices objectify her as the erotic object of the male gaze within a patriarchal symbolic order, she uses her exhibitionistic performance to subvert that very structure. At a particularly passionate moment, the rose drops from her hair and her tresses fall loose—stylized gestures (like those in a similar scene from *Muerte de un ciclista*) that become inscribed as the iconography of gypsy melodrama and that are pushed to the point of parody. Most excessive are the series of successively tighter facial close-ups as she becomes more sexually focused on Angelillo, pursuing her own desire. When Amaya's pimp becomes jealous and provokes a fight with Angelillo, she signals a friend to turn off the lights, as if she were the director controlling both the mise-en-scène and montage—and stabs her oppressor in the back. When the lights return, her pimp lies dead and all the extras have fled, leaving Angelillo, the soloist, artfully framed and poised to take the rap. Aranda perceptively observes, "Unable actually to dignify an unpardonable genre, Buñuel chose instead to exaggerate it, to accumulate its most awful conventions in order to carry the style to a kind of delerium. . . . In asking her to exaggerate a style that was already in itself an exaggeration, [he] laid the foundations of the dancer Carmen Amaya, later famous" (108, 110). No wonder Buñuel remembered her as the star and considered this dance sequence "the best thing in all his work at Filmófono" (Aranda, 110).

From the standpoint of sound, the most important film from the Filmófono period is *Don Quintín, el amargao.* One innovative sequence actually narrativizes the new sound technology by making it the primary focus of the action. As café patrons sing along with a phonograph record of a popular song that mocks the temperamental Don Quintín, the camera cuts from one singer to another, reflexively calling attention to the technical process of synchronization and playing with the comical mismatch of body and voice. When Don Quintín enters the café, the owner quickly turns on the radio to drown out the offensive song, but the radio broadcasts the same tune. Not only is this coincidence essential to the humor of the scene (which ends with the impetuous Don Quintín smashing the phonograph record, once he discovers what it contains) but it also acknowledges the historical connection between the newly emerging talkies and the existing sound media of radio and the recording industry—a connection that has only recently been theorized by Amy Lawrence in *Echo and Narcissus: Women's Voices in Classical Hollywood Cinema.*

In another key sequence, where two stepsisters are lamenting their oppressive lives with their abusive father, one leafs through popular magazines, fantasizing about becoming "the Spanish Greta Garbo" or "the Spanish Marlene Dietrich"—the glamorous European stars who succeeded in Hollywood's melodramatic talkies of the 1930s with their sexy voices. This is a fantasy that also appealed to Buñuel, as we have seen, and one that he would return to in his last film, *Cet obscur objet du désir* (That Obscure Object of Desire, 1977), a rival version of the von Sternberg/Dietrich Hollywood melodrama, *The Devil Is a Woman* (1935). No wonder, then, that *Don Quintín* is the only film from the Filmófono period that Buñuel would later remake in Mexico, changing the title to *La hija del engaño* (The Daughter of Deceit, 1951).

CULTURAL CONTINUITY AND NARRATIVE EXPERIMENTATION IN MEXICO AND SPAIN

Aranda observes that as a Spanish exile in Mexico, Buñuel did not have to overcome a foreign language or culture.

Not only the idiom and the race, but the physical types, the dry and dusty landscape, the impassioned speech, the attitudes to life and death, the religious problem, the social structure which he attacked, all combined to restore him to conditions in which he could be himself. From the very first film his personality and his *Spanishness* were engaged, while he observed, understood and analysed the idiosyncrasy of the Mexican people with a greater profundity than any of the cinèastes who had preceded him. (130)

Although Buñuel also noted this cultural continuity, it was forged by a painful colonialist past, whose legacy still can be detected in Aranda's condescending tone.[32] Although many of Buñuel's Mexican films present stories and characters that could easily be transposed to Spain (and sometimes say so in the text),[33] they tend to emphasize the legacy of that colonialist history through an emphasis on class— from the abandoned children in *Los olvidados,* whom Buñuel refuses to sentimentalize, to the trapped haute bourgeoisie in *Exterminating Angel,* the class he subjected to the severest irony and to which he himself belonged.[34]

Although many of his best Mexican films suggest a strong parallel with at least one of the films he made in Spain, there is usually a pivotal inversion of class or gender, two registers that are frequently combined (or opposed) in his texts as agents of subversion. For example, despite their obvious differences, both *Exterminating Angel* and *Land without Bread* are ensemble films where characters are divided between insiders and outsiders (the guests trapped inside the mansion versus the servants locked outside, or the Hurdanos who are trapped in poverty versus the visiting bourgeois narrator who comments on their misery). In both cases, a woman—the Virgin who performs a ritual of repetition or the poor old woman ringing the death bell—arouses some hope of liberating the insiders. Though the insiders at first seem to be the only ones who are trapped, the films eventually reveal that the outsiders (and by extension, we spectators) are caught in the same social structures on a larger scale. Yet the insiders in the Spanish film are poor, whereas the insiders in the Mexican film are rich—an ironic inversion of expectation when set against the colonialist past. Moreover, though deeply surrealist, both films present a surface style and genre (comedy of manners or documentary) that seem transparently realistic. Both works also function as prophetic parodies of genres whose popularity was to come—the disaster film and the ethnographic film, respectively.[35] This is an irony that extends the temporal absurdities and distortions beyond the boundaries of the texts.

As many other critics have observed, *Nazarin* and *Viridiana* can also be seen as a pair, since both deal with the ironic disillusionment of a good samaritan (a former priest or novice) who sincerely tries to aid the poor and whose religious passion arouses erotic desire in others less devout. The connection is strengthened by having Francisco Rabal, the Spanish actor who was Nazarin, also play the sardonic materialist cousin who finally triumphs over Viridiana, as if his prior experience playing a Spanish priest in that Mexican adaptation of Galdós is the reason for his cynicism. There are other ironic inversions: whereas in the Mexican picaresque narrative the do-gooder is a celibate who wanders through the countryside in a state of abject poverty, relying on the charity of others and inadvertently breaking a strike, the Spanish tale is a religious melodrama confined to the bourgeois family estate, where two heirs (the corrupt modern cousin and the feudal Viridiana) represent the two sides of Spain, fiercely opposed over how to make the best use of their patrimonial legacy. Here the beggars are grotesque rapists and thieves who are treated with the comic detachment of Spanish esperpento.

Despite vast differences in tone and production values, *Ensayo de un crimen,* aka *La vida criminal de Archibaldo de La Cruz* (The Criminal Life of Archibaldo de La Cruz, 1955), and *Tristana* (1970), an adaptation of a novel by Galdós, are both ironic discourses on fetishization, in which the titled character is a stunted child who becomes fixated on an object associated with sex and murder—little Archie's music box that is playing when his governess is accidentally shot to death and Tristana's nightmare image of the phallic bell clapper that is transformed into her guardian's decapitated head. The traumatic events associated with these fetishes turn these lost innocents into killers. In both cases, the most eroticized object is a woman's leg: in the former, a wax leg that is slowly and graphically burned in a fiery furnace; and in the latter, a real leg that is amputated and fetishized through lack (causing Alfred Hitchcock to repeatedly sigh, "Ah, that leg, that leg").[36] While Archibaldo is an empowered member of the bourgeoisie and a successful ceramist, as a Bluebeard he is impotent, for he never succeeds in killing any of his intended female victims before they die by other means. Conversely, as a subordinate female, Tristana's association with the art world depends on her lover (a successful painter) and (since she is a poor relation) her membership in the bourgeoisie depends on her patriarchal guardian, who deflowers her and whom she ultimately marries and murders. As in *Viridiana,* the issue of patrimonial legacy is central—for Don Lope as well as for his young ward. The inversion of gender gives far more social resonance to *Tristana,* as does the ironic parallel with the subversive maid Saturna and her deaf son Saturno, who parody the relations between the mutually devouring Don Lope and Tristana on a different class register.

Finally, there is *El* (literally He but known in English as *This Strange Passion,* 1952), which evokes the strongest parallels not with a film made in Spain but with *L'age d'or,* since both films center on un amour fou (one in the context of surrealism, the other in commercial melodrama), which flowers in the garden of an elegant mansion during an elegant party and which results in the gentleman's erotic frustration and jealousy being displaced onto violence. Both include servants, who start disturbances in the closet and whose outrageous behavior (the seduction of a chambermaid or the killing of a son) elicits absurd responses from the bourgeois masters (the firing of the maid or mild curiosity). Both are framed with a prologue and an epilogue, which mock the church and which "play [an] . . . erotic 'trick' on religion by using it as [an] aphrodisiac." Both narratives are marked by radical ruptures and ellipses, which are associated with "sexual/social transgressions."[37] Yet while *L'age d'or* works intertextually with Sade's *120 Days of Sodom, El* adapts a novel written by a woman, Mercedes Pinto, and plays with the melodramatic conventions and masochistic aesthetic of the woman's film.

Although these films made in Mexico and Spain appear much more conventional on the surface than Buñuel's earlier and later films made in France, the best are deeply subversive. Advancing the project started in *La hija de Juan Simón,* they make a much bolder adaptation of the surrealistic strategies to commercial melodrama and simultaneously introduce virtually all of the main lines of experimentation that Buñuel would explore in the later French films of the 1960s and 1970s.

I will concentrate on three texts—*El, Viridiana,* and *Tristana*—to demonstrate how in all three, the Hispanic patrimonial legacy is subverted by a young woman, who (like Amaya in *La hija de Juan Simón*) temporarily captures control of the narrative and the camera's point of view. Most attention will be devoted to *El,* because it is the most radical and excessive of the three and also the least written about and also because (as we have seen in chaps. 4 and 5) it had such an important influence on Saura and Bigas Luna.

El can be read as a case study of a paranoid schizophrenic, who (Buñuel claims) is studied like an insect and with such precision that Jacques Lacan is reported to have used this film in his classes to illustrate this mental disorder. Yet the madness is presented not merely as the perversion of a lone individual but rather as the product of repressive institutions that Spain and Mexico have in common—Catholicism, the patriarchal family, feudal class divisions, and machismo.

Don Francisco (Arturo de Córdova) is obsessed both with his wife Gloria (Delia Garcés), of whom he is insanely jealous and on whom he projects his paranoid fantasies and fears, and with regaining his grandfather's land, which was lost during the Mexican revolution. Thus, his madness can be traced to a series of losses, which can be read on different registers: history (Spain's loss of its empire in the New World), biography (Buñuel's loss of his fatherland), Lacanian psychoanalysis (Francisco's fear of castration that he displaces onto his wife, literally trying to sew up her vagina), and epistemology (the loss of reason and distortion of perception, with which both the characters and spectators are threatened). As a manic depressive, Francisco experiences wild swings between delirious optimism and abject feelings of impotence. In his struggles with the law, he calls on his wife to charm a young lawyer (which evokes the Oedipal conflict and justifies his insane jealousy) and also to write a letter for his case (which leads him to resent his infantile dependency on the maternal and her intrusion into the symbolic order). Yet these excesses are hidden behind a false persona of the perfect Catholic gentleman, which only she can penetrate. Blaming the lawyer for his loss of property (both his land and his wife), Francisco is overwhelmed by frustration, which is converted into violence; he tries to kill Gloria by throwing her from a bell tower (a scene that probably influenced Hitchcock's *Vertigo*). After finally driving her away with his insane violence, he returns to the church, which has structured his desire through repression, and attacks the performing priest (his close friend and father confessor), demonstrating that the church has always provided a theater of displacement.

Fetishization (both of the erotic and religious varieties) is central to this drama. For it functions as a means both of disavowing the hero's losses and of suturing together the film's two rival discourses of personal and colonial history. Silverman helps explain why he becomes so obsessed with Gloria when she observes, "The motivating desire behind conventional fetishism [is] to inscribe lack onto the material surface of the female body, and in so doing to construct a fetish capable of standing in for all those discoveries and losses suffered by the male subject in the course of his cultural history."[38]

The two discourses of eroticism and colonialism are masterfully combined in the brilliant opening sequence, which dramatizes both the genesis and perversion of Francisco's l'amour fou and its dependence on fetishization. It takes place in a church during Holy Week, where Christ's passion becomes the sadomasochistic model for all eroticism, a dynamic clearly understood in Spain and its colonies. Performing the traditional foot-washing ritual, a Europeanized priest leans down to kiss the foot of a young androgynous peasant of Indian descent, who wears a wanton expression on his sensuous mouth; the camera moves in to a homoerotic close-up of the kiss, fetishizing not only the foot but also the close-up and camera move. Consistent with the conventions of the Counter-Reformation, the ritual is highly specularized. The theatrical space of the church contains a mass

In the opening sequence of Luis Buñuel's *El* (This Strange Passion, 1952), a Europeanized priest leans down to kiss a peasant's foot in a close shot that fetishizes the foot, the kiss, and the close-up.

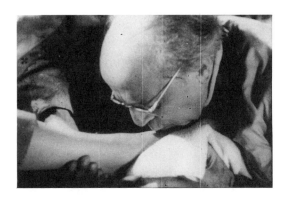

The androgynous peasant wears a wanton expression on his sensuous mouth.

In several shots the mass audience in the church entirely fills the frame, specularizing the ritual.

Don Francisco (Arturo de Córdova) discreetly turns his eyes aslant.

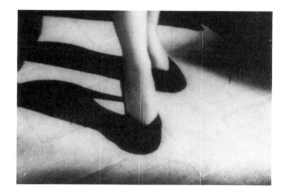

Don Francisco's perverted gaze is captivated by a pair of black pumps.

audience, which sometimes entirely fills the frame and which is clearly mesmerized by the visual spectacle and choral chanting of the ritual. This specularization also suggests an analogy with cinema (particularly in the silent era), which also uses erotic spectacle and music to structure patriarchal desire.

The effect of this fetishistic ritual is immediately demonstrated when we see Don Francisco discreetly turning his eyes aslant, and a reverse shot sutures us into his perverted gaze as it slowly moves along a line of well-heeled feet, until it is captivated by a pair of black pumps that (like the humble Indian kissed by the priest) become the object of his conquest. He pans up from the feet to Gloria's lovely face and is instantly smitten. In this chain of fetishization, the shoes do not stand in for Gloria but vice versa; both substitute for a former object of desire, the Holy Virgin, whom Francisco has been trained to worship (and with whom he later explicitly compares Gloria); and the Madonna, in turn, is an authorized fetish for his mother, his original object of desire. When later describing this magical moment of "love at first sight," Francisco proclaims, "It's a love nurtured from infancy!" The mass is presented as a realm of the imaginary in which no words are spoken, forcing Francisco to express his love only with his eyes. (Later, on his honeymoon, he will attack an imagined rival by poking a knitting needle through the keyhole he imagines him to be spying through, as if eyes were an erogenous zone). When Francisco follows Gloria outside the church in hot pursuit, he is awakened from his erotic reverie by the church fathers, who break the silence with a line that dampens his spirits and deflates the dogma: "If it's important, then a Christian has no business doing it." The narrative then turns to conventional melodrama—until the next major rupture. Thus, this opening sequence is like a germinal dream (or historical primal scene) out of which the rest of the film is spun; it is as resonant for the ideological discourse as for the obsessive romance.

During the courtship and conquest that follow, we adopt Don Francisco's point of view, though we are presented with an omniscient narrative that seems to be "naturalized" as the truth, as in conventional Mexican or Hollywood melodramas. Yet several disjunctive perceptions provoke a surrealistic tremor: when Francisco goes to see his rival, Gloria's fiancé Raoul, at his engineering office, the sign under his name reads, "S.A.D.E., c.v."; at the dinner party to which Francisco invites Raoul, Gloria, and her mother, he quips, "I'll make love to the mother"; when an exchange of erotic looks between Francisco and Gloria reaches a sexual climax, a loud noise comes from the closet, where the butler is desperately trying to find a lost object; although the priest claims that Francisco's father designed and built this Gaudiesque house "that is an expression of pure feeling," a few moments later Francisco tells Gloria it was built by

In *El*, Francisco lives in a gaudiesque house with theatrical drapes that evoke a proscenium arch.

his grandfather (a contradiction that warns us there is a problem with Francisco's patrimonial legacy).

The most noticeable ruptures are disjunctures between sound and image. The first instance (the scene in which Francisco spies on Gloria and Raoul in a restaurant) begins with what looks like an ordinary interior two-shot of the couple facing each other across the table, but when they begin to speak, we cannot hear what they are saying. Then the camera pulls back, revealing a curtained window through which Francisco is shown watching the scene. We realize that the camera is not positioned inside the restaurant as we had first assumed (without necessarily thinking of camera position at all) but outside with the voyeur. Moreover, the curtain evokes the proscenium arch in theater and is part of the pattern of theatrical sets that recur through the film (from the opening church ritual to many shots of similar drapes in Francisco's art deco house), which gives the whole melodrama the feeling of staged fantasy. Thus, the rupture on one register (sound) leads to the acknowledgment of other enunciative agencies (camera position, camera movement, and mise-en-scène). Yet these discursive marks do not prevent us from perceiving the psychoanalytic level, of Francisco reenacting the primal scene in this love that was "nurtured from infancy"; in fact, they facilitate it by displaying the dynamics of visual pleasure. Later, in the dinner party sequence, a disjuncture of sound and image recurs, only this time we see a shot of Francisco and Gloria through the window. The formal repetition positions Francisco to replace Raoul as the lover and us spectators to replace Francisco as voyeur. Much later, when Francisco's paranoid delusions take over, these disjunctures of sound and image (and jump cuts) are recoded as madness.

The film's major rupture comes with conquest, with Francisco and Gloria's first kiss, which (like the foot-kissing ritual in the church) is represented by the camera rushing in for a close-up. But this time the kiss is followed by a big bang, which not only comically stands in for the orgasm but also explodes the narrative. The explosion occurs at a dam site, where Raoul is apparently working, but only after hearing confusing dialogue about his reluctance to return to Mexico City do we realize that a major temporal ellipsis has occurred. Then after a second ellipsis, we see Raoul driving in city traffic and nearly running over Gloria, who at first tries to flee and then reluctantly enters his car. These narrative disjunctures are so extreme that the first time I saw the film, I thought that the projectionist had put on the wrong reel.[39]

Raoul's car functions as a narrative vehicle that introduces a shift in mode (as it had earlier, in carrying Gloria away from the erotic revery in the church into the low mimetic reality of domestic melodrama, and as it will again later, in transporting Francisco into his paranoid fantasies about Gloria's imagined elopement with Raoul). In this instance, the shift is in point of view (from an omniscient narrative focalized on Francisco to Gloria's first-person account told to Raoul in flashback), gender (from his to her version of the romance), genre (from romantic melodrama to a woman's film like *Gaslight*), and narratee (from anonymous spectators whose presence is not even acknowledged to a prejudiced spectator-in-the-text). Within her inset narrative, we witness Gloria and Francisco competing for credibility with other narratees (her mother and his confessor, who are spokespersons for the patriarchal family and church, respectively); but these spectators prove to be as prejudiced as Raoul, who represents the competing institution of romantic love.

Even though we narratees are positioned (along with her former lover) to believe and identify with Gloria, her account is peppered

In *El* Raoul's car functions as a narrative vehicle that introduces the shift to Gloria's first-person flashback.

with incongruities that force us to recognize it as another fictional construct. For example, in the representation of the scene in which Francisco beats her, what we see is not the violent encounter but the butler being awakened in his room by her screams, which Gloria could not possibly have seen. In another scene, Francisco shoots her at point blank; then the film cuts back to the car, where Gloria tells Raoul, "Don't worry, I didn't die, it was only blanks," perhaps evoking Billy Wilder's use of a dead narrator in *Sunset Boulevard*. Through such absurdities, the inset narrative blatantly problematizes the issue of point of view. Once the tale reverts back to third-person omniscience, we can no longer take it as the "truth" and are therefore prepared for Francisco's hallucinations.

Gloria's narrative also contains formal oppositions that go beyond its borders and thus belong to the enunciation of the whole text. For example, a contrast is established between the close-up (which eroti- cizes the object of the gaze) and the overhead long shot (which is associated with Francisco's fantasies of infantile omnipotence, espe- cially when he tells Gloria on their honeymoon that they make everything look "clean and pure" and when, just before trying to push her off the tower, he observes that they make people look like "insects who should be squashed"). This dialectic helps intensify and politicize the film's major narrative rupture, when the extreme close-up of Francisco and Gloria's kiss is followed directly by an

The overhead long shots in *El* become associated with Francisco's infantile fantasies of omnipotence.

equally extreme overhead long shot of the dam site, in which the jilted lover Raoul and his anonymous workers are reduced to the size of ants.

Another formal dialectic is between the straight line and the zigzag, a figure that is introduced in the flashback to the wedding night on the train, where an almost imperceptible "z" is momentarily created by the brief superimposition of the two trains going in opposite directions and where it is linked to Francisco's wild swings from aggressive accusations to abject pleas for forgiveness. It recurs more blatantly in the powerful scene in which, after a violent encounter with Gloria, Francisco zigzags halfway up the staircase, then sits down in despair, grabbing a bar (which is briefly shown in a fetishized close-up) and then beating it with a masturbatory rhythm against the bannister, as if desperately pursuing the pleasure principle to make his anxiety cease. When the camera pulls back to an extreme long shot of his small huddled figure and the pace of the beating accelerates, he is transformed into a savage or animal performing a primitive ritual, perceptions that bring to mind both Freud's essay, "A Child Is Beating Beaten," and Buñuel's description of the drums of Calanda.

In the final image of the film, after the visit of Gloria, Raoul, and their son to the monastery where Francisco has sought quiescence,

When the paranoid Francisco peers into a shop window in Luis Buñuel's *El*, he evokes a similar shot from Fritz Lang's *M*.

In the final shot of *El*, Francisco zigzags his way down a path toward the monastery, whose black doorway looks like a gaping mouth ready to swallow him.

the penitent in his robe zigzags his way down a primrose path toward a low building in the background whose black doorway looks like a gaping mouth. Although the head monk has discouraged the visitors from seeing the disenfranchised Francisco ("Why lay bare old wounds?") and has assured them, "His faith will be a shield against reality," the zigzag confirms that he is as mad as ever and that his castration fears were justified, particularly now that he has has been totally swallowed by the church. He has lost not only his land and his wife but also his son (whom Gloria has named Francisco and whom, when pointedly asked by the Father Superior, Raoul refuses to acknowledge as his own). Yet Francisco persists in seeing that child as tangible proof that his paranoid jealousy was justified, unaware that he is passing on his own loss of patrimonial legacy to the next generation.

More subtly, the zigzag also evokes the Gaudiesque arabesques of Francisco's family mansion, a structure that contains no straight lines and that seems to have helped shape him as a schizophrenic subject. Yet linearity is as suspicious as the zigzag, for it is merely a form of secondary revision that smooths over primary process eruptions and that "shields" subjects against psychic and political reality—whether it is Francisco's aspirations for perfection, his love of symmetry, his refusal to relinquish his patrimonial inheritance (which was only partially overthrown by the Mexican revolution), or his story's linear plot (which is only periodically disrupted by surrealistic jolts). Finally, the zigzag functions as a figure for the whole film (like Henry James's "figure in the carpet")—one that is appropriate for this wildly humorous, manic-depressive narrative, with its delirious swings between omniscient and subjective points of view, between close-ups and long shots, between secular and sacred settings, between an erotic and a colonialist discourse.

In Buñuel's two Spanish features, *Viridiana* and *Tristana,* the narrative experimentation is much subtler. In *Viridiana,* the subversiveness appears to lie more in the sacrilegious content and images, particularly the parody of the Last Supper, which led to its being attacked by the Vatican and subsequently censored in Spain. Thus, very little attention has been paid to the narrative. In the case of *Tristana,* even though it has been called by Aranda "the most Spanish film of Buñuel" (242), both the form and the content were widely perceived to be fairly conventional and realistic, which led to a lukewarm reception in Spain.[40]

Interestingly, although Buñuel emphasizes that both of these films are totally "Spanish," foreign actresses are cast in the title roles: Mexican actress Silvia Pinal as Viridiana and French star Catherine Deneuve as Tristana. Despite his claims in the case of Deneuve or insinuations in the case of Pinal that these actresses were foisted on him by his producers (see Aranda, 193 and 239), their foreignness (like Amaya's "Otherness" as a gypsy) gives an additional edge to the characters' status as eccentric outsiders, who try to take over the narrative. This dimension is also intensified by having both characters adopted and corrupted by a Spanish patriarch, who is played in both films by one of Spain's best-known actors, Fernando Rey.

In *Viridiana,* the most extreme instances of a female capturing the gaze are performed by characters from a lower class than Viridiana. The maid's daughter (a wild, high-spirited girl who plays with a jump rope) spies first on the religious masochistic rituals of Viridiana and then on the erotic rituals of Don Jaime. This double specularization underscores the parallel not only between these sacred and profane acts but also between these rituals and her own acts of voyeurism and play. In the latter instance, the girl watches Don Jaime kissing Viridiana, who has been dressed in the wedding dress of her aunt (who died on her wedding night) and then drugged into a state of unconsciousness that stands in for death (just as the kiss substitutes for rape). Thus, the girl's initiation into the forbidden knowledge of sexuality (whose mythic dimension is underscored by her having to climb a tree to reach the optimum vantage point) encompasses the most extreme taboos of incest and necrophilia and involves the complicity not only of the patriarch who kisses and perhaps performs the rape and of her own mother, Ramona, who helped him dress and drug Viridiana for the deflowering but also the victim herself, whose own masochistic rituals seem to have prepared her for this sacrificial role.

When this scene is read against other texts from Buñuel's canon, the young girl prefigures the young victim in *Diary of a Chambermaid* (1964) who is brutally raped and murdered by a Fascist servant and who inspires the title character to seek revenge both against the killer and against the entire patriarchy. When read against what is to come in *Viridiana,* this violation sets off a chain of repercussions: the patriarch's suicide (in the same tree that the girl has climbed and with her jump rope, which becomes a fetish like Viridiana's crown of thorns), a death that imposes his patrimonial legacy (both his property and his corruption) onto his niece; Viridiana's renunciation of the convent and of her feudal vision and faith; a second attempt to rape

Viridiana, this time by one of her beggars who uses the same jump rope to hold up his pants; and the seduction and leveling ("in the dark all cats are gray") of both Viridiana and the girl's mother by Don Jaime's bastard son.

The child's act of looking gains even greater resonance when read against the third subversive moment of female spectatorship, which takes place during the parody of the Last Supper. Enedina (one of the beggars, played by Lola Gaos, who is even more raggedy than Ramona's daughter) mockingly pretends she is photographing the sacrilegious scene. Then she lifts up her dress exposing her naked genitals (which she calls the instrument "Papá gave me"), substituting this spectacle for the phallic camera and thereby performing a sex change on both the fetishistic cinematic apparatus and its referent. Her defiant act appropriates and conflates both sides of the gaze—voyeurism and exhibitionism, which are traditionally gendered male and female, respectively.

Thus, this obscene gesture marks the moment in the film that is most subversive on several registers: religion, class, gender, and cinematic enunciation. It also evokes the earlier acts of voyeurism performed by the young girl, whose spirited play with the jump rope and precocious knowledge may enable her to grow up to be another Enedina. In all three of these moments, carnal knowledge destroys illusions, particularly when the female controls the gaze, a dynamic that prefigures Viridiana's final shift in perception.

Tristana is the story of a young girl who (like a combination of Viridiana and Ramona's daughter) is shaped as a subject by her precocious knowledge of sexuality. Though she is sexually initiated by her libertine guardian Don Lope while she is still an innocent young girl, she already has had an erotic fantasy in which his head replaces the phallic bell clapper in the church tower. The problem for her (and for us) is how to read her sexual experience. For not only is their incestuous relation exploitive but it also transforms her into a sexual subject who is capable of pursuing her own desire—a liberty not ordinarily granted to a woman under patriarchy. Yet once she accepts the conventional attitude toward their incestuous relation, she rejects her seducer and seeks revenge. In some sense, she is as corrupted by this shift in reading as by the sexual relation itself.

One of the most interesting things about the film is that despite its apparently "realistic" surface, the narrative is highly elliptical (especially concerning motivation) and the characters extremely inconsistent. Not only does this lack of coherence encourage spectators to fill in the gaps by projecting their own fantasies and values onto the text but it also serves the interests of those patriarchs who designed it. As Don Lope tells Tristana, "I am your father and your husband, and I can be one or the other as and when it suits me."

In one crucial scene, in which Tristana goes for a walk with the maid Saturna (also played by Lola Gaos, the actress who was Enedina in *Viridiana*), the two women reach a crossroads in the twisting streets of Toledo. When they learn that a rabid dog is loose and that the guardia civil are in hot pursuit, Saturna decides to follow the action, but Tristana chooses to take the other path, which leads to a different genre (bourgeois romance rather than lowlife picaresque adventure). She wanders along until she happens upon a scene where a handsome young artist is painting a portrait of a Catalán. Amazingly, he and his artistic gaze (which is focused on his male model) become the object of Tristana's erotic gaze. This double specularization establishes a set of choices, like the forked paths. In this instance, the camera (as well as the editing) privilege Tristana's control over the scene (rather than the artist's), as a subject pursuing her own desire and narrative. Later, this young man Don Horatio will offer her an alternative to her life with Don Lope—as young bohemian lovers (rather than an incestuous couple) living in Paris (rather than Toledo), where she will develop a different form of resistance and illness, which will lead to the loss of her leg (rather than her virginity.) Thus, ironically, as in *Exterminating Angel,* this new liberating path proves to be merely another version of the original trap. Even here in the scene of their first meeting, we are reminded that an absent enunciator stands outside of Tristana's narrative, for the film intercuts between the two alternative episodes—the scene in which Tristana sees the young man Don Horatio and the episode of the mad dog that Saturna follows as a spectator. What is most fascinating is that in intercutting between these two episodes, we miss the dramatic climax of both—the shooting of the dog and the crucial part of the conversation between Tristana and Horatio—just as, in moving between these two men, Tristana ends up rejecting both. This double ellipsis of the two climaxes resonates with the earlier crucial scene, in which Don Lope and Tristana have sex for the first time, but, much to our frustration, the camera, narrative, and we spectators are locked outside the room with the family dog.

In the film's most notorious scene, Tristana (after having lost one of her legs) stands on a second-story balcony, propped on her crutches, and calls to Saturno (the deaf-mute son of the maid) to watch as she opens her kimono and exposes her deformed body. Like Enedina in the most subversive moment in *Viridiana* (and Amaya in *La hija de Juan Simón*), Tristana appropriates and conflates both sides of the gaze—the exhibitionism that invites and controls the male gaze and the voyeurism that studies his response. Her counterstare is so intense that it makes Saturno draw back so that he can masturbate in private. In contrast to classical Hollywood melodrama, rather than merely serving as the passive site of projection for "the male subject's castration, . . . specularity, exhibitionism and narcissism,"[41] Tristana uses this subversive "display" of her body to force men to confront their own deformity, impotence, and lack. In both *Tristana* and *Viridiana*, not only is the erotic spectacle of the female body subverted by grotesquery but its symbolic identification with "lack" is parodied through exaggeration (by being explicitly inscribed with the lack of other fetishistic substitutes for the phallus—a leg and a camera). Clearly the lack is not restricted to the female gender but is shared equally by all the disempowered males, not only by the mute servant Saturno and Enedina's fellow beggars but also by the impotent bourgeois patriarchs and their young replacements. In this particular scene in *Tristana*, the deaf male voyeur is literally as deformed as the female object of his gaze. Thus, these two stunted children of different genders and classes provide a mirror image for each other that is centered around loss—of innocence, language, and phallic empowerment.

Like *El, Tristana* is totally structured around loss but much more subtly. This dynamic also occurs in characterization, for the more contradictory qualities the characters acquire, the more the distinctions between them are erased—not only between Tristana and Saturno or Tristana and Don Lope but also between her two lovers. For example, Don Lope is presented as the aging libertine who lavishes more care on his beard as he ages, narcissistically admiring it in the mirror and combing and dying it, as if fetishizing it in compensation for his waning sexual powers. Later, Don Horatio's growth of facial hair is used as a key sign that during the two-year ellipsis when Tristana is living with him in Paris, he is becoming a younger version of Don Lope. These changes are never developed or explained. Like the tumor and gangrene that grow in Tristana's fetishized leg and necessitate its amputation, the facial hair becomes a symbolic substitute for a psychological explanation that could account for her growing domination over Don Lope and Don Horatio and for her growing sexual and emotional estrangement in both relationships. The choice of a beard is particularly clever, since, as we have seen, its iconography is so ubiquitous in Spanish cinema, yet in this context, it is used as an empty signifier—like Hitchcock's Maguffin. On the narrative level, these fetishized body parts stand in both for the waning power of the phallus (which is repeatedly brought to mind by the recurring nightmare of the bell clapper and its replacement by Don Lope's bearded decapitated head) and for the absence of continuity and motivation in a highly elliptical story whose inconsistent characters verge on incoherence. This incoherence would be pushed much further in the final phase of Buñuel's narrative experimentation in France.

THE ABYSS BETWEEN SPAIN AND FRANCE   When Buñuel first went to Paris in the 1920s, he claimed that "the abyss between Spain and France widened with every passing day" (*My Last Sigh*, 79). When he returned to Paris in the mid-1960s and 1970s as a famed international auteur to make his final glossy masterpieces in Eastmancolor, all co-written with his French collaborator Jean-Claude Carrière, he bridged that abyss with a cross-cultural dialectic that helped to structure his films. Even his career was artfully framed by these two periods of voluntary exile in France, which helps explains why there are such striking parallels (as Williams has persuasively argued) between his first and last two pairs of films.[42]

During this final phase of artistic exile, although Buñuel was already deaf, he was still experimenting with sound-image relations, only now instead of introducing a subjective space of memory or fantasy that was identified with a specific character, disjunctive sounds tended to represent an alternative discourse that was suppressed from the narrative. The competition between sound and image was frequently related to an analogous rivalry between the discourses of sex and politics, which competed for control over the narrative, image, and sound tracks. Rooted in the surrealist concept of l'amour fou (a mad love so extreme that one is willing to destroy all bourgeois values to pursue it) and in the movement's early attempts to synthesize Freud and Marx, this dialectic between sex and politics runs through Buñuel's entire canon, yet the competition between these two discourses becomes much more intense in his last three films, made in Paris, where they are further complicated by being interwoven with the dialectic between Spain and France.

The two nations represent competing cultural and linguistic grids against which sensory perceptions (both sounds and images) are read; they narrativize percepts and thereby anchor their meanings in quite different ways, performing a cultural secondary revision that is also provided by master narratives (such as the Oedipal myth) and conceptual frameworks (such as Freudian psychoanalysis, Marxism, and Catholicism), with which they overlap. One of Buñuel's most characteristic strategies is to force his spectators to shift abruptly from one of these grids to another, which is analogous to the kind of shift an exile must make when moving from one culture to another (or that a filmmaker must make when moving from silent to sound cinema). Such shifts demonstrate that any particular framework is neither natural nor inevitable but ideological and arbitrary. It is merely one framework among many others that has been selected from a paradigm of paradigms, and to make this point, Buñuel's subversive texts (in contrast to Hollywood classical narratives) pointedly reveal the whole menu of choices. Another way he initiates these subversive shifts is by making the percepts so disjunctive that they cannot be incorporated into a conceptual framework without seriously compromising its coherence or without threatening the whole symbolic order. This struggle between conceptual frameworks and renegade perceptions was central to *Exterminating Angel* (made in Mexico in 1962), where disorienting repetitions of dialogue and images ultimately lead to the total breakdown of civilization.

The Spanish-French dialectic first emerges in *Belle de jour* (1966),[43] where the character Hyppolite (played by Francisco Rabal, the Spanish actor who had played the Spanish priest in *Nazarin* and the seductive cousin in *Viridiana*) sings gypsy songs in Spanish, as if to foreground his nationality. Hyppolite is a father figure to the young French anarchist Marcel, who is played by Pierre Clementi (consciously evoking the gangster hero of Godard's French new wave classic, *Breathless*). Though Rabal's Spaniard is a minor character, he brings Marcel to the Parisian brothel, where the perverse Severine (Catherine Deneuve) is working incognito as Belle de Jour. He generously turns her over to his young protégé (even though he fancies her himself), boasting, "I'd have slit my father's throat for less, but friendship comes first!" When she disappears from the brothel, he is the one who tracks her to her bourgeois home base and gives the address to Marcel. Even though Hyppolite brings these French lovers together, he evokes the Spanish version of the Oedipal narrative, where the relationship between father and son is more important than the desire for any woman. He also reminds us that Spain is the historic source for anarchy, particularly as a political force.

Belle's erotic experiences are full of French literary allusions, for erotic fantasy thrives on intertextuality. For example, the Madame's name Anaïs evokes the erotic narratives of Anaïs Nin, the visit from the masochistic judge is reminiscent of Genet's *The Balcony,* and the impersonation of the Duke's dead daughter brings to mind Sade's *120 Days of Sodom* (as well as Buñuel's earlier allusion to this text at the end of *L'age d'or* and the violation of Viridiana in the bridal gown of her dead aunt).

Belle's encounter with the Duke is the most subversive in the film in terms of sex (in acting out incestuous necrophilia and finally "letting the cats loose") as well as on the registers of religion (he calls it "a religious ceremony") and class. While Belle finds the rejection of her bourgeois class position and its restrictive morality to be a turn-on and becomes most enamored with the lowlife Marcel, in the episode with the Duke she is the social inferior, who is mistreated accordingly by the aristocrat's misogynist servant. Thus, sexual fantasy is represented as a social drama that requires subject positions to be cast with figures carefully selected from the appropriate paradigms of gender, sexual orientation, class, race, physical type, and so on. Earlier, in the gynecologist's masochistic fantasy, Belle is temporarily miscast in the role of punishing mistress (because she also yearns to be mastered by "a firm hand"), but she is perfect in the role of the Duke's incestuous daughter—a part for which she has been trained by a whole string of patriarchs.

The key issue appears to be selection, for the brothel is repeatedly described as a structure in which men choose among women and in which women have no choice at all. Clearly the Duke has chosen Belle, and he even has his servant tell her (as Marcel will do later) that "those who preceded you would like to be in your place." Yet in Buñuel's texts, freedom is always a phantom; the issue is therefore reformulated as who created the fantasy, a question that is avoided in most Hollywood classical melodramas, where the marks of male enunciation for women's bourgeois fantasies usually are suppressed. It is the foregrounding of this question that makes the encounter with the Duke so subversive on the narrative plane. Not only is it the only erotic episode that is consummated outside the brothel (implying that she is entering his rival sadistic aesthetic where he wields a camera rather than he entering her masochistic realm of the imaginary run by women where she looks through a peephole) but it is also the one that unravels the previously accepted boundary between fantasy and reality. Although the Duke recruits her for this encounter from an elegant open-air restaurant, which we at first think belongs to her "ordinary" bourgeois life but which she confesses she visits "every day in [her] thoughts," she is carried to his château in the horse-drawn coach (consistently introduced by the sound of horses and bells), which has previously functioned as the narrative vehicle for *her* subjective reveries of escalating punishment. But with the Sadean

Duke ("a man from another epoch . . . where people still had a feeling for death"), punishment and sex are totally fused. And with this fusion, the whole narrative begins to unravel.

The unraveling first takes us back to the preceding sequence in the brothel, where the bulky Asian customer with the mysterious black box succeeded in ringing Belle's bells and in nearly replicating (with the maid's innocent blonde daughter) her fond childhood memory of being molested by a plumber of similar build. Ultimately, the unraveling embraces the whole narrative, for we perceive that the fantasies are structured like a series of Chinese boxes: the Duke's sadistic ritual is positioned inside Severine's chain of erotic daydreams, which are, in turn, positioned within Buñuel's cinematic fantasy that is tellingly framed by the image of the coach and its Pavlovian bells (a sound that is paired in the opening with a whistle of a train that is nowhere in sight and at the end with the loud meowing of "those damned cats" who are never seen or explained). Moreover, the director's presence as male enunciator is actually acknowledged on screen, for just before the Duke approaches Belle in the restaurant, Buñuel appears in the center of the frame sitting at a table on the terrace, that staging point for the film's erotic fantasies.

Thus, in this sequence, our attention is displaced from the story to its enunciation—the discursive means through which the story is told. It will take the introduction of a new pair of mysterious characters—the dope dealers Marcel and Hyppolite, with their French/Spanish dialectic—to draw us back into the plot. But in all of Buñuel's subsequent films made in France, our attention remains primarily focused on the discourse.

La Voie Lactée (The Milky Way, 1969) is a subversive road movie made in the wake of May '68, a theme that would recur in all of Buñuel's subsequent films. A pair of pícaros of different generations (a variation on Marcel and Hippolite) make a pilgrimage from France to Spain. The film opens with the image of a map, the camera panning down from Paris to northern Spain as a male voice-over gives a historical explanation of "The Milky Way"—a road taken by over 500,000 pilgrims annually since the eleventh century to the shrine of St. James in the city of Santiago de Compostela. This prologue suggests that the film will be a documentary or historical docudrama, a premise that is still viable when the film cuts to a montage of modern freeways and highways in France but that is promptly subverted when the two fictional pilgrims encounter another traveler on a deserted country road.

Acting like an angel of capitalism ("He who has no money shall have none; . . . he who has some, shall have much"), a demonic figure in a Spanish cape commands the two French pilgrims to go take "a wife of whoredom" who will bear them two sons, whom they should call "You are not my people" and "No more compassion" (names that are especially resonant in the context of Spanish exile). As he departs, a dwarf and a dove mysteriously appear at his side (as if parodying the Holy Trinity). After his departure, the young pilgrim Duval (a student activist) tells his elder Christian companion Dupont, "He liked your beard. It inspires confidence." This remark reminds him of what his mother used to say and leads into a flashback. But instead of seeing Dupont's personal memory, what we see is a parodic version of Holy Scripture, where Mary tells Jesus, "Don't shave, my son, . . . you look wonderful in a beard." Obviously, this incident parodies the Spanish iconography of beards, which can be found in most of Buñuel's films,[44] perhaps most notoriously at the end of *L'age d'or,* where the bearded Duke de Blangis, who doubles as Christ and Sade, returns to the screen sans beard, after having murdered his final female victim.[45] In both instances, Buñuel calls attention to how different groups represent religious experience, an issue that was central to the Counter-Reformation (whose legacy still survives in Spain) and that is also the central focus of the catalog of heresies in *The Milky Way.*

In the representation of these heresies, there is virtually always a competition between word and image. A prologue originally designed to introduce the film (part of which is retained in the closing credits) suggests it may be a docudrama after all:

Everything in this film concerning the Catholic religion and the heresies it has provoked, especially from the dogmatic point of view, is rigorously exact, except for error on our part. The texts and citations are taken from the Scriptures, modern and ancient works on theology and ecclesiastical history. . . . Throughout the film, apparitions, miracles and accounts of miracles will be treated with the utmost seriousness, in accordance with the traditional representations given by the Church, without any spirit of deformation.

Deformation occurs, nevertheless, for the visual and narrative contexts (who speaks them, in what setting, with what effect) change the connotative meaning of the words, frequently making them absurd. One of the best examples is the student recital at the Lamartine Institute where the prologue of religious intolerance and its chorus of "anathemas" are rendered comical through the incongruity of the ambience (a festive bourgeois picnic), epoch (1969), and characters (a chorus line of pampered little girls in uniform), especially when the performance is intercut with Duvall's visions of student demonstrators executing the pope and with an exemplum from the Spanish Inquisition.

The dialogic encounter between the two generations of pilgrims and their respective historical imaginaries reflects the mutual influence between Buñuel and Jean Luc Godard and between the politicized surrealist and French new wave movements.[46] Buñuel's pilgrims carry the rebellious visions of May '68 back to Francoist Spain, which in 1969 was still immersed in the kind of Catholic orthodoxy being parodied, yet the French student movement of the 1960s also had things to learn from Hispanic culture. When discussing *The Milky Way* in his autobiography, Buñuel explicitly compares the French students to the surrealists, observing they had "the same ideological themes, the same verve, the same schisms and romance with illusions, and the same difficult choice between words and actions," but then he adds,

Like me, the students talked a great deal but did very little. . . . I told myself that if this had been happening in Mexico, it wouldn't have lasted more than two hours, and there would surely have been a few hundred casualties to boot, which is exactly what happened, of course, in October on the Plaza de las Tres Culturas. (125)

In *The Milky Way,* the student terrorist begins to be an important figure, no longer merely a romantic gangster like Marcel but part of a culturally specific historic movement, whether in France, Spain, or Mexico.

In *Le charme discret de la bourgeoisie* (The Discreet Charm of the Bourgeoisie, 1972) the French/Spanish dialectic at first appears to be insignificant. Hispanic culture is limited to Miranda, the fictional Latin American republic, which is represented by a corrupt ambassador, an émigré played by Buñuel's favorite Spanish actor, Fernando Rey. The name Miranda itself designates an elevated place that commands a prospect view—a perspective that is visualized when the ambassador shoots at the pretty student terrorist from the second-story window of his embassy and that is associated with the kind of privileged overhead long shot so coveted by Don Francisco in *El* because it reduces all other people to insects who can be crushed. Similarly, in Miranda, we are told, student activists are swatted down like flies. Thus, the political discourse on student terrorism is deftly transferred from French to Hispanic culture, which is underscored when the ambassador tells his female captive, "¡Adios, muchacha!"

The French/Spanish discourse reaches its climax at the colonel's party, where a catalog of stereotypical insults concerning Latin American corruption leads the ambassador to insult the French army, which provokes a fatal duel with his French host. This event proves to be merely a dream, yet (as in *Belle de jour*) the identity and nationality of the dreamer of this chain of interlocking dreams remain mysterious. Since the Hispanic ambassador (despite his elegant demeanor) functions as the less civilized Other and Miranda as a foreign imaginary dystopia where all charges of political corruption can be displaced, we might conclude this is a French fantasy, yet Fernando Rey is the last to awaken. Clearly it is a hybrid, a cross-cultural dream of multinational corruption spun by an exiled Spaniard (cum Mexican) and his French collaborator as well as by the dominant ideology in Western culture that is the object of their satire.

The competition between sound and image is directly related to the suppression of political discourse in this film. Virtually every time there is a political discourse (e.g., the pretty terrorist's speech quoting Mao that proves he does not understand Freud and the minister's explanation of why the police must release the charming bourgeois dope dealers), it is drowned out by some familiar urban noise (traffic, a typewriter, or a plane passing overhead) that is foregrounded in an aural close-up. To make sure that spectators realize the suppression of this information is intentional, the censorship is repeated. Our attention is also constantly drawn to the visual surface—to the gorgeous clothes worn by the beautiful women, to the luxurious furnishings of the elegant interiors, to the glossy color of the film's lush style (which is so uncharacteristic of Buñuel's earlier periods), all of which we are invited to savor *avec plaisir,* a line that recurs in the dialogue like a musical refrain. Thus, in contrast to Hollywood classical cinema where all choices are naturalized, here the spectator is constantly made aware of the implications not only of what is included but also of what is excluded both from the visual and audio tracks (e.g., the sex scene between the married couple hidden behind the bushes, the scars of the unfaithful wife concealed behind her organdy blouse, the soldier's train dream that we do not have time to hear, or the reasons that the poor woman hates Jesus). As a result, despite the emphasis on repetition, it is always impossible to predict what will happen next.

The film repeatedly demonstrates that cultural expectations are crucial for contextualizing the reading of signs—an issue that is introduced in the opening scene when the guests first notice that their host's fire is unlit and the table unset and that is extended to the issue of narrative enunciation when the rebellious young sister-in-law seems to notice the cinematic frame that substitutes for the missing "fourth wall" of the set. In a later scene, when a restaurant's menu offers coffee, tea, and milk, its patrons naturally expect those options to be accessible, and the violation of these expectations proves to be far more disturbing to the bourgeois consumers than adultery or patricide. In fact, the violations represented in the film range from a minor breach of etiquette (gulping a martini) to murder and revolution.

Cultural expectations also shape the reading of a film's narrative and generic conventions (like the ambience, epoch, and main characters from Buñuel's synoptic table). To exert some control over spectator expectations, Buñuel repeatedly uses repetition to force them to recognize functional differences—whether it is the central organizing structure of the recurring dinner parties, which are always interrupted by unpredictable events related to sex, death, or dreams, just as they are socially bound to feature a change in menu; or the subtle variations in the recurring picaresque image of the bourgeois characters walking down a highway, scenes that coherently divide the film's narrative into three discrete sections (although they lack narrative coherence themselves); or the more blatant differences in the film's array of mini-Oedipal narratives, which all center on generational conflicts in scenes that are darkly lit and that contain strange ambient sounds (including church bells) but with shifting thematic emphases that gradually politicize the violence. The emphasis shifts from patricide (in the lieutenant's childhood memory of poisoning his stepfather to avenge his mother) to incestuous desire (in the soldier's dream of reuniting with his dead mother) to class conflict (in the bishop's deathbed shooting of the murderer of his parents, a humble gardener whom they mistreated) to overt political action associated with May '68 (in the cries of the student activist who was tortured by the police). As with his own experience of exile or his charting of Hollywood conventions in his synoptic table, Buñuel tends to display the whole paradigm, or as Barthes puts it, "to extend a paradigm onto the syntagmatic plane," a form of "semiotic transgression" around which "a great number of creative phenomena are situated."[47]

In *Le fantôme de la liberté* (The Phantom of Liberty, 1974), this "extension of a paradigm onto the syntagmatic plane" controls the entire structure of the film. From the opening sounds and images, we are made aware of the menus from which each sign is selected. It is not merely a matter of whose fantasies are represented but who is making the choices and combinations and in which national context (Spanish or French)—a question that must be raised not only

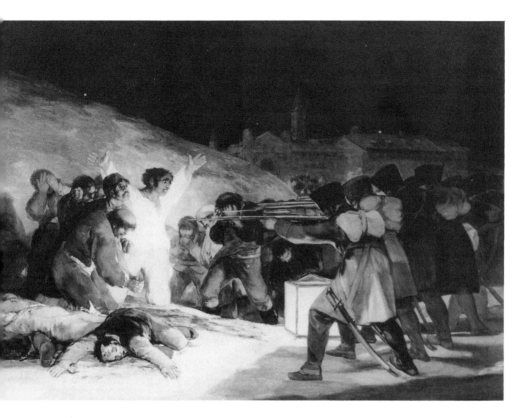

Buñuel's *Le Fantôme de la Liberté* (The Phantom of Liberty, 1974) opens with a still image of Francisco de Goya's *El 3 de Mayo de 1808 en Madrid* (The Third of May 1808 in Madrid), one of several signs that the film's artistic roots lie in Spain. Museo del Prado, Madrid.

on the levels of biography, psychoanalysis, and production but also on the registers of language, culture, and ideology, as the professor makes explicit in his lecture to the police.

Even before the film begins, we are presented with a printed statement acknowledging the fictional status of the characters that is followed (in the American version) by the logo for its Hollywood distributor 20th Century Fox, which reveals the economic dimensions of its multinational enunciation. The film itself opens with reminders of its artistic roots in Spain and its political roots in a historical discourse of French/Spanish rivalry: a still image of Goya's painting, *The Third of May*, over which is added first the contrapuntal sounds of church bells and gunfire and then a printed title that reads, "The action of this film begins in Toledo, in 1808, during the occupation of the city by Napoleon's troops. Inspired by a tale by Gustavo Adolfo Bécquer, a Spanish romantic poet." When we move to a live-action dramatization of the execution, we probably expect to see a historical film about the Napoleonic invasion of Spain, but we are unsure whether what is being represented is a dramatization of the painting, the literary tale, or the historical events they depict, an array of choices that foregrounds the issue of representation. We are also soon confronted by two incongruous percepts, which can easily be missed or misconstrued: the visual presence of Buñuel himself, dressed as a monk, among the captive Spaniards (an authorial presence who is immediately killed off) and the incongruous cry from one of the dying Spaniards (foregrounded in a close-up), "¡Vivan las caenas!" (literally, Long live the fallen!), which is translated "Down with freedom!" in the English subtitles, which means precisely the opposite. Although the Spanish version of the published screenplay gives the line as "¡Vivan las caenas!" a footnote acknowledges, "The original screenplay specifies: ¡Vivan las cadenas! [Long live chains!] is a famous cry in Spain. It was uttered by the multitude in Madrid when King Fernando VII returned, after the abdication of Napoleón.'"[48] Thus, the screenplay is apparently as contradictory as the film.

When the drama moves inside the church where a sacrilegious

French officer is about to kiss the statue of a beautiful dead Spanish señora, the genre shifts from history to romance; and when her stone consort strikes the offender, the blow marks another shift to the Gothic subgenre and also serves as a cue for an intrusive female voice-over that begins to narrate the bizarre events. When the French officer retaliates against the jealous statue by exhuming the corpse of the woman (whose face is miraculously preserved "fresh as a rose" by "the mysterious hand of death"), the body of the female narrator is also revealed by the mysterious hand of the editor—a disclosure that transforms the voice-over into a voice-off. The Toledo tale is abruptly displaced by a contemporary Parisian scene where two dowdy women sit on a park bench, one reading to the other.

The subversive power of this narrative rupture is intensified by the issue of gender, since (as Mary Ann Doane and Silverman have observed) disembodied voice-overs are usually exclusively male, and the female voice is usually synchronized with the image so that it can remain closely identified with (and thereby subordinate to) the spectacle of the female body.[49] Thus, the classical conventions are simultaneously exaggerated (by pairing the female voice with the miraculous spectacle of the exhumed corpse) and violated (by temporarily withholding the body of the female narrator). Moreover, in this subversive instance, the woman's voice leads us into the next disjunctive episode where the two women are discussing the word "paraphernalia," which one defines as "the personal property of a married woman," observing that the meaning is broader in England than in France and thereby revealing the cultural constructedness of these gendered conventions. Like the voice-over, this kind of intellectual semantic discussion is rarely assigned to women, particularly from this class and culture.

The reader is played by the same actress who was the woman who hated Jesus in *Discreet Charm,* but unlike that character or the student terrorist from *Miranda,* she is allowed to make her inset story heard because its subversiveness seems to be limited solely to the formal narrative plane. But in the narrative segment that follows, when she turns out to be a maid who is unfairly dismissed by her employers, the "Foucaulds" (whose name, despite the variant spelling, evokes the well-known French philosopher Michel Foucault), she also voices a class discourse about punishment, power, and property. She belongs to the paradigm of maids (frequently played by the same actress) who are mistreated by perverted bourgeois families in Buñuel texts (perhaps most pointedly in the Mexican *El* but most pivotally in the French *Diary of a Chambermaid*) and who thereby help insert a political discourse of class conflict into what otherwise looks like a psychoanalytic tale of erotic perversity.[50] Like all of the characters in this movie (and to a lesser degree in *Tristana*), she operates not as a realistic representation of a well-rounded individual or unified subject but as a set of narrative functions that need not be coherent.

By presenting this menu of contextualizing frameworks (which are conventionally used to anchor the meanings of raw percepts) and by extending this paradigm of paradigms onto the syntagmatic plane (whose linearity is emphasized by an almost compulsive attention to transitions), Buñuel undermines the stability of all meanings. As Suleiman observed in the most insightful reading of this film yet published, "The narrative of *Phantom* is more linear, not less so, than that of 'normal' narrative; but it is this very excess of linearity that constitutes the narrative's 'abnormalcy,' its madness."[51]

There are several instances in the film where the array of paradigms is actually dramatized in a visual figure (like the zigzag in *El* or the forked paths in *Tristana*). The best example occurs in the inn, which has a long tradition as a reflexive stopping point (or chapter break) in Spanish narratives that can be traced back to *Don Quixote* and picaresque fiction. Here the several rooms off the hallway provide a perfect visualization of the mini-stories that compete for control over the narrative. Doors repeatedly open and slam shut as characters rush in and out of the main hallway—and the foreground of the main narrative. The camera can choose to follow any of these characters into a separate room and tale. Or, switching to the figure of a card game (also prominently featured at the end of *Viridiana* and after Severine turns her first trick in *Belle de jour*), it can shuffle and deal them into ingenious syntagmatic combinations. For example, at the inn, a prayer meeting turns into a poker game, in which the players (one woman and four Dominican monks) and the chips (Medals, Virgins, and Sacred Hearts) make us realize that all the characters and their perversities can be similarly categorized into suits (Dominicans or Franciscans; masochists or sadists; incestuous aunt and nephew substituting for incestuous mother and son). Even the spectators are chosen with care, for although practically everyone is recruited as the audience for the whipping of the masochist by his maitresse, these performers (like Buñuel) clearly prefer to outrage the monks. The paradigms also interweave the dialectics of sound/image and Spain/France, especially when a Spanish flamenco dancer and guitarist in one room provide the erotic background music for the incestuous French couple down the hall.[52] Characters can also reject a musical track for their erotic encounters, as when the masochist rudely shuts the gypsies' door or later when the police commissioner who loves Brahms's "Rhapsodie" objects to the "canned music" in the bar.

The process of choosing from a paradigm is also dramatized in casting, particularly when more than one character is playing the same role—a strategy that would be developed much further in *That Obscure Object of Desire*. In *Phantom,* it first occurs when the incestuous middle-aged aunt played by Helene Perdriere is replaced by a young Danish model in the shot where she displays her nude body to her nephew. Her body is as miraculously preserved as that of the dead señora earlier exhumed from the tomb, making them members of the same paradigm.

The prime instance, however, is the doubling of the police commissioner, after the character whom we have quite naturally accepted in this role is arrested as an imposter. He is played by Julien Bertheau, the same actor who was the bishop in *Discreet Charm,* where his identity as patriarchal official was also compromised when he changed into the gardener's outfit. The "authentic" police commissioner is played by Michel Piccoli, the actor who was cast as minister of the interior (with a similar suit, palacial office, and corrupt agenda) in *Discreet Charm.* When the two commissioners confront each other in a symmetrical two-shot, they face each other in a mirror relation, affably compare notes on the role they are both playing, and then plan the next scene—the police crackdown on the student demonstrators at the zoo. The striking similarities in their costuming, demeanor, and repressive ideology indicate that the key point is to determine not which of them is the "real" commissioner but what characteristics make both of them belong to the same paradigm.

The process of choosing a single option from a paradigm is also frequently dramatized. Once we realize how the narrative works, we are always guessing which object or character will serve as a transition into the next episode. Sometimes we are surprised, particularly in the sequence of the sniper, when we follow the anonymous customer rather than the bootblack's dog, who is privileged by the dialogue and camerawork. The sniper and camera lead us to an empty high-rise, where together they choose the floor, room, angle, and victims for his crime. The sniper's rifle is compared to the camera, for both are represented as powerful phallic instruments (wielded only by men) that select their victim with a viewfinder before shooting. Frequently, we are presented with shots that include several potential targets, so that we are positioned to identify with the sniper's point of view and to predict who will be hit next. This camera/gun analogy is further reinforced when we see a tourist photographing the violence. The depiction of the violence is not graphic; in fact, as soon as we see the first drop of blood (a moment that is specularized when a passerby stops to look and touch it), the power relations switch gears. Suddenly the point of view and narrative are captured by two policemen, who aim their rival phallic apparatus, a pair of high-powered binoculars, at the sniper, trapping him in an iris. Ultimately, the camera proves to be the true pícaro, whom we follow from shot to shot.

As in *Discreet Charm,* we are made aware of what is omitted from the narrative. It is presented as if it were merely a question of "artistic choice," even when what is omitted is beyond representation—like the police chief's "astonishing" explanation of how the little girl (who was never really lost) was found, or his dead sister's explanation of "the true mystery of death."

The film also confronts us with contradictions between our perceptions and narrative coherence and, as in *Exterminating Angel,*
mocks any attempt to devise an explanation that will reconcile these
incongruities, as in the cases of the little girl who is allegedly missing
and of the sniper who is found guilty and then promptly freed.
Sometimes it is a matter of inverting the cultural coding of antonyms,
for example, reversing which end of the digestive process is repressed
(eating instead of shitting) or casting police in the role of rebellious
students reading leftist journals. Other times it is a matter of which
channel is privileged in the representation, as in the case of the final
massacre at the zoo. Though we see the police led by the two
commissioners, the only signs of the students are the sounds of
the violence (again paired with church bells) and the same cry of
";Vivan las caenas!" that we heard in the opening (again incongru-
ously translated "Down with Freedom!"). What we *see* of the demonstration is only a sweeping pan that reduces the action to a blur
and incongruous close-ups of the caged animals who (like the pigeon
shot by the sniper along with his human victims) are cast in the same
paradigm as the students. These aural repetitions not only signal
narrative closure, but also categorize the French police with the
Napoleonic soldiers and the student activists with the fallen Spanish.
No wonder Buñuel took credit for the sound effects.

In *Cet obscur objet du désir,* the whole narrative constantly shifts
between two paradigmatic choices—not only between Seville and
Paris as ambience and between Carole Bouquet and Angela Molina
as the mysterious character Conchita in a discourse on France and
Spain but also between psychoanalysis (which dominates the narrative frame and story) and a rival political discourse of terrorism and
class conflict (which subverts this story of l'amor fou from the
margins and background with explosive incidents and sounds). There
is also a competition between Buñuel's radical text and the nineteenth-century French novel it adapts, Pierre Louÿs's *La femme et le
pantin* (The Woman and the Puppet), whose title was based on a
Spanish painting by Goya and which is another French exploitation
of the well-known españolada stereotype popularized in Spain. And,

of course, there is the additional rivalry with von Sternberg's Hollywood adaptation of the same novel, *The Devil Is a Woman* (1935), where (as in the loathed *Dishonored,* 1931) the femme fatale is played by Marlene Dietrich.[53] This opposition may have inspired Buñuel to perform his most explosive parody of those Hollywood conventions he had so carefully charted and studied in the 1930s.

Those critics who have offered perceptive psychoanalytic readings of the film tend to ignore the political level entirely. For example, Williams treats the bombings solely as a parody of orgasm and dismisses the political level "because there is no political program to these terrorist acts" (193), and Paul Sandro claims that the acts of terrorism are mere "background noise" that "threaten the telling of the story" (150). Yet neither satisfactorily explains why this strain of terrorism is so persistent throughout Buñuel's French films, where it is usually the political explanations that are drowned out by "noise," or why it finally appropriates the foreground in the final image. Nor do they satisfactorily explain why the Parisian dwarf psychiatrist in the frame (the privileged narratee for Don Mateo's erotic tale) is a visualized pun on shrink. To read this or any other Buñuel text solely in psychoanalytic terms, I would argue, is to seriously shrink its meaning.

From the sound of the flamenco guitar and the image of the Andalusian palms behind the opening credits, we know this text is rooted in Spain, even if the protagonist books a train to Paris in the very first scene. Almost immediately our attention is drawn to the issue of class by one of Buñuel's perceptual incongruities. After Don Mateo clearly asks for a "second-class sleeper," the ticket clerk asks, "You said first class, didn't you?," to which he emphatically replies, "Yes!" Nothing more is said about this contradiction, but later we see him board a second-class train, then throw a bucket of water from the window of a first-class car onto Conchita, who promptly boards a second-class sleeper.

As in *El* and *Tristana,* there are several "structuring absences" that are at least as important as what is there—for example, the omission of any explanation for why there are two Conchitas or what is in

Mateo's burlap bag; the lack of sexual consummation, which sustains his desire; and the omission of the scene of violence that substitutes for sexual fulfillment. Moreover, the film fetishizes this absence, not only in the celebrated image of the woman in the shop window darning the bloody hole in the white lace garment but also in the comic scene in which Mateo and his friend sit in a restaurant, staring at the empty chair that signifies Conchita's absence. The political discourse is similarly fetishized by being restricted to the background, allowed only to erupt in six terrorist events (and several more allusions) that punctuate the erotic episodes. Although these explosions may function metaphorically as orgasms, half of their targets are cars or planes (which, like the train in the frame, are visual puns for the narrative vehicle).

Conchita also uses her recurring absences to inflame Mateo's desire, yet her character remains as mysterious and inconsistent as the terrorists. Besides her double casting, her dual names (the idealized Concepción versus the sensual nickname Conchita), and her dual Franco/Hispanic nationality, she incarnates an array of paradigmatic female figures from Buñuel's whole canon, including the dubious virgin, the deceptive whore, the rebellious young woman, the good daughter, the sexually precocious young girl, the "undesirable alien," the flamenco dancer from the españolada stereotype that the French imposed on the Spanish, the mistreated maid, and the student terrorist. The cultural specificity of the terrorists and of Conchita's class position fluctuates with the changes in casting and nationality, changes to which Mateo is totally oblivious, yet she always remains "obscure" in the double sense of "ambiguous" and "humble." In contrast, he is consistently the bourgeois gentleman, no matter what outrage he performs. Thus, his stable class identity enables him to indulge his erotic tastes and to buy a young girl from her mother (as if she were a trinket).

As in *Bilbao* (and in contrast to *El, Viridiana, Tristana,* and *Belle de jour*), the narrative never presents the woman's point of view (which is rendered virtually impossible by the double casting). Thus, the subversive female voice is suppressed along with the political discourse. Yet, as in Bigas Luna's film, Don Mateo's story of erotic obsession is clearly bracketed, for it is put in a comical frame that exaggerates coincidence, shrinks the psychoanalytic paradigm, throws cold water on sex and violence, restricts its audience to the bourgeoisie, and is finally exploded by the political subtext it suppresses at its own peril.

Such bracketing is one more strategy of the exile that enables Buñuel to position his subversive texts in that liminal slipzone between Spanish and French cultures, between sexual and political discourse, between sound and image, between surrealism and commercial melodrama, between the margins and the center.

BORAU *ON THE LINE* OF THE
NATIONAL/INTERNATIONAL INTERFACE

> Steinbeck would be nothing without American weapons. I think the
> same is true of Dos Passos and Hemingway. If they had been born
> in Paraguay or in Turkey, who would read them now? A country's
> power determines who the great writers are. As a novelist Galdós is
> often on a par with Dostoevski, but who has heard of him outside of
> Spain.

This quotation from Buñuel's autobiography, *My Last Sigh* (222),
is the epigraph to an essay called "Without Weapons" by fellow
Aragonese filmmaker José Luis Borau. Significantly, the essay was
published in a special issue of *Quarterly Review of Film Studies* (Spring
1983) on "New Spanish Cinema" edited by Katherine Singer Kovács, which was the first book-length study of Spanish cinema to be
published in the United States. In defense of exile, Borau's essay
argued that by making films abroad (even as a Mexican citizen),
Buñuel contributed far more to Spain's international stature than he
would have if he had stayed at home in Spain.

> It is not all that clear that if you go away you stop helping your peo-
> ple. Did Picasso hurt Spain or Miró undermine Catalonia in any
> way by leaving? . . . Could anyone say that about Buñuel, even

though he changed his nationality? On the contrary, aren't they the best proof in the world (and maybe the only one aside from the bullets and blood of the Civil War) that we Spaniards are still alive and breathing? Would it have been better if they had stayed home? . . . Who would have recognized the importance of their contributions? Whom would they have helped?[1]

More important than defending Buñuel (who hardly needed any defense in 1983), this essay was justifying Borau's own decision to make *Río abajo* (literally translated Downstream but titled in English *On the Line*, 1983–84) in an artistic exile of his own choosing, the final realization of a lifelong dream of working in Hollywood that was soon to turn into a nightmare. As Borau put it, when I interviewed him in Los Angeles in June 1985,

Ever since I was a child, I always loved movies—films by Fritz Lang, Alfred Hitchcock, John Ford. I wanted to do a film here. I thought it would be possible. I came here eight years ago. I bought a house. I brought the money from Spain, but it was a long, long suffering. It took more than five years of my life.[2]

Although *Río abajo* has been considered by many Spaniards (including filmmaker Victor Erice, critic Antonio Lara, and former general director of cinema Fernando Méndez-Leite)[3] to be one of Borau's best films, it did poorly in the international market, and since he had invested his own money in the project, it nearly ruined him financially. In fact, he is still working to pay off that debt. Rather than focusing on the consequences of this disaster for Borau's career in a strictly auteurist context, this chapter will explore its broader implications for the national/international interface of Spanish cinema made abroad.

In her introduction to the same issue of the *Quarterly Review* that contained Borau's essay, Kovács described the economic crisis that faced Spanish filmmakers in the post-Franco period, after the "euphoria" that followed Franco's death and the end of political censorship had begun to fade and a new realization emerged that few Spanish films could expect to survive in the home market, particularly with the dramatic decline in the number of tickets being sold and in the number of movie theaters and with the spiraling increase in production costs and in the competition from big budget Hollywood movies and other formerly censored foreign films that were then flooding Spain. The number of total spectators who attended movies in Spain decreased from 331 million in 1970 to 101 million in 1985, and by 1985, Spanish films held only 17.5 percent of that diminishing home market as opposed to 30 percent in 1970. By 1989, Spanish film production was to fall to a new low of forty-seven films and to earn less than 8 percent of what was taken in at the box office.[4]

In December 1977, a new law on cinema was passed which ended censorship and which required all exhibitors to show one day of Spanish film for every two days of dubbed foreign film. Although these measures were designed to help Spanish filmmakers, their situation was still desperate. Here is how the situation was described by filmmaker Miró, who was appointed general director of cinema by Felipe González almost immediately after the Spanish Socialist Workers party (PSOE) won the elections in October 1982:

At the beginning of 1978 the government owed producers almost fifteen million dollars in subsidies. . . . Film production became semiparalyzed. . . . The always insecure income from the protection fund, the bad administration, and corruption—remainders of the former government—had caused this situation. . . . Distributors who were also producers stopped making films because they did not need Spanish productions any more to obtain import licenses. Other producers made fewer films for lack of capital as a result of government debts. And theater owners showed old Spanish films to comply with the screening quota, or they did not comply at all in view of the guaranteed financial success of the enormous amount of foreign productions that used to be prohibited. The crisis reached its peak when a Supreme Court decision of 1979 found the obligation for theater owners to program one day of Spanish film for every two of dubbed foreign ones to be unconstitutional.[5]

Hopewell observes that this decision to abolish the distribution quota was reached "in a fit of liberalism [by] Adolfo Suárez's UCD government . . . [and] under pressure from the American-backed Federación de Empresarios."[6]

To address this situation, a new law was introduced in January 1980 stipulating "that there be a minimum of one day of showing Spanish films for every three days of foreign films dubbed in any official language, during every natural four-month period" (Miró, 41). These provisions assured that Spanish films would no longer be purposely screened in the worst times of the year—the way Borau's *Hay que matar á B* had been treated in summer 1974. By the end of 1980, Spanish television also provided a new source of funding for Spanish filmmakers, granting $2 million for film production in exchange for television rights two years after the theatrical release of the film.

Once Miró was appointed general director of cinema (the first time this position was held by a filmmaker), she helped introduce a new law (in December 1983) with even more radical measures for protecting Spanish films which "allowed [no] more than four dubbing licenses for each Spanish film" and dramatically increased government subventions. She claims, "Subsidies were granted the same way as in other European countries: a project received an advance payment of 50 percent of the expected box office results if the film was not expected to be a commercial success, and films of 'special value' received 25 percent on top of their gross box-office income" (45). Despite these measures, the situation still grew worse, for, as Hopewell reports, "Spanish box-office takings have gone down drastically, precisely at the time when Spanish advance subsidies have gone up drastically."[7]

Miró's critics attacked her for encouraging "self-indulgent" artists to ignore the current realities of the marketplace and of the changing Spanish audience—the very factors to which Almodóvar's early successes seemed to be so responsive.[8] They also accused her of favoring her friends from the "old liberal tradition of filmmaking"—a group that would certainly include Borau as well as many of the other filmmakers from the opposition whose works are discussed in this book. According to Hopewell, "Viewed with hindsight, the films subsidized by Pilar Miró since 1984 represent the culmination of a central tradition of filmmaking in Spain, a tradition which was born most clearly with Juan Antonio Bardem's *Muerte de un ciclista . . . ,* systematised by titles in the New Spanish Cinema of the 1960s, popularized by transition hits such as *Furtivos* and institutionalized by socialist film-funding policies since 1983."[9]

Although Hopewell (along with Miró's defenders) attributes this post-Franco slump primarily to the dramatic increase in TV spectatorship, the boom in domestic video consumption, and the concomitant drop in the number of movie theaters, he sees these difficulties as part of a larger pattern of economic crisis that has always plagued Spanish cinema from its inception and that remained problematic even after Miró's subvention plan was suspended in 1989. "Lacking ready capital, the Spanish cinema has veered giddily between the devil and the deep blue sea: dependence on, hence potential domination by, a meddlesome volatile state (1940–1962, and even more so between 1962–69 and 1983–89), or independence and recession in a nearly free market economy (1969–73, 1977–80 and 1989 onwards, the Spanish industry feared last year)."[10] Moreover, there seemed to be little hope for the future—unless Spain could develop a cinema that was capable of appealing to an international market or at least to the newly consolidated European community. This prospect hardly seemed viable until Almodóvar broke through to the world market in 1988 with *Women on the Verge of a Nervous Breakdown,* yet even this success seemed more of an exception than a trend. As Hopewell observed, "In 1990 Spain's population remains a modest 38 million, hardly the demographic base for more than a modest industry."[11]

Thus, in the global context, Spain was not only "without weapons" but also without economic clout. As Berlanga observed in 1983, "Instead of the political and ideological censorship that we used to have we are now feeling the effects of what one might call economic censorship."[12] In light of these conditions, it is hardly surprising that the political exile imposed on Buñuel in the 1930s would now be replaced in the 1980s by an economic exile freely chosen by Borau. The issue was still creative survival—both for the individual and for the culture.

In his essay "Without Weapons," Borau challenged European filmmakers and critics who argue that it is only the deep immersion in one's own cultural specificity that makes a film have universal appeal and thereby enables it to rival Hollywood in the world market, an argument that was perhaps most powerfully articulated by Jean Renoir.

> Naïvely and laboriously, I did my best to imitate my American teachers; I had not understood that a Frenchman living in France, drinking red wine and eating Brie cheese in front of a grisaille of Paris, could only create works of quality by following the traditions of people like himself. . . . Now I am beginning to be aware of how I must work. I know that I am French and that I must work in an absolutely national sense. I know also that, by doing this, and only by doing this, I can reach the people of other countries and create works of international standing.[13]

The validity of this statement was supported by the historic stature eventually achieved by films like *Boudu Saved from Drowning, Toni, Rules of the Game,* and *Grand Illusion* as well as by Renoir's subsequent failure in Hollywood with *The Diary of a Chambermaid* and *The Woman on the Beach.*

Similar arguments for cultural specificity were used by Bazin in his early defense of neorealism, particularly in distinguishing this Italian aesthetic from other national cinemas,[14] and by those who adapted the neorealist aesthetic to their own national context—not only Spaniards like Bardem and Berlanga, as we have seen above, but also Third World filmmakers like Satyajit Ray.[15]

Like Buñuel before him, Borau rejected this "fallacy" of "try[ing] to reach universality by delving into the particular" because he saw it as "the ultimate pacifier, devised to calm the creative urges of disinherited authors (you know, the ones from the countries without weapons)" (89). Yet Borau's own career—both his failure in Hollywood and his successes in Spain—lend support to that so-called fallacy.

For Borau, the dream of making international films in Hollywood (like earlier European émigrés, such as Lang, Hitchcock, and Ford)[16] was never one of cultural erasure. Rather, it was a quixotic dream of reasserting the power of Spain's contributions to Western Civilization, particularly in the face of "an incredible lack of knowledge of and interest in Hispanic culture" (85). His projects were therefore chosen very carefully, to emphasize that clash between Hispanic and Anglo culture, between European and American cinema, and between the national and international dimensions of filmmaking. As Erice has perceptively observed, it was a dream designed to recapture the cosmopolitan classical Hollywood of the 1940s and 1950s, which had successfully assimilated so many European émigrés, and to show its superiority over the postmodernist Hollywood of the 1980s, now dominated by what Borau calls "the childishness of Lucas's and Spielberg's movies" that faithfully reflect "prevailing patterns of regressive behavior in this country" ("Without Weapons," 88). According to Erice,

Borau's American adventure implies, on the one hand, the accomplishment of a personal desire (to work in the United States, following an itinerary similar to those of some of the legendary European cineastes: Lubitsch, Lang, Renoir, Hitchcock, Ophuls, Sirk . . .) and, on the other hand, the verification of the abysmal difference that exists between the Hollywood of yesterday and that of today, between the cinema of the past and of the present.[17]

Certainly this passion for Hollywood classical cinema is not unique to Borau; it is shared by many Spanish filmmakers, including some whose work has been more successful in the U.S. market than Borau's, such as Garci (whose *Volver a empezar* won an Oscar for best foreign film in 1983) and Almodóvar (whose rich intertextuality with

Furtivos (Poachers, 1975) was the first Spanish film to present a negative portrait of a civil governor, superbly played by the film's director, José Luis Borau (who is here seen holding a rifle). (Photo courtesy of El Imán.)

Hollywood melodramas help make his outrageous comedies more accessible to international audiences). Nor, as we have seen, does the combination of Hollywood conventions and Spanish specificity have a structural function only in works by Borau. As Hopewell has remarked, "It is noteworthy that Spain's two most successful young filmmakers—Pedro Almodóvar and Fernando Trueba—both mix Hollywood modes . . . with Spanish genres or references."[18] Nor is Borau the only distinguished Spanish auteur who has managed to make a film in Hollywood and to suffer the consequences; Bigas Luna also experienced financial failure with *Reborn* in 1981.

Yet it is only Borau whose entire career has been structured around this paradoxical relationship with Hollywood and who has been willing to stake many of his best creative years and his own personal fortune on this dream. As Hopewell observes, one "both insidious and beneficial result of the Miró decree has been to allow Spanish directors to continue [the tradition of liberal filmmaking associated with the New Spanish Cinema] while releasing them from countervailing market pressures, which would derive from investing substantial sums of their own money in a project."[19] Borau was the prime exception, partly because of the degree of his commitment to the *Río abajo* project and also because it fell on the border between two regimes: the liberalizing free market measures of Suárez and the new Socialist subventions of Miró. Thus, during the post-Franco era, it is only Borau who has commuted between Madrid and Hollywood, between the language of the European art film and the generic conventions of Hollywood classical cinema, between exerting tremendous influence on other Spanish filmmakers as one of the pivotal figures in the New Spanish Cinema and working in self-chosen exile as an international auteur.

A BRIEF OVERVIEW OF BORAU'S CAREER   Borau's career is marked by a central paradox.[20] On the one hand, he is the director, co-writer, and producer of *Furtivos,* a film released on the eve of Franco's death and generally credited with being a turning point in Spanish film history. The first film to present a negative portrait of a civil governor (superbly played by Borau himself), it also became the first film to be exhibited in Spain without an official license. Exposing the cruelty and deception that lay beneath Franco's deceptive image of Spain as "a peaceful forest," this powerful work proved to be one of the top-grossing Spanish films of all time as well as the film that went the farthest in pushing against the remaining censorship codes during those two years of increasing liberalization immediately preceding Franco's death.

Borau also is the producer and co-writer of other courageous Spanish films made both before and after Franco's death. *Mi querida señorita,* directed and co-written by Armiñán, challenged sexual borders with a sympathetic portrait of a transsexual, exploring the rigid boundaries that bourgeois institutions impose around gender and class. Nominated for an Oscar for best foreign film, ironically it lost out to Buñuel's *The Discreet Charm of the Bourgeoisie.*

Camada negra, directed and co-written by Gutiérrez Aragón (who was Borau's former student and also the co-writer of *Furtivos*), was one of the few films made in the early post-Franco transition that was still threatened by official censorship and theater bombings. A satirical portrait of a Falangist family of brothers who are choirboys by day and terrorists by night, the film focuses on the making of a Fascist.[21]

These three films are all deeply immersed in Spanish specificity, all very intense in their coupling of sex and politics, all very controversial in their reception inside Spain, and all highly respected in the international context. They are primarily responsible for establishing Borau's reputation as a major force within the New Spanish Cinema.

On the other hand, Borau has always been a great admirer and emulator of Hollywood classical cinema—its fast-paced action genres, its transparency and coherence, and its high production values and technical expertise—an aesthetic that can be found in virtually *all* of his films, whether they are exclusively Spanish or international coproductions. Saura has been quoted as saying, "Borau is the Spanish director who is best at directing. He knows a very great deal about technique, and he likes to exercise it."[22] Yet technique is usually invisible in Borau's films. Unlike Saura, he chooses not to emphasize the signifier. Like dominant Hollywood cinema, he focuses the spectator's attention entirely on the signified.

I think when people go to see a movie, there's some kind of contract. You go to see the film and suppose the camera doesn't exist. As soon as you see the camera move, it begins to develop its own personality and becomes somebody else. And I don't need anybody else. In order to express myself, I need only the audience and me. . . . If you say, "how marvelous the landscape and the photography," then you are not thinking about the story. I want the audience to be watching the human beings in action, not the photography or the moving camera.[23]

In some ways, this stylistic approach is similar to Buñuel's rejection of "pretty shots" and to his reliance on total conceptualization as the primary site of radical subversion. In describing his film *Tata mía,* Borau observed,

My films always look very ordinary, but they are very strange from the inside. That way, the audience doesn't expect the strangeness. When you make a film that is blatantly symbolic or surrealistic, then the spectator comes prepared for peculiarity. I think it's stronger to surprise them.[24]

The problem with this strategy is that the audience sometimes fails to perceive the strangeness and consequently misinterprets the film. Borau's aesthetic differs from the "indirect style" associated with the productions of Querejeta, where the ruptures and deviations may be difficult to interpret but are impossible to miss. Yet, under a regime of censorship when audiences were still prone to look for implicit meaning, this transparency could also provide an alternative means of subversion, particularly when treating politically charged material, as it did so successfully in *Furtivos* and *Mi querida señorita.* In these instances, the irony was aimed not at the film conventions but at the Spanish social and political issues to which they were being applied. Indeed, one could argue that Borau's "purest" application of the Hollywood classical aesthetic can be found in *Furtivos* (which is generally considered the most "Spanish" of his films), for here there are few discursive marks of reflexivity, except perhaps for Borau's presence in the role of the infantilized governor.

However, in those films where the reinscription of Hollywood conventions was emphasized at least as much as the Spanish context, the likelihood of misinterpretation was greater. Both before and after the death of Franco, Borau wrote, directed, and produced a number of action films that fit comfortably within established commercial genres and that were designed for an international market and yet subtly twisted those familiar conventions from inside. This strangeness was frequently misread, for it could easily be dismissed as merely a failure to understand or master the genre or as merely a result of the transcultural adaptation to the Spanish context.

Such works include Borau's first two features, which were in some ways ahead of their time. *Brandy* (1963), subtitled *El sheriff de Losatumba*, was a Spanish-Italian western (coproduced by Alberto Grimaldi) that predated Sergio Leone's successful spaghetti westerns. While Hopewell describes it as "a loving pastiche of the Western," he also acknowledges that "the endearing thing about Brandy was that he was a rotten cowboy and a thoroughly nice guy" and that "the two things are probably related."[25] Yet he fails to observe that this connection implies an ironic commentary on the genre.

Crimen de doble filo (Doubled-edged Murder, 1964) is a highly specularized, psychological thriller with explicit homages to Hitchcock and Lang. With an almost expressionistic mise-en-scène and a taut, suspenseful plot that are characteristic of noir, this film tells the story of Andrés, the stunted son of a famous concert pianist, who feels inadequate as a musician in comparison with his dead father and who appears almost infantile in relation to his nurturing wife, Laura. When an old man is murdered in the basement of their apartment building, Andrés sees a stranger leaving the scene of the crime and concludes he must be the killer. Imagining he is being shadowed by this mysterious American (who happens to be a Hitchcock fan), Andrés becomes totally immersed in this Oedipal scenario and finally murders the American double. Later, he discovers that the man he killed was his wife's lover and that she was the one who killed the old man in the basement.

Though both of these films flaunt the Hollywood influence and are designed to have international appeal, they were shot in Spain with a Spanish cast and aroused little or no interest outside the home market. Although Borau was not satisfied with how either of them turned out, they nevertheless demonstrated his growing skill in playing with generic conventions and mastering his craft.

During a ten-year leave from directing, Borau established his own independent production company, El Imán. As Hopewell observes, "Two films were enough for Borau to realise that artistic freedoms entailed far greater economic independence" (98). At the head of El Imán (which was founded in 1967), Borau produced and co-wrote films directed by others: *Un, dos, tres, al escondite Inglés* (Hide and Seek, 1969), directed by Iván Zulueta, and *Mi querida señorita* (1972). During this period, Borau also was teaching screenwriting at the Escuela Oficial de Cinematografía (EOC), from which he himself had graduated in 1961 and where he exerted a strong influence on his colleagues and students, many of whom would later be his collaborators on future film projects. Both through his teaching and producing the movies of other filmmakers, Borau's personal impact on the New Spanish Cinema went far beyond his own directorial efforts. This ten-year leave from directing also gave him time to carefully plan a project that could take him to the next stage of international filmmaking, the European coproduction.

Hay que matar á B   Borau returned to directing with *Hay que matar á B* (B Must Die, 1973), a Swiss (Taurean Films, 50%)/Spanish (Borau 25%, Megino 25%) co-production that was made in English and later dubbed into Spanish. The film was co-written by Borau and Antonio Drove, and the director of production was Luis Megino, a former student at the EOC who had previously worked with Borau as executive producer on *Mi querida señorita* and who in 1973 established his own production company. *Hay que matar á B* helped launch Megino on a career that would soon lead him to be, along with Borau and Querejeta, one of the top creative film producers in Spain.

Despite its sophistication and international appeal and its selection by Spanish critics as "the Best Film of 1973," *Hay que matar á B* bombed at the box office—largely because of the way it was distributed. Although the film was shot in 1973, it opened in Barcelona in July 1974 (one of the worst months of the year) and was not shown in Madrid until June 1975. Calling distribution "the bane" of adventurous Spanish filmmakers, Hopewell observes,

Since the American film industry's boycott of Spanish imports between 1955 and 1958, distribution in Spain had effectively become an appendage of American multinationals, whose films were distributed either through subsidiary companies or through exclusive rights agreements. With the complacent connivance of a supposedly nationalist regime, foreign capital was allowed to call the shots in the Spanish cinema. Pre-production deals allowed the distributors to dictate terms to Spanish producers, whose less profitable films they were required to buy by law (the 4:1 distribution quota) but could release in the worst cinemas at the most unpopular times of the year. . . . All Spanish films risked the fate of *Hay que matar á B,* . . . released in the summer of 1975 with very little publicity when most of Madrid was on holiday.[26]

The film featured an international cast including Darrin McGavin, Burgess Meredith, Patricia Neal, and Stéphane Audran. In a complex plot evocative of both Lang and Hitchcock, McGavin played a Hungarian exile named Pal Kovac who was set up to perform a political assassination and then murdered by those who had hired him. Set in an undetermined South American country, this politicized noir thriller originally involved Basque characters, but government censors made Borau change their nationality so that the political implications would be less threatening to the Franco regime.

The film is extremely ingenious in using a popular genre like noir for a "double-edged" critique, which is aimed both at the current political situation in Spain and at the generic conventions themselves. This strategy is similar to the one used by Bardem in *Muerte de un ciclista,* only here it is disconnected from the cultural specificity of a Spanish setting. Like the Orson Welles character in *Lady from Shanghai,* Pal has a weakness for blondes, which leads him to be framed in a highly complex plot that he never understands. Like most noir narratives, the plot is Oedipal. Although Pal thinks he is motivated by love and idealism to kill a corrupt patriarch, he is actually being manipulated by the corrupt patriarchy to commit a political assassination.

The genre conventions are masterfully controlled and politicized. Instead of making Pal a likable antihero with whom we can identify, Borau enables us to see his stupidity and political obtuseness. Early in the film, Pal's pride in being "an independent operator" contributes to the death of Jani, the young son of the Hungarian woman he lives with (Patricia Neal). Eager to earn enough money to return to his native land, Pal ignores a general strike. When he tries to break through a blockade, his companion, Jani, who earlier warned him about the strike, is killed. In generic terms, it is the "rugged individualism" of the noir hero that causes not only the senseless death of the boy[27] but also his own entrapment. Thus, we are almost immediately put in a position of cognitive superiority in relation to Pal, carefully tracking the political background he ignores.

Unfortunately, these subtleties were missed by most of the public and by many critics. Hopewell perceptively observes,

Critical reaction to Borau's film was that it was not a particularly original variation on the theme of an individual victimised by the secret state. Yet it was designed to be exactly the opposite, . . . a call for collective action, for a new political consciousness in self-satisfied Spaniards. The butt of the film's criticism, Drove has explained, is the adventurer of such films as Anthony Mann's *The Far Country* and King Vidor's *Man Without a Star.*[28]

Thus, just as *Brandy* anticipated the spaghetti western, *B Must Die* prefigured that subgenre of romantic thriller set against Third World intrigue that became so popular in the 1970s and 1980s in films like *Cuba, Missing, Under Fire,* and *The Year of Living Dangerously.* Yet while those films ultimately abandon political analysis in favor of the personal tragedy or romance, *B Must Die* critiques this kind of resolution.

This dimension is expressed through the film's double framing. At its outer limits, the film is framed by images of a filing cabinet being opened and a file marked "Kovac" being removed or replaced. Presumably, this action is being performed not only by the omnipotent plotters, who have orchestrated the political assassination and framed Kovac within the diegesis, but also by the screenwriters and the director who have constructed the story and cast the roles. While the male antagonists are played by American actors McGavin and Meredith, the femme fatale is Chabrol's wife, Stéphane Audran (who in her husband's French reinscriptions of Hollywood noir frequently evoked the prototypical Hitchcock blonde but who here brings to mind the blond Rita Hayworth in Welles's *Lady from Shanghai*). By acknowledging these two levels of plotting, the framing distances us from the fiction, forcing us to become aware of a larger reality.

The second framing is introduced after the credits with the killing of the ocelot, whom we see through the iris of the gunsight, presumably from Pal's point of view. Thus, the traditional suture not only immediately invites us to identify with the hunter or killer but also identifies the camera as a weapon. Yet, at the end of the movie, it is Pal who turns out to be the prey, precisely at the moment that he captures B in his gun sight in a similar shot and then is gunned down himself. This pattern also evokes an earlier voyeuristic shot in the restaurant scene with Susana, where Pal thinks he is the seducer, unaware that he is the one being seduced. Immediately preceding the assassination, Pal has a final meeting with Susana, who now tries to

In Borau's *Hay que matar á B* (B Must Die, 1973), the obtuse noir hero (Darrin McGavin) is framed by the blonde femme fatale (Stéphane Audran). (Photo corutesy of El Imán.)

In *Hay que matar á B*, we are positioned to feel superior to the noir hero, tracking the political action he ignores at his own peril. (Photo courtesy of El Imán.)

take some of the blame. But he responds, "No, this is all my responsibility, only mine. All my life I've made mistakes and blamed others. No, this one is all mine. I want someone to get some good out of this." In any other context, this "heroic" speech would represent his moment of existential redemption—as it does in *Muerte de un ciclista* when Juan delivers a similar "heroic" speech on responsibility that is to be taken straight. But here it is merely an echo of the same naive romanticism that has plagued Pal throughout the film and that lies at the core of most American genres.

As Hopewell correctly points out, this double critique of Spanish politics and Hollywood cinema is also developed through visual choices in Borau's direction. A good example is the scene in the movie theater, where Pal first meets Susana. At first we see newsreel footage of political violence in the capital, and then the camera pulls back to reveal the glamorous silhouettes of Pal and Susana against the screen (a shot reminiscent of the aquarium scene in *Lady from Shanghai*). When one of the spectators (who is *not* distracted by romance) shouts out a political remark, the management interrupts the newsreel and turns on the light, which sets the stage for the romantic encounter between the glamorous stars. When the projection resumes, the film they are watching is neither political propaganda nor a Hollywood romantic thriller but Borau and Armiñán's *Mi querida señorita,* which mediates between the two.

The ironic opposition between the film noir couple and the political context is handled most brilliantly in the sequence where they make love in the middle of a political demonstration. The competition between the two discourses of politics and romance is developed through an effective use of specularization, size relations, and an interplay between interiors and exteriors. The sequence begins in a bar with Pal watching a demonstration on television as he waits for Susana. The political action is represented in two contrasting spaces and modes: the black and white documentary footage being broadcast on television (which explains the political background for the assassination Pal will ultimately commit) and the live-action coverage in color which is visible through the window of the bar and which is part of Borau's generic contextualization in noir. The view through the window is soon masked by shutters (which are pulled down as the proprietors prepare to close the bar); similarly, in the television documentary, the view of one of the cameras is blocked by the hand of a participant shielding his identity. Within the TV coverage, there is a further visual contrast between shots where the political action is confined within the small screen and others where it takes over the entire frame.

Once the lovers go outside the bar, the positioning of the two discourses is reversed. Pal and Susana are now surrounded by hundreds of demonstrators who are marching in the opposite direction and who become the visual spectacle that captures the entire screen. Fleeing the demonstration, the lovers seek refuge in a bus. Visually their romantic action is confined within the cramped space of the vehicle, just as earlier the political action was confined within the small space of the TV set. In one shot, the crowd peers in at them through the windows of the bus, as if watching an erotic spectacle on television. Once they kiss, a huge facial close-up of the lovers takes over the entire screen, blocking out the political demonstration that is now reduced to the audio background for the lovemaking. If he had paid attention to this political background, Pal's perspective could have been broadened beyond his narrow romantic and nationalist desires of getting the girl and getting back home. As Fiddian correctly observes, this is the first of four Borau films (*Hay que matar á B, Furtivos, La Sabina,* and *Río abajo*) to focus on "the insidious appeal and blinding effects of nationalism"[29]—a theme ideally suited to his goal of international filmmaking.

La Sabina   Following the critical and commercial success of *Furtivos* and *Camada negra,* Borau had the funds to pursue his goal of international filmmaking on an even more ambitious scale. The Swedish state company Svenska put up 30 percent of the 74 million–peseta budget (about 1 million dollars) for this European coproduction, which was shot in color. *La Sabina* (1979) was Borau's first directorial effort written without a collaborator.[30] Although it is set in Andalusia, the film features a well-known international cast, including Swedish actress Harriet Andersson, British actors Jon Finch and Simon Ward, American actress Carol Kane, and Spaniards Angela Molina, Ovidi Montllor, and Fernando Sánchez Pollack. As

The three women in Borau's *La Sabina* (1979) present contrasting cultural sterotypes: (from left to right) the "Strindbergmanesque" wife Monica (Harriet Andersson), the Andalusian flamenco dancer Pepa (Angela Molina), and the aging American ingénue Daisy (Carol Kane). (Photo courtesy of El Emán.)

Fiddian observes, the multinationalism of the cast is used to "illustrate a clash of cultural values in contemporary Andalusia, and . . . [to] interrogate myths of national character" (302). Against a flamenco score by Paco de Lucia, the Andalusian stereotypes from the españolada (e.g., a flamenco-dancing heroine, her mute and deformed idiot brother, and a local legendary monster) are juxtaposed with the British stereotype of two latent homosexual mates (who are trapped in a sexual rivalry that dates back to early childhood); an aging American ingénue, who is emotionally needy despite her material resources; and an aggressive, manipulative Bergmanesque (and Strindbergesque) wife. Borau explains,

At first I wanted to make a film with Manolo Gutiérrez in which a dragon appeared. Manolo agreed, provided that the dragon would go. The project was abandoned and, later, I thought about shooting a film in Andalusia with two very different women, Geraldine Chaplin and Angela Molina, attending to their national, physical, material and class differences. Finally, after a trip to Sevilla, it ripened into the idea of foreigners in Spain. I wrote the script thinking of Angela, Geraldine, Ovidi Montllor and some well-known foreign actress like Harriet Andersson. . . . The one who could not participate was Geraldine. We wanted to substitute Mia Farrow, but . . . finally we contracted Carol Kane.[31]

Working with actors who come from such varying cultures and acting traditions presents a formidable challenge to any director. It is a challenge that Borau does not totally master. Both Fiddian and Kovács argue persuasively that the inconsistency of tone in the performances is functional; or as Kovács puts it, "Borau uses contrasts in acting styles to embody the clash of different cultures."[32] This dialogic effect is heightened by the clashes in accents (which unfortunately were lost in the dubbed version of the film) and by the casting and naming of the characters, especially the women. For example, Harriet Andersson plays Monica, a name that evokes her debut in Ingmar Bergman's 1952 film *Summer with Monika* (his first film to arouse international interest, particularly from French new wave critics like Truffaut and Godard). Yet the decadent middle-aged literary agent in *La Sabina* is very different from Bergman's young sensual Monika, who lived totally in the moment—a contrast that perhaps suggests the dramatic changes in international filmmaking that have evolved since the 1950s. The emotionally dependent, childish American is called Daisy, a name that evokes both the corrupt Daisy from F. Scott Fitzgerald's *Great Gatsby* and Henry James's *Daisy Miller*, which is about an innocent young American girl going abroad, where her actions are misunderstood by Europeans. As interpreted by Carol Kane, who (like Mia Farrow) is known for comic roles in Woody Allen movies and who plays the humor very broadly, she seems to belong to another movie or to parody this one (particularly in the scenes where she tries to imitate Pepa's flamenco dancing or where she asks Pepa's retarded brother Mani to open his pants). These two foreign women are contrasted with the Spanish Pepa, whom Fiddian claims is the film's central character:

As the linch-pin of Borau's project, Pepa is presented in terms of the contrast between native and foreign values which underpins the film. Played by Angela Molina, who was much in demand as an actress after her performances in *Las largas vacaciones del '36* by Jaime Camino (1976) and *Cet obscur objet du désir* by Buñuel (1977), Pepa embodies the stereotype of *la lozana andaluza* whose associations include a natural sensuality and a certain primitiveness supposedly alien to northern Europeans and other races. (Fiddian, 303)

Unlike Molina's versatile Pepa (who is a formidable rival for the two foreign women and an object of desire for virtually all of the men), the Spanish actors are more narrowly restricted to Spanish cinema and its cultural stereotypes, without much appeal to foreign characters or spectators. This insularity applies both to Ovidi Montllor, who also played a stunted figure (Angel) in *Furtivos,* and to Fernando Sánchez Pollack, who (as we saw in chap. 4) also played a peasant committed to and exploited by the traditional patriarchy in *La caza* and *Los desafíos.*

Fiddian reads *La Sabina* as an exploration of the "social constructs, or myths, about women and . . . their effect on the minds of individuals"—not only the myth of La Sabina, the insatiable female dragon who lures men into her cave and then devours them, but also the traditional role imposed on Pepa by her repressive culture, which is played out in her engagement to her young Spanish fiancé Antonio and violated in her relationship with the British writer Michael for whom (despite the presence of both his mistress Daisy and his wife Monica) she becomes another Concha or Carmen, the exotic object of an erotic obsession. Ultimately, Fiddian concludes that "for all their foreign idiosyncrasies, Daisy and Monica represent two extremes on a spectrum of female behaviour which, while degraded in both cases, coincides exactly with the local scale of values, itself structured around two polarised images of women: the innocent Virgin Mary and the monstrously sexual La Sabina,"—a polarity that is visualized in a float during the "fiesta de la patrona" where we see "a statue of the Virgin Mary . . . with a black dragon beneath her feet" (308). While I find this reading convincing, it omits another important dimension of the film: the latent homoerotic backstory that helps to structure these female stereotypes of the Virgin and the whore (or in Oedipal terms, the incestuous mother and the sphinxlike monster).[33]

Significantly, this homoerotic backstory is most explicit in the opening and closing moments of the film. *La Sabina* opens with Pepa leading her retarded brother Manolín through the village, defending him against the taunts of young boys who ask to see his penis, which was half devoured by the monster when he was a child as punishment for watching at the mouth of the cave. Pepa delivers the first line of recognizable dialogue to the boys: "Why don't you ask that of your father, maricón!" This line introduces the homosexual subtext of the film, in which the castrated Spaniard (evocative of the Black Legend) is an important figure but which is played out most fully by the British writers, Michael and Philip, who were loving boyhood friends and who have been intensely competitive ever since. We learn that Philip took away Michael's wife, Monica, just as he now seduces

Michael's current passion, Pepa, as if this is a way of acting out the repressed eroticism between them. This displacement finally leads Michael to draw Philip down into the cave where they can be devoured by La Sabina. But in fact it is Michael who cuts the rope that is their lifeline and who sets a fire in the cave, thereby committing murder and suicide. These desperate acts are motivated less by the impulsive actions of Pepa (who functions as the human version of La Sabina) than by the obsessive struggle between the two fiercely competitive buddies. Thus, here as in the story of Oedipus, the devouring sphinxlike monster and the incestous desire for the woman both mask the repressed backstory of homoerotic desire.

The homoeroticism is not a "foreign idiosyncrasy" restricted to Michael and Philip; it also crosses national borders. The first time Manolín sees Michael (who is as popular an erotic object as Pepa), the Englishman walks out of Daisy's house naked to have a shower. Instead of avoiding Manolín's persistent stare, Michael asks him to hose him down—an action that is obviously pleasurable to both men (even if the sexual dimension of the act is not as blatant as it is in the famous hosing scene in Almodóvar's *La ley del deseo*). When Pepa sees their interaction, she chides her brother, almost as if she is jealous. This interaction is later repeated in the cave of La Sabina, when Michael goes there alone one night and challenges the siren by taunting her with insults and by pissing in the cave. Again, he is observed by Manolín, who is still drawn as a voyeur to the eroticism of the cave, despite his first traumatic encounter with the Circe-like siren.

Michael is also capable of experiencing homoerotic desire, which is even directed toward his Spanish rival, Antonio. Driven by his obsession with Pepa, Michael goes to the village during the *fiesta de la patrona*, where he watches a group of young Andalusian men performing a local folk dance while wearing fringed shawls and feminine hats decorated with flowers and carrying long phallic sticks. Michael selects Antonio from the group, staring at him with the same kind of intense concentration that the camera lavishes on the icon of the Virgin. In the same carnivalesque scene, the younger boys taunt

La sabina ends with the
powerful image of Pepa
standing in silhouette at the
mouth of the vaginal cave of
the female monster,
screaming for Michael. (Photo
courtesy of El Imán.)

Manolín, as they did in the opening of the film where the homoerotic theme was introduced—a dynamic that suggests the combination of male bonding and sadistic antagonism that fueled the deep boyhood connection between the young Michael and Philip. These juxtapositions call attention to the festival's transgressive potential, especially on the register of gender.

Thus, the film is populated by latent homosexual or stunted men and by devouring females—not only the monster La Sabina and the three female rivals who overwhelm Michael with their sexuality (Pepa), emotional dependency (Daisy), and manipulative power games (Monica) but even figures in the background like the towering icon of the Virgin and the middle-aged woman who teaches the young male folk dancers how to wield their phallic sticks. While these male and female figures compete for control over the narrative, the women clearly dominate the mise-en-scène. In fact, most of the action is set within their territory, especially in Daisy's house, which is being painted by Pepa. These are not merely passive spaces to be invaded by active male heroes but power zones in which the female inhabitants exert their force. This dynamic is most resonant in the cave of La Sabina—the realm of the primal uterine mother, the abyss where sexuality merges with madness and death. This setting is represented with the greatest sensory power, particularly at the end of the film, when Pepa stands at the mouth of the gaping entrance in silhouette screaming for Michael and the sensuous moans of the siren merge with the flamenco guitar. This final image expresses not only the male fear of female sexuality and of their desire for original plenitude but also the woman's protest against these male constructions of sexuality that are so destructive to both genders.

Río abajo: The Production   The very next year, 1980, Borau started working on the script for *Río abajo,* a border film that placed him "on the line" of the national/international interface. As in the case of *Hay que matar á B,* Borau had been laying the groundwork for this project for several years. In 1977, he established residency in Hollywood by purchasing a home in Sherman Oaks (a suburb of Los

Angeles), where, over the next nine years, he spent six months of each year, hoping to realize his long-term goal of making a film in Hollywood.

This time the project was to be a Spanish-American coproduction, a commercial genre film made in North America with a predominantly American cast and Spanish crew. This time Borau would be working in self-chosen exile, shooting both in Laredo, Texas, and in Mexico on both sides of the Río Grande. The subject appeared to be a conventional love story between an American boy and a Mexican girl, an interracial romance set against the political context of illegal immigration. Several Spanish critics treated *Río abajo* as part of a trilogy of border films that also included *Furtivos* and *La Sabina,* yet this time there would be no explicit references to Spain.[34] Like Buñuel, Borau would be risking the charge that he was abandoning his country and culture. But, as we have seen, he had already answered those charges in his essay "Without Weapons," which was published while the film was in production.

While Borau correctly anticipated the criticism he would receive for choosing a non-Spanish subject, he seriously underestimated the difficulty he would have in finding American funding. American writer Barbara Probst Solomon originally proposed that she and Borau collaborate on a border film and that he obtain one-third of the budget from Spain while she would raise the other two-thirds in the United States. Although Borau succeeded in getting his share ($600,000) from the Spanish government for the first year of shooting, Solomon never raised a penny. Moreover, he wrote all of the many versions of the screenplay himself, while she only "translated" his original treatment and first draft of the script. Seeking another American collaborator (this time a coproducer), Borau turned to Steven Kovács (a Hungarian émigré who had worked for Roger Corman and written a book on surrealist cinema and who had met Borau through his wife, Katherine Singer Kovács, who had already written about Borau's earlier films).[35] Kovács eventually raised $50,000 outside of Hollywood, which is the only money in the film that did not come from Spain. In addition to the $600,000, Borau raised $250,000 to pay the Spanish crew in Spain and got an additional $350,000 from the Spanish government for the second year of shooting. In addition, there was $100,000 for preproduction expenses (covering travel to Texas and New York, translations, localizations, etc.). Thus, the cost of the film was close to $1,350,000, without certain salaries (such as those for Borau, Kovács, the editors, and some actors) that never were paid. This figure does not include the interest and penalties on the loans from the banks.

Although Kovács later succeeded in getting International Film Investors (the company that had produced *Ghandhi* and *The Killing Fields*) interested in *Río abajo,* the deal was undermined by larger political and economic pressures in both countries. According to Borau,

International Film Investors was getting a government loan from the small business program. It was the only film company involved in this program. They had to wait for a government approval of a loan, and Reaganomics froze the situation. It was Summer of '82, and we were waiting for the money, and they were waiting for the government approval. I had permission to take money out of Spain in Summer of '80 and this permit expired on December 31, 1982. I knew that a new law was coming in Spain—new elections were coming in October and clearly the Socialists would win and the government policies would be changed. So I knew I had to start the film before December. I asked Steve, "Do we have enough money just for the shoot?" All we had was the $600,000 I had brought from Spain, plus money spent in Spain. We paid Victoria Abril, the cinematographer, the photographic crew, the technicians, in Spanish money. They were all Spaniards. Steve said yes, so we went ahead.

It was a good thing Borau did not wait, because by the time International Film Investors got an approval of their loan, they were no longer interested in *Río abajo.*

While Borau realizes that this situation is not unique, that similar difficulties have been suffered by many foreign directors (particularly Eastern Europeans) trying to make their first American film, he points out, "Directors like Kadar, Forman, Polanski—they came here themselves—they didn't bring the money from their home country as I did" (Borau interview, June 1985).

Río abajo as Border Film   Like earlier Borau films, *Río abajo* works the boundaries between sexual and political discourse—the same border zone explored by Buñuel. As Erice puts it, "The border, and the combination of experiences that it engenders, constitutes the paradigm of José Luis Borau's cinema" (164). Like *Touch of Evil,* this border film explores the ambiguous line between good and evil; in fact, Kovács told me that to make this connection explicit, Borau had originally hoped to cast Orson Welles in the cameo role of "El Gabacho," the philosophical old gangster who finances the border crossings, a role that was played in the film by Sam Jaffe shortly before he died.

Although on the surface *Río abajo* seems to fit totally within the conventional border film and the dominant Hollywood stylistic, a number of tensions create a subtext that interrogates the genre's sexual and political codes. *Río abajo* tells the story of Chuck (Jeff Delger), a young American very naive both sexually and politically, who comes to Laredo with his buddy Jonathan (Paul Richardson) to become a border guard like his Uncle Willy Bryant (David Carradine). While looking for his uncle, who has since become a "coyote" (a paid guide who helps Mexican illegal aliens cross the Río Grande into Texas), Chuck meets up with Mitch (Scott Wilson), his uncle's racist alter ego, who is one of the most aggressive members on the force. These antagonist macho models, who are both morally ambiguous, lead Chuck across the border where he meets and falls in love with Engracia (Victoria Abril), a beautiful young Mexican whore, whom all three men patronize and desire. Eventually Chuck marries Engracia, sneaks her across the border, and, when she is sent back to Mexico, even crosses over to his uncle's side to help him smuggle Mexicans across the Río Grande. Functioning as the primary obstacle to all border crossings both on the sexual and political registers, Mitch hounds his macho rival Bryant and oversees his arrest, sexually harasses Engracia and reports her to Immigration, and torments Chuck by describing his own sexual exploits with Engracia and forces him to choose one side of the border. Significantly, it is

Engracia, the female object of exchange and the victimized Mexican stereotype, who ultimately proves most potent. Though neither male nor North American—the sexual and political categories normally associated with power within the border film genre—she is the one who gets revenge against Mitch by stabbing him to death for herself, her gender, and her people as well as for Chuck and Uncle Willy.

As is readily apparent, these dynamics are very similar to those that lie at the center of *La Sabina,* where the latent homoerotic attraction and antagonism between Michael and Philip is displaced onto the rivalry over the Spanish girl, Pepa, who (like Engracia) is also involved with an innocent young boy (Antonio). Despite their subordinate class position, inferior education, and identification with Hispanic stereotypes (la lozana andaluza and the Mexican whore, respectively), these Hispanic women (particularly when played by strong Spanish actresses like Angela Molina and Victoria Abril) are the object of desire for all of the Anglo men and also their moral superiors. Yet in the border context of *Río abajo* and in the economic crisis of the 1980s in which it is set, these dynamics become more blatantly politicized.

The opening action sequence is effective in identifying the genre and establishing the ambiguities against which the film is to be read. It opens with a long shot of the Río Grande just before sunrise, the border between night and day, with the dark figure of Bryant leading about twenty illegals across the river, urging them on in his broken Spanish and also communicating by walkie-talkie in English with someone on the other side. Suddenly a plane flies overhead from which an amplified voice (which, we later learn, belongs to Mitch) shouts, "Coyotes, you're going in the wrong direction." Mitch is introduced as a man who loves playing a "deus ex machina"—whose position as border guard and whose air power give him an inflated sense of his mission, leading him to focus his wrath and his "hunt" not on the "wets" but on the treacherous "coyote" who used to be on the force. He booms out his violent threats as if they were divine commandments: "If you cross this river again, you're putting your life on the line!" Once on the ground, Mitch's voice loses its divine resonance and develops almost a tremorous whine, yet his distorted sense of his own moral superiority is still apparent in his swaggering walk and in his sneering grin. This opening sequence also establishes Bryant's moral ambiguity. Though he is encouraging to the Mexicans during the crossing, like Mitch, he also refers to them as if they were livestock: "We'll have 'em to the derrick and then we can pack 'em." . . . All we got to do now is let 'em loose." We know he's in it for the money: we are as yet unsure whether there is any other motive.

The film's second main sequence introduces the young protagonist, Chuck. With his first appearance the film begins to falter, partly because the opening led us to expect that Bryant and Mitch would be the two main antagonists but primarily because of the weak performance of the inexperienced Jeff Delger, whose lines had to be redubbed.

Though the performances of David Carradine and Sam Jaffe are both strong and the characters they play intriguing, unfortunately neither role is developed very fully. Kovács explained that these parts were enlarged once these two well-known American actors agreed to do the film. Jaffe's "El Gabacho" remains a mysterious gringo in Mexico who contributes very little to the plot but who strengthens the intertextuality with other Hollywood action films (in one shot he looks at the same calendar he had admired in John Huston's *Asphalt Jungle*) and who delivers some of the film's most explicit political lines: "Things look different from here, don't they. All these people want is to go to the States and make a decent living. I see nothing wrong with that."

While Carradine's Willy Bryant is crucial to the narrative, he appears in relatively few sequences. In fact, one of Carradine's best scenes—the one in which Bryant appears most morally ambiguous—was originally intended for Mitch. Suggesting that Chuck and Jonathan do some target practice, Bryant tries to goad them into shooting animals instead of beer cans and taunts them with a rattlesnake to test "who has the balls." Though Jonathan (who has left home to escape his reverend father) shows he is a better shot than Uncle Willy, as soon as there is a live target (the rattlesnake that

The scene in *Río abajo* where Bryant (David Carradine) tries to goad Jonathan (Paul Richardson) and Chuck (Jeff Delger) into shooting a rattlesnake was originally written for Mitch (Scott Wilson). (Photo courtesy of El Imán.)

threatens Chuck's life), Bryant outshoots him, proving that the only test that counts is when there is a life on the line. The Oedipal rivalry in the original target practice scene would have intensified the sexual tensions between Mitch and Chuck, but once reassigned to Bryant, the scene helps to strengthen his symbolic connections as Mitch's antagonistic double. In fact, after shooting the head off the snake, Bryant implies that this feat of machismo questions the manhood not only of the boys but also of his archrival Mitch. Laughing, he says, "Guess you kids are still tied to Mitch's apron strings." In a later scene when Bryant is caught smuggling aliens across the border and Jonathan's sharpshooting causes the death of a young Mexican, Bryant reminds him of his earlier righteousness: "Ah, the animal lover, . . . guess you prefer to practice on people."

Another of Bryant's strongest scenes is his first meeting with Chuck, who has been brought by Mitch to Boystown, the authorized Mexican zone of prostitution where Engracia works and where Bryant frequently hangs out. Chuck's first view of his uncle is of a naked man lying face down with his legs spread wide on a pool table under a bright light while a group of Mexican whores dutifully pick cactus spines out of his backside. Apparently, he acquired these spines in the opening sequence while running away from Mitch and the border patrol. Though he is literally caught with his pants down, Bryant still manages to maintain his arrogant machismo. More important, this strikingly provocative image introduces the highly charged sexual atmosphere, not only in which Chuck becomes sexually drawn to Engracia but also in which the repressed homosexual subtext gets started. Mitch even quips, "I didn't know acupuncture was a turn-on."

The film's most interesting male character is Mitch, particularly as played by Scott Wilson. He embodies the cruelty and sexual repression that drive the plot forward and also enrich the subtext and connect this film to Borau's other Spanish works. He is a corrosive force who is effective in projecting his own malice and desire onto others. Playing an Iago to Chuck's Othello or a Claggart to his Billy Budd, Mitch's nervous energy, emotional intensity, verbal dexterity,

In *Río abajo* Engrácia (Victoria Abril) is one of the whores picking spines out of Bryant's backside as he sprawls naked on a pool table. (Photo courtesy of El Imán.)

and ironic sense of humor make him charismatic in a hateful sort of way. These qualities are best displayed in the scenes that most clearly reveal his sexual dynamics with Engracia and Chuck.

After roughing up a Mexican TV journalist covering the hearing on the border killing, Mitch asks Chuck to go with him to Boystown. His anger makes him reveal how his political and sexual behavior are intertwined, how his racist machismo forces him to repress his own homosexual desire and to treat all Third World people as whores: "Those dirty Mexicans been fucking us long enough. Now we're gonna fuck them." When Chuck refuses to go, Mitch purposely arouses his jealousy, telling him he will go to see Engracia himself but then waits for him in a bar. Once drunk, Mitch delivers a long seductive monologue full of strategic pauses in which he gauges Chuck's nonverbal responses—a monologue that, in using Engracia as a sexual go-between, clearly articulates the latent homosexual dynamics that underlie so many male-dominated buddy movies in so many American action genres.[36]

Chuck is so deeply shaken by this encounter that it drives him immediately to send a telegram proposing marriage to Engracia, presumably so that he can have her all to himself but also so that he can escape the latent homoerotic attraction that exists not only between Mitch and himself but also between Mitch and Bryant and between Chuck and his buddy Jonathan. Not only is Bryant an antagonist double for Mitch but the boys also double for the older generation of buddies before they were estranged—with Jonathan in the role of Mitch and Chuck as Uncle Willy. In a later scene, when Jonathan unknowingly helps Chuck transport Engracia illegally across the border, the two young men stop at a motel, where Jonathan insists on sharing a room. Instead of revealing that Engracia is in the trunk of the car, Chuck uses homophobia as an excuse for why they need separate rooms: "People come here just to get a quick lay. I don't want them to get any funny ideas about us being together."

Mitch's second powerful scene is an explicit sexual encounter with Engracia (a payment for his promise to help her get back into

Boystown after her unsuccessful attempt to cross the border into the United States as Chuck's bride). His lines reveal that he is still more turned on by the verbal mind-fuck than by the physical sex act. As in the scene with Chuck, Mitch tries to demonstrate the superiority of his own power position and to project his own desires onto her. But unlike Chuck, Engracia talks back, and her physical moves demonstrate that she thinks *she* is in control. The scene is like a battle between moves and words. As she unbuttons his shirt and trousers and kisses his neck, chest, and nipples, Mitch passively sits back smiling and asks, "You heard from Chuck?" While the implication is that he knows she is probably fantasizing about making love to Chuck, the same could hold true for Mitch. When she expresses her anger at Chuck for not telling her he was with Immigration, Mitch responds, "You people don't exactly love us." Just as he had earlier used Engracia with Chuck, now he identifies himself with the young man as if that will make her transfer the desire she feels for her husband onto him. When Engracia begins to go down on him (a sex act that could as readily be performed by another man), Mitch passively lies back with a sneering smile and says, "Somebody has to do the dirty work. For instance, you don't like me but I pay you good. . . . Don't you get a certain satisfaction outa doin' somethin' you don't like—and knowin' you do it better than anybody else?" Designed to humiliate her and to show that he is in control, this line makes us recall that in the earlier sexual monologue with Chuck, Mitch had also projected the satisfactions he derived as a border guard onto Engracia as a "real pro" who does her job "better than anybody else." As Mitch talks, there is a strange, revealing close-up of his face. Then Engracia looks up and confronts him with her silent gaze, acknowledging that they are both professional whores, equals. As if to deny this insight that his own words have generated, in his first active physical move, he pushes her head back down to his groin. Then the image cuts to a close-up of Chuck (from the next scene), the missing member of their sexual triangle who brings them together and whom they both desire.

The strongest character in the film is unquestionably Engracia, partly because of the stunning performance by one of Spain's leading young actresses, Victoria Abril, who was virtually unknown to North American audiences at the time of the film's release. Her sexuality and screen presence are so strong that she overwhelms Jeff Delger, making him appear even more inept and inexperienced than he is as an actor or than the character Chuck is probably intended to be.

The force of Engracia's screen presence is also intensified by the vibrant colors with which she is associated. Her lushly colored costumes—such as her bright turquoise robe, scarlet chemise, and royal blue low-cut wedding dress—and the vivid reds and greens of her bedroom at Boystown help convey the bright flash of Hispanic flamboyance that she brings to virtually every scene, particularly in contrast to the drab grays, browns, and greens of many of the Texas settings. (Her first close look at the United States is the seedy site where Chuck lets her out of the trunk of his car—a garbage dump under the distant tower of a Hilton hotel.) The blue-and-lavender butterfly outlined in white neon at the El Papillon nightclub and the red neon windmills function as images of Engracia's powers of transformation. The rose tattoo displayed on her chest in the final sequence, according to Borau, is a deliberate allusion to that torrid Tennessee Williams melodrama, in which another great European actress, Anna Magnani, made her Hollywood debut. Intending to entice and then murder Mitch, Engracia wears a seductive black dress with sequined stripes, which hypnotically holds the gaze of her intended victim as well as of the spectator. When she plunges the knife into Mitch, his bright red blood splatters on her face, marking not her guilt but the extravagant flair with which she carries out the deed. It also signals a shift in generic conventions from the Hollywood border film to Hispanic melodrama.

Engracia's character draws additional strength from being the center of a subtext on language, which was also a primary thematic concern in *La Sabina*. As she becomes involved with Chuck, we watch Engracia learn how to speak and write English by means of a toy computer game called "Speak and Spell"—a process that shows both her capacity for intellectual growth and acculturation and the price of infantilization demanded from émigrés by the imperialist culture whose language has colonized the world. The scene in which

Engracia first sees this linguistic toy is one of the most interesting in the film, for it is one of the few times when the Spanish language dominates the sound track and one of the few sequences where the political issues transcend the melodrama. We see Engracia sitting among a group of whores with their small children watching on a TV set the Mexican news coverage of the inquiry into the border incident in which a Mexican boy was killed. When the women recognize Mitch as the border guard attacking the Mexican TV reporter (in a mediated vérité replay of what we had earlier seen from a different perspective and in a different style), this gringo is suddenly trans-formed into a villain. In fact, the word *cabron* (bastard) immediately appears on the child's "Speak and Spell." Even though these media—computer toys, television, and movies—are normally associated with the cultural imperialism of the United States, this scene suggests that they can have a subversive effect when put into the hands of the Third World.

Even before learning to write English, Engracia demonstrates her sensitivity to the political implications of language, a dimension that is even stronger in the screenplay than in the film. In her very first scene, when Mitch asks her the racist question of whether she is "getting ready to make the jump . . . to America," she points out that he has dismissed Central and South America, by replying, "What do you mean by 'America'? The States?" In the film she merely answers, "What for? I'm still doing fine in my own country." In both versions, she is proud of being a Mexican and is not apologetic for being a whore. Boldly groping her prospective clients, she is the sexual aggressor both with Chuck (because of his inexperience) and with Mitch (because of his sexual tastes).

For Engracia, making love is another means of communicating with the alien. When she offers to teach Chuck her language, she tells him that "the best place to learn Spanish is in bed." When Chuck first tells her his name, she explodes, "That's not a name, that's just a noise." Then imitating the driving of a train, she syncopates the sound, singing, "Toot, choc-a-choc-a-choc-a-choc," which sounds like it comes out of a Carmen Miranda routine but which Engracia manages to make very sexy. By drawing our attention to the name, she makes us see that phonetically it is closer to Chac, the Mayan god,

Engrácia sits with a group of prostitutes and their children, watching the TV coverage of the inquiry into the border shooting in *Río abajo*. (Photo courtesy of El Imán.)

than to the royal name Charles, which she fails to recognize on his telegram proposing marriage. Engracia enables us to realize that acculturation potentially moves in both directions—despite the racist structures of imperialism. Later, after Chuck has left the force, when Engracia asks whether he will be able to find any work in Mexico, a Mexican cynically replies, "This is the real land of opportunity, especially for a gringo!" After the murder (and with the aid of "Speak and Spell"), Engracia finally succeeds in writing her first letter in English to Chuck in prison as Bryant dumps Mitch's corpse into the Río Grande. She ends her letter with the saying that Mitch attributed to Mexicans but which she attributes to North Americans: "What goes downstream belongs to nobody." In killing Mitch, she symbolically destroys the obstacle to all forms of border crossings, yet the institutional obstacles remain intact. Nevertheless, the film ends with Engracia reaffirming the values of acculturation and rootlessness.

The strongest scenes in *Río abajo* are those between Engracia and Mitch, not only because they are the best characters built on the best performances but also because the dynamic between them carries the greatest force both on the sexual and the political registers. These scenes repeatedly show Engracia proving her equality and also reveal that those in power, like Mitch, always try to colonize others by putting them in the subordinate role of female or child and by using economic support to reduce them to the status of whore. Despite the censorship codes, the focus on sexual discourse was always one of the most powerful means of dealing with political issues within the repressive Franco regime—a common strategy that Borau pushed to its extreme in films like *Furtivos* and *Mi querida señorita*. In *Río abajo*, he adapts that strategy to the international context, to an economically ravaged Third World country like Mexico (embodied in Engracia) and to a Western European nation just emerging from cultural isolation like Spain (represented by Borau). The film implies that both nations are struggling for equal partnership and political independence within their unequal relationship with an arrogant world power like the United States.

Given who Engracia is, how she is developed, and who is playing her, it is hardly surprising that she is the character with whom Borau most strongly identifies. For in making *Río abajo*, he was also affirming the possibilities of acculturation—willing to risk the dangers of infantilization, to speak the language of the commercial Hollywood cinema, without sacrificing his Hispanic pride or his allegiance to his own national cinema or his status as a highly accomplished professional. Erice observes,

In the great metropolis of cinema, for the legal heirs of the men who founded it (all children of television), the cineaste of *Río abajo* is a second class citizen, one more "mojado." Hence the profound feeling of recognition and solidarity that the author demonstrates in his work toward the character of Engracia, the prostitute played by Victoria Abril.[37]

Borau fully acknowledged this dimension in "Without Weapons," where he accurately predicted the American reaction to his film.

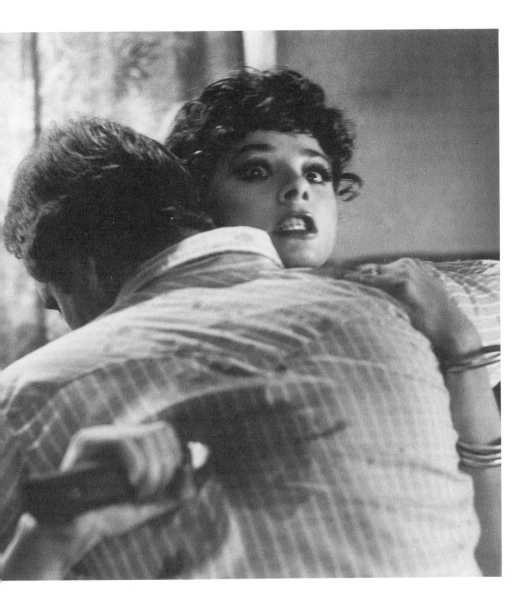

In killing Mitch, Engrácia
symbolically destroys the
obstacle to all forms of
border crossings in *Río abajo*.
(Photo courtesy of El Imán.)

Today's movies have not only a homeland but even a passport which the viewers demand to see whenever they sit down in the theater—or what's worse, even before they enter. They have become like those customs agents who have favourite countries whose visitors are received with a warm smile, and others which they find bothersome and suspect, and whose natives are promptly disinfected or vaccinated. As if this were not enough, if one of those unwelcomed foreigners claims to speak about their lives in their own language, the spectators—or rather, those who have set themselves up as their direct representatives, the distributors and critics—will ask the newcomer for his documents and will inspect his suitcases, concluding with an air of superiority, "No, none of this is useful here. You don't understand what the distinguishing characteristics and idiosyncrasies of our people (they really mean 'audiences') are. We are special (they really mean 'superior'). Why don't you criticize your own country? You'd have enough to dig up there." (86–87)

The Reaction to Río abajo

It's so ironic. In November of 1980, I was on the jury at the Chicago Film Festival with Claudia Cardinale, and we became friends. Werner Herzog came to see her to talk to her about doing *Fitzcarraldo*. At that time I already had the screenplay for *Río abajo*, and I had the money to do it, and the film still hasn't opened in the U.S. But *Fitzcarraldo*, the legendary problem film, has been made, released, argued about, and has become legendary. In *Fitzcarraldo* you can see the problems because they are dramatized in the plot, but in *Río abajo* you can't see them. (Borau interview, June 1985)

Although *Río abajo* has proved to be a critical and commercial success in Spain, because of the limited size of the home market, that success could pay only the interest on the Spanish loans that Borau had incurred to make the film; to make back the principal, the movie would have to do well outside of Spain—in Latin America, in Europe, and most important, in the prime market for which it was intended, the United States. According to Kovács,

Counting the interest that has accumulated on the loans over the past four years, the film cost over three million dollars. It would be almost impossible for Borau to recoup his losses on this film—even if it did receive adequate distribution. But so far American distributors have dismissed the film as a dirty Mexican picture. To them all Spanish-speaking people are alike—Spaniards, Mexicans, Argentinians—filthy, conniving, subhumans.[38]

Kovács claims that most of the American distributors who saw *Río abajo* thought it was not "arty" enough to be European or "commercial" enough to be American. In other words, it was "on the line."

When I interviewed Borau in June 1985, he told me, "The film opened in Spain in November of 1984. It's due to open here in the States in September or October, to be distributed by New World Pictures. It will open in six markets with an advertising budget of $250,000." But when I spoke to Borau again in July 1986, he reported that the deal with New World Pictures had fallen through. After Borau had his overseas agent, Robert Little (of Overseas Film Group), sell *Río abajo* in twenty-five foreign markets both for theatrical and video release (see fig. 1) to recoup the costs of redoing the sound track for the American version, New World was no longer willing to pay the $250,000, which had been their offer for total world rights. Borau rejected their new offer and continued to search for a company that would put up a more substantial advance. Eventually, the film was sold to Miramax for $370,000 and released theatrically in the United States in six markets. Although the film did better in home video and pay television than in the theaters, Borau is still paying off his debts.[39]

Traditionally, the primary way that a Spanish (or any other foreign) film gets distribution outside of its own country is by doing well at international festivals. But when the Spanish government tried to place *Río abajo* in competition as an official Spanish entry at the annual festivals in Berlin, Venice, and Moscow, it was refused on the grounds that "it has the appearance of a North American production and is not very representative of Spanish cinema." This same excuse was cited again as one of the primary reasons that *Río abajo* was not chosen by Geoffrey Gilmore of the UCLA Film Archive for inclusion in its August-September 1986 program of eighteen "recent Spanish films by Spain's most talented new generation of filmmakers."

The rejection by the Berlin Film Festival was the most disturbing, since Spain's Socialist government had used Germany (its old Francoist ally) as their primary European model. They chose Germany because it was most successful in challenging the United States economically and also because it was so effective in using a modernist film movement of the 1970s to help transform its tainted national image from that of a repressive Fascist loser to that of a progressive democratic winner within postindustrial consumer capitalism.

Thus, when *Río abajo* was rejected at Berlin, Miró (then general director of cinema) wrote a strong letter of protest to one of the officials connected with the festival. Pointing to recent selections at the Cannes and San Sebastián festivals in 1984, she noted that Werner Herzog's *Where the Green Ants Dream,* Wim Wenders's *Paris, Texas,* and Volker Schlöndorff's *Swann in Love* were all shown in competition as official German entries without anyone questioning *their* national identity. Yet, "all of these German films had a subject that was not specifically German and were shot outside of Germany with technical equipment and artists that were not for the most part German."[40] She declares that "in spite of the difficulties, we will continue opening new roads like cineastes, looking for our place in the worldwide cinematographic panorama, as the German cinema does." More specifically with reference to Borau, she insists that "*Río abajo* is a Spanish film. The American coproducer [International Film Investors] withdrew when the production began, and it had to be taken over and totally financed by the Spanish producer José Luis Borau. It has Spanish actors and technicians, and its conception is Spanish." Indeed, despite Borau's original intention, the only sense in which *Río abajo* could still technically be called a Spanish-American coproduction is that it was jointly produced by the Spanish company El Imán and by the American company Amber Films, both of which are totally owned by Borau himself. For this reason, Miró concludes her letter by saying, "José Luis Borau has communicated to me that he cannot accept the kind offer that the committee made him of presenting his film at Berlin outside of competition, and, with all respect, I agree." Most important, this glaring inequality of treatment leads her to ask with sarcasm,

Is the Spanish cinema condemned to try only typical Spanish subjects, to offer only the image that others have of our culture? We will make *Carmen,* but we will also make stories about subjects which we consider an interesting contribution from our point of view. We value, nowadays, whatever social, political, or cultural problematic of the world affects us. Or is it that we don't have anything to say about the situation of Latin Americans in relation to the United States?

The clear implication is that the fate of all films at international festivals and in the world market is largely determined by the position of their home nation in global politics—precisely the same point that Borau had made in "Without Weapons" and that Buñuel had made earlier in *My Last Sigh* in the epigraph with which this chapter began.

Since joining the NATO alliance, the Common Market, and the European Community, Spain has been eager to take its place among other Western European nations and also to maintain its independence from the imperialist policies of the United States in Latin America. Thus, the Socialist government's support of *Río abajo* has larger political implications; Borau's film seriously challenged the boundaries of the Spanish cinema by venturing into international terrain precisely at the moment when post-Franco Spain was most eager to transcend its cultural isolation and, more specifically, to improve its image in Latin America. According to distinguished Mexican novelist Carlos Fuentes (who recently wrote a television series on Spain and the Hispanic world called "The Buried Mirror," coproduced by the Smithsonian Institution and England's Channel 4), Spain has already made considerable progress toward achieving these goals.

Throughout Spanish America, we used to see Spain and say: Look at that toothless hag, sitting on the church steps, reeking of incense and urine, dressed in rags and begging alms. We shrugged in resignation. We are as we are because Spain is what she is.

No longer. Fifty years after the Battle of Spain, the lady is sleek, modern, beautiful and, we hope, willing to admit us into her bright new bedroom.[41]

Acknowledging that "perhaps no other country in Europe has been, to such a degree, the victim of foreign perceptions," Fuentes claims this perception began to change in his own nation largely through exile and diaspora—when Mexican President "Lazaro Cardenas received almost 200,000 refugees from Franco's Spain . . . [who] revitalized our culture . . . [and] taught us that Spain had another tradition, a democratic tradition." Now in the post-Franco era, Fuentes predicts that "Spain can play a greater role in mitigating conflict between Latin America and the United States. It can even fill in many vacuums in current hemispheric relations." Spain took a step in this direction in July 1992 by hosting the Ibero-American Summit in Madrid. And this was also precisely the direction in which *Río abajo* was moving by presenting a Hispanic perspective on border issues.

In light of these broader implications, the particular case of Borau's self-chosen exile in Hollywood provides a crucial lesson on the national/international interface for Spanish filmmakers of the 1980s. As was observed by Erice, his friend and colleague (whose own ambivalence toward Hollywood was explored in chap. 3),

To hear José Luis narrate his vicissitudes in the United States during the production of *Río abajo* . . . is a lesson not to be forgotten. Its negative balance is especially pronounced, since it proceeds from an auteur whose admiration for the great classical American narratives is very evident. In this sense, his decision to transgress the border which separates European cinema from the American (and we are not saying anything here besides, about the treatment of a Spanish director), with its disappointing final result, closes a chapter of an extraordinary experience which appears integrated, in an unconscious way, into the very fiction of the film.[42]

This lesson was reinforced by the stunning success of Borau's latest project *Celia,* a high-rated six-part television series broadcast by TVE on Tuesday evenings in prime time from January 5 to February 9, 1993. Based on Elena Fortún's popular series of children's stories from the pre–Civil War period, this work is as culturally specific as *Furtivos* and is the first project directed by Borau that has come close to matching its success.

Yet Borau has not totally abandoned his dream of international filmmaking. While living in Los Angeles, he wrote a book called *El caballero d'Arrast* (which was published by the Festival Internacional de Cine de San Sebastián in 1990), a meticulously researched, handsomely produced critical biography of the French/Basque émigré director Henri d'Abbadie d'Arrast (1897–1968), who was known in Hollywood as Harry d'Arrast and whom Borau credits with inventing screwball comedy. This biography seeks "to make the necessary amends" to a European exile who has been forgotten by most film historians.[43] At the end of his prologue to this biography, Borau makes the analogy between d'Arrast and himself explicit.

Although definitely a victim of the stupidity and cruelty that have always dominated Hollywood, he was just as much a victim of his own demons. It takes two to tango. . . . This book . . . should be interpreted as the tribute of a grateful spectator who, for generally very different reasons and a few that are identical, didn't fare too well himself in Hollywood. (12)

If d'Arrast could be recuperated, then perhaps there was still hope for Borau's dream of working in Hollywood. But as of this writing, Borau has not found an American publisher for this book, even though his Spanish publisher has paid for the English translation. The story sounds strangely familiar. Moreover, it suggests that the following quotation from d'Arrast (with which Borau closes his biography) might apply equally well to the director of *Río abajo* and (with a minor emendation) might serve as an equally appropriate conclusion to this chapter.

Hollywood, by dint of its constant blowings, extinguished a tiny flame which burned within me, and the [Hollywood] cinema, that I loved as I would have loved a woman, no longer held any more interest for me than a woman who tells you a lie. (177)

Former ETA member Mikel
(Imanol Arias) leads a
demonstration for Basque
independence in Imanol
Uribe's *La muerte de Mikel*
(The Death of Mikel, 1984).

BLOOD CINEMA · IV

MICRO- AND MACROREGIONALISM

8 ▪ MICRO- AND MACROREGIONALISM IN CATALAN CINEMA, EUROPEAN COPRODUCTIONS, AND GLOBAL TELEVISION

REGIONALISM AND THE LOCAL/GLOBAL DIALECTIC   Since regionality (like nationality) is an ideological construct, "regional film" and "regional television" are relativistic concepts. Like a linguistic shifter, "regional" means "marginal" in relation to some kind of geographic center or dominant cultural practice, and in the case of cinema, that frequently means Hollywood. As Ed Buscombe and others have observed, every national cinema is inevitably related to Hollywood, for it is this relation as an alternative to the dominant global practice that helps define its cultural distinctiveness.[1] Such statements imply that in the context of the world market, all national cinemas are regional cinemas and that there is always a close connection between regionalism and nationalism. As John Hartley puts it in a statement on television (which could just as readily be extended to include national cinemas),

Neither television nor nations can be understood at all, in fact, except in relational terms. They have no pure, intrinsic properties but only differences from other related domains. . . . Like signs, nations are constructs not of any external, referential world but of discourses.[2]

Given this relativism, regionalism clearly may refer to geographic areas that are both *smaller* and *larger* than a nation. Thus, the terms "microregionalism" and "macroregionalism" help us to understand the regional/national/global interface.[3] Most important, because micro- and macroregionalism function codependently, fluidly shifting meaning according to context, they thereby serve as an effective means both of asserting the subversive force of any marginal position and of destabilizing (or at least redefining) the hegemonic power of any center. Once regional structures and the "center" come to be seen as sliding signifiers, then there is a movement toward the proliferation and empowerment of new structural units both at the micro and macro levels.

A vivid example of these dynamics was provided by the television coverage of the Persian Gulf War. Within the United States, the definition of "network news" was almost instantly transformed and globalized by the 24-hour reporting of CNN, whose broadcasts could be received in over one hundred nations, forming a new macro region. Within the United States, CNN's coverage of the Gulf War made national networks look regional, causing many to question whether U.S. *national* news would survive in George Bush's so-called new world order. Moreover, CNN's exclusively international focus made microregional news coverage by local stations appear more essential. As Lawrence Grossman, the former president of NBC News, was quoted as saying, "With CNN becoming the place where viewers turn for breaking news in a crisis, and local news also assuming a stronger role, the traditional dinner-hour network news is becoming an anachronism."[4] Yet many foreign viewers perceived this development as a strengthening of North American hegemony, for CNN refused to transmit the stories of Spanish and other European journalists who still remained in Baghdad, seeing them as competition rather than as colleagues in the global reporting of the war.[5] Thus, once again (as in the cold war era), world events were being monitored and mediated primarily by the voice of America.

The regional/national/global interface is increasingly important in our world of global mass media where satellites circle the earth, easily transgressing and redefining all existing boundaries. Nowhere are these changes more dramatic than in Europe. As William Boddy observes, "The changes in TV delivery systems represented by cable and direct broadcast satellites, the ongoing consolidation of the telecommunications and computer industries, the shifting political and regulatory policies regarding broadcasting, and the growth of significant new trans-national entrepreneurs in the new media environment all point to the 1990s as the decade of greatest change in broadcasting in Western Europe since the widespread adoption of television in the 1950s."[6]

One important dimension of these changes is the simultaneous creation of both a macroregional "Eurotelevisión sin fronteras" (European television without borders) and a proliferation of diverse forms of microregional broadcasting. Appropriating the role formerly played by national and regional cinemas, these new developments in television promise to play a pivotal role in redefining the political, social, economic, and cultural boundaries of the European community as well as in challenging many key assumptions that have shaped our vision of the world. Seeing "the emergence of both enlarged (continental Europe) and restricted (local, regional, provincial) conceptions of citizenship," David Morely and Kevin Robins insist that "we need to focus on the . . . new forms of bonding, . . . being forged out of the global-local nexus," which are increasingly undermining "the fundamental principles for political attachment in capitalist societies, . . . national and nationalist identities."[7] Yet, within this period of massive global restructuring, nationalism is not only being challenged at the macroregional level but is simultaneously proliferating in the microregional context. Some Spanish critics are calling this new phase "the great European cultural revolution," claiming it will prove "more decisive and important" than the French Revolution or the Russian Revolution (whose accomplishments have recently been unraveled).[8] And undoubtedly, this cultural revolution will increasingly rely on global mass media—including both film and television—to shape and disseminate this new world order. Although this new revolution will increasingly rely on global mass media to redefine cultural boundaries, it will not eradicate nationalism. For, as Benedict Anderson has observed, "nation-ness" will continue to function as a malleable cultural artifact like religion and kinship (rather than as a specific ideology like fascism) and to flourish as "the most universally legitimate value in the political life of our time."[9]

Within this new revolutionary context, Spain, with its miraculously rapid and peaceful transition from fascism to democratic socialism (which prefigured many of the other miraculous transitions to come in Eastern Europe), is an ideal European case study for the global-local nexus. Moving quickly from hermetic isolation to a full participation in Western Europe, from a monolithic Castilian hegemony imposed by the central government to a legal division of the nation into seventeen "Comunidades Autonómicas," Spain is widely perceived both by Spaniards and by other Europeans as uniquely suited for the simultaneous development of a Eurotelevisión sin fronteras and a rich diversity of regional broadcasting. For example, Peter Zimmerman, secretary general of CIRCOM Regional, observes that the change in Spain's constitution has made "the conditions for regional television . . . extremely favorable," enabling it to develop a "bottom up" organization that was previously unique to the Federal Republic of Germany.[10] Within Spain, Pedro Orive Riva, author of *Europa: Guerra audiovisual* (Europe: Audiovisual War, 1990), asserts, "Since the diversity and variety offered by our Nation's different territories are the richest in Europe, the communication model that we are developing must maintain constant inter-regional communications . . . ; it can only become reality if a microsystem functions at the level of each autonomous community, . . . intensify[ing] the accent of the endogenous actions . . . , but always with an equal emphasis on the national and international levels."[11]

In *Variety*'s special Global Report on Spanish cinema (published in September 1990), where Besas reported the sharp decline in Spanish film production to a new all-time low of forty-seven films in 1989 and a similar downward spiral in home video sales, he also described an equally dramatic growth in Spanish television which was occurring both at the microregional level (with seven new regional networks broadcasting in regional languages and being run by provincial governments) and at the macroregional level (with three new private networks at least partially controlled and financed by outside European interests—"Telecinco, 25% controlled by Italian media mogul Silvio Berlusconi, airing mass-market programming; Antena 3-TV, controlled by a mixed group of newspapers and local and foreign banks, emphasizing 'traditional' programming; and Canal Plus, a feevee operation which offers feature films and is one-quarter controlled by France's Canal Plus"). Besas also observed that in addition to these new stations, "RTVE, the once-complacent government monopoly, is still a major television force in Spain, with two channels and a $1.45 billion budget for 1991."[12] Moreover, between 1980 and 1989, advertising sales for Spanish television had increased sevenfold, a faster rate of growth than for any other nation during that same period.[13] Thus, Besas concludes, "With spot ad revenue of close to $2 billion per year at stake, Spanish TV has become one of the most competitive and hectic markets in Europe, if not the world."[14]

Nevertheless, in the early 1990s, RTVE experienced a financial crisis, which was attributed to mismanagement and which threatened to put it on the verge of bankruptcy and forced it to decrease its funding of feature film production. Quickly becoming a highly charged political issue, the crisis was minimized by the Socialist government and exaggerated by their opponents—a situation that may have helped the right-wing opposition to defeat the Socialists in local elections within certain regions (such as Valencia) in the early 1990s and which certainly emphasized television's crucial ideological role in constructing national identity.[15] Whether one emphasizes the phenomenal growth or mismanagement of Spanish television, its national identity has clearly been destabilized, for it is now being challenged simultaneously both at the regional and global level.[16]

It is precisely this decentralizing tendency of Spanish television that makes it so appealing as a European model, particularly since Spanish radio and television were earlier used by the Francoist regime as an ideological state apparatus to disseminate propaganda and to impose a Castilian hegemony over other cultural regions, and therefore both the cultural diversity of the regional stations and the internationalism of the private networks could effectively be used to demonstrate the openness and "new mentality" of the Socialist government. But Besas does not address the political dimensions of these changes, since his optimistic global report in *Variety* is directed primarily to potential North American advertisers and investors. Many Spanish commentators, however, are less optimistic. For example, Pedro Fernaud Casais observes that although recent laws were apparently designed to "depoliticize public radio and television," Spanish television has remained an important site of political struggle, in which the interests of the public have been subordinated to those of the government as well as to those of specific politicians and political parties—a situation that is even more intense in the regional stations, despite their ideological differences from Madrid (69, 79).[17]

Spanish television also makes us rethink its borders with cinema, for now in Spain, as in most other parts of the world, the respective fates of these media are inextricably fused. It is not merely a matter of television *displacing* cinema as the dominant vehicle for defining national and regional identity, for many Spaniards are hoping that these new configurations of television will help revitalize Spain's national cinema, which has been plagued by economic crises throughout the post-Franco era. Given that Spanish spectators currently prefer to see feature films on small screens at home rather than in movie theaters and prefer movies over any other form of television programming,[18] some critics are predicting that Spanish regional television will provide the "infrastructure" for strengthening a regional cinema that would otherwise remain merely "a sporadic rupture of silence throughout the marginalized regions."[19] As Pedro Fernaud Casais puts it, "The reordering of the new Spanish audiovisual landscape must take into account and evaluate the strategic interests of cinema, . . . its systems of financing, production, distribution and exhibition" (81). Even at present, with Spanish cinema deep in crisis, advertising and television are sustaining many of Spain's most highly respected auteurs.[20] Moreover, the present developments in global mass media can lead to a new understanding of regional cinema from the past, and it is hoped this historical recuperation will, in turn, bring a fuller understanding of the local/global nexus in Spain's "new audiovisual landscape."

Catalan Microregionalism   A paradigmatic case of microregionalism is the Catalan cinema, which flourished in the 1930s under the Republic and was suppressed after the Civil War along with Catalan language and popular arts. This act was grave, for the distinctiveness of Catalan identity is based primarily on language and culture rather than on race or religion, and their suppression evoked earlier historic wounds, such as the banning of Catalan language in 1714 after Barcelona had supported Austria against Spain. Since it was the granting of political autonomy to Cataluña that partly motivated Franco to join the military rebellion that launched the Civil War, it was hardly surprising that one of the consequences of the Nationalist victory was the suppression of Catalan culture. During the Francoist era, the dominant cinema in Spain was made in Madrid and in Castilian, as dictated by Franco, who tried to use a unified language in speech and cinema to impose a cultural and ideological unity on the nation.

In the 1960s as Francoist Spain moved toward the macroregionalism of Western Europe, which opened the nation to tourism and foreign investments, there was a revival of Catalan language and culture that drew on its rich literary heritage and its sophisticated, indigenous cinema from the 1930s. As D'Lugo observes, what emerged in the Catalan cinema of the 1960s was "the Civil War ideal of Barcelona as the tolerant, generous city of the Republic," frequently with plots that focused on "personal myths" as substitutes for more direct representations of regional or national history.[21]

During the Francoist era, any difference in verbal or filmic language in the Catalan cinema carried subversive implications, even when the plot seemed more personal than political. Within this period of destabilization, Catalan cinema had to compete against two different dominants—Castilian cinema and foreign imports, primarily from Hollywood. One way this microregional cinema could subvert Castilian dominance was by exposing it as marginal (and regional) within the international context, thereby allying itself with other dominant cultural centers, like Paris or Hollywood. Consistent with Bakhtin, by "participating in alien cultures and languages," Catalan cinema demonstrated the arbitrariness of Castilian dominance in the national realm, revealing that it was "only one among other cultures and languages."[22] As David Gilmour has observed, these dynamics had a long history.

In the Middle Ages, when Madrid was a meager provincial town, Barcelona was the center of a Mediterranean empire which included Sicily, Sardinia and Majorca. In the nineteenth century, when Madrid was perhaps the most backward and corrupt capital in Europe, Barcelona led Spain's industrial revolution, while today it is the largest city anywhere on the Mediterranean. Only bad luck and, in Catalan eyes, fiendish inequity could have determined that the greater city should have had to serve its inferior. . . . The Catalans' traditional reaction to this situation has been to claim that they are more European than Spanish, to declare that they have more in common with Paris than with Madrid, and to clamor periodically for independence.[23]

When Catalan cinema became totally authorized in the post-Franco era and when Cataluña became one of the seventeen autonomous regions authorized by the new constitution, Catalan cinema lost some of its political effectiveness. D'Lugo claims, "In many ways this new freedom of expression and the government incentives to develop previously interdicted Catalan themes only seemed to dilute the force and even the appeal of the enterprise for once the obstacles to expression had been removed, very few filmmakers have taken seriously the interrogation of Catalanism" ("Catalan Cinema," 140).

Nevertheless, the definition of regionalism by language, thematics, and cast is still crucial for Catalan cinema, for it determines whether a film qualifies for special subsidies by the regional government (which go to producers, exhibitors, and local distributors) and for advance supplements from the Catalan television network, TV-3. According to *Variety*'s Madrid correspondent, Besas,

> About $3 million is earmarked by the Generalitat [the Catalan regional government] each year for subsidies to local filmmakers for the approximately 10 features annually lensed in the region. . . . Maximum amount available for each subsidy is $220,000, but more often coin allotted is in the range of $160,000 to $180,000 per pic. Among the conditions are that film must be shot in Catalan, using mostly local crew and cast. Under a new law passed in June, producers can now get up to 10% of a film's budget even if the pic is shot in Castilian, with an additional subsidy if pic is released in Catalan. Should the film prove a commercial success, an additional $100,000 may be forthcoming.[24]

Miró has severely criticized the Catalan government for wasting its subventions on "the production of shallow comedies or confusing historical superproductions, such as the six-hour *Victoria* (1984) by Antoni Ribas," and for spending most of its film budget "subsidizing the dubbing of great American productions into Catalan, using a criterion that is very similar to the law of 1941 by which the use of any language that was not Castilian was prohibited."[25] Moreover, she contrasts their strategy with what she calls "the much more intelligent approach" of the Basque government, which "subsidized up to 25 percent of the costs of productions filmed on Basque locations, with Basque themes, and with Basque technicians and actors"—a policy that resulted in a number of interesting art films like "*La fuga de Segovia* (1981) and *La muerte de Mikel* (1984) by Immanol Uribe, *La conquista de Albania* (1983) by Alfonso Ungría, and *Akelarre* (1984) by Pedro Olea" (45). Actually, these works were more like the films Miró had subsidized during her tenure as general director of cinema. In fact, many of the most internationally well known Basque figures in cinema—like producer Querejeta (whose Basque identity is well known, largely because of his former career as a soccer star) and directors Erice (who was born in San Sebastián) and Eloy de la Iglesia (who was born in Zarauz)—are usually treated solely as Spaniards working within a national tradition (such as the New Spanish Cinema), except in texts featuring issues of regionalism, such as José María Unsain's *El cine y los Vascos.*[26]

Apparently there is some substance to Miró's criticism, for few films in the Catalan language focusing on Catalan thematics have done well outside of Cataluña in broader Spanish or international markets. Besas reports that "the last such case was a sexy pic, *La Senyora,* which grossed a neat $800,000 around Spain last year, dubbed into Castilian outside Cataluña" (80). The more common situation is for a Catalan film to do well in Barcelona but poorly throughout the rest of Spain, as in the case of Rosa Vergés's more recent comedy, *Boom Boom* (1990).

Television offered greater support than cinema for regional discourse in Cataluña, primarily because when the autonomous communities were established, the television industry was dramatically expanding (rather than declining like the film industry) and also because it was considered more important for local, national, and international news (than for drama) to be mediated through the Catalan language and consciousness. As José Luis Ibáñez reports, by 1989 in Cataluña, there were six television channels being received, two private channels (Antena 3 and Tele 5) and four public channels (two national channels, TVE1 and TVE2, which both include a certain degree of regional programming specific to the Autonomous Catalan community, and two autonomous channels, TV-3 and Canal 33, which originate from the region and which broadcast programming in the Catalan language).[27] Warning against any simplistic division of television into national, regional, and local categories, Inma Tubella observes that the meanings of these terms have been destabilized by the interplay between micro- and macroregionalism:

We all agree . . . that when we say "regional television," we are talking about a television that does not broadcast over the totality of whatever territory that we are adopting as a point of reference. Following this reasoning, then, TVE [usually considered national television in Spain] is a regional television if we take Europe as our point of reference, and TV3 [usually considered a regional channel] is a national television if the point of reference is Cataluña.[28]

Nevertheless, Orive Riva claims that the successful existence of the interregional structure depends on "the operative strategies" of local television within the "microsystem" of each autonomous unity, for these strategies can resist Madrid's attempt to pass off its own regional programming as the authentic "national" culture (168, 171).

Some of the regional networks have even grander ambitions of competing with Madrid as the center, particularly in 1992 with the World Exposition in Seville and the Olympic Games in Barcelona.[29] Even though the television coverage of the Olympics was handled by an organization created solely for this purpose, Radio Televisión Olímpica 92 (RTO 92), which was cofounded in February 1989 by the national public channel, RTVE, and the regional Catalan network, TV-3, this event proved to be the perfect vehicle to globalize Catalan television and to justify the city's ambitious claims of being not only the most cosmopolitan center of the Autonomous Catalan region and of the entire Spanish nation but also the cultural capital of Europe and (at least temporarily) the sports capital of the world.[30] Indeed, the host city of Barcelona was widely perceived as the most impressive star of the 1992 Olympics. In the opening ceremonies (where Catalan, Spanish, French, and English were the four official languages and where both Catalan microregionalism and the macroregionalism of the European Community were prominently orchestrated into the festivities and mise-en-scène), Spain's King Juan Carlos I greeted the crowd in Catalan before officially declaring the games open in Spanish, a gesture that was considered an important concession to the region's autonomy. Yet the operatic spectacle that preceded and followed still reaffirmed the old "national stereotypes" by featuring flamenco and Bizet's *Carmen*.

Spain's Participation in Macroregionalism   Operating within the international context, macroregionalism can be applied to works made by a number of nations who share common economic interests (such as coproductions between members of the European Community), or a common language (as in the case of Latin American cinema), or a common historical experience, such as having been colonized (as in Third World cinema and Eastern European cinema). Belonging to more than one macroregion, Spain is tied both to the Latin American cinema through language (and has recently increased its financial support of Latin American productions)[31] and to the European cinema through geopolitical interests (which are reaching a new stage of consolidation in 1992). Virtually all of these macroregional groups are economically motivated, for they are trying to compete with Hollywood's domination of world markets.

Hollywood itself recently became a denationalized macroregion when several of its major studios were purchased by Japanese-, European-, and Australian-owned multinational corporations and as Los Angeles (the postmodernist city within which Hollywood is positioned) has increasingly been absorbed within the Pacific Rim. While American politicians and analysts worry that this decentering will weaken U.S. domination over global mass culture, Europeans fear that the alliance with Japan will make Hollywood's hegemony even more formidable. For example, Gubern of Barcelona warns,

Today in mass culture Europe faces a double challenge, . . . the consolidation of the new Los Angeles–Tokyo axis of audiovisual power, in place since Sony bought the record division of CBS (1987) and the productive Columbia Pictures (1989), followed by the Matsushita (1990) purchase of MCA-Universal and the setting up of film production in Hollywood with Japanese capital. . . . Indeed, with these operations it has produced a denationalization without precedent in the North American audiovisual industry, and as if in compensation has produced a strong Americanization of world cinema, subjecting it to its aesthetic-ideological hegemony. . . . In the next five years, Europe will need some 16,000 hours of fictional narrative for programming its televisual networks, while its productive capacity is no more than 2,500 hours. We already know who will fill this vacuum.[32]

Commentators from all nations are predicting that the main "trade wars" of the 1990s will focus on mass media, which will redefine and reshape the world to come. In 1991, movies and television programming represented the second-largest export of the United States, which the European Community is determined to curtail, hoping to reduce the percentage of U.S. programming on European television from 80 to 50 percent by 1993. While the United States has successfully marketed and naturalized its own national product as a global mass culture capable of colonizing the world, the Japanese have perfected the opposite strategy—the ultimate postmodernist simulacrum that imitates, improves, and thereby conquers and replaces the alien Other. Yet both models eradicate difference. In contrast, the European Community is developing a strategy that retains and highlights cultural diversity, and that is why the combination of micro- and macroregionalism is so central to its enterprise. While Tubella claims that regionalism can provide a realistic infrastructure for retaining cultural diversity within a unified Europe that is increasingly decentralizing the traditional state, Jesus Arilla Perez elaborates on the paradoxical nature of this combination:

The Region is a privileged platform for the construction of real European unity by means of being a concrete realm, humanized in scale. It is a depository of cultural, linguistic and sentimental elements, which form part of the undeniable patrimony of European citizens from the great continent. This depository is more than capable of integrating its diversity without destroying their peculiarities, but even more capable of protecting them for the purpose of enriching a patrimony that is common rather than unique. (249)

Within these "new forms of bonding being forged out of the global-local nexus," Morley and Robins claim that "the most apparent tendency is, perhaps, towards a new or renewed localism." They conclude that "the key issue" is whether "such affiliations will necessarily be conservative, parochial and introspective, or whether it is possible to reimagine local communities in more cosmopolitan terms" (22).

I am arguing that the unique history of Cataluña provides a model precisely for this "cosmopolitan" vision of the global/local nexus— not in the post-Franco era when Madrid surpassed Barcelona as Spain's most liberated center of cosmopolitan culture and Catalans were perceived by outsiders as provincial in promoting the exclusive use of their own language and in redefining Barcelona "as the capital of its own Catalan nation within the Spanish state,"[33] but in the 1940s and 1950s when Cataluña fought hardest against Francoist xenophobia. Nowhere was this vision more powerfully expressed than in a fascinating Catalan film of the 1940s, Lorenzo Llobet Gràcia's *Vida en sombras* (Life in Shadows, 1947–48). This film was only recently rescued from obscurity when the Spanish Filmoteca's reconstruction of the original was shown at the Valladolid Film Festival in 1984—a context in which its cosmopolitan micro-/ macroregionalism could at last be fully appreciated.

The rest of this chapter will move backward and forward in time, exploring how this cluster of issues surrounding micro- and macro- regionalism was addressed by *Vida en sombras* at the end of the 1940s and how they are now being redefined in the post-Franco context, where Spain is being refigured as a member of the newly unified European Community through the new social formation of global and regional television (as we have seen) as well as through European coproductions like Trueba's *El sueño del mono loco* and Vergés's *Boom Boom* and through the stunning international success of recent films by Almodóvar.

MICRO-/MACROREGIONALISM IN *VIDA EN SOMBRAS*   Described by Hopewell as "the masterpiece" of the *telúricos* movement (a Barcelona-based group of film buffs in the 1940s who were very attuned to foreign films and who engaged in advanced formalist experimentation), this Catalan film presents Barcelona as an international center in touch with Paris and Hollywood, despite its subordinate position within a xenophobic Spanish nation.[34]

Vida en sombras tells the story of a cinephile named Carlos Durán, played by actor-writer-director Fernando Fernán Gómez. Carlos

Carlos Durán (Fernando Fernán Gómez) is obsessed with filmmaking in Lorenzo Llobet Gràcia's reflexive melodrama, *Vida en sombras* (Life in Shadows, 1947–48).

Durán is also the name of an actual Catalan filmmaker born in 1935, who was only twelve when the film was produced and who started in documentary filmmaking like Llobet Gràcia and his protagonist. This real-life Durán was a core member of the "Barcelona school," a group of filmmakers active in 1967–68 who rejected the Castilian cinema of opposition represented by Berlanga, Bardem, and Saura. D'Lugo claims the "essence" of their critique was "the ideological cleavage between cosmopolitan, universalist culture in Barcelona, strongly identified with the intellectual and artistic currents of the rest of Europe, and the Francoist Castilianism of Spanish culture and film which was, in their eyes, provincial and anachronistic" (138). While this "cleavage" was already operative in *Vida en sombras,* Llobet Gràcia's film alludes not only to European works (as did the Catalan films of the 1960s) but also to Hollywood movies—a combination that makes it more similar to the kind of Castilian cinema of opposition that Berlanga, Bardem, and Saura were developing in the 1950s and 1960s as well as to the Catalan cinema of the post-Franco era, which relies so heavily on popular Hollywood genres.

After literally being born in a movie theater in 1906 during the screening of early films by the Lumières, Méliès, and Segundo de Chomón, the fictional Durán grows up to be a documentary filmmaker. When the Civil War breaks out on July 18, 1936, he goes out into the streets of Barcelona to shoot live footage of the action; meanwhile, at home, his pregnant wife Ana is accidentally killed by a stray bullet. Blaming himself for her death, he renounces his camera and career. Thus, the suspension of Durán's filmmaking is linked with the suppression of Catalan culture, both brought by the Civil War and the Nationalist victory. They are liberated from this cultural freeze, not through a political thaw as the nation moves toward macroregionalism with Europe (as was the case in the Catalan films from the 1960s) but rather *through* cinematic spectatorship and reflexive intertextuality. Durán returns to filmmaking after seeing Hitchcock's 1940 film *Rebecca* and becomes romantically involved with another young woman. The film ends as he begins to shoot the semiautobiographical movie we are now seeing.

In this regional context, intertextuality becomes politicized, anticipating the way Erice would use the James Whale *Frankenstein* in *El espíritu de la colmena,* or the way Armiñán would use Marlon Brando in *El amor de Capitán Brando,* or the way Garci would explore in *Mi Marilyn* (1975) how Marilyn Monroe functioned as "a passport to . . . a pleasure out of reach" for young Spanish boys coming of age in the repressive atmosphere of the 1950s. In the post-Franco period, this form of intertextuality would be perpetuated and exaggerated, especially by Almodóvar, whose films frequently include excerpts from Hollywood melodramas (e.g., *Duel in the Sun* in *Matador, Splendor in the Grass* in *What Did I Do to Deserve This?*

and *Johnny Guitar* in *Women on the Verge of a Nervous Breakdown*)—allusions that generate more outrageous excesses by his pleasure seekers who (like their creator) disavow all knowledge of Francoist repression. Yet, like the young protagonists whose emotional lives were deeply affected by the Civil War and its aftermath in *El espíritu de la colmena, El amor de Capitán Brando,* and *Mi Marilyn,* Llobet Gràcia and his filmmaker/hero use politicized intertextuality to escape the traumatic experiences (both personal and historical) that permanently stunted their growth.

As has been noted by Ferrán Alberich, the Spanish critic who directed the documentary about Llobet Gràcia that accompanied the Valladolid screening of *Vida en sombras* and who wrote a monograph that was distributed at the festival, Llobet Gràcia's film has many autobiographical dimensions.[35] Born in Barcelona in 1911 (only five years later than his fictional alter ego), Llobet Gràcia was also a passionate, precocious film fan who was encouraged by his father to become a filmmaker. Like his hero, he also won a prize for one of his early documentaries and (in 1936) married his childhood sweetheart. As his widow describes in voice-over their first meeting, courtship, and marriage, Alberich's film shows clips from *Vida en sombras* that dramatize these events. In the Civil War, Llobet Gràcia lost his father, who had fought on the Republican side.[36] Curiously, the fictional death of Durán's wife not only substituted for that of his father but also prefigured the sudden death of the director's seven-year-old son, which occurred in summer 1948 while Llobet Gràcia was editing the film. Blaming himself for not being there when his family needed him most, Llobet Gràcia suffered a mental breakdown, which led to his confinement in a psychiatric hospital for several months (in late 1948 and early 1949). During this period he also had considerable difficulties with the film; it was given an unfavorable classification by the censors, which prevented it from being exported, necessitated several cuts, and delayed its release for several years. In fact, *Vida en sombras* was not commercially released in Spain until 1953, when it was shown in the Cine Actualidades in Madrid without any advance promotion or publicity. Consequently, it was ignored both by critics and by the public and was quickly withdrawn from the theater. Tragically, the 35-mm negative and prints were lost, leaving only a couple of 16-mm copies in poor condition, which were still being screened at film clubs in the 1970s and which served as the basis for the Filmoteca's reconstruction of the film in the 1980s. Unlike his hero, Llobet Gràcia did not make a comeback; he died in 1976 without having directed another feature and without knowing that *Vida en sombras* would ever be recuperated.[37]

Although the autobiographical parallels are intriguing, I am more interested here in the three larger historical contexts within which Durán's biography is positioned: the histories of mass media, of twentieth-century wars, and of Cataluña's relationship with Spain. Within this structural embedding, film history guides us in reading broader cultural histories. As D'Lugo observes of the Catalan films from the 1960s, "The conceptualization of history and the inter-textual construction of a Catalan historical referent [would] play a pivotal role in the development and evolution of modern Catalan cinema" (133). This conceptualization is already clearly operative in Llobet Gràcia's film.

Vida en sombras is remarkable not only as an early reflexive film, which does *not* rely on a genre already known for reflexivity (such as comedy, as in Keaton's *Sherlock Jr.* and *The Cameraman,* or the musical, as in Busby Berkeley's *Footlight Parade*), but one that explores the ideological potential of reflexiveness, as in the work of Vertov and Godard. Like *Citizen Kane* and *8½,* *Vida en sombras* positions bio-graphical and cinematic reflexivity within the international genre of melodrama, while stressing the regional/national/global interface (the influence of France and Hollywood on the development of a distinctively Catalan cinema) and the film medium's historic con-nections with photography, radio, and other early forms of mass entertainment. Like *Citizen Kane,* through the fictionalized biogra-phy of one man, the film provides a critical commentary on the history of his nation. But in the case of *Vida en sombras,* it was a part of history (the Civil War) and a regional culture (Cataluña) that were repressed by the Francoist government, which restricted the repre-sentation of history to an idealized version of Spain's glorious past. Apart from propagandistic Francoist epics like *Raza, Vida en sombras* is the first Spanish film to represent the Spanish Civil War, particularly from a perspective that is sympathetic to the losing side, which is one reason that it had so much trouble with the censors. As Bardem and Saura were to demonstrate later in the 1950s and 1960s with *Muerte de un ciclista* and *La caza,* Llobet Gràcia seemed to realize that though the representation of the Civil War was repressed at home, it might be recognized abroad as a powerful seme of Spanishness.

The film opens and closes with the same image of Durán's parents posing for a still photographer, suggesting how the family would anchor the photographic medium of cinema within the domestic province of melodrama.[38] In his perceptive psychoanalytic reading of *Vida en sombras,* Jesús González Requena argues that the circularity of its structure (the framing of the film by these images of his parents) helps entrap the protagonist in the imaginary where he is castrated and impotent and from which he never escapes.[39] Yet the inset excerpts from foreign films demonstrate that moviegoing can provide a temporary magical release from this entrapment within the frozen image and frozen culture.

We see this dynamic occurring at least three times: first, when the maternal spectator gives birth to the hero just as the magician on screen pulls a baby out of a hat; second, when Carlos and his fiancée Ana go to see George Cukor's 1936 version of *Romeo and Juliet* and the light beam from the projector seems to magically empower their kiss, which segues directly to a wedding ring being put on her finger;[40] and third, when Durán's viewing of *Rebecca* enables him to be blessed by photographic images of his dead wife, so that he can regain his potency in art and romance. Within this Francoist context, cinema is figured as a mass medium that combines Méliès-type magic with the minor miracles of the Madonna. In substituting for the idolatrous gaze of religion and for taboo images of sex, the spectatorial gaze of cinema gains the power of fetishizing foreign icons that were otherwise forbidden in Spain.

Significantly for the regional discourse, these reflexive dynamics are set in Barcelona around the turn of the century. After being photographed, Carlos's bourgeois parents wander through the 1906 Exposition where they see all the latest fads from Paris, including desirable cinematographic hardware like the toy zoetrope, which the husband purchases for his wife, and a Lumière projector. In the birth sequence, we see a scene from one of Segundo de Chomón's pioneering trick films that he made in Paris in 1908 for Pathé, *Les vêtements cascadeurs* (Cascade of Clothes, or Transformations). The excerpt features a magic act in which men are magically replaced by dolls, and a woman removes their legs. This castrating image is emblematic of the regional filmmaker's plight; for both Chomón at the beginning of the century and Llobet Gràcia in the Francoist period were cut off from a receptive home audience and prevented by the xenophobic provincialism of the dominant Castilian culture from expressing their sophisticated modernist views (which *Vida en sombras* quite pointedly associates with France).[41]

As Durán grows up, the ellipsis between his birth and his emergence as a young spectator in the cinema is covered over by a montage of historical images from World War I. The end of the war is broadcast over the family radio, with the announcer claiming, "Paris goes wild with enthusiasm," implying that France still sets the trends for spectators of war as well as of cinema. But little Carlos is oblivious to history; he is far more interested in playing with his mother's zoetrope. This scene prefigures the later introduction of the Civil War, whose outbreak is also announced over the radio and where the zoetrope is replaced by Carlos's movie camera.

The ellipsis between Durán's boyhood adventures and his emergence as an adult played by Fernando Fernán Gómez is also covered by a montage of historical images—this time of a 1929 International Exposition, which presents Barcelona as the cosmopolitan city where Carlos launches his moviemaking career. We are reminded—again, by a radio broadcast, this time of music from *The Jazz Singer*—that this is the precise historic moment when the medium acquires sound. This development would immediately transform cinema from, in Borau's words, "a poetic series of silent images without national identity" into movies "that have geographical, political, and literary dimensions" and that "are nationalistic in ways that jump out at you from the very first frame."[42] The conversion made cinema an effective vehicle for accentuating both Catalan autonomy under the II

Republic (which was born only two years later in 1931) and Spain's technological backwardness in comparison with Hollywood and other European nations. When Carlos hears the music from *The Jazz Singer,* he quips, "I love cinema, I don't believe in mechanical progress."

Apparently, this attitude toward progress was common in Spain, particularly in Madrid. For, according to Augusto M. Torres, when *The Jazz Singer* premiered in Madrid in June 1929, it was at first shown without sound since Spanish movie theaters were not equipped for sound projection and "the owners of cinemas [were] reluctant to invest in what they consider[ed] a passing fad."[43] Thus, the only way to hear the sound track in Spain was on the radio. Torres observes,

Western Electric sound equipment, which quickly captures the market after an initial patents war, is very expensive. . . . So they continue to screen silent movies or close down, waiting for the sound fever to pass. . . . From over seventy films that are made annually in Spain, production plummets to a mere five movies between 1929 and 1931. Furthermore, the films are shot in Spain without sound and are dubbed abroad due to the lack of Spanish sound studios. ("1896–1929," 26–27)

Positioning these industrial conditions within the larger political and economic context, Torres explains why the transition to sound in Spain was "not as easy as . . . in most of the major film industries around the world":

The arrival of sound motion pictures coincides with the great international economic depression and with the end of the dictatorship in the Spain of General Primo de Rivera, which was succeeded for a few months by that of General Berenguer. At a time when the film industry needs to invest heavily in new sound equipment for both recording and reproduction purposes and in building sound studios, the peseta is tottering, capital is being sent out of the country and investors are discouraged. ("1896–1929," 27)

Thus, it was the new Republic that provided the setting for the revival of Spanish cinema and, more specifically, the emergence of "talkies" that could speak Catalan. But in the Francoist context of 1947–48 when *Vida en sombras* was being made, the sound track now emphasized Castilian's dominance over regional languages like Catalan, as well as over the languages of foreign imports (since a new law imposed in 1941 required that all films be dubbed into Castilian). Yet, as in the transitional period to sound, Spanish sound tracks continued to be technically inferior to their counterparts from Hollywood and Europe, a problem that Llobet Gràcia himself was not able to overcome and that still persists today. This dimension is emphasized in the excerpts from Cukor's *Romeo and Juliet* and Hitchcock's *Rebecca,* which demonstrate the literary richness of their Anglo-American sources (which range from a Renaissance giant like William Shakespeare to a popular contemporary writer like Daphne Du Maurier and which Hispanic and Catalan culture could rival) as well as the technical richness of Hollywood sound tracks (which could not be satisfactorily reproduced either in Barcelona or Madrid).

Although these historical backstories are all subordinated to the personal biography of Durán, his linear "progress" is soon interrupted by the Civil War. Taking his camera rather than a gun, he goes out to shoot the early action in scenes that appear very staged and theatrical but that clearly violate the Francoist prohibitions against showing realistic footage of the Civil War. Linked melodramatically to the death of his pregnant wife (who is blatantly associated with the Virgin), this transgression of the taboo is severely punished on screen. The Civil War becomes a historical primal scene and the hero one of those stunted "children of Franco." Requena reads this moment as a form of castration, which is underlined by the symbolic decapitation of the statue of the Virgin. While I agree with this reading, what seems more interesting historically is that the film offers a model for how to use a personal romantic/sexual discourse to talk about political topics that were otherwise suppressed. Although this film failed to influence others, it prefigured what was to come in the oppositional cinema of later decades both from Madrid and Barcelona.

When Durán's castration is read against both his birth in the theater during a showing of early trick films (made in Paris for Pathé by Chomón, who was born in Teruel) and the hero's later rebirth after seeing *Rebecca* (Hitchcock's first Hollywood film, which launched his success as an international auteur), we realize that cinema can be seen as an imaginary form of exile. This exile applies not only to brilliant world-class cinematic émigrés like Hitchcock, Chomón, and Buñuel but also to ordinary spectators, for it suggests that seeing foreign films in Barcelona can function as a potent form of inner exile or resistance against the xenophobic Francoist culture.

Vida en sombras is most advanced in the way it explores spectator/text relations. It shows us the history of the growing sophistication of moviegoers in what they are able to understand and enjoy and how they can be manipulated by the image—to laugh or cry, to fight or fall in love. It demonstrates the dynamics of the gaze and its ability to suture spectators into emotional identification with the image. And it dramatizes the use of film equipment and photographic images as a fetishistic substitute for the absent object of desire. These effects are most powerfully dramatized in one amazing sequence. After watching the scene from *Rebecca* in which Joan Fontaine and Laurence Olivier are looking at home movies from their own happier past, Durán (who physically resembles the young Olivier) returns to his room to watch home movies of himself and his dead wife. This act of double spectatorship enables him to find a way out of his own entrapment. Gradually, the close-ups of him as spectator replace his screen image in the home movie. He is able to suture himself into that imaginary scene from the past and as an empowered spectator to actively draw a blessing from the ambiguous image and words of his dead wife. Like the scene in John Ford's *Young Mr. Lincoln* (1939) in which the hero consults his dead love about whether to study the law, Durán uses the recorded words of his dead wife ("What do you want me to say?") to authorize his own desire to resume his pursuit of cinema.

Moreover, this sequence is contrasted with an earlier scene in which Durán returned to the movie theater where he was born and

Vida en sombras shows the responses of early moviegoers to cinematic violence and tracks the growing sophistication of spectatorship.

where he had seen *Romeo and Juliet* with Ana. Although this earlier scene contained a flashback to their magical kiss, its subjective interlude was framed by still photos of Leslie Howard and Norma Shearer, which Durán was unable to animate. Thus, there he remained stuck in the tragedy of the past, which (as in Fascist and neo-Catholic discourse) fetishizes heroic death. But *Rebecca* is pure melodrama, not tragedy, and it specifically teaches the spectator how to escape the castrating power of the frozen domestic image—the fetishized portrait of the dead wife.

After seeing the moving images both from *Rebecca* and his own home movies, Carlos stares at Ana's still photograph, which miraculously smiles. It is a minor miracle; but it is also the spectator's power of animating the still image that is fundamental to all cinema. By frequently foregrounding Ana's photographic representations and by having other characters comment on the "tenderness" of her gaze, the film has transformed her into an icon of the Madonna, whose moral blessing is granted to her spiritual children. In fact, when Durán earlier claimed that his "passion for cinema" was responsible for his wife's death, he accused himself of "extinguishing her gaze"—as if he had lost the singular spectator whose desire made his art worthwhile.

There is a sophisticated awareness here that the whole cinematic process—its production, its hardware, and its reception—are emotional substitutes for original plenitude, a dynamic that is the primary source of its intense pleasure and of its power to repeatedly draw us back to the screen. And yet there is also the recognition that these pleasures still cannot totally compensate for the loss of that original object of desire—whether it is Hitchcock's evil Rebecca, or Durán's martyred wife, or total fusion with his mother's body, which he lost at the movies, or Catalan autonomy, which was lost in the Civil War. Nevertheless, in the historical context of cultural entrapment, such spectatorship and intertextuality provide temporary ideological relief. Like Almodóvar's suicidal lovers in *La ley del deseo,* Carlos seeks this blessing from a pop version of the Holy Virgin, who is enshrined in the intertextuality of a cinema that is both deeply personal and strategically international.

INTERNATIONAL COPRODUCTIONS OF THE LATE 1980S AND EARLY 1990S: *EL MONO LOCO* AND *BOOM BOOM* AS MACROREGIONAL CINEMA   A more recent strategy for international filmmaking currently being tried by Spanish filmmakers both from Madrid and Barcelona is the European coproduction. In fact, Spain is one of nine member states of the European Community (along with Belgium, Denmark, France, Greece, Ireland, Italy, Luxembourg, and Portugal) who signed "on 10 February 1987, at the invitation of the French government, a declaration of intent with the aim of setting up a multilateral support mechanism for the coproduction, distribution, transmission and promotion of film and audiovisual works, known as EURIMAGES," a pact that became operational in January 1989.[44]

Yet there is some ambiguity as to whether Spain's coproductions are aimed primarily at the European or the U.S. and Latin American markets. In a study sponsored by the European Institute for the Media, which assesses the international coproduction in the context of the new European Community, André Lange and Jean-Luc Renaud conclude,

It would certainly be a mistake for Europeans to focus their attention exclusively on the U.S. market, since they will never be able to make more than a marginal or tangential impact on it. . . . The main thrust of a European policy to deal with the world market should begin with an increase in the number of European programmes in circulation within the European market itself. In this sense, the policy which the European Commission has been pursuing vigorously since 1986 is a coherent one. (315, 322)

Acknowledging that the coherence of that policy is somewhat compromised by the specific "linguistic, historical and cultural links" that these European nations have with other regions they formerly colonized (e.g., Spain/Latin America, France/Africa, United Kingdom/Commonwealth), Lange and Renaud report that Latin America currently represents nearly 40 percent of Spain's market for television productions, in contrast to the United States and Canada (which represent only 13 percent) and with the rest of Europe (representing 47 percent).[45] Yet their figures also indicate that whereas the number of cinema tickets sold in the entire European community has steadily been dropping (from 994 million in 1980 to 649.6 million in 1986), the number sold in the United States has remained fairly constant (from 1,021 million in 1980 to 1,017 in 1986). Moreover, of all the European countries being assessed, Spain has experienced one of the most dramatic declines—from 176 million in 1980, when it was second only to Italy (241 million), to 87 million in 1986, when it fell far behind France (163.4 million), Italy (124.8 million), and West Germany (105.2 million; Lang and Renaud, table 11, p. 84). Thus, one can hardly be surprised that despite the economic failure of Borau's *Río abajo* and Bigas Luna's *Reborn* and *Anguish*,[46] Spanish filmmakers are still trying to repeat Almodóvar's success in the North American market, particularly since film tickets sold in the United States far surpass those sold in all of Europe and Japan combined.

A diverse range of fascinating Spanish films have recently grappled with these pressures. For example, Antonio Drove's *El tunnel* (The Tunnel, 1987), a highly sophisticated erotic thriller based on an Argentine novel by Ernesto Sabato and shot in Spain and Argentina, was made both in English and Spanish with a well-known international cast, including Peter Weller, Jane Seymour, and Fernando Rey. Basilio Patino's *Madrid* (1987) stars Rudiger Vogler (well known for his roles in Wim Wenders's road movies) as a German director who has been hired by Spanish television to make a documentary on the fiftieth anniversary of the Spanish Civil War. Although the subject appears to be very Spanish—a city symphony of Madrid that draws on archival footage of the Civil War—the film is multilingual (Spanish, German, and English), and its mode of discourse emphasizes conceptual issues of representation that transcend national and generic boundaries. Gonzalo Suárez's *Remando al viento* (Rowing with the Wind, 1988), a Spanish/Norwegian coproduction made both in English and Spanish with a predominantly British cast, focuses on Mary Shelley's writing of *Frankenstein,* drawing heavily on Goya and the surrealists for its stunning visual imagery while suggesting historic links between Spanish painting and English romanticism; it was a big critical and box office success in Spain (and in summer 1991, it was still playing in Madrid).[47] Saura's *El dorado* (1988), a Spanish/French coproduction, presents another version of the story of Spanish conquistador Lope de Aguirre, which was designed to challenge and surpass that of Werner Herzog's German masterpiece, *Aguirre, The Wrath of God;* the most expensive production in Spanish film history, it unfortunately proved to be both a commercial and a critical flop.

Saura's more modest *¡Ay, Carmela!* (1990), a Spanish-Italian coproduction starring Carmen Maura, fared much better in the international market both commercially and critically, perhaps partly because it returned to the subject of the Spanish Civil War. Guerin's *Innisfree* (1990), a Catalan feature-length documentary (coproduced by France's Channel 7), explores the small Irish town where John Ford was born and where he made *The Quiet Man* and the traces that the film and its director left behind; despite its Irish/American focus, this reflexive film emphasizes themes of exile, memory, and historical recuperation, which are very familiar both in Spanish and Catalan cinema.

Of the forty-two Spanish features released in 1990, ten were international coproductions whose foreign partners were based in France (2), Italy, England, Belgium, Switzerland, Mexico, Peru, Argentina, and Morocco, and three others were coproductions between Madrid-based firms and companies based either in Barcelona (2) or the Basque region (1). While the emphasis has shifted to *European* partners (60 percent as opposed to 33 percent), the actual number of coproductions is consistent with those for 1988, when there were nine coproductions—whose foreign partners were based in Italy (2), the United States (2), Mexico (2), Peru, Cuba, Colombia, France—and three domestic coproductions between Madrid-based firms and companies based either in Barcelona (2) or San Sebastián; but the percentage of international coproductions was considerably lower in 1988 (14 percent as opposed to 24 percent), since there were sixty-four features released that year.[48]

The macroregionalism in these coproductions tends to destabilize not the economic infrastructure they were designed to challenge but rather the cultural identity of Spanish and Catalan cinema. Having had little impact abroad, these films seem to have more influence at home, where they help Spaniards and Catalonians redefine how they see themselves in relation to the changing world order.

One of the best examples of these dynamics is *El largo invierno* (The Long Winter, 1991), directed by Jaime Camino, one of the most important Catalan filmmakers in the post-Franco era. This

Catalan/Spanish/French coproduction evokes Camino's earlier film, *Las largas vacaciones del 36* (The Long Vacation of '36, 1975), which depicted the outbreak of the Civil War (also in the generic context of family melodrama) and was a commercial success at home. Clearly designed for an international audience, this new version features Vittorio Gassman as an Italian servant, French actors Jean Rochefort and Jacques Penot as the Red members of the rich Catalan family he serves and betrays, and English actress Elisabeth Hurley as the American leftist love interest, with well-known Spanish star José Luis López Vázquez and Catalan actors Adolfo Marsillach, Sergi Mateu, and Teresa Gimpera in supporting roles. Beginning in the winter of 1939 just before Franco's troops reached Barcelona, the story centers on the fate of the Casals family, a name that evokes one of the most internationally famous Catalan exiles, Pablo Casals (who was featured in another Camino film about the outbreak of the war, *Dragón Rapide,* 1986). Like Camino's masterful three-hour documentary on the Civil War, *La vieja memoria* (Old Memory, 1977), *El largo invierno* conflates the destruction of Catalan autonomy with the fall of the Republic and specifically calls attention to the issue of language (when the names of family members are forcibly changed from Fernán to Fernando and from Jordi to Jorge), yet the bilingual version of the film (in Catalan and Spanish) was shown only in Cataluña, whereas the Spanish version was shown throughout the rest of Spain and (with subtitles) in Europe. When the film was shown at the AFI International Film Festival in Los Angeles (June 26, 1992), Camino claimed that this was the only way the film could get distribution.

I have chosen to focus my discussion on two earlier international coproductions, *El sueño del mono loco* and *Boom Boom,* primarily because their mixed reception most fully illuminates the regional/national/global interface at the turn of the decade. Both are genre films (a reflexive psychological thriller and a romantic comedy, respectively) that try to duplicate the success Almodóvar earlier achieved with these forms in *La ley del deseo* and *Mujeres al borde de un ataque de nervios. El mono loco* is a Spanish/French coproduction made in Paris and in English by a well-established madrileño auteur, Fernando Trueba, in collaboration with one of Spain's "most active" producers, Andrés Vicente Gómez. *Boom Boom* is a Spanish/Belgian coproduction made in Barcelona in three versions (Catalan, Spanish, and French) by a young regional feminist, Rosa Vergés,[49] in collaboration with an up-and-coming television producer, Rosa Romero. In discussing these works, I will focus as much on their reception, particularly on the critical response in the popular press, as on the films themselves, for I am primarily interested in how they were perceived by Spaniards.

El sueño del mono loco   One of the most striking examples of a European coproduction at the end of the 1980s is Trueba's *El sueño del mono loco* (1989, released in the United States under the title *Twisted Obsession*), a project the director had wanted to make for over ten years and that he consciously conceived as a model for a new macroregional cinema.

There are six characters, . . . two Americans, two English, and two French, and my intention is to do it with actors of those nationalities. Since the English-speaking protagonists predominate, I will shoot it in that language with direct sound. I believe that this film can be a good example of what we call European cinema, a coproduction with France and with a budget of between three and four million dollars.[50]

In many ways, this project is similar to Borau's international coproductions from the 1970s (*Hay que matar á B* and *La Sabina*), which may have been ahead of their time. *El mono loco* also had European financing, a prominent international cast with at least one well-known American actor (Jeff Goldblum), a plot evoking Hitchcock's psychological thrillers with stylized touches of noir, a fast-paced narrative, and a highly crafted visual surface. But in contrast to Borau's situation, now the timing was right: *El mono loco* was partially funded by Spanish public television (TVE); it was selected as Spain's official entry for the 1990 Venice Film Festival; it won five Goya awards;[51] and it was highly praised for its international qualities by some of Spain's most influential critics. For example, Antonio Lara hailed it as an "ambitious" work that "transcends the conventional limits and inevitable provincialism which usually restrict Spanish cinematographic projects" and that leads "the Spanish film industry to embark on a new road."[52] Javier Maqua placed it in that international genre of reflexive movies about filmmaking, a connection that Trueba strongly encouraged in his interviews.[53] For example, he reported that when his leading actor, Jeff Goldblum, said "we wanted to make another *Last Tango in Paris, . . .* I replied that we were going to shoot the *Sunset Boulevard* of the 1980s."[54] Trueba also endorsed the comparison with Hitchcock's reflexive thrillers, observing, "if there is a point of reference to find, it is more in *Vertigo* than in *Psycho*."[55]

Although these international dimensions were highly appreciated in Spain, where the film was shown both in the original English with Spanish subtitles and in a totally dubbed version and where it did fairly well at the box office (grossing 108 million pesetas by December 1990), like Spain's earlier international coproductions, it did not fare as well in France (and even had trouble obtaining distribution in England) and flopped in the United States, quickly disappearing from the theaters without much publicity, critical attention, or box office. Even at the Venice Film Festival, it was coolly received and won no awards—partly because "the film did not seem Spanish, but international."[56] Moreover, when he was accused of compromising his material for commercial considerations, Trueba disavowed his earlier claims of pioneering a new form of European filmmaking and instead defended his artistic integrity.[57] When Spanish journalists charged that most of the pesetas from the film's inflated budget went into Goldblum's pockets and that the new estimate of $5 million was a very large sum, even for a film trying "to internationalize the Spanish cinema," Trueba defended himself by distinguishing between the national and macroregional contexts.

That's true if we look at it from the Spanish point of view, which is very poor economically; in this way it can be defined as a luxurious film. But considering that it has involved the participation of international actors and that it was shot in Paris, one could say that we have neither skimped on the costs nor exaggerated the expenses. The price is reasonable.[58]

The film was coproduced by Emanuel Schlumberger of French Producciones and Andrés Vicente Gómez of Iberoamericana Films, who is actively seeking new ways of coping with the Spanish film industry's current crisis. According to Hopewell, "Vicente Gómez... is launching an ambitious slate of Spanish "A" titles—Fernando Trueba's *El Mono Loco* . . . and Carlos Saura's *¡Ay, Carmela!* (1990) are the latest examples—which offset their high budgets by substantial takings at home and piecemeal sales abroad, by [his] differentiation into theatrical and video distribution of large U.S. and European art films, and by sales of his large film library archive to television."[59] Ironically, the international distribution of *El mono loco* begins to sound similar to that of Borau's *Río abajo*—only fortunately for Trueba, he did not invest his own money in the project and therefore is still eager to try again.[60]

Based on a 1976 novel of the same name by Christopher Frank (who was born in London and raised in Paris), *El sueño del mono loco* tells the story of Dan Gillis (Jeff Goldblum), a writer living in Paris. Accusing him of being a child, his French wife Marianne abandons him, leaving him to take care of their five-year-old bilingual son Danny.[61] At the urging of Malcolm Green (Dexter Fletcher), a young avant-garde British filmmaker, Dan's French producer hires him to collaborate on adapting his own novel, a perverse variation on Peter Pan, which he wrote before becoming a commercial screenwriter and which Green now wants to direct. Gillis is ambivalent about the project until he meets Green's teenage sister Jenny (Liza Walker), whom Malcolm exploits sexually, not only as erotic spectacle in his soft core movies but also as a prostitute to advance his career and as the object of desire in their own incestuous relationship. Even after Gillis discovers that Malcolm is a demented junkie and that his producer has been seduced into the project by Jenny's sexual favors, he sticks with the film because he has also become erotically obsessed with this suicidal Tinkerbell. He recklessly pursues Jenny until he finds her corpse eerily floating in a tank in an old deserted factory, along with the bloated nude bodies of other stray victims of murder and suicide. Like the runaways in *Peter Pan,* these anonymous corpses appear to be freed from growth and decay, suspended between life and death. After facing this grisly sight, Gillis is consoled by his beautiful British agent Marilyn (Miranda Richardson), who conveniently doubles as his mistress.

The most mysterious characters in the film are the two femmes fatales. As an elusive Tinkerbell, young Jenny may prove to be as exploitive and ambitious as her brother; but her motives remain as inaccessible as her death. As a morally ambiguous Wendy, the matriarchal agent Marilyn (despite her confinement in a wheelchair) controls not only clients and lovers like Gillis but also the orphaned Greens, whom she apparently adopted and exploited in England.

Trueba's film, like the Gillis novel that Green wants to adapt to the screen, focuses on the tragedy of growing up. As Trueba puts it, "It is perhaps a film on the inquietude of Peter Pan, on the inability to grow up. The infirmity and the disgust of the man who clings too hard to adolescent dreams."[62] Both Gillis and the Greens are the mad monkeys, the lost children hooked on adolescent dreams who are abandoned by a cold mother and manipulated by a crippled queen. A far cry from Spielberg's optimistic *Hook* (1991), Trueba's perverse adaptation of *Peter Pan* has a deep structure that is recognizably Spanish, even if its cultural specificity is internationalized and disguised.

Within the Spanish Oedipal narrative that lies at the heart of this melodrama, one still finds many of the patterns we have analyzed in earlier chapters. For example, the submerged rivalry between the young girl and the older woman (ending with the death of the former) evokes the Snow White/Wicked Queen rivalry and its ironic variations that we traced through the Spanish Oedipal narrative in *Camada negra, Amantes, Furtivos,* and *Bilbao* as well as the pairing of the incestuous desire for the sister with the matricidal urge toward the phallic mother, which proved so violent in *Pascual Duarte* and *Tras el cristal.* Moreover, within this Spanish Oedipal narrative, one still finds the displacement of patricidal impulses onto the bad mother—both onto Gillis's wife Marianne, the repressive patriarchal mother who abandons the hero (the archenemy of the surrealists and their homoerotic successors like Almodóvar and Villaronga), and onto his agent Marilyn, the crippling phallic queen, who is still formidable, even in her regal wheelchair.

We also find the quintessential shaving scene, which is assigned to Gillis's five-year-old son Danny, who cuts himself while shaving with his father's razor. This shaving scene triggers Gillis's nightmare in which Jenny attempts suicide by jumping out the bathroom window, a dream that acknowledges the suicidal nature of Danny's so-called accident with the razor and Gillis's conflation of Jenny with his son, both as erotic doubles and rivals. These acts occur after Danny has witnessed his father performing cunnilingus on Jenny's shaved pudendum (which, as in Bigas Luna movies, is featured as the primary object of erotic spectacle in brother Malcolm's soft core films). The boy deeply resents his father who is also his rival and whose childishness has driven his mother away, yet Danny simultaneously desires him and is jealous of Jenny, with whom he perversely identifies (the way Rena comes to identify with Angelo in *Tras el cristal* and Marcelino with Miguel in *Marcelino, pan y vino*). Thus, in the shaving scene, not only "is a child being beaten" according to the orthodox Freudian scenario but this particular form of castrating self-mutilation has special cultural resonance in the Spanish context. Moreover, Gillis's obsession with the underage Jenny begins to eroticize his relationship with Danny, enabling homoerotic incest between father and son to rival the heterosexual incest between brother and sister. This implication is strongest in the sequence in which Jenny suddenly emerges out of the shadows of Danny's bedroom, watching him and confiding to his father that the child is only pretending to be asleep because *she* (his rival) is there. Then as soon as she abandons Gillis, he carries his son to his bed and embraces him as if to console the child, but clearly he himself is the one being consoled. For he is using Danny as a substitute for his lost androgynous love, just as he will later use his agent Marilyn for consolation after discovering Jenny's corpse. This sequence acknowledges the homoerotic backstory of the Oedipal myth, which became blatant in many post-Franco films.

El mono loco has several superficial similarities with *Vida en sombras*. Both are reflexive melodramas about moviemaking, where the obsessiveness of the childlike hero makes him lose his wife and contributes to the death of his love (who are here divided into two characters); both rely on intertextuality with world cinema at a key moment of global reconfiguration; and both focus on the psychodynamics of spectatorship as a form of inner exile or escape. Yet, in contrast to *Vida en sombras* and Borau's international coproductions from the 1970s, Trueba's film disavows its specific political implications and its cultural traces of Spanishness, which appear to be merely an inflection of the melodrama. Given that the protagonist is an American screenwriter living in Paris, his emotional stuntedness and his "tragedy of growing up" are rooted not in traumatic events from Spanish history but in the Anglo-Saxon myth of Peter Pan; the fetishization of death is not linked with fascism and Catholicism but (as in Almodóvar's *¡Atame!*) with the hybridization of horror and porn. Perhaps what *El mono loco* demonstrates is that for Spain, the real "tragedy of growing up"—of moving into the new world order of the united European Community, that macroregionalism of the 1990s—may be the risk of cultural erasure.

Boom Boom Less ambitious than *El mono loco, Boom Boom* is a sophisticated screwball comedy that tries to woo international audiences by presenting Barcelona in the way Almodóvar has represented Madrid; that is, as a freshly distinctive yet cosmopolitan urban setting, where the complex interrelations among its characters can be spatialized within a specific neighborhood—as tenants, neighbors, and porters in high-rise luxury apartments, as doctors and patients in nearby professional buildings, and as vendors and consumers in local newsstands, shops, and bars. Thus, unlike *El mono loco,* it exaggerates rather than disavows its cultural specificity, a strategy more suitable to its microregional context.

What is most impressive about this debut feature is its visual wit and narrative stylization. Director Vergés calls it "an urban comedy with few displacements."[63] Sharing with Almodóvar the common influence of Billy Wilder, *Boom Boom* skillfully choreographs the erratic movements of its ensemble of mismatched zany characters through kaleidoscopic couplings within a fast-paced, hyperplotted narrative.[64] Noting the connection both with Almodóvar's *Women on the Verge of a Nervous Breakdown* and with recent American comedies it rivals, Spanish critic José Luis Guarner claims Vergés succeeds in creating a film that departs from "the traditional provincial tone of the Catalan cinema" and that cultivates the kind of "Almodovaresque touches that today so definitely convey the look of modernity."

Her obvious models are the screwball American comedy and the ironically elaborated sentimental intrigues of [Alan] Rudolf—the cocktail bar here serves a function that is similar to the bar in *Choose Me*—not copied imitatively but assimilated in order to express what finally is revealed as a personal style.[65]

As in *Women on the Verge of a Nervous Breakdown*, the protagonist is an attractive career woman in her thirties (a sexy dentist named Sofía), who breaks up with her married lover and whose fate is affected by a potent tomato-based brew containing a mysterious ingredient. Yet since *Boom Boom* is far less outrageous (and less sexually explicit) than Almodóvar's films, the Bloody Mary works more like the magical dust in *A Midsummer Night's Dream* than like the drugged gazpacho in *Women on the Verge*. Vergés describes it as "a film about love without sex. What is important and entertaining are the characters and situations of the four persons who are in their thirties."[66] Sofía finds a new romance with her neighbor Tristan, who has just been dumped by his bride and who is adopted as a model of masculinity by Angel, a young bartender from a neighborhood bar. Like the Almodóvar characters frequently played by Antonio Banderas (sometimes called Angel), this Angel is also struggling to break free from his possessive mother and his repressive aunts. He is a puckish changeling who helps drive the narrative—both as Sofía's patient and secret admirer and as Tristan's temporary roommate and double.

The comic resolution of the film is more conventional than its opening. In the romantic precredits teaser, a woman gets out of a car. At first, we see only her sexy black dress and a fetishized close-up of her bare feet. Her male companion brings her shoes and kisses her passionately, following her into a modern urban high-rise, leaving the voyeuristic camera to loiter outside. Accompanied by romantic guitar music, the camera rises up in a crane shot that follows the gliding movement of the elevator, which is reminiscent of the one featured in *Last Tango in Paris* and which carries the lovers up to her flat. Then the camera moves into a shot through the window just in time to see her discreetly close the shutters.

The sound of a pulsing heartbeat begins with the credits, creating comic distance from the romantic theme and calling attention to the syncopated stylization of the editing and narrative. At the end of the credits, the camera is still waiting at the window. When the shutters are raised, we see the same couple arguing; she throws out her married lover, and the tango music resumes. With few words spoken, this mini-narrative concisely captures the peak and nadir of the romance. Like a perfume commercial, it also establishes the hotness of the affair and of the heroine, the fetishized focus on shoes and other visual details, and the rhythmic use of ellipsis. We know very little about the characters or the setting; the scene could occur in any modern city. Nor do we know where the film will go from here; whether this is merely a prologue, or one scene from a steamy on-again, off-again affair, or one episode in an anthology film on romance.

The following scene makes the third option seem most likely. An overhead shot reveals a bride and groom getting out of the same elevator. Then the camera follows them to the door of their apartment and stays there to record elliptically the rapid deterioration of their marriage, until she leaves with a new lover. At this point, the narrative seems to be developing in the iterative like Chantal Akerman's boldly original film *Toute une nuit* (All through the Night, 1982), which is totally composed of a series of brief elliptical scenes of numerous couples uniting and parting in a Parisian suburb.[67] But Vergés abandons this radical path when her camera pulls back to show the two unhappy lovers—Sofía brooding alone on her balcony above and Tristan sulking on the terrace below. The spatial unity poses the question, how and when will these miserable misfits meet and become lovers? The narrative game is to withhold the answers as long as possible, particularly since the meeting is so clearly inevitable.

The elaboration of the plot follows the familiar conventions of romantic comedy. Original variations are provided by the traces of stylization carried over from the opening—the pulsating sound of the heartbeat (which gives the film its title and accentuates its linear drive), the narrativizing of the foot fetish (by making Tristan the owner of a local shoe store and by giving Sofía a pair of smashing red pumps that rival Dorothy's famous ruby slippers), and, most effective, the film's narrative obsession with pairing (not only of lovers but also of misplaced or mismatched shoes, gloves, scenes, and shots). After the opening, the film also plunges into Catalan specificity, which becomes another means of delaying and complicating the romance.

From the beginning, *Boom Boom* was conceived as a project that could negotiate the local/global nexus, as a regional Catalan film that could succeed in an international market—an achievement, as Besas has noted, that was previously accomplished only by Jordi Cadena's "sexy pic," *La senyora,* which was successfully distributed in fifteen countries outside Spain. Or as Diego Muñoz puts it, "*Boom Boom* was born as a film destined for Europe: A Hispanic-Belgian coproduction shot in three languages . . . ; with Spanish actors . . . and Belgian actress; and, above all, in a comic tone on today's amorous relations."[68] Shot in seven weeks, *Boom Boom* cost only 125 million pesetas, 25 percent of which was raised by its Belgian coproducer, Benoit Lamy, who describes the film as "contemporary and very international."[69] The film also received subventions at the microregional level (from TV-3, the regional Catalan television channel, and from the autonomous regional government, the Generalitat de Cataluña), at the national level (from the Spanish Ministry of Culture), and at the macroregional level of the European Community (from

Entrepreneurs de l'Audio-visuel Europeén, EAVE, which selected it as one of twenty European projects to be funded).

Its Catalan dimension is strongly represented by the two women who made it, the two Rosas who were both born in Barcelona in the mid-1950s. Despite her relative youth, before making her directorial debut Vergés had worked as an assistant on many of the most important Catalan films of the post-Franco period: Aranda's *La muchacha de las bragas de oro* (The Girl with the Golden Panties, 1980), Salgot's *Mater amatísima* (Beloved Mother, 1980), Betriu's *La Plaza del Diamant* (Diamond Square, 1982), Bigas Luna's *Lola* (1985) and *Angústia* (Anguish, 1987), and Villaronga's *Tras el cristal* (1985). In 1986, she became part of the Commission for the Evaluation of Cinematographic Projects by the Ministry of Culture and the Generalitat de Cataluña, both of whom were later to help fund *Boom Boom.* She describes the film as "very *barcelonés,* but with characters who can appeal to all types of audiences over 15 years of age."[70]

Rosa Romero has been associated with TV-3 since 1983, primarily as coordinator of popular cutting-edge programs like "Estoc de Pop," "Max Headroom," "Clip-Club," "Arsenal," and "Arsenal-Atlas." In 1988, she founded Arsenal Films, a company whose first feature was *Boom Boom.* Previously, she produced shorts and documentaries for television. As one of the twenty European producers selected to participate in the first seminar on production that was sponsored by EAVE (an organization that is part of the Media Plan of the new European Community), she helped to get the subvention from the macroregional level. Keenly aware of the importance of television in the local/global nexus, she insists, "It is very important for us to shoot a Catalan film in Catalan with vistas that can be exhibited not only as a feature but also on television."[71]

The third important woman making her feature debut on the project is the actress playing Sofía. Viktor Fleming (whose name comes from the character played by Paul Henried in *Casablanca*) was formerly a successful Parisian model and a popular international jazz singer (whose records are especially successful in Japan). Fluent in

French, English, Spanish, German, Italian, and Dutch, this multi-national Mulatta actress (who was born in Belgium of an English mother from Grenada and a French father from Martinique) slides across many boundaries of gender, language, culture, ethnicity, and race.

The rest of the cast is primarily Catalan, including Sergi Mateu (Tristan), who is best known for his role in Bellmunti's Catalan classic black comedy *Radio Speed* (1985), and Fernando Guillén Cuervo (Angel), who had a small role in Almodóvar's *Law of Desire* (1986). There are also small bits by Angel Jové (the lead actor in Bigas Luna's *Bilbao*) as the nearly mute browbeaten spouse of the bossy apartment porter, and by well-known French actress Bernadette Lafont as Angel's powerful boss at the bar.

Despite this carefully designed formula for international success, the film flopped at the box office when it first opened in Madrid—repeating on the national level what *El mono loco* had suffered abroad. Although Besas attributes this failure to the film's rootedness in Catalan culture, Spaniards tell a more complicated story, which is reminiscent of the disastrous openings of Llobet Gràcia's *Vida en sombras* and Borau's *Hay que matar á B*. According to Vergés,

My film was premiered in twenty Spanish cities on the 8th of June. It's not that I think that I've made the best film in the history of cinema, but the multinational company [United International Pictures] that distributed it launched it right in the middle of the World Football match and that was a nightmare, except in Barcelona where it remained in the theaters for 19 weeks.[72]

The film was saved in Barcelona by word of mouth and in other markets by its success at international festivals like Cannes, Montreal, and Venice (where it was one of ten films, chosen out of 160, that were invited to participate in the International Critics Week). According to Angel Fernández-Santos, it was better received at Venice than most of the films from the official selection (and clearly did better than *El mono loco* had done the previous year). This positive critical reception at the festivals helped to sell it in several other countries (including Germany, Holland, Belgium, France, Portugal, French Canada, Japan, Italy, and England) and helped bring it back for a new opening in Madrid in October. Diego Muñoz observes, "*Boom Boom* . . . managed something unusual in the industrial racket of Spanish cinema: to be revived in a city like Madrid, whose theaters are so dominated by North American cinema" (ibid.). Fernández Santos is much more explicit in pointing the finger at those who are to blame.

It is not unfair to say that *Boom Boom* is better than 90% . . . of the total celluloid, distributed with puffery and gossip on favorable and productive dates during this year by the distribution company that massacred this little jewel of the current Spanish cinema. . . . We must remember that the film is distributed by a multinational North American company, which premieres Spanish films at their own convenience, only to cover the obligatory quota that the law requires in order to obtain licenses for dubbing their own films. . . . If he wants to, a distributor can destroy the film that he distributes. *Boom Boom* is a flagrant case of this . . . type of aesthetic crime, which has victimized through its distribution not only this Spanish film, but many others as well. ("Resurrección de un bello filme")

I have dwelt so long on the details of *Boom Boom*'s distribution in Spain because it is symptomatic of a familiar problem that still persists and in fact has been intensified by the increasing globalization of mass culture—a problem that will undoubtedly be addressed by the development of new regulatory policies to protect the European market against the Hollywood/Japanese audiovisual hegemony. Vergés concludes,

I hope that this history of *Boom Boom* serves as an example and a reflexion for other Spanish films, because it demonstrates that in our country there is no money to promote the films that we make and, since they stay such a short time in the theaters, the public cannot even find out that they exist. . . . I believe that the Spanish public does not see more Spanish cinema because they are not allowed to, because they are not given enough time to do it.[73]

With all of the expanded hours on regional, national, and European television, this medium may provide the time that is needed for Spanish and European spectators to see and finally support Spanish and Catalan cinema. But to survive, the films themselves may also have to change. Perhaps what is needed in the 1990s to succeed in the global market without totally sacrificing cultural specificity is a more radical cultural reinscription of existing practices—as radical as the dialogizing of neorealist and Hollywood conventions that was achieved by Spanish filmmakers in the 1950s in carving out the language of the New Spanish Cinema, or as outrageous as the subversion of melodrama that was performed from a position of exile or marginality by internationally acclaimed mavericks like Buñuel and Almodóvar.

REINSCRIBING THE MARGINAL AS THE CENTER   These issues of micro-/macro-regionalism are not limited to international coproductions or to films made in so-called marginal regions like Cataluña, Galicia, or the Basque provinces. For example, in the 1950s, the issue of regionalism was crucial to a ground-breaking film like *¡Bienvenido, Mr. Marshall!* which mocks the absurdity of making Andalusian regionalism the cultural stereotype for all Spain (particularly for international spectators) and which reveals the dreams of poor Spanish villagers to be (in Bakhtin's terms) parodic reenvoicements of popular movie genres—not only the Francoist historical epic that celebrates the macroregional Golden Age conquests of the New World but also foreign imports from major imperial world powers—like the Hollywood western and the Soviet Socialist realist epic. Thus here, too, a dialogism of micro-/macrocultural images became the means of widening the cracks in the Francoist monolith of Castilian culture.

These micro-/macroregional dynamics were turned inside out by Almodóvar in the post-Franco era. Although his films are always

Homosexuality, drugs, and violence are linked with the struggle for Basque autonomy in Eloy de la Iglesia's Oedipal melodrama, *El pico* (The Shoot, 1983).

centered in Madrid, his debut feature, *Pepi, Luci, Bom y otras chicas del montón* (Pepi, Luci, Bom and Other Girls on the Heap, 1980) was produced and distributed by the Barcelona-based Figaro Films, which in 1978 had produced two other outrageous post-Franco films by regionally based filmmakers that succeeded in breaking through to an international market by politicizing marginality: Bigas Luna's *Bilbao* and Eloy de la Iglesia's *Il diputado* (The Deputy). In *Bilbao,* not only are Bigas Luna's perverse protagonist and plot grounded in Barcelona, the capital of Cataluña, but their female victim is associated with other regional languages—both on the microregional level through her Andalusian accent and her name Bilbao and on the macroregional European level through her name's envoicement by Lotte Lenya in the "Bilbao song," which is compulsively repeated on the sound track. Though Iglesia's protagonist and plot in *Il diputado* are centered in Madrid, the marginality of the hero's closeted homosexuality substitutes for the marginality of the filmmaker's closeted Basque regionalism, which are blatantly linked in other Iglesia films like *El pico I* and *II* (The Shoot, 1983–84) and in a more radical Basque film like Uribe's *La muerte de Mikel.*

In *El pico* a homosexual sculptor (top) is more supportive to the delinquent teenage buddies than either of their macho fathers, a *guardia civil* (opposite), and a leftist politician who supports Basque autonomy (bottom).

Elaborating on these connections forged by Bigas Luna and Iglesia, Almodóvar succeeded in establishing this eroticized marginality as a new stereotype for post-Franco Spain, particularly for foreign audiences. It is a marginality associated with drugs, transsexuality, homoeroticism, and terrorism. Exaggerating his break with Spanish film traditions from the past, Almodóvar cast himself as the embodiment of the "new Spanish mentality."

> I think my films . . . represent . . . this kind of new mentality that appears in Spain after Franco dies. Above all, after 1977. . . . Stories about the new Spain have appeared in the mass media of every country. Everybody has heard that now everything is different in Spain . . . but it is not so easy to find this change in the Spanish cinema. I think in my films they see how Spain has changed, above all, because now it is possible to do this kind of film here, . . . a film like *The Law of Desire*.[74]

When *The Law of Desire* proved critically successful at the 1987 Berlin Film Festival and did well commercially in foreign markets, the Socialist government touted its universality and used it to promote Spain's culture industry—a strategy that was similar to Franco's earlier use of oppositional figures like Saura, Querejeta, and Buñuel to promote a more liberal image of Spain abroad. Thus, despite the film's graphic homoerotic sex scenes and its backstory of homosexual incest, an editorial in Spain's oldest and largest circulation film journal, *Fotogramas y video,* lavishly praised *The Law of Desire* and heralded it as a model for Spain's macroregional cinema of the future.

> The recent Berlin Festival has demonstrated an important fact for Spanish cinema: the interest that our cinema can arouse abroad, not only at the level of interchange or cultural curiosity but as an exportable and commercially valid product. . . . Spanish cinema is trying to leave the national "ghetto" and join a movement that proclaims the necessity and urgency of a "European cinema" which transcends nationalities without renouncing their specificity.[75]

In Imanol Uribe's *La muerte de Mikel* (The Death of Mikel, 1984) the hero's relationship with a transvestite alienates him from both his repressive mother and his radical comrades in ETA.

Thus, through a strategy that was similar to that used by Catalan films like *Vida en sombras,* Almodóvar subverted the center by re-defining it as the marginal. But this time, the center was located in Madrid rather than Barcelona, and, ironically, the inversion helped to demarginalize Spanish cinema in the world market.[76] In fact, as of the date of this writing, six of the top thirteen Spanish exports to the United States of all time were directed by Almodóvar: *Women on the Verge of a Nervous Breakdown* (#1), *Tie Me Up, Tie Me Down!* (#2), *Law of Desire* (#6), *Matador* (#8), *What Have I Done to Deserve This?* (#11), and *Labyrinth of Passion* (#13).[77] Undoubtedly, *High Heels* will join the list. No wonder he can afford to publicize his hatred of the television medium.

Six of the top thirteen Spanish exports to the United States of all time were directed by Pedro Almodóvar, including (top) *¿Que he hecho yo para merecer esto?*, 1984 (photo by Antonio Debenito); (bottom) *Matador*, 1986 (photo courtesy of Pedro Almodóvar); (opposite, top) *Mujeres al borde de un ataque de nervios*, 1988 (photo courtesy of Orion Pictures); and (opposite, bottom) *¡Atame!*, 1989.

The popularity of Almodóvar movies like ¡Atame! (1989) helped make it possible in 1992 for Antonio Banderas to co-star in *Mambo Kings* and for Victoria Abril's performance in *Amantes* to get wide commercial distribution in the U.S. (Photo by Paca Navarro, print courtesy of Miramax Films Release.)

The most powerful acknowledgment of this reversal of marginality and center is perhaps that dramatic moment in Madonna's documentary *Truth or Dare* (1991), when the reigning queen of global pop culture confesses that the only person in the world whom she ardently desires to meet is Antonio Banderas, the star of those Almodóvar movies that she loves. Though she mispronounces and misspells Banderas's name (as if to punish him for rejecting her and for having a wife), the film stages their first meeting at a party hosted by Almodóvar in Madrid, which is figured as a universal center of subversive pleasure and desire. By the following year, the rest of the world shared her passion, for Banderas was costarring as a Cuban émigré in the Hollywood hit *The Mambo Kings* and was introduced by Billy Crystal at the 1992 Oscar awards as "the sexiest man alive."

While the "marginal" may have replaced the "regional" as the primary seme of Spanishness (especially for international spectators of Almodóvar's Madrid movies), the post-Franco Catalan and Basque cinemas reappropriated the marginal for their own regional discourse. In films as diverse as Vicente Aranda's *Cambio de sexo* (Sex Change, 1977), Ventura Pons's *Ocaña: Retrato intermitente* (Ocaña: A Partial Portrait, 1978), Eloy de la Iglesia's *El pico* (1983), Imanol Uribe's *La muerte de Mikel* (1984), and Montxo Armendáriz's *27 horas* (27 Hours, 1986), these same marginal practices (homophobia, terrorism, and drug trafficking) were refigured as international problems, which have cultural specificity in their particular regional context where they are linked to class issues. As doubly marginal, they speak both to the wider Spanish and heterosexual majorities, seeking like Almodóvar to appropriate "the center." By addressing these current international problems that are not being solved by the national government, the films expose the continuing inadequacy and provincialism of the so-called center and demonstrate the potency of a micro-/macroregional discourse.

Some of these regional films—like *Cambio de sexo, Los placeres ocultos* (Hidden Pleasures), *Il diputado, Navajeros* (Knife-fighters), *Colegas* (Mates), *El pico, La muerte de Mikel,* and *Tras el cristal*—would also find viewers in a new marginal macroregionalism, the gay

Problems with teenage
suicide and drug addiction are
linked to issues of Basque
autonomy in Montxo
Armendáriz's *27 horas*
(1986).

market that distributes both films and videos for a specialized international audience. In this context, Iglesia was hailed as the Spanish
Fassbinder, Almodóvar was celebrated as a cross between Billy
Wilder, Douglas Sirk, and David Lynch, and Villaronga's brilliantly
perverse debut feature *Tras el cristal* was read as a homoerotic Hitchcock thriller.

Though not a regional film, Antonio Giménez-Rico's *Vestida de azul* (Dressed in Blue, 1983), a documentary portrait of six transvestites who have come to Madrid from various regions throughout Spain to change their gender and live a "modern life," also belongs to this macroregional context of global gay culture. Consistent with Almodóvar's postmodernist melodramas, it dramatizes the replacement of the old españolada with the new transgressive stereotype in the young gypsy transvestite Juan Muñoz, who literally combines both images, particularly when imitating the great flamenco dancer Isabel Pontoja. Muñoz also evokes the Black Legend of Spain with poignant childhood stories about having been beaten by her father and with images of the grim poverty in which her family still lives. In one scene set in a flamenco bar, she is confronted by the proprietor who criticizes how she is dressed. At first, we think he is objecting to the gender of her costume, but then we realize that he is objecting to its vulgarity. This incident makes us see that these transvestites are cross-dressing in terms of class as well as gender. It is no coincidence that the gypsy subculture is both the most impoverished and the most macho within Spain. Thus, the gypsy conversion of gender is an act with symbolic resonance, for it evokes Spain undergoing the radical "cultural transformation" from neo-Catholic fascism to socialist democracy. David Garland has argued persuasively that "*Dressed in Blue* seems finally to posit contemporary Spanish transsexualism as an ideologically unstable and ambiguous lightning-rod for shifting boundaries between and within religion on the one hand and class on the other."[78]

Eight years later, the phenomenal international success of Jenny Livingston's independent American documentary *Paris Is Burning* (1991) made one see *Dressed in Blue* in a new global context. Along with a Catalan film like *Ocaña* and an American short like *Queen,* both films belong to an international genre of transvestite documentaries. The striking similarity between *Paris Is Burning* and *Dressed in Blue* also enables one to distinguish the cultural specificity of each group of transvestites—the distinct cultural values they are trying to mimic and appropriate and the particular combination of class, race, and gender oppression in which they are inscribed. Interestingly, when Livingston appeared with her film in Los Angeles in October 1991, she described one of her next projects as a fictional New York comedy "in the mode of Almodóvar." Thus, like Madonna, Livingston also acknowledged the international postmodernist appeal both of Almodóvar and of the transsexual vogueing he has come to symbolize worldwide.[79]

In addition to Almodóvar's predictable successes, Aranda's *Amantes* proved to be a surprise hit in the global market, winning Goyas for best picture and best direction in Spain and the best actress award for Abril in Berlin and enjoying a long successful commercial run in the United States. In New York and Los Angeles, it was in first-run theaters for over four months; according to the *Hollywood Reporter* box office report of August 11, 1992, after nineteen weeks in release it had grossed $1,182,303 and was still going strong. On both coasts, it received enthusiastic reviews praising it as one of the "hottest" films of the summer. In the *Los Angeles Times,* an advertisement for the film even quoted a remark that Madonna had made about *Amantes* on the popular Arsenio Hall television show: "It made me want to go home to *** my boyfriend!" The success of *Amantes* in the United States can probably be attributed at least partially to the film's sexual explicitness (which is compatible with the new stereotype of a transgressive Spain) and to the familiarity both of its noir conventions and of its brilliant star, Victoria Abril, whom American spectators already knew from her earlier performances in Almodóvar's *¡Atame!* and *Tacones lejanos.* The success of *Amantes* in the world market has already begun to help Aranda's next project, *El amante bilingüe* (The Bilingual Lover, an adaptation of Juan Marsé's novela), which has received from the Instituto de Cinematografía (ICAA) one of the largest subventions of the year, 65 million pesetas, out of a total fund of 625 million for the session and 1,800 million for the year.[80]

While Almodóvar movies and surprise hits like *Amantes* may have succeeded in redefining the marginal as central both in Spain and in international perceptions of Spanishness, this strategy cannot be expected to solve the severe economic crisis of the Spanish cinema, which (with a few exceptions) still remains marginal worldwide. Perhaps a more optimistic way of interpreting the current crisis is to read it from the synergistic perspective of the 1990s, that is, to see it as a moment of massive historical restructuring that demands cultural resilience. Now that the concepts "cinema," "nation," and "national cinema" are increasingly becoming decentered and assimilated within larger transnational systems of entertainment, Spanish cinema is bound to be radically transformed as it continues to move between micro- and macroregionalism, subvention and commercialism, blood cinema and global mass media.

EL SOL ALSO RISES

In the first three days of June 1992, Spanish filmmakers held a conference in Madrid entitled Audiovisual Español 93 to call attention to the dire crisis that Spanish cinema is currently facing. Participants urged the government and, more specifically, the current minister of culture, Jordi Solé Tura, to introduce a new audiovisual law to protect it from the total domination of Spanish screens by Hollywood movies and by North American multinational distributors and from the "europuding" coproductions of the new European community that threaten to erase the cultural specificity of Spain and its diverse autonomous regions. The most explosive moment of the conference came on the second day when Antonio Recoder, president of the Federation of Distributors of Cinema (Fedicine), the group that represents Spanish distributors and affiliates of the North American companies operating in Spain, proposed that the exhibition of Spanish cinema be limited solely to television, while film theaters be reserved for Hollywood movies that draw large crowds. Not surprisingly, this proposal provoked angry responses from Spanish filmmakers, such as producer Andrés Vicente Gómez who was quoted as saying, "The North American multinationals already control 80 percent of cinema in Spain—do they now want to have 100 percent?" and director José Luis Cuerda, who responded,

"It is an effrontery that the distributors play innocent, when they have contributed in great part to the decline of Spanish cinema."[1]

Sounding in many ways like a new Salamanca congress with which the modern Spanish cinema of the 1950s began, this three-day conference was organized by several professional groups (including the Federación de Asociaciones de Productores Audiovisuales Españoles and the Academia del Cine de España) with the approval of the Ministry of Culture's Instituto de Cinematografía. Like its forerunner at Salamanca, the conference was designed to consider the social, economic, and political dimensions of the crisis and came up with an equally dire diagnosis of Spanish cinema, this time not voiced by a leftist filmmaker like Bardem but quoted by the president of the conference, Román Gubern, from an editorializing interview with Almodóvar in the distinguished French film journal *Cahiers du cinema:* "Metastasis of television, gangrene from the American enemy and paralysis of the central neuropolitics."[2] According to the cover story in which the diagnosis appeared, this condition has made Almodóvar want to continue his filmmaking outside of Spain.

Like Salamanca, Audiovisual Español 93 turned into (as actor-producer Juan Luis Galiardo put it) "a symbol of protest," for it also apparently failed (at least, as of this writing) to achieve its immediate goals. Although the ministry agreed to create a commission to study the matter, it claimed it was unnecessary to pass a new audiovisual law or to create an autonomous entity charged with coordinating the problems of the cinema. Former ministerial general directors of cinema Fernando Méndez-Leite and Pilar Miró (whose "Miró decree" of 1983 had expanded the ministry's support of Spanish cinema until it was dismantled by the "Semprún decree" of 1989) assigned part of the blame to the government's present unwillingness to preserve its national film industry, a failure that critic Angel Fernández Santos has called "cultural genocide."[3] Even well-known actress Carmen Maura, who is the niece of the former minister of culture, Jorge Semprún, has acknowledged her uncle's pivotal role in initiating the government's withdrawal of support: "He is a very nice, very intelligent uncle, but at the moment it seems to me that he is very far removed from the reality of Spanish cinema, that he came to it with a very French mentality."[4] Yet, as Gubern pointed out, the French government is now actively protecting its audiovisual industry, and unless Spain follows its example, "we will be the lackeys of Jack Valenti [the president of the Motion Picture Association of America]," and in 1995, instead of celebrating the centennial of Spanish cinema, "we will celebrate its funeral."[5]

The key issue is whether the Spanish government should financially support an industry that cannot survive on its own, a question that has become much more complex in the current economic climate of European macroregionalism. Now that the government of Felipe Gonzalez is determined to make Spain one of the elite members of the EC—that is, those who meet the 1997 deadline for passing the economic criteria (agreed on at Maastrict in December 1991) and who thereby qualify for economic and monetary convergence—it must quickly catch up with the living standards of other European nations. According to a survey recently published in *The Economist,* Spain may have been "Europe's superstar" for the five years between 1986 and 1990, when its "GDP grew at an average rate of nearly 5% a year [and] business investments expanded by more than 10% a year," but growth is not one of the Maastrict criteria.[6] In fact, as of May 1992, Spain could pass only one of the tests—a public debt that does not exceed 60 percent of GDP. In the wake of the European monetary crisis (which was triggered by the rise in interest for the German mark and which has seriously jeopardized the Maastrict goals for economic convergence) and exacerbated by the huge expenditures that Spain had invested in the Barcelona Olympics and the Sevilla World Expo, the Spanish peseta suffered two devaluations in quick succession (5 percent on September 17, 1992 and another 6 percent on November 22). This situation has raised serious doubts throughout the nation about the economic policies of the Gonzalez government. Given the pressures to meet the other Maastrict criteria and "with harder times ahead," *The Economist* claims,

The answer is to cut subsidies, fraud and bureaucracy. . . . All that is needed is a government bold enough to wield the axe. It could begin by chopping subsidies to big lossmakers. (19)

A crucial question for Gonzalez's government, then, is whether the film and television industries should be exempt from these cuts, since (despite their losses) they manufacture unique cultural products that construct images of national identity for world consumption (at least, at international festivals) even if they fail to draw spectators at home. In contrast to 1982, when Gonzalez was eager to demonstrate Spain's ideological transformation and therefore supported the Miró decree, in 1992 he is now far more interested in demonstrating fiscal responsibility, especially to his European peers (which is one reason that the comparison with France keeps recurring). According to Berlanga, Spain should follow the example of France not only in protecting the home market against Hollywood but also in "converting Spanish cinema into a real industry," one capable of regaining the kind of mass audience in Spain that his films and those of Bardem had enjoyed in the 1950s when they helped launch the New Spanish Cinema and, one might add, that politically daring films like *La prima Angélica, Furtivos, Camada negra,* and *El crimen de Cuenca* attracted at key moments of transition in the 1970s and that Almodóvar's postmodernist melodramas have consistently been able to reach on a global scale in the 1980s and 1990s.[7]

CANNES 1992   The alleged two poles of Spanish filmmaking (the commercial and the artistic) are represented at their best by Almodóvar and Erice, respectively, who have both made commercially successful films of great artistic merit. They came together at the Cannes Film Festival in spring 1992, with the former as a member of the international jury and the latter as the author of an "art film" in competition, *El sol del membrillo* (The Sun of the Quince). Despite speculations that Erice would never win a jury prize with Almodóvar on the selection panel and reports that spectators had walked out of the screenings in droves, the film nevertheless received two of the festival's most highly prestigious awards—the International Critics Prize and the Jury Prize (which it shared with Vitali Kanesvski's *An Independent Life* from Russia).

Erice's long-awaited third feature is a stunning documentary on the well-known Spanish painter Antonio López and his attempts to paint and then draw a quince tree that he planted in his backyard. Co-written by Erice and Antonio López with cinematography by Angel Luis Fernández (who shot most of Almodóvar's films) and Javier Aguirresarobe, *El sol del membrillo* is a study of representation, demonstrating that any work of art is a self-portrait of the artist and his subject as well as of their historical and cultural moment. Both López's painting and Erice's filmmaking capture the traces of what is perceived and remembered: the street noise, aromas, and visitors that invade the painter's garden; world events and media culture that are transmitted on radios and television screens; memories and dreams that color the present moment; intense conversations with family and colleagues, especially with López's vibrant friend Enrique Gran. This unique combination of perceptions transforms both the painting and the film by giving them their distinctive texture. Thus art is conceived as perception (which engages all the senses), as work (which grows more intense with age), and as process (which involves a constant struggle for a fullness and perfection that can never be totally achieved).

Like Chávarri's *El desencanto* (discussed in chap. 5), *El sol del membrillo* is a documentary on a celebrated Spanish artist and his family at a pivotal moment in Spanish history. Although Erice's portrait, period, and characters are all far more positive than those in Chávarri's film, they are still used to represent a much broader subject that is never depicted directly, and the emphasis is still on death and decay. Thus, both films acknowledge the structuring absence that lies at the core of all visual representation. In his perceptive essay on *El sol del membrillo,* Carlos Heredero quotes John Berger to make precisely this point: "The visual image is always a commentary about an absence. The description comments on the absence of that which it describes."[8]

Like Wim Wenders's film about Nicholas Ray, *Nick's Film, Lightning over Water* (1979–80), Erice's movie is a productive collaboration between two artists as subject and object. Both works erode the boundaries between documentary, fiction, and the avant-garde as well as between realism and reflexivity, black-and-white and color, film and video; in the case of Erice, his movement between film and video echoes López's movement between painting and drawing. Both films display the conscious process of subject positioning that the artists build into the text, inscribing their own image and point of view as essential components of the work that help manipulate spectator response; in the case of Erice and López, the process involves positioning the camera and making footmarks. Both films document the subject's collaboration with his family and friends; in the case of López, that includes his wife María Moreno who resumes work on her portrait of him sleeping and gradually moving toward death, his son who studies English and paints in a more abstract style than his parents, and his old friend Enrique Gran whom he has known since art school. Ultimately, both films explore how art forestalls death through its representation of time, whether documenting the effects of cancer as it destroys a human body (*Nick's Film*) or tracking the changing light of the sun and the seasons as they ripen and then rot the fruit of a quince tree (*El sol*).

Like Erice's own *El espíritu de la colmena* (discussed in chap. 3), *El sol del membrillo* uses an elliptical, repetitive style to create the iterative mode, representing time as habitual daily (or annual) actions and exploring subjectivity within the flux of growth and historical change. Erice's jump dissolves and time-lapse shots not only both mask and mark the temporal gaps (as in his earlier works) but also evoke López's strategy of starting again the following year with the new fruit of the tree and his own strategy in *El sur* of using black fades between resonant images. Also as in *El sur, El sol* emphasizes the resonant image of the pendulum, in this case, as López's instrument for measuring the subtle movements of the fruit and as the inverted shape of a modern tower on the Madrid skyline, both powerful spatiotemporal representations.

While the film is very concretely focused on this single action by López, the depiction of the quince, its subject is rich and abstract. In this way, it demonstrates what one of López's art teachers called "fullness," a concept that he and Enrique Gran did not understand when they were students but that has now become the primary goal of their art. This concept of fullness is embodied not only in the maturation of the fruit and the growing heaviness of the tree but also in the painters working in their prime at full strength. It is also narrativized in López's dream of dwelling in Paradise with his parents, realizing their mortality and acknowledging his own fear of death—a dream that develops the biblical resonance of the quince tree. Though the film is positioned precisely in the present (starting on Sunday, September 30, 1990), it looks back to earlier personal experiences of López and Enrique in Francoist Spain and to earlier influences on their work, such as Michelangelo's self-portrait on the flayed skin of Saint Bartholomew in his *Last Judgment*. Though the film is located in Madrid and grounded in Spanish specificity (with a song celebrating the Andalusian city of Seville), it documents the nation's involvement in the changing world: through images of a postcolonial film like *Sammy and Rosie Get Laid* flickering on television screens through the windows of high-rise apartment buildings; through radio allusions to the Gulf War, the Eastern European revolutions, and the post–cold war era; through the inclusion of Polish workers remodeling López's house and Chinese artists coming to look at his paintings. Like Spain's three exhibits at the 1992 World Exposition in Seville, Erice's film combines an acknowledgment of Spain's great cultural heritage in painting (at one point using a mirror shot to make a visual allusion to *Las Meninas,* the Velázquez painting that Michel Foucault helped establish as Western culture's privileged instance of modernist representation)[9] with a demonstration of its current mastery of contemporary multimedia, its openness to other cultures and languages, and its engagement with international issues.

The fact that a brilliant, demanding, and culturally specific work like *El sol del membrillo* can win two prizes at Cannes, the most important film festival in the world, is as heartening a sign for Spanish cinema as the recent commercial successes of artistically innovative films by Aranda and Almodóvar. Yet, as of this writing, Erice's film still does not have a North American distributor. These facts should help convince Spain's ministry as well as international spectators that Spanish cinema is well worth protecting and perpetuating as a key contributor to the lifeblood of both Spanish and global culture.

INTRODUCTION

1. Before the publication of these two books, the only extended works on Spanish cinema available in English were a brief monograph by Vicente Molina Foix, *New Cinema in Spain* (London: British Film Institute, 1977), and a special issue of *Quarterly Review of Film Studies* (Spring 1983), "New Spanish Cinema," edited by Katherine S. Kovács. For a fuller discussion of Besas's and Hopewell's works, see my book reviews in *Film Quarterly* (Fall 1986: 30–36 and Spring 1988: 49–51). Other English-language books in this category include the Spanish Ministry of Culture's anthology, *Spanish Cinema, 1896–1983* (1986), which was updated and reprinted as *Cine Español (1896–1988)* in 1989, Virginia Higginbotham's *Spanish Film under Franco* (Austin: University of Texas Press, 1988), J. M. Caparrós-Lera and Rafael de España's *The Spanish Cinema: An Historical Approach* (Madrid: Film Historia, 1987), and Ronald Schwartz's *The Great Spanish Films: 1950–1990* (Metuchen, N.J.: Scarecrow Press, 1991). A similar work in French is Emmanuel Larraz's *Le cinéma espagnol des origenes à nos jours* (Paris: Editions du Cerf, 1986).

2. Yet *Blood Cinema* draws on Marvin D'Lugo's excellent *The Films of Carlos Saura: The Practice of Seeing* (Princeton: Princeton University Press, 1991), which provides persuasive readings of his works against the cultural and political history of the nation and industry; and on the prolific writings of Agustín Sánchez Vidal, whose perceptive auteur studies are clustered together to highlight specific cultural issues either within a single volume, as in *Lorca, Buñuel y Dali: El enigma sin fin* (Barcelona: Editorial Planeta, 1988) and *Tres aventuras americanas* (of Buñuel, Saura, and Borau) (Zaragoza: Diputación General de Aragon, 1990), or in his more extensive series of separate volumes on the Aragonese auteurs Réy, Buñuel, Saura, and Borau. The auteur study, especially consisting of interviews, is the most common form of critical film text published in Spain, though this is currently not the case in the United States. Besides D'Lugo's study of Saura, other

English-language auteur studies of Spanish filmmakers include Ronald Schwartz's *Spanish Film Directors, 1950–1985: 21 Profiles* (Metuchen, N.J.: Scarecrow Press, 1986) and Nuria Vidal's *The Films of Pedro Almodóvar* (Madrid: Ministerio de Cultura, 1988).

3. *Challenges to Authority: Fiction and Film in Contemporary Spain* (London: Tamesis Books Limited, 1988): 2–3.

4. "Introduction: Narrating the Nation," in *Nation and Narration,* ed. Homi K. Bhabha (London and New York: Routledge, 1990): 5.

5. Among one-volume history texts on world cinema published in English during the 1980s and early 1990s, only William Luhr's *World Cinema Since 1945* (New York: Ungar, 1987) comes close to providing sufficient space to the Spanish cinema, with an essay by Virginia Higginbotham entitled "Spanish Film under Franco: Do Not Disturb." Another exception is David Shipman's *The Story of Cinema: A Complete Narrative History from the Beginnings to the Present* (New York: St. Martin's Press, 1982), which includes eighteen pages on Spanish cinema. Yet two-thirds of that discussion is devoted to Buñuel (the chapter is significantly entitled "Luis Buñuel and His Followers"), and it is unfortunately as critically obtuse on Buñuel as on his so-called followers. In his newly "revised and updated" *History of World Cinema* (New York: Stein and Day, 1981), David Robinson includes only one paragraph on Spanish cinema, hardly more than a listing of names and titles. David Cook's widely used *History of Narrative Film* (New York and London: W. W. Norton, 1981) relegates Spanish cinema to a single foot-note, full of condescending judgments; and his revised second edition (1990) actually reduces that footnote by two-thirds, reallocating the space to photos from five Spanish films that are neither discussed nor otherwise even mentioned. Although Robert Kolker's highly politicized *Altering Eye: Contemporary International Cinema* (New York: Oxford University Press, 1983) ends with a glowing celebration of Buñuel as the ultimate modernist, he grants only one sentence to the "Spanish national cinema"—a passing reference to Manuel Gutiérrez Aragón's *Black Brood* (with the filmmaker's name misspelled). In the fourth edition of his *Short History of the Movies* (New York: Macmillan, 1985), Gerald Mast devotes *his* one sentence to Saura; Bruce Kawin's 1992 update (5th ed.) expands that sentence to a paragraph on post-Franco cinema, with two accompanying illustrations from films by Saura and Almodóvar. *Flashback: A Brief History of Film* (Englewood Cliffs, N.J.: Prentice Hall, 1986), by Louis Giannetti and Scott Eyman, omits Spain entirely. Understandably, these one-volume world film

histories frequently have to depend on the primary scholarship of others, which has been very sparse on Spanish cinema. Yet, after the publication of the books by Besas, Hopewell, and Higginbotham in the mid-1980s, there should no longer be any excuse for such misunderstandings and omissions. Nevertheless, only Luhr seems to have paid any attention to these basic histories on Spanish cinema.

6. See Thomas Elsaesser, *New German Cinema: A History* (New Brunswick: Rutgers University Press, 1989).

7. Christian Metz, *The Imaginary Signifier: Psychoanalysis and the Cinema*, trans. Celia Britton, Annwyl Williams, Ben Brewster, and Alfred Guzzetti (Bloomington: Indiana University Press, 1982): 14.

8. One concrete example of this dynamic is the way it changed my understanding of the iterative (a temporal mode described by French narratologist Gerard Genette, which narrates once what happens many times) and its application to cinema. Though I had first started working on the iterative in a paper on Chantal Akerman, by applying the concept to Spanish films of the 1950s, I discovered how it functioned as a significant means of distinguishing between the neorealist and Hollywood stylistics, which were being dialogized by these Spanish filmmakers. For a fuller discussion of this issue, see my essay, "The Subversive Potential of the Pseudo Iterative," *Film Quarterly* 43, no. 2 (Winter 1989–90): 2–16.

I: THE IDEOLOGICAL REINSCRIPTION OF NEOREALIST AND HOLLYWOOD CONVENTIONS IN SPANISH CINEMA OF THE 1950S

1. Besides DeSica's 1948 neorealist classic, *Bicycle Thief* (which was both a critical and commercial success at home and abroad), and live appearances by Cesare Zavattini and Alberto Lattuada, the Italian film week in Madrid featured screenings of three additional films that were not commercially successful but that illustrated the various directions in which the movement was going as it began to face its demise in Italy at the end of the 1940s: Antonioni's first feature *Cronaca di un amore* (Chronicle of a Love, 1950), a melodrama that seems to come out of American noir but that is treated with a neorealist class discourse and a modernist elliptical plot; *Il camino della speranza* (The Path of Hope, 1950) by Pietro Germi (who had been called a "popularizer" by Rossellini and a "director of compromise" by others for trying to make neorealism compatible with mainstream commercial filmmaking); and Visconti's *Bellisima* (1951), a comedy starring

Anna Magnani. According to Besas in *Behind the Spanish Lens: Spanish Cinema under Fascism and Democracy* (Denver: Arden Press, 1985), "Bardem marked [this] film week sponsored by the Italian authorities in Madrid as the most decisive event of his formative years as a filmmaker. . . . Those films by Antonioni, Germi, DeSica, and Visconti shown in the Gran Via and Rialto cinemas, plus others in the Italian Institute, were celluloid proof of their aesthetic theories. Instead of making historical epics in studios, the Italians had shot their films in the streets. They had captured the pulse of day-to-day life" (34). Higginbotham claims that even earlier, "in 1950, a copy of Rossellini's *Open City* crossed the Spanish border in a diplomatic pouch to be viewed by a small group of film aficionados" and after the Italian film week in 1951 "students at the National Film School were able to screen films that up to then had been banned, including Antonioni's *Chronicle of Love* (1950), DeSica's *Bicycle Thief* (1948) and *Miracle in Milan* (1951), Rossellini's *Open City* (1945) and *Paisa* (1946)" (*Spanish Film Under Franco* [Austin: University of Texas Press, 1987]: 26). Yet Borau claims *Bicycle Thief* was shown theatrically in Madrid in 1950 and even won the Best Foreign Film award at the Círculo de Escritores Cinematográficos (Writers' Cinema Circle) and that neither it nor *Miracle in Milan* was ever banned in Spain.

2. This same principle of denial was later repeated when, in responding to inquiries from the American Academy of Motion Picture Arts and Sciences, which was considering *Canciones* for an Oscar nomination as Best Foreign Film, the Spanish Ministry of Culture claimed that the film did not exist "legally."

3. Raymond Carr, *Modern Spain, 1875–1980* (New York: Oxford University Press, 1980): 164.

4. Louis Althusser, "Ideology and Ideological State Apparatuses (Notes Towards an Investigation)," in *Lenin and Philosophy and Other Essays,* trans. Ben Brewster (New York and London: Monthly Review Press, 1971): 127–186.

5. Carr, 164.

6. In Bardem and Berlanga's debut film, *Esa pareja feliz* (That Happy Couple, 1951), a comedy about a working-class couple whose passion for cinema is a means of escaping their depressing reality, the wife proposes to the husband that they go to see a double bill—"one Spanish and one with Rita Hayworth." Her symbolic resonance as a Hispanic signifier of Hollywood's cultural imperialism was greatly enhanced in the late 1960s by the international success of Manuel Puig's brilliant Argentine novel, *Betrayed by Rita Hayworth* (1968).

7. Diego Galán, "1950–1961," in *Spanish Cinema, 1896–1983* (Madrid: Ministerio De Cultura, 1986): 146.

8. Román Gubern, "1930–1936: II Republic," in *Spanish Cinema, 1896–1983: 34–37*. Also see Daniel Pineda Novo, *Las folklóricas y el cine* (Huelva: Festival de Cine Iberoamericano, 1991), and Carlos Aguilar-Jaume Genover, *El cine español en sus interpretes* (Madrid: Verdoux, S. L., 1992).

9. Mira Liehm, *Passion and Defiance: Film in Italy from 1942 to the Present* (Berkeley, Los Angeles, and London: University of California Press, 1984): 101.

10. Peter Bondanella, *Italian Cinema: From Neorealism to the Present* (New York: Ungar, 1983): 86–87.

11. J. M. Caparrós Lera, *El cine español bajo el régimen de Franco (1936–1975)* (Barcelona: Ediciones de la Universitat de Barcelona, 1983): 232–233.

12. At Cannes, it was the Americans who protested against *¡Bienvenido, Mr. Marshall!* Edward G. Robinson, who was a member of the jury and who had been a strong supporter of the Republican cause during the Civil War, tried to block the screening of the film because of the brief shot, after the unsuccessful "welcoming" celebration, where one can see an American flag (and a Spanish flag) floating down a stream amid other debris.

13. John Hopewell, *Out of the Past: Spanish Cinema after Franco* (London: British Film Institute, 1986): 56–57.

14. José Luis Guarner, *30 años de cine en Español* (Barcelona: Kairos, 1971): 67, as quoted by Iván Tubau in *Crítica cinematográfica española, Bazin contra Aristarco: La gran controversia de los años sesenta* (Barcelona: Publicacions Edicions Universitat de Barcelona, 1983): 16. Tubau is an excellent source for a fuller treatment of the critical controversies in the Spanish film journals of this period.

15. A Spanish critic writes in *Objetivo,*

> None of the films that we have examined can be considered a masterpiece; but together they demonstrate to us that Italian neorealism, in spite of having gone far away from its origins, has found a new indisputable vitality, extending the themes of its action, . . . discovering unexplored human and social territories, and, above all, reclaiming fresh energies for the cinema. (Giovanni Calendoli, "Neorealismo: 1955," *Objetivo,* no. 9 [Septiembre–Octubre 1955]: 24).

16. For an elaboration of this speech, see Juan Antonio Bardem, "Informe Sobre la Situación Actual de Nuestra Cinematografia," *Objetivo,* no. 6 (Junio 1955): 7–8.

17. Emmanuel Larraz, *El cine español* (Paris: Masson et Cie, 1973): 50.
18. As quoted in Besas, *Behind the Spanish Lens*, 41.
19. As quoted by Hopewell, *Out of the Past*, 52.
20. *Continuismo* meant the continuation of the existing political system by whatever means necessary. Admiral Carrero Blanco was assassinated by Basque terrorists in 1973, two years before the death of Franco, thereby destroying continuismo as a viable alternative for post-Franco Spain.
21. According to Besas, *Alba de America* was "a 'reply' to David McDonald's *Christopher Columbus* (1948) starring Frederic March, which was offensive to Spanish officialdom and was considered to be anti-Spanish" (*Behind the Spanish Lens,* 30). *Alba* also helped to reinforce Franco's obsession with national unity by glorifying its historic roots in the 1469 marriage between Ferdinand of Aragón and Isabel of Castile, which unified Christian Spain both politically and religiously, enabling it to expel the "infidel" Moors and Jews and conquer America and its "savages" for church, queen, and country. Instead of focusing on the potential action of the voyage and discovery of the new land and its natives (an inadequacy that is parodied in one of the dream sequences in *Bienvenido*), *Alba de America* spends most of its screen time on Columbus's attempts to win the support of the church and the court, allowing for a triple celebration of female power as embodied in the Virgin, Queen Isabel, and Columbus's folkloric fiancée. Yet the lavish finale demonstrates the colonizing power of cross-cultural spectacle, by having the naked savages function as exotic spectacle for the Spanish court while the cathedral and queen who baptizes them are figured as awesome spectacle both for the colonized natives and for us spectators.
22. Román Gubern, *La imagen pornográfica y otras perversiones ópticas* (Madrid: AKAL/Comunicación, 1989): 51.
23. In *Fascism: Comparison and Definition* (Madison: University of Wisconsin Press, 1980), Stanley G. Payne, one of the leading historians of European fascism, observes,

> The term fascist is used not for the sake of convention alone but because the Italian movement was the first significant force to exhibit those characteristics (or at least most of them) as a new type and was for long the most influential ideologically. It constituted the type whose ideas and goals were the most easily generalized, particularly when compared with racial National Socialism. (7–8)

Payne claims "that Spain and Italy have shown more points of similarity during the modern period than have any other two large European countries, . . . particularly in politics" (140).

24. Marcia Landy, *Fascism in Film: The Italian Commercial Cinema, 1931–1943* (Princeton: Princeton University Press, 1986): 4–5. Also see James Hay, *Popular Film Culture in Fascist Italy: The Passing of the Rex* (Bloomington: Indiana University Press, 1987): i–xvii.

25. Luis Buñuel, as quoted by Francisco Aranda in *Luis Buñuel: A Critical Biography,* trans. David Robinson (New York: DaCapo Press, 1976): 165, 185.

26. As quoted in Besas, *Behind the Spanish Lens,* 18.

27. For a fuller discussion of this parallel with German cinema, see my essay, "José Luis Borau *On the Line* of the National/International Interface in the Post-Franco Cinema," *Film Quarterly* (Winter 1986–87): 35–48.

28. Stanley G. Payne, "Spanish Fascism," *Salmagundi,* nos. 76–77 (Fall 1987– Winter 1988): 101–112. In attempting to account for this process of defascistization, Payne explains,

> The revolt of July 17–19, 1936 that finally began the Civil War was almost exclusively the work of certain sectors of the Spanish Army officer corps who accepted the cooperation of Falangists and of right-wing civilian groups only as subordinate adjunct forces. . . . Yet once in power, in order to avoid repeating the "Primo de Rivera mistake" of operating a short-term military dictatorship without developing a firm new ideology and institutional basis, . . . [Franco] turned soon to the Falange as the only viable new force of modern and authoritarian nationalism that might provide the political vehicle for a modern new single-party state. . . . When Franco incorporated the Falange as his new state *partido unico* in April 1937, he did so by merging it with the Carlist and other rightist groups, creating to some extent a new syncretistic government party, the Falange Española Tradicionalista y de las JONS (FET). (105)

29. Carr, 161, 168.

30. In 1963, García Escudero would draft an explicit list of codes that censorship boards were obliged to follow, thereby meeting one of the key demands of the Salamanca Congress in which he had participated. He would also initiate a new "special interest subsidy" designed to promote more sophisticated "art" films with a strong international appeal and to replace the old "national interest subsidies" of the 1940s and 1950s which had supported escapist films that were ideologically "correct" but artistically "regressive."

31. M. M. Bakhtin, "Discourse in the Novel," in *The Dialogic Imagination,* ed. Michael Holquist (Austin: University of Texas Press, 1981): 360, 345–346.

32. Roland Barthes, "The Rhetoric of the Image," in *Image, Music, Text,* trans. Stephen Heath (New York: The Noonday Press, 1977): 48–49.

33. As Robert Graham observes in his foreword to *Spain: A Nation Coming of Age* (New York: St. Martin's Press, 1984), now in the post-Franco era there is "a wealth of publications on the Civil War in all its minutiae" while "the long period of Franco's rule was virtually ignored as if an embarrassment." Both the former repression and the current imbalance (which now extends to cinema) helped to intensify the fetishization of the Civil War as a signifier of Spanishness, both for Spaniards and for foreigners. For an insightful analysis of how the Spanish Civil War has been represented in post-Franco cinema, see Román Gubern's essay, "The Civil War: Inquest or Exorcism," *ORFV* 13, no. 4 (1991): 103–112, and his book, *1936–1939: La guerra de España en la Pantalla* (Madrid: Filmoteca Española, 1986).

34. As Higginbotham points out, "*For Whom the Bell Tolls* (1943) was prohibited in Spain, while scenes of the Spanish conflict were cut from *Snows of Kilimanjaro* (1952) . . . because they portrayed the Republican (losing) side" (17). A notable exception is Lorenzo Llobet Gràcia's brilliant reflexive film from the Barcelona School, *Vida en sombras* (Life in Shadows, 1947–48), which was not released until 1953, when it quietly slipped into oblivion. The film was rediscovered by critic Ferrán Alberich in the 1980s, when it finally began to receive the recognition it deserved.

35. Landy, 303.

36. Because Bardem was a jurist at Cannes, *Muerte de un ciclista* could not be selected as Spain's official entry in the festival. Yet, the film still won the International Critics Prize.

37. Hopewell, *Out of the Past,* 56.

38. Ernesto Laclau, *Politics and Ideology in Marxist Theory: Capitalism-Fascism-Populism* (London: Verso Editions, 1979): 102.

39. Christine Gledhill, "The Melodramatic Field: An Investigation," in *Home Is Where the Heart Is: Studies in Melodrama and the Woman's Film,* ed. Christine Gledhill (London: British Film Institute, 1988): 36–37.

40. Carr, 156–159.

41. "*Surcos* escapes by giving us a Virgilian explanation of the peasants' exodus to the city. If there is an exodus, there must be a reason. *Surcos* doesn't look for it. It escapes." Juan Antonio Bardem, "Informe sobre la situación actual de nuestra cinematografía," *Objetivo,* no. 6 (Junio 1955): 7.

42. For a perceptive reading of this film in relation to the 1942 sound version (also directed by Florián Rey), see Agustín Sánchez Vidal, "Florián Rey y las dos versiones de *La aldea maldita*," *Artigrama,* no. 4 (1987): 309–324.

43. Payne, *Fascism,* 7, 12–13.

44. Geoffrey Nowell-Smith, "Minnelli and Melodrama," in *Movies and Methods,* II, ed. Bill Nichols (Berkeley, Los Angeles and London: University of California Press, 1985): 192.

45. Soviet expressionism is repeatedly evoked and ideologically reinscribed in the Fascist nationalist epic *Raza,* particularly in several historical montage sequences. But, in contrast to the dialectic interrogation of Eisenstein's montage, here the superimpositions and cross-dissolves help to construct a monolithic space in which images from past, present, and future, and footage from newsreels and fiction, and fates of individuals and collectives are all united in a single diegetic space, creating a seamless idealized historical narrative that supposedly tells "the universal truth of any people who refuse to perish . . . when provoked by communism."

   As in *Surcos,* the parodic fusion of conventions from American and Soviet cinema also occurs in one of the dream sequences in *¡Bienvenido, Mr. Marshall!* where a plane drops a new tractor for the needy Spanish peasants below. The tractor may be labeled as coming from the U.S.A., but the style of its filmic representation comes from the USSR and the official aesthetic of Socialist realism (particularly from films by Pudovkin). Similarly, the three generous donors in the plane may be wearing American military uniforms, but their beards, crowns, and other physical characteristics mark them as the three wise men whose iconography is so familiar to Spaniards in their own Catholicism and its traditional pictorial arts. The sequence conflates the supposedly opposed materialisms of the Catholic church and of the other two great world powers (communism and capitalism), showing how dreams help to function as an internal mechanism of ideological reinscription. Another scene (in which the mayor addresses the villagers from a balcony) is sometimes called "the Pudovkin shot."

   La aldea maldita was also strongly influenced by Soviet expressionism, more specifically, by Olga Preobranskaia's *Women of Liaison* (1927, also known as *The Village of Sin*), which was shown both in Spain and in Paris, where Florián Rey spent time in the 1920s.

46. For a detailed discussion of the iterative in cinema and its relationship to the neorealist and Hollywood aesthetics, see my essay, "The Subversive Potential of the Pseudo Iterative," 2–16.

47. This spectatorial function of the mob is not unique to *Surcos,* for one can also find it in Edgar Neville's social comedy *El último caballo* (The Last Horse, 1950), where, after being discharged from the nationalist cavalry, a private quixotically tries to save his faithful horse from death in the plaza

de toros and tries to survive in Madrid, which is undergoing a materialistic modernization that he strongly opposes. When the horse is surreptitiously left overnight in the courtyard where he devours one of the tenant's prize flowers, the other tenants roar with laughter as the distraught woman accuses the beast of murder.

48. Thomas Elsaesser, "Tales of Sound and Fury: Observations on the Family Melodrama," in *Movies and Methods,* II: 168.

2: THE SUBVERSIVE REINSCRIPTION OF MELODRAMA IN *MUERTE DE UN CICLISTA*

1. Peter Brooks, *The Melodramatic Imagination: Balzac, Henry James, Melodrama, and the Mode of Excess* (New Haven: Yale University Press, 1976): ix.

2. Gledhill, "The Melodramatic Field," 13.

3. Ortega y Gasset, "The Dehumanization of Art," in *Velázquez, Goya and the Dehumanization of Art,* trans. Alexis Brown (New York: W. W. Norton, 1953): 74–75. He also claims, "A conversion of a more radical kind was inevitable; it became necessary to eradicate personal sentiments from music." Thus, paradoxically, Wagner's melodramatic music provided both the emotional grounding and the ironic detachment for the surrealist l'amour fou.

4. Román Gubern, "Teoría del melodrama," in *Mensajes icónicos en la cultura de masas* (Barcelona: Editorial Lumen, 1974): 225. Also see Gubern's *Melodrama en el cine español (1930–1960)* (Barcelona, 1991): 11–28. Another brilliant exception is Kathleen Vernon's essay "Melodrama Against Itself: Pedro Almodóvar's *What Have I Done to Deserve This?*" (*Film Quarterly* 46, no. 3 [Spring 1993]: 28–40), which I heard her read at a conference at Clark University in April 1990, after I had finished writing this chapter. In applying some of the recent work on melodrama by Anglo feminist film theorists to post-Franco cinema, Vernon makes several points that are similar to ones that I am presenting here.

5. Thomas Elsaesser, "Tales of Sound and Fury," in *Movies and Methods,* 173–176.

6. Geoffrey Nowell-Smith, "Minnelli and Melodrama," in *Movies and Methods,* II: 190.

7. Besas, *Behind the Spanish Lens,* 34.

8. Landy, *Fascism in Film.*

9. Antonio Lloréns, *El cine negro español* (Valladolid: Semana de Cine de Valladolid, 1988): 3.

10. The emphasis on fathers and sons in cine negro español can be contrasted with the emphasis on mothers and daughters in Edgar Neville's *El crimen de la Calle Bordadores* (1946), a murder mystery that Lloréns cites as an important precursor of cine negro and that one Spanish critic describes as being "closer to cine negro than to a detective film" but which is actually closer to a maternal melodrama like *Mildred Pierce* or even *Stella Dallas*.

11. In his "Teoría del melodrama," Gubern claims, "In its historical origin, melodrama was born in Florence at the end of the sixteenth century, in an attempt to return to the purity of Greek tragedy" (225–226).

12. Gubern, "Teoría del melodrama," 242.

13. I. L. McClelland, *Spanish Drama of Pathos, 1750–1808,* II, *Low Tragedy* (Toronto: University of Toronto Press, 1970): 349–396.

14. Although McClelland finds this fusion with parody as early as the Spanish reaction to Rousseau's *Pygmalion* (which was already burlesqued by Ramón de la Cruz in his 1770 sainete, *La despedida de los cómicos*), he claims it reached new heights in Rodriguez de Arellano's *El Domingo* (1791), where it became difficult to distinguish serious melodrama from its parody.

> It is just as well that Arellano described the *sainete* as a burlesque, otherwise an audience of the later nineties might have taken this Domingo seriously, so faithful is his reasoning to the logic of melodramatic "thought." . . . His self-analytical passage from one mental phase to another follows the course originally laid down for all enlightened dramatists by the analytical characters of [Samuel] Richardson under the influence of popular philosophers which was the eighteenth-century equivalent of the popular psychology of the day. (McClelland, 374)

15. Ortega y Gasset, *Velázquez, Goya and the Dehumanization of Art,* 114–116.

16. The most exalted noblemen adored them, duchesses sought their company, and every evening the populace came to blows defending the superiority of the actress each group idolized. . . . As a result, authors began to make their characters fit the people who played the parts, and rather in the manner of Hollywood, gave them star-vehicles to shine in. This was the case with Ramón de la Cruz, who held sway in the theatre for twenty years . . . [and] who composed innumerable *sainetes, zarzuelas, loas* (prologues), *tonadillas* and *jácaras,* and who also translated French and Italian tragedies. (Ortega y Gasset, ibid.)

17. The clash between these two great factions was intense and harsh. . . . The *illustrados*—the men of learning—fought against *majismo*, attempted to suppress the bullfights and at times succeeded, and fiercely attacked poor Don Ramón de la Cruz for his burlesques. (Ortega y Gasset, ibid., 117)

18. The intelligent would . . . employ their detective instinct—as active in the eighteenth century as in the twentieth, . . . to check practically, by the gestures, postures, revealing silences, and pointed music, the complexity of human experience which the protagonist only half explained in words. Melodrama might have been a show for the epoch's eyes and ears. But, in its rudimentary way, it was also a mental exercise in close analysis and coordination as well as a histrionic training school in controlled expression. (McClelland, 385)

19. According to Gubern,

   Premiering on May 6, 1957, in the Rialto cinema in Madrid, it played for 325 consecutive days, that is, almost an entire year, a phenomenon without precedent for a Spanish production. Despite the influential ecclesiastical authority which classified the film in the disfavorable 3R category, *El último cuplé* was to become the most important commercial success in Spanish cinema since 1939 and one of the most important successes in Latin American markets, including the Puerto Rican communities in the United States. ("Teoría del melodrama," 252)

   Although Sarita Montiel had earlier been successful both in Mexican and Hollywood films, working with Robert Aldrich in *Veracruz,* Sam Fuller in *Yuma,* and her husband, Anthony Mann, in *Serenade,* her triumph in *El último cuplé* was so enormous that she decided to stay at home in Spain, where she made all of her subsequent films.

20. Diego Galán, "1950–1961," in *Spanish Cinema,* 162.

21. Gubern, "1930–1936: II Republic," in *Spanish Cinema,* 32–34.

22. According to Borau, Florián Rey and Imperio Argentina claim that during the Civil War they went to Paris to make a coproduction, which fell apart. Having little money, they went to Cuba where their film *Morena Clara* was playing and where they were helped by Cifesa's representative, Norbeto Soliño, who arranged personal appearances. When they accompanied the film to Mexico, they received a cable from Germany inviting them to make a coproduction with UFA, which was eager to enter the South American

market. In Berlin they met Goebbels, who wanted them to make a new version of *Lola Montez,* but Rey refused because he claims that he found the script "too political." Instead, he proposed a new version of Carmen, which resulted in *Carmen, la de Triana* (1936). Falangist reviewers criticized the film for relying for its inspiration on "such a cheap foreigner" as Merimée. The Republican side, however, banned *Morena Clara* because Rey and Argentina were working at the Nazi studios. Yet, neither was ever a Falangist, and Argentina claims she always hated Franco.

23. José Ortega y Gasset, "Sobre el Fascismo," in *Obras completas,* II (Madrid: Revista de Occidente, 1954).

24. Gubern observes,

> The great explosion of baroque art in the West, from the end of the 16th century to the middle of the 18th century, was in great measure a consequence of the Catholic Counter Reformation. . . . Because of the eclecticism at the end of our century, it's difficult for us to understand the scandalous rupture which the eruption of baroque art entailed. . . . To the great aesthetic traditionalists . . . the baroque seemed a disordered extravagance, confusing and void of rules in opposition to the measured classical and neo-classical rationalism. . . . In spite of its exuberance and its violent ruptures with classical tradition, the Catholic art of the epoch was an extremely normative art, which typified canonically its subjects of representation and its modes of representation. (*La imagen pornográfica,* 24–25)

Also see Mary Hivnor, "The Baroque Equation in Spanish Films," *Partisan Review* 17, no. 4 (1990): 616–620.

25. One of the first neorealist films with a bourgeois protagonist, *Cronaca di un amore* (1950) tells the story of a pair of lovers (she, the wife of a rich industrialist, and he, her former working-class lover) who were separated seven years ago by the accidental death of his fiancée (which they could have prevented) and who now conspire to murder her husband in a car crash. Although his death ironically proves to be an accident, their complicity destroys their relationship. Not only is the heroine played by Lucía Bosé (who also stars in *Muerte de un ciclista*) but the lover is Massimo Girotti (who played a similar role in Visconti's *Ossessione*). Though the film looks back to *Ossessione* in its use of a narrative situation loosely modeled on Cain's *The Postman Always Rings Twice,* it looks forward to Bardem's *Muerte de un ciclista* in its ideological contrasts between the stylized luxurious interiors of

the bourgeoisie and the realistic streets scenes of the Milanese suburbs and in its brilliant stylistic hybridization of both neorealism and noir.

26.   The importance of the Hitchcock thriller to Spanish cinema is also demonstrated in the reflexive film *Vida en sombras,* where a filmmaker, who had renounced filmmaking because his passion for the art contributed to the tragic death of his wife during the Civil War, is drawn back to movies by seeing *Rebecca,* the splashy Hollywood debut of Hitchcock, who was previously known to him only as the director of the British thriller, *39 Steps.*

27.   The undischarged emotion which cannot be accommodated within the action . . . is traditionally expressed in the music and, in the case of film, in certain elements of the mise-en-scène. . . . The mechanism here is strikingly similar to that of the psychopathology of hysteria. . . . The "return of the repressed" takes place, not in conscious discourse but displaced on to the body of the patient. In the melodrama . . . a conversion can take place into the body of the text. (Nowell-Smith, 193)

28.   Ortega y Gasset, "Teoria de Andalucia," in *Obras completas* (Madrid: Revista de Occidente, 1961): 112.

29.   Marvin D'Lugo, *The Films of Carlos Saura: The Practice of Seeing* (Princeton: Princeton University Press, 1991): 203.

3: BREAKING NEW GROUND IN *LOS GOLFOS, EL COCHECITO,* AND *EL ESPíRITU DE LA COLMENA*

1.   According to Francisco Aranda, Films 59 "were eventually only nominally coproducers of the film [*Viridiana*]; the effective producer was UNINCI." Moreover, Mexican producer Gustavo Alatriste claims that he was the only one who really put money into the film. Nevertheless, Aranda acknowledges that the crew on *Viridiana* was partly composed of the same young technicians as *Los golfos* (*Luis Buñuel: A Critical Biography,* 191–193). UNINCI was founded by Joaquin Reig, a politically ambiguous figure who produced *¡Bienvenido, Mr. Marshall!* but who had been in Berlin during the Spanish Civil War and who had organized the Spanish film productions that were made in Germany under the Third Reich. Hopewell describes UNINCI as "an umbrella company backed by the Spanish Communist Party" whose "associates included Buñuel, Ferreri, Azcona, Berlanga, Bardem, Fernán-Gómez, Saura, Portabella, Querejeta, Picazo, and even a young Gutiérrez Aragón"; he also notes that Bardem resigned from the company over a

financial dispute (*Out of the Past,* 250). Besas observes that in 1957, during the shooting of Bardem's *La venganza,* Bardem was invited to rejoin the company, which was now to be "a kind of Spanish version of United Artists . . . pooling the top talent of the day. The project, however, was doomed to failure" (*Behind the Spanish Lens,* 45). When *Viridiana* was denounced by the Vatican and banned in Spain (forcing Buñuel to change the film's nationality to Mexican), even though it had won both the Golden Palm and the French Critics' Prize at Cannes, general director of cinema José Muñoz-Fontán (who had accepted the prize for Buñuel) was fired and UNINCI was liquidated. According to Besas, this meant that "the film's shooting permit was cancelled retroactively, causing the production company, UNINCI, to remain comatose until 1983 when Bardem reactivated it and a Spanish court under the Socialists finally conceded Spanish nationality to *Viridiana*" (50).

2. Higginbotham, *Spanish Film under Franco,* 11.
3. D'Lugo, *The Films of Carlos Saura,* 33.
4. *Films and Filming* (November 1960): 9.
5. *Temas de cine,* no. 4, "Numero especial dedicado a la película *Los chicos de Ferreri.*" *Temas de cine,* no. 6, "Numero especial dedicado a la película *El cochecito* invitada al Festival de Venecia, 1960." *Temas de cine,* nos. 8–9 (Octubre-Noviembre, 1960), "Numero especial dedicado al film de Carlos Saura, *Los golfos.*" For a recent edition of the *El cochecito* script, see Rafael Azcona's *Otra vuelta en El cochecito* (Lograño: Biblioteca Riojana, 1991).
6. Santiago San Miguel, "Cuatro notas a *Los golfos," Nuestro cine,* no. 13 (Octubre 1962): 8.
7. "Coloquios internacionales de Venecia sobre el nuevo cine y la 'nouvelle vague'" (orig. published in *Schermi*), *Temas de cine,* no. 2 (Marzo y Abril, 1960): 22–37. Besides Rossellini, Wajda, and Truffaut, other participants included Leónide Móguy, Ettore Giannini, Bruno Beneck, Jerzy Kawale-rowicz, Giulio Pontecorvo, Luigi De Sanctis, and Francesco Maselli. Throughout these conversations, Truffaut functioned both as the primary example of and spokesman for the nouvelle vague. Godard was never mentioned. The transcription also included a more elaborate attack by Rossellini against Hollywood cinema and a more specific attack by Wajda against Bardem's latest film:

I believe that no producer can force me to make a film that I don't feel. For example, I don't understand how Bardem, a director who has made *Muerte de un ciclista* and *Calle mayor* can shoot scenes so banal and so void of imagination as those we have seen last night in his film, *Sonatas.*

Within this same issue of *Temas de cine,* Bardem's previous film, *La Venganza* (Revenge, 1957), was also discussed by García Escudero (along with *Serjeant York* and *The Bridge on the River Kwai*) in an essay called "Pacifism in the Contemporary Cinema," which demonstrates the continued preoccupation with this topic of political engagement in Spanish film criticism at this time.

8. In this same article, Saura also acknowledges the influence of foreign films about the Spanish Civil War (which he had seen at Montpelier, France, in 1957 during a Hispanic film week, along with three films by Buñuel— *Tierra sin pan,* 1932, *Subida al cielo,* 1951, and *El,* 1952). D'Lugo claims that it was during this international conference that Saura began consciously to explore "the meaning of his own cultural isolation"(27). One way to deal with that cultural isolation was to document what was distinctively Spanish and to confront the taboo subject of the Spanish Civil War, which, as a signifier of Spanishness, had tremendous international appeal outside Spain—an insight he would later act on in *La caza.*

I was profoundly impressed by all of the documentary parts and by noticing that, indeed, they were revealing the true human face of the Spaniard. (Saura, 6)

9. Elsaesser, *New German Cinema.*
10. This celebrated generation of '98 included many famous Spanish writers such as Miguel de Unamuno, Pío Baroja, Jacinto Benavente, Antonio Machado, Ramiro de Maéztu, and José Martínez Ruiz "Azorin."
11. For a more elaborate discussion of the historical context of Valle-Inclán, see José Luis Cano, "Valle-Inclán and Contemporary Spain," trans. José Sánchez, in *Valle-Inclán: Centennial Studies,* ed. Ricardo Gullón (Austin: University of Texas, 1968): 97–122.
12. Marco Ferreri, as quoted by Juan Carlos Frugone, in *Rafael Azcona: Atrapados por la vida* (Valladolid: International Cinema Week at Valladolid, 1987): 56.
13. Saura, *Temas de cine,* nos. 8–9 (Octubre-Noviembre, 1960): 7.
14. Carr, 164.

15. Bullfighting is also used negatively within a class discourse in Edgar Neville's social comedy *El último caballo* (1950), where it represents the plebeian sport, supported and exploited by the bourgeoisie in opposition to the aristocratic "Old World" traditions of chivalry and the cavalry, which are both centered on the horse. Bullfighting is introduced in a scene in which the quixotic Fernando (who has just been discharged from the Nationalist army) leads his beloved horse past a group of young ruffians who are playing at being toreros. Neville's vision is totally antithetical to that represented in Ernest Hemingway's *Death in the Afternoon,* where the horse is figured as inherently inferior to the noble toro and the machismo it represents.

16. Though Saura claims he had not seen *Los olvidados* before making *Los golfos,* Buñuel also introduces his Mexican hooligans with the Hispanic signifier of bullfighting as a means of distinguishing them from their international counterparts. Buñuel's film opens with a documentary-style prologue, in which a voice-over narrator tells us "this film is entirely based on actual events and all characters are authentic" (the same claims made by Saura for *Los golfos*) and that this same problem of hungry delinquents occurs in other modern "pits of misery" such as New York, London, and Paris (which are illustrated with a montage of familiar tourist shots from these progressive urban centers). Then there is a dissolve to a long shot of the impoverished suburbs outside Mexico City, where a group of young boys simulate a bullfight, a transitional image that both completes the prologue and launches the narrative. This image of bullfighting evokes both the Hispanic cult of masculinity and Buñuel's own cultural specificity as an exiled filmmaker, who had previously worked in Paris, New York, and Spain before settling in the commercial film industry in Mexico.

17. The motor is also the symbol of modernization in Edgar Neville's right-wing comedy, *El último caballo,* where it replaces the horse, with whom the quixotic protagonist is similarly obsessed. Yet the hobbyhorse in Neville's film is treated not with the distancing irony of esperpento but with an affectionate, admiring humor.

18. Ricardo Gullón, "Reality of the *Esperpento,*" trans. Miguel González-Guth, in *Valle-Inclán: Centennial Studies,* 125–131.

19. José María García Escudero, *Temas de cine,* nos. 8–9, 24. Manuel Villegas Lopez, "En la ruta del humor español," *Temas de cine,* no. 6.

20. Landy, *Fascism in Film,* 24–25.

21. Ortega y Gasset, "The Dehumanization of Art," in *Velázquez, Goya and the Dehumanization of Art,* 77.

22. According to Baena,

> On various occasions, in the hallway especially, where it was not possible to use a dolly or traveling for the movements of the camera and actors, my second operator had to shoot seated in a wheelchair. Some shots were shot where the camera accompanying the movements of the characters traveled the hallway (approximately 18 meters long by 0.80 wide) from front to back, and then back to front, making it impossible for us to permit anyone to remain in the set except the second operator, the focusists and a machine operator, who moved with the actors. (*Temas de Cine,* no. 6, 13–14)

23. In the special issue of *Temas de cine* devoted to the film, Baena writes,

> Before beginning the shoot of *El cochecito* Marco Ferreri and I had spoken many times about the character that the photography must have. In those days I was finishing the shoot of *Los golfos* with a very different atmosphere and theme. Ferreri wanted for the picture, and I agreed with him, a high contrast photography, but without any effects. The basic plot, the character that Alarcón was going to give to the decor, as well as the condition of the characters, made desirable a photography of whites and blacks, with the scale of grays very reduced. At the same time we were proposing to offer an image completely realistic in atmosphere. . . . We had abundant natural interiors and, as in the studio, my intention has always been to save the light that exists in reality. For that reason, I exploited to the maximum all the possibilities that were offered to me by each set—doors, balconies, patios, etc.—as principal references, and then I created the lighting for the rest by enclosing the lights of the scene in the latitude of the emulsions, trying always to save the most realistic. (Baena, 13–14)

24. Though there is a similar scene in *El pisito,* where two characters having hysterics in the foreground and background, respectively, vie for the space, there it is not handled in the same way stylistically with two kinds of contrasting lighting.

25. Quoted by Hopewell, *Out of the Past,* 65.

26. For a fuller analysis of this adaptation, see my article, "The Children of Franco in the New Spanish Cinema," *Quarterly Review of Film Studies,* ed. Katherine S. Kovács (Spring 1983): 57–76.

27. See André Bazin, "In Defense of Rossellini," *What is Cinema?* vol. 2, trans. Hugh Gray (Berkeley and Los Angeles: University of California, 1972).

28. Gerard Genette, *Narrative Discourse: An Essay in Method,* trans. Jane E. Lewin (Ithaca: Cornell University Press, 1980): 123. For a more detailed discussion of how the pseudo-iterative can be applied to the opposing aesthetics of Hollywood melodrama and Italian neorealism, see my essay, "The Subversive Potential of the Pseudo-Iterative," 2–16.

29. Elsaesser, "Tales of Sound and Fury: Observations on the Family Melodrama," 170.

30. Kinder, "The Subversive Potential of the Pseudo-Iterative," 11.

4: SACRIFICE AND MASSACRE

1. Hopewell, *Out of the Past,* 27.

2. As quoted by Besas in *Behind the Spanish Lens,* 183.

3. In 1987, Bill Nichols proposed an anthology of theoretical and cross-cultural essays entitled *Representations of Violence,* which was originally to be an American Film Institute Reader and which was to include this chapter. Unfortunately, the project was aborted when Nichols ceased being editor of the AFI Monograph Series.

    In a chapter from *La imagen pornográfica y otras perversiones opticas* entitled "The Cruel Image," where noted Spanish critic Gubern deals with the representation of violence in world cinema, interestingly, he dwells mainly on American genre movies, with brief commentary on films made in Japan (especially Oshima's *In the Realm of the Senses*) and in Europe (especially Pasolini's *Salo*) but without mentioning a single Spanish film, unless one counts Buñuel's *Un chien andalou* or documentaries on the Spanish Civil War made by foreigners Roman Karmen, Ivor Montagu, and Joris Ivens (111–130).

4. Both models had always been an important influence on the films of Buñuel, which had been observed by André Bazin in 1951 in a collection of his essays called *El cine de la crueldad de Buñuel a Hitchcock.* In a review of *Los olvidados,* Bazin links the "affection for the horrible," the "sense of cruelty," and "the expression of the most extreme human decadence" less to surrealism than to the Spanish painting tradition of Goya (and of others like Zurbarán and Ribera). André Bazin, "*Los olvidados,*" in *El cine de la crueldad de Buñuel a Hitchcock,* trans. into Spanish by Béatrice Meunier de Galipienso (Bilbao: Ediciones Mensajero, 1977): 74. According to Valle-Inclán, both of these models from Goya also helped to inspire and create the esperpento in his own drama and fiction, where death is consistently linked

with eroticism and where the victims of the cruelest violence are frequently innocent children. For a fuller discussion of this issue, see Ildefonso Manuel Gil, "'Innocent Victims' in the Works of Valle-Inclán," trans. Douglas Rogers, in *Valle-Inclán: Centennial Studies,* 43–62.

5. Fred Light, "El moralismo del arte de Goya en el contexto de su época," *Goya y el espíritu de la ilustración* (Madrid: Museo del Prado, 1988): 91.

6. As noted art historian Light observes, "In many ways, the *Disasters of War* are an exhibition of human depravity, of such dimensions and such intensity that all moral speculation becomes irrelevant. In a world where scenes like *Esto es peor y Por qué?* can occur, all reason, all logic, all hope for human dignity appears absurd or blasphemous" (ibid., 98).

7. René Girard, *Violence and the Sacred,* trans. Patrick Gregory (Baltimore and London: Johns Hopkins University Press, 1977): 134.

8. Georges Bataille, *Erotism: Death and Sensuality* (1957), trans. Mary Dalwood (San Francisco: City Lights Books, 1986): 186.

9. Gubern, *La imagen pornográfica,* 24.

10. Miguel de Unamuno, "The Spanish Christ," in *Perplexities and Paradoxes,* trans. Stuart Gross (New York: Greenwood Press, 1968): 75, 76, 79.

11. Federico García Lorca, "Teoría y juego del duende" (Theory and Play of the Duende, 1928), in *From the Havana Lectures,* trans. Stella Rodriquez (Kanathos, 1981): 70, 72.

12. Tzvetan Todorov, *The Conquest of America: The Question of the Other,* trans. Richard Howard (New York: Harper & Row, 1984): 133.

13. Spain's ground-breaking modernism was to be found not only in this conception of violent massacre or in Cortés's perception of history and the Other (in contrast to the medieval assumptions of Columbus), as Todorov has argued, but also in the rupturing reflexivity of artistic works like Calderón de la Barca'a *La vida es sueño* (which was a key source for Girard's anti-Freudian reading of the Oedipal myth), Cervantes's *Don Quixote,* and Velázquez's *Las meninas.*

14. Spain's paradoxical combination of an advanced modernism and regressive feudalism was not restricted to earlier centuries. At the beginning of our own century, we can still see advanced modernists like Picasso and Buñuel reaffirming that their artistic roots lay in the sacrificial art of bullfighting or in the fierce spirituality of the Middle Ages. Buñuel writes in his autobiography,

In my own village of Calanda, where I was born on the twenty-second of February, 1900, the Middle Ages lasted until World War I. It was a closed and isolated society, with clear and unchanging distinctions among the classes. The respectful subordination of the peasants to the big landowners was deeply rooted in tradition and seemed unshakable. . . . I'm lucky to have spent my childhood in the Middle Ages, or, as Huysmans described it, that "painful and exquisite" epoch—painful in terms of its material aspects perhaps, but exquisite in its spiritual life. What a contrast to the world of today! (*My Last Sigh,* trans. Abigail Israel [New York: Vintage Books, 1984]: 8, 18)

15. Stanley Payne, "Spanish Fascism," 107.
16. Georges Bataille, "Sade," in *Literature and Evil,* trans. Alastair Hamilton (New York and London: Marion Boyars, 1985): 122–123.
17. Gilles Deleuze, *Masochism: An Interpretation of Coldness and Cruelty,* trans. Jean McNeil (New York: George Braziller, 1971): 33–34.
18. Allan Stoekl, *Politics, Writing, Mutilation: The Case of Bataille, Blanchot, Roussel, Leiris, and Ponge* (Minneapolis: University of Minnesota Press, 1985): 108.
19. "Modern thinkers continue to see religion as an isolated, wholly fictitious phenomenon cherished only by a few backward peoples or milieus. And these same thinkers can now project upon religion alone the responsibility for a violent projection of violence that truly pertains to all societies in- cluding our own" (Girard, 317).
20. "Although traces of the mimetic conception are scattered throughout Freud's work, this conception never assumes a dominant role. It runs counter to the Freudian insistence on a desire that is fundamentally directed toward an object; that is, sexual desire for the mother" (ibid., 169).
21. Girard's theory is compatible both with the definition of fascism offered by a traditional historian like Stanley Payne and with the far more radical theory of fascism developed by Klaus Theweleit, which is based on the fantasies of the Freikorpsmen, who began as volunteer armies fighting for Germany in World War I and ultimately became the core of Hitler's SA and key functionaries of the Third Reich. Specializing in "death production," these Fascist warriors waged a perpetual war, which, according to Theweleit, was undertaken to escape women, whom they dread as a source of dissolution and annihilation. In a foreword to Theweleit's book, Barbara Ehrenreich observes,

The dread arises in the pre-Oedipal struggle of fledgling self, before there is even an ego to sort out the objects of desire and the odds of getting them: it is a dread . . . of being swallowed, engulfed, annihilated. Women's bodies are the holes, swamps, pits of muck that can engulf. . . . This is what the fascist held himself in horror of, and what he saw in communism, in female sexuality—a joyous commingling, as disorderly as life. In this fantasy, the body expands . . . and we are at last able to rejoice in the softness and the permeability of the world around us, rather than holding ourselves back in lonely dread. This is the fantasy that makes us . . . revolutionaries in the cause of life. (*Male Fantasies,* Vol. 1. *women floods bodies history,* trans. Stephen Conway [Minneapolis: University of Minnesota Press, 1987]: xiii–xvii)

This revolutionary fantasy of plenitude and infantile desire, which so terrified the Fascists, is a positive vision of Girard's generative sacrificial crisis in which all boundaries and distinctions disappear; like the Freikorpsmen, he sees it as the ultimate threat to social order, which all religious rituals and cultural myths are supposedly designed to forestall. This fantasy and the fear it arouses are disavowed in the escapist Francoist cinema where women are frequently idealized; but they are obsessively explored in the cinema of opposition, particularly in films like *Furtivos* and *Pascual Duarte,* where repressed sons dread the devouring mother and where excessive violence and rebellious patricidal impulses lead to matricide.

22. The role played by women in the religious and cultural structure of a society—or rather, the minor importance of that role—is graphically illustrated by the social framework prevailing in certain South American villages—in those of Bororo, for example. . . . The women inhabit the houses on the periphery of the circle and unlike the men they never move to another house. This immobility of the women was one of the factors that led early researchers to affirm the existence of a "matriarchy." In fact, far from attesting to women's importance, this very stability suggests that women are only passive spectators at a masculine tragicomedy. (Girard, 140)

There is nothing incomprehensible about the viewpoint that sees menstrual blood as a physical representation of sexual violence. We ought . . . to inquire whether this process of symbolization does not respond to some half-suppressed desire to place the blame for all forms of violence on women. By means of this taboo a transfer of violence has been affected and a monopoly established that is clearly detrimental to the female sex." (Ibid., 34–36).

23. No one today [1957] could deny that impulses connecting sexuality and the desire to hurt and to kill do exist. Hence, the so-called sadistic instincts enable the ordinary man to account for certain acts of cruelty, while religious impulses are explained away as aberration. By describing these instincts in

masterly fashion then, deSade has contributed to man's slow growing awareness of himself. . . . The history of religion, then, has given our consciousness but little assistance in its reassessment of sadism. The definition of sadism, however, has shown us that religious experience and behavior need not
be regarded as something bizarre and inexplicable. (Bataille, *Erotism,* 183)

24. Unamuno also extends this opposition (between the sadistic alliance of
father and daughter and the masochistic alliance of mother and son) to the
contrast between Christianity and classical mythology:

Pagan mythology offers us . . . a male god who, without recourse to woman,
begets a daughter: for Jupiter begot Minerva from his own head. . . . Virility, will *ganas* are one thing; quite another is faith, feminity, woman and the
Virgin Mary. . . . Christ was born of woman! Even the historic Christ, who
came back from the dead." ("The Virility of Faith," in *The Agony of Christianity and Essays on Faith,* trans. Anthony Kerrigan [Princeton: Princeton
University Press, 1974]: 51–53)

25. Emilio Sanz deSoto, "1940–1950," in *Spanish Cinema,* 124–125.
26. For a recent discussion of the representation of war in this film, see Antoni
Rigol and Jordi Sebastián's essay, "España aislada: *Los últimos de Filipinas*
(1945) de Antonio Román," *Film historia* 1, no. 3 (1991): 171–184.

27. The only unique feature of the fascist relationship to violence was the theoretical evaluation by some fascist movements that violence possessed a certain
positive and therapeutic value in and of itself, that a certain amount of continuing violent struggle, along the lines of late nineteenth century Social Dar-
winism, was necessary for the health of national security. (Stanley Payne,
Fascism: Comparison and Definition, 12)

28. César Santos Fontela, "1962–1967," in *Spanish Cinema,* 179–180.
29. Hopewell observes,

At a time when the Francoist regime was increasingly courting foreign opinion, Querejeta was attributed with far-reaching influence over the foreign
media, which he did not go out of his way to deny. Of all Spain's producers
he was the last a supposedly reformist regime wanted to disaffect.
    By the 60s at least a filmmaker's evasiveness served not only to distract
attention from hidden themes but also to persuade the censor that the film's

impact would be limited to an intellectual, dissenting minority whose existence the regime was resigned to. This market factor explains in part Saura's
relative toleration by the censor. It is doubtful whether in Spain in political
terms his films did much more than preach to an already converted
minority. . . . Saura's importance was the fact that he was tolerated in Spain
despite his clear opposition to its dictatorial regime. It is hardly surprising
that when the Francoist government attempted to establish a wider, more
liberal base for continuance in 1974, one of its most influential moves was
to champion a Saura film, *La Prima Angelica,* which made an acid attack on
the extreme right. (*Out of the Past,* 76)

30.   In *El cine de Carlos Saura* (Zaragoza: Caja de Ahorros de la Inmaculada,
      1988), Agustín Sánchez Vidal denies the validity of this connection, ac-
      cepting Saura's emphasis on his own originality and disavowal of his sources.

      Although there is no lack of appreciations that have presented it [*Llanto por
      un bandido*] as an actualization of an old tradition of films about bandits in
      the light of strands like *Salvatore Giuliano* by Francesco Rosi or *Viva Zapata*
      by Elia Kazan, Saura has distanced himself from them and also from docu-
      mentaries of the type of *Bandits of Orgosolo,* shot in Sicily by the young doc-
      umentary filmmaker Vittorio DeSeta in 1961. As has been said, he was try-
      ing to move toward his own aesthetic. (37)

      Though using documentary conventions, *Bandits of Orgosolo* was the first
      fictional feature of DeSeta and was shot in Sardinia.

31.   D'Lugo observes,

      The anti-Francoist playwright, Antonio Buero Vallejo, played the town crier,
      and seven prominent opposition writers, including the outspoken playwright,
      Alfonso Sastre, were to play the seven bandits. Of the original sequence, only
      a brief set of images of Buñuel and Buero Vallejo remain. (*The Films of Car-
      los Saura,* 48)

32.   Saura, as quoted by Gail Bartholomew, "The Development of Carlos
      Saura," *The Journal of the University Film and Video Association,* no. 35.3
      (Summer 1983): 23.

33.   Even when the hunting metaphor is not central—as it is here in *La caza*
      and later in Borau's *Furtivos* (1975), Berlanga's *La escopeta nacional* (The
      National Shotgun, 1977), and Camus's *Los santes inocentes* (The Holy

Innocents, 1984)—it is significantly operative in those films in which the depiction of violence is most political, as in Saura's *El jardín de las delicias* (The Garden of Delights, 1970) and *Ana y los lobos* (Ana and the Wolves, 1972), Borau's *Hay que matar á B* (B Must Die, 1974) and *Río abajo* (On the Line, 1984), Franco's *Pascual Duarte* (1975), Gutiérrez Aragón's *Camada negra* (Black Brood, 1977) and *El corazón del bosque* (The Heart of the Forest, 1978), Miró's *El crimen de Cuenca* (1979), and Chávarri's *Dedicatoria* (A Dedication, 1980). Although Saura did not invent the hunt metaphor as a vehicle for political commentary, he helped establish it as a subversive cinematic convention that was acceptable to Spanish censors.

García Escudero seems for instance to have been aware of Saura's insinuations in *La caza:* "That the film's got secondary intentions is evident," he wrote in his diary. "But whether that's enough to prohibit it is another matter. That it's got quality can't be doubted. The script was given "special interest" status. (Hopewell, *Out of the Past,* 76)

34. Maximiliano Alonso, "Entrevista con Carlos Saura," *Joven crítica cinematográfica* 13 (Junio 1968): 7–8.
35. Hopewell, *Out of the Past,* 76.
36. Saura has been quoted as saying, "I saw *El* a number of times, something I rarely ever do, and even today it continues to fascinate me and seems to be one of Buñuel's finest films. Buñuel oriented me in a definitive way." Enrique Brasó, *Carlos Saura: Introdución incompleta* (Madrid: Taller de Ediciones Josefina Betantor, 1974): 40.
37. Bernard Cohen, "Entretien avec Carlos Saura," *Positif,* 110 (Noviembre 1969): 29.
38. Girard, *Violence and the Sacred,* 102.
39. Steven Kovács, *From Enchantment to Rage: The Story of Surrealist Cinema* (London and Toronto: Associated University Presses, 1980): 224–225.
40. According to Juan Hernández Les,

This film was born out of a proposition made by two young North American residents in Spain, who were associates at that time, 1968–69, Dean Selmier, who wanted to be an actor, and an ex-marine, Bill Boon, who wrote for the Spanish press. Both offered to Querejeta a conversion into dollars and the opportunity for the Spanish producer to make any films that he wanted to make, the only way possible of collaborating with him. Then the idea occurred to him of reuniting Egea, Guerin, and Erice, three young promising graduates from the EOC [Escuela Oficial de Cinematografía].

According to the producer, the idea was to divide the film into three tales that narrate historical variations on the theme of violence and have them form the basis for which Selmier was to be the vehicle, the object of that violence, except in Erice's episode. (*El cine de Elías Querejeta, un productor singular* [Bilbao: Ediciones Mensajero, 1986]: 63)

41. According to Hernández Les, "Rafael Azcona intervened on the three stories, but Erice maintained such strong disagreements with him that finally practically nothing remained of his participation in that episode" (63).
42. Lorca, "Teoría y juego del duende," 72, 66, 69.
43. In *La caza,* the gamekeeper Juan (Fernando Sánchez Polack, the same actor who plays Benito) is also left to put out the fire that gets out of hand.
44. Juan Carlos Frugone, *Rafael Azcona: Atrapados por la vida* (Valladolid: International Cinema Week at Valladolid, 1987): 108.
45. Laura Mulvey, "Visual Pleasure and Narrative Cinema," *Screen* 16, no. 3 (1975). For the best discussion of the masochistic version of the scopic drive in cinema, see Gaylyn Studlar, "Masochism and the Perverse Pleasures of the Cinema," in *Movies and Methods,* II: 602–621.
46. Among the films discussed thus far, Querejeta's productions include the anthology film *Los desafíos,* Saura's *La caza, Peppermint frappé, La prima Angélica,* and *Cría cuervos,* and Erice's *El espíritu de la colmena* and *El sur.* Considered by some critics as an important Spanish auteur in his own right, Querejeta is a creative producer who developed a distinctive cinematic style that appeared in the work of many directors from the 1960s to the 1980s. His remarkable collaborative team included Luis Cuadrado, the brilliant cinematographer who was known for cultivating the "blackness" that was found in Spanish paintings by Goya and by seventeenth-century masters like Murillo, Ribera, Zurbarán, and Velázquez; camera operator Teo Escamilla, who replaced Cuadrado when he went blind and who became Spain's next preeminent cinematographer; Pablo G. Del Amo, who made his editorial debut on Orson Welles's *Mr. Arkadin* (1955) and who developed a highly original elliptical style of editing that would serve a wide range of narrative functions; and Luis de Pablo, whose expressive, minimalist musical scores frequently worked in counterpoint to the image, exerting tremendous control over the narrative (anticipating events, connecting images that are far apart in the plot, shifting the tone to heighten suspense or to parody the action, fading in and out in unpredictable patterns, and sometimes suggesting musically what could not be said explicitly). The auteurist approach

to Querejeta is probably best represented by Juan Hernández Les in *El cine de Elías Querejeta, un productor singular.*

47. For an excellent discussion of the adaptation issue, see Kathleen M. Vernon's essay, "La politique des auteurs: Narrative point of view in *Pascual Duarte,* novel and film," *Hispania* 72, no. 1 (March 1989): 87–96.

48. See Denis Hollier, ed., *The College of Sociology: 1937–1939* (Minneapolis: University of Minnesota Press, 1988).

49. One way of seeing the difference between *Salò* and *Tras el cristal* is to contrast their use of close-ups. Although *Salò*'s inset verbal narratives make it quite explicit that concrete detail helps to arouse desire, its close-ups are not used to fetishize or eroticize individuals or actions, as in *Tras el cristal.* Instead they are usually linked to recruitment or the process of selection, to demonstrate who has been chosen from the paradigm for a particular performance. The key example occurs in the "circle of blood," when one of the voyeuristic masters watching the torture suddenly turns his magnifying glasses around and the action immediately becomes distanced and easier to watch. The close-ups have an abstract categorizing function, for example, the face of pain on the victim versus the face of pleasure on the torturer, but they never suture us into identification with either. While this strategy enables us to analyze the relationship between violence and eroticism with the safe distance of satire, *Tras el cristal* demonstrates the connection through its emotional impact, which we experience even against our will. *Salò* risks losing its audience if they are bourgeois spectators who are horrified by the torture and who fail to understand the subversiveness of the design, but it does not really risk converting anyone to the pleasures of sadism and thus is far less threatening than *Tras el cristal.* A similar distinction can be made between the satiric distance of the eroticized violence in Kubrick's *A Clockwork Orange* and its emotional impact in Peckinpah's *Straw Dogs* (which is much closer to the Spanish aesthetic).

50. Quoted by Carlos Balagué, "Entrevista con Ricardo Franco," *Dirigido por . . . ,* no. 37 (Octubre 1976): 15.

51. "Entrevista con Ricardo Franco," 14.

52. Camilo José Cela, *The Family of Pascual Duarte,* trans. Anthony Kerrigan (New York: Avon Books, 1966): 91.

5: THE SPANISH OEDIPAL NARRATIVE AND ITS SUBVERSION

1. Some notable exceptions are George L. Mosse's groundbreaking work, *Nationalism and Sexuality: Middle-Class Morality and Sexual Norms in Modern Europe* (Madison: University of Wisconsin Press, 1985); Kay Schaf-

fer's brilliant study *Women and the Bush: Forces of Desire in the Australian Cultural Tradition* (Cambridge: Cambridge University Press, 1988); and a valuable anthology edited by Andrew Parker et al. entitled *Nationalisms and Sexualities* (New York and London: Routledge, 1992).

2. In my article "The Children of Franco in the New Spanish Cinema," I examined seven influential films (made between 1973 and 1980) and described some of the patterns, which I will be elaborating on here. The seven films were Erice's *El espíritu de la colmena,* Saura's *La prima Angélica* and *Cría cuervos,* Armiñán's *El nido,* Chávarri's *A un dios desconocido,* Gutiérrez Aragón's *Camada negra,* and Borau's *Furtivos. Quarterly Review of Film Studies,* "The New Spanish Cinema," ed. Katherine S. Kovács, vol. 8, no. 2 (Spring 1983): 57–76.

3. Ernesto Laclau, *Politics and Ideology in Marxist Theory: Capitalism-Fascism-Populism* (London: Verso Editions, 1979): 156–159.

4. Leopoldo Alas, *La Regenta,* trans. John Rutherford (Middlesex, England, and New York: Penguin Books, Ltd., 1984): 328.

5. Gilles Deleuze, *Masochism: An Interpretation of Coldness and Cruelty,* trans. Jean McNeil (New York: George Braziller, 1971): 49.

6. For a discussion of the collaborative relationship between director Vicente Aranda and actress Victoria Abril, see Rosa Alvares and Belen Frias's *El cine como pasión* (Valladolid: Semana Internacional de Cine de Valladolid, 1991).

7. Sophocles, *Oedipus the King,* in *Greek Tragedies* I, ed. David Grene and Richmond Lattimore (Chicago and London: University of Chicago Press, 1942): 152.

8. Laura Mulvey, "The Oedipus Myth: Beyond the Riddles of the Sphinx," in *Visual and Other Pleasures* (Bloomington: Indiana University Press, 1989): 192.

9. George Devereux, "Why Oedipus Killed Laius," *International Journal of Psycho-Analysis* 34 (1953): 132–141. Marie Balmary, *Psychoanalyzing Psychoanalysis: Freud and the Hidden Fault of the Father* (Baltimore and London: Johns Hopkins University Press, 1982). For a development of this argument from a gay perspective, also see Bernard Sergeant, *Homosexuality in Greek Myth* (Boston: Beacon Press, 1986): chap. 5. I am indebted to Stephen Tropiano and Grigoris Daskalagogorakis for first bringing these arguments to my attention.

10. Girard, *Violence and the Sacred,* 169.

11. Quoting from the *Purifications* by Empedocles, Girard writes,

"The father takes hold of his son *who has changed form,* and in a fit of madness, sacrifices him. . . . The demented father cuts the son's throat, and prepares an abominable feast in his palace. Similarly, the son seizes the father and the children of their mother, kills them all and devours their flesh."

. . . As in *The Bacchae,* we are witnessing the degeneration of a rite into a form of reciprocal violence that is so irrational it conjures up the monstrous double. That is, it harkens back to the very origins of the rite and thus closes the circle of religious compositions and decompositions that preoccupied the pre-Socratics. (Girard, 164).

12. For a discussion of this genre, see Antonio Lloréns, *El cine negro español* (Valladolid: Semana de Cine de Valladolid, 1988).

13. Susan Rubin Suleiman, *Subversive Intent: Gender, Politics, and the Avant-Garde* (Cambridge: Harvard University Press, 1990): 161.

14. Benito Pérez Galdós, *Fortunata and Jacinta: Two Stories of Married Women,* trans. Agnes Moncy Gullón (London and New York: Penguin Books, 1988): 158.

15. This woman, by name Magdalena Ventura, was a native of the Abruzzi, in the Kingdom of Naples. At the age of 37, she grew a beard and moustache. She had seven children, three of whom were born before the beard grew, and the other four afterwards. She was married twice, and is shown in the picture with her second husband, Félix, and suckling her last child, born when she was 52 years of age. When this woman was presented to the Viceroy of Naples (the third Duke of Alcalá), he was so struck by her that he commissioned Ribera to make the portrait in 1631, so as to bring this extraordinary case to the knowledge of King Philip III.

16. This attempt by patriarchs to appropriate the Madonna's breast is also represented in some of the paintings that depict San Bernardo's vision of the Virgin. In Alonso Cano's version, *San Bernardo y La Virgen,* the kneeling white-robed saint squats in the center of the composition with open mouth, ecstatically receiving the holy milk that squirts from the Virgin's erect breast in a dramatic arc, whose shape evokes both a rainbow and a spume of urine from an erect penis. The saint clearly holds center stage, appropriating the starring role of the Christ child who passively sleeps in the Virgin's arms. In Murillo's version, *Aparición de la Virgin a San Bernardo,* it is not clear whether the Madonna is squeezing her breast to draw milk for the saint or protecting it against his appropriation. In either event, the infant Jesus

clearly wears a skeptical expression on his face, wary of the saint who kneels in the foreground with arm extended, as if negotiating for the holy emission. (Both of these paintings are at the Prado Museum in Madrid.)

17. Goya's parody of the Ribera painting prefigures Marcel Duchamp's dadaist parody of Leonardo's *Mona Lisa,* which Susan Suleiman reads as "a classic Oedipal scenario in its 'ascendant' phase":

> If we focus . . . on the mustache and beard, it becomes obvious that the two V's . . . are mirror images of each other—and are also fairly standard iconographic representations of a woman's pubic hair. It would appear that by a humorous "displacement upward," Duchamp has produced not, or not only, the Mona Lisa as a sexpot . . . , nor the Mona Lisa as a young man, but the Mona Lisa as a phallic mother (pubis plus "appendages")—indeed, a phallic mother doubly marked, redundantly phallic. We are no longer in Oedipus but in its fetishistic perversion: sexual difference no sooner recognized than denied. (152–153).

18. Agustín Sánchez Vidal, *José Luis Borau: Una panoramica* (Teruel: Instituto de Estudios Turolenses, 1987): 19–20.

19. Now Queen Isabella (and the founder of Opus Dei, Josemaría Escrivá de Balaguer) are candidates for sainthood, though Pope John Paul II thus far opposes the move. See Kenneth L. Woodward, "Saint Isabella? Not so Fast," *Newsweek* (April 15, 1991): 67.

20. Alexander Mitscherlich, the director of the Sigmund Freud Institute in Frankfurt, has described a similar dynamic in Nazi Germany, which he called the "Fatherless Society." Elsaesser writes,

> Nazism, according to Mitscherlich, could exert such a firm ideological hold even before the war because it . . . encouraged the original attachment to the mother to transfer itself onto substitute love objects, abstractions such as nation, race, the State: in turn symbolically represented by the Führer. . . . Hitler projected himself not as the ideal father, but as the dutiful son of a beloved mother, and thus as a representative of the primary love object, prior to and outside Oedipal division. The Nazi sympathiser would thus be a Narcissist who had bypassed repression and failed to acquire the ego-ideal modelled after the Father who was either absent, inaccessible or overshadowed by the mother's authority. Fathers became pure objects of hate and aggression in a psychic world dominated by masochistic and sadistic impulses. Mitscherlich saw in Nazism a regressive solution to the "fatherless

society," a solution which led to latent and disavowed homosexuality and manic-depressive personality structures. (*New German Cinema*, 240–241)

21. As quoted by Suleiman, *Subversive Intent*, 165.
22. Diego Galán, "1950–1961," in *Spanish Cinema*, 152–154.
23. Miraculously, a remake of *Marcelino, pan y vino* appeared in 1991 in color. This Spanish-Italian-French coproduction, directed by Italian filmmaker Luigi Comencini with a six-year-old Italian boy (Nicolo Paolucci) in the role of Marcelino, also featured well-known Spanish actors Fernando Fernán Gómez and Alfredo Landa as two of the monks. The success of the original film in the international market must have encouraged the producers of the remake to try it again as a European coproduction in the new world order of the 1990s.
24. Gubern, *La imagen pornográfica*, 33.
25. *Erotism*, 248.
26. Their encounter suggests perverse intertextual relations with the opening homoerotic murder scene in *Tras el cristal*, where the young boy is positioned as the suspended martyr. In his discussion of the "formal" similarities between martyrdom and masochism, Theodor Reik notes three common features, which are foregrounded both in *Marcelino* and *Tras el cristal:* the specific fantasy of identification ("the desire to die for him in order to be united with him"), suspension (or prolonged anticipation), and the demonstrative factor (the importance of specularizing the display of the tortured body). Theodor Reik, *Masochism in Modern Man*, trans. Margaret H. Beigel and Gertrud M. Kurth (New York: Farrar & Rinehart, 1941): 352–353.

While *Marcelino* is deeply masochistic both in form and content (both erotically and religiously), *Tras el cristal* uses the masochistic aesthetic to glamorize sadistic murders that glorify the patriarchy. The difference is most apparent in their treatment of the maternal, which the former celebrates and the latter brutally rejects. As if describing the plot of *Tras el cristal*, Deleuze observes,

In sadism the Oedipal image of woman is made, as it were, to explode: the mother becomes the victim *par excellence*, while the daughter is elevated to the position of incestuous accomplice. . . . Sadism is in every sense an active negation of the mother and an exaltation of the father who is beyond all law. (*Masochism*, 52)

27. Sara Medialdea, "Sánchez Silva: 'Escribí el cuento para que los padres lo contasen a sus hijos,'" *Ya* (25 Agosto 1989).

28. Unamuno, "Agony," in *The Agony of Christianity and Essays on Faith,* 11.

29. The English subtitles translate their exchange of dialogue as follows:

Marcelino:	I'm wondering where your mother is.
Jesus:	My mother is with yours in heaven.
M:	What are mothers like?
J:	Very giving, . . . they give everything. They give life to their sons.
M:	Are they ugly?
J:	Mothers are never ugly.
M:	Do you love your mother?
J:	With all my heart.
M:	I love mine more . . .
J:	Would you like to be a friar like Friar Soup, or do you prefer to be with Manolo?
M:	I prefer to see my mother and yours.
J:	Right now?
M:	Yes.
J:	You have to sleep, . . . I'll put you to sleep.

When my eight-year-old son saw the movie and was confounded by the ending, he wondered why Marcelino didn't ask Jesus to bring his mother *and* father (whom he never mentions) back to life, or why Jesus didn't think of this solution himself. Good questions.

30. Marsha Kinder, "Pleasure and the New Spanish Mentality: A Conversation with Pedro Almodóvar," *Film Quarterly* (Fall 1987): 43.

31. In a 1990 interview published in Iberian Airlines' monthly magazine, Almodóvar described an intermediate version of the project that showed the gradual process of transformation and that contradicted his comments in Los Angeles.

What I am writing changes every day. . . . It's the story of a great vengeance. For the first time I am trying to construct an evil female character, and it's proving difficult. . . . It's the story of a girl's revenge against her mother. . . . I'll try to make a really brutal melodrama like Bette Davis's old films. My protagonist is a television newscaster. The film begins with her husband [being] murdered and [her] confessing to all of Spain that she killed him. . . . Most of the movie takes place in prison. . . . The relationship between a sensitive mother and an only daughter is very special. I remember a humiliating scene in the film, *Sonata de otoño* [Autumn Sonata], with Ingrid Bergman showing her daughter how to play a Chopin sonata well, a very simple scene but terrible. (Miguel Angel Arenas, Paco Navarro, Mimmo Cattarenich, "Interview with Pedro Almodóvar," *Ronda Iberia* [September 1990]: 62–71)

32. Kaja Silverman, *The Acoustic Mirror: The Female Voice in Psychoanalysis and Cinema* (Bloomington: Indiana University Press, 1988): 124.

33. Marvin D'Lugo, "Almodóvar's City of Desire," *Quarterly Review of Film and Video,* special issue, "Remapping the Post-Franco Cinema," ed. Marsha Kinder, vol. 13, no. 4 (1991): 63–64.

34. The mother . . . is traditionally . . . the one who first organizes the world linguistically for the child, and first presents it to the Other. The maternal voice also plays a crucial part during the mirror stage, defining and interpreting the reflected image, and "fitting" it to the child. Finally it provides the acoustic mirror in which the child first hears "itself." The maternal voice is thus complexly bound up in that drama which "decisively projects the formation of the individual into history," and whose "internal thrust is precipitated from insufficiency to anticipation." Indeed, it would seem to be the maternal rather than the paternal voice that initially constitutes the auditory sphere for most children, although it is clearly the latter which comes to predominate within the superego. (Silverman, *The Acoustic Mirror,* 100)

   Also see Amy Lawrence's *Echo and Narcissus: Women's Voices in Classical Hollywood Cinema* (Berkeley, Los Angeles, and Oxford: University of California Press, 1991). The title *Tacones lejanos* also sounds like *Tambores lejanos,* the Spanish title for Walsh's *Distant Drums* (1951), a classical Hollywood film that was very popular in Spain.

35. Silverman, *The Acoustic Mirror,* 32.

36. Pilar Miró, "Ten Years of Spanish Cinema," trans. Alma Amell, in *Literature, the Arts and Democracy: Spain in the Eighties,* ed. Samuel Amell (Rutherford, Madison, and Teaneck: Fairleigh Dickinson University Press, 1990): 41.

37. Linda Williams, *Figures of Desire: A Theory and Analysis of Surrealist Film* (Chicago: University of Illinois, 1981).

38. According to Giuliana Bruno, in Naples both the train and department store were early analogues for silent cinema. "Dora Film: Street Walking Around

Plato's Cave," an unpublished paper read at the conference, Feminist Theory and the Question of the Subject, at UCLA on May 17, 1990.

39. Sigmund Freud, "The Interpretation of Dreams," *Standard Edition* IV (London: Hogarth Press, 1962): 262.

40. See Mary Ann Doane, "Film and the Masquerade: Theorising the Female Spectator," *Screen* 23, nos. 3–4 (September-October 1982): 87.

41. Teresa DeLauretis. *Alice Doesn't* (Bloomington: Indiana University Press, 1987).

6: EXILE AND IDEOLOGICAL REINSCRIPTION

1. Rockwell Gray, "Spanish Diaspora: A Culture in Exile," *Salmagundi*, no. 76–77 (Fall 1987–Winter 1988): 53.

2. As quoted both by Gray (57) and by Paul Ilie, in *Literature and Inner Exile* (Baltimore: Johns Hopkins University Press, 1980): 21.

3. Hamid Naficy, "Cross-cultural Syncretism and Hybridity in Exile," unpublished paper delivered at the Society for Cinema Studies, 1990, 4.

4. Some alternative approaches would be to trace the impact of the large mass of Spanish émigrés through Latin America and Europe, extending the work that Román Gubern did in his ground-breaking study, *Cine español en el exilio, 1936–1939* (Barcelona: Editorial Lumen, 1976); or to examine the impact of foreign émigrés within Spain—figures as diverse as Argentinian-born writer/actor/director Fernando Fernán-Gómez, who emigrated to Spain at the age of three and whom Hopewell and many other critics consider "the most Spanish" of all filmmakers (*Out of the Past, 236*); Samuel Bronston, the American mogul whose efforts to make Madrid "a Hollywood in Spain" helped (in Besas's words) "to train and influence a whole generation of Spanish technicians" (*Behind the Spanish Lens, 53*); Marco Ferreri, the Italian filmmaker who made his first features in Spain during the 1950s, which helped combine Italian neorealism with Spanish esperpento; and, perhaps most interesting, Enrique Guerner (born Heinrich Gartner), an Austrian Jewish cinematographer who worked in Berlin with Robert Wiene and who brought elements of the expressionist style to Spain, where he trained Alfredo Fraile, José Aguayo, and Cecilio Paniagua and developed a new cinematographic style that can be found in three of the greatest popular successes of the Francoist cinema—*Raza* (1941), *Los últimos de Filipinas* (1945), and *Marcelino, pan y vino* (1955). For the fullest treatment of cinematographic style in Spain, see Francisco Llinás's *Directores de fotografía del cine español* (Madrid: Filmoteca Española, 1989).

5. Corrine Marchand had just starred as a free-spirited pop star in Agnes Varda's *Cleo from 5 to 7*, a film that was reviewed by Erice in the April 1962 issue of *Nuestro cine* and whose screenplay was excerpted in the same issue.

6. Homi Bhabha, "Introduction," *Nation and Narration* (London and New York: Routledge, 1990): 4.

7. For a perceptive analysis of the dynamics behind this award, see Robert Dickinson's essay, "The Unbearable Weight of Winning: Garci's Trilogy of Melancholy and the Foreign Language Oscar," *Spectator* 11, no. 2 (Spring 1991): 6–15.

8. For a fuller treatment of how exile is represented in post-Franco cinema, see Gubern's essay, "The Civil War: Inquest or Exorcism?" *Quarterly Review of Film and Video* 13, no. 4 (1991): 103–112, and Thomas Deveny's "In Search of the Past: The Return of the Exile in Spanish Cinema," a paper read at a conference on post-Franco cinema at Clark University, April 1990.

9. "A Survey of Spain: After the Fiesta," *The Economist* 323, no. 7756 (25 April–1 May 1992): 1–24.

10. Carlos Giménez, a professor at the Universidad Autónoma in Madrid, as quoted by Begoña Aguirre, "'Madrid aún puede evitar los guetos de inmigrantes,' dicen los expertos," *El país* (11 Junio 1992): 4.

11. Hamid Naficy, "Culture in Exile: Fetishized Iranian TV in the U.S.," paper read at the Society for Cinema Studies Conference in Bozeman, Montana, June 1988.

12. Luis Buñuel, *My Last Sigh,* trans. Abigail Israel (New York: Vintage Books, 1984): 9.

13. For an elaboration of this case, see Alfonso E. Pérez Sánchez's introduction to the official catalog entitled *Ribera, 1591–1652,* ed. Alfonso E. Pérez Sánchez and Nicola Spinosa (Madrid: Museo Del Prado, 1992): 15–17.

14. While Williams asserts that "*Un chien andalou* and *L'age d'or* are perhaps the only unquestionably Surrealist films, . . . the only 'pure' examples of filmic Surrealism," Kovács concludes that "it took Luis Buñuel . . . to create films which have not only expressed Surrealist concerns, but which have become artistic landmarks in the history of film." See Linda Williams, *Figures of Desire: A Theory and Analysis of Surrealist Film* (Urbana: University of Illinois Press, 1981): xii; and Steven Kovács, *From Enchantment to Rage: The Story of Surrealist Cinema* (London and Toronto: Associated University Presses, 1980): 41. In *The Altering Eye,* Robert Kolker even extends this claim to all of modernism, insisting that Buñuel is the ultimate modernist filmmaker "whose career all but encompasses the history of film" (93, 392).

15. Cook, *A History of Narrative Film,* 528. In his revised and updated second edition (1990), as if to acknowledge my critique of his coverage (published in *Film Quarterly*), Cook added after the phrase, "the work of Buñuel," the clause, "which, of course, was done mainly outside of Spain." Yet in this new edition, Cook's description of the rest of Spanish cinema was even briefer and more derogatory ("badly retarded" rather than "almost uniformly undistinguished") than in the original version of the footnote (659).

16. Francisco Aranda, *Luis Buñuel: A Critical Biography,* trans. and ed. David Robinson (New York: Da Capo Press, 1976): 190.

17. Borau, "Without Weapons," *Quarterly Review of Film Studies* 8, no. 2 (Spring 1983): 85.

18. Carl Mora, *The Mexican Cinema: Reflections of a Society, 1896–1980* (Berkeley, Los Angeles, London: University of California Press, 1982): 91.

19. These limitations are apparent in many of the books on Buñuel, for example, in the auteurist studies by Linda Williams and Paul Sandro that stress his narrative experimentation but totally ignore the Spanish cultural context and its political implications, or in Aranda's informative critical biography that is so condescending toward other Spanish and Mexican filmmakers. For example, in describing Buñuel's triumph with *Los olvidados* at Cannes, Aranda (a Spaniard) observes, "It was moreover an important discovery for Europe, to learn that Mexico had another cultural aspect than the vapid folklore drama which was familiar through the films of Emilio Fernandez" (143). In contrast, in *Third World Filmmaking and the West* (Berkeley, Los Angeles, London: University of California Press, 1987), British film historian Roy Armes treats Fernandez as the single most important Mexican filmmaker, partly because he is one of the few Third World filmmakers who comes from the subproletariat class rather than from the bourgeoisie, and he values him for representing precisely that Indian culture, which Aranda dismisses as "vapid folklore" (171). Aranda's contempt for folklore is probably partially determined by the perverse history of the españolada stereotype in Spain, from whose influence an earnest leftist Brit like Armes would probably be immune.

20. Besas, *Behind the Spanish Lens,* 51.

21. José Luis Borau, "A Woman without a Piano, A Book without a Mark," *Quarterly Review of Film and Video,* special issue on "Remapping the Post-Franco Cinema," ed. Marsha Kinder, vol. 13, no. 4 (1991): 11.

22. Buñuel tells an anecdote about "a reunion in 1980 with a few friends in a medieval castle not far from Madrid where we surprised everyone with a

drum serenade imported directly from Calanda"—an experience that was particularly moving for those Spaniards, like Buñuel, who had spent considerable time outside their homeland.

> Many of my closest friends were among the guests—Julio Alejandro, Fernando Rey, José-Barros—and all of them were profoundly moved, although unable to say exactly why. (Five even confessed to having cried!) I don't really know what evokes this emotion, which resembles the kind of feeling often aroused when one listens to music. It seems to echo some secret rhythm in the outside world, and provokes a real physical shiver that defies the rational mind. . . . I myself have used their somber rhythms in several movies, especially *L'Age d'or* and *Nazarin*. (*My Last Sigh*, 19–20)

23. Cook, *A History of Narrative Film*, 330. For a perceptive detailed analysis of how early sound conventions were codified in Hollywood, see Amy Lawrence's *Echo and Narcissus*.

24. Aranda perceptively observes,

> The technical defects of the recording do not prevent the sound track of *L'Age d'or* from being the most important in this first stage of sound film. . . . Buñuel is really putting into practice the image-sound counterpoint theoretically discussed by Eisenstein, Pudovkin and Alexandrov in their famous *Manifesto on Cinema Sound* of 1928. It is not known if Buñuel was acquainted with the manifesto. . . . For the first time the music of gramophone records was used with the images not as a rhythmical accompaniment, but as an intellectual discovery. . . . Fragments of romantic symphonies, ideals of bourgeois society, collide with the crudity and brutality of the visuals. It is a matter of a scandalizing counterpoint, which instead of making the visuals sweeter, makes them still more insolent. The same idea impels the off-screen commentaries accompanying the documentary fragments. (83–84)

25. For the best treatment of the sound track in Spanish cinema, see Carmelo Bernaola's *Evolución de la banda sonora en España* (Madrid: Festival de Cine de Alcalá de Henares, 1986).

26. Although all four films were attributed to other directors, Agustín Sanchez Vidal claims that "it was Buñuel who actually controlled them" (*Luis Buñuel: Obra cinematográfica* [Madrid: Ediciones J.C., 1984]: 25.) According to Hopewell,

Buñuel's directorial contribution varies from film to film. He was on set with [Luis] Marquina shouting to lead actress Ana María Custodio to ham it up; he worked out shot movements for Sáenz de Heredia in *La hija de Juan Simón,* as can be seen in some Buñuelish frontal set-ups with lateral pans following character movements and belated cuts to closeup. But in *¿Quién me quiere a mí?* Sáenz de Heredia was given "almost complete control," and Buñuel only directed scenes from *¡Centinela alerta!* when Grémillon had a toothache. (*Out of the Past,* 20)

27. Now he had an opportunity to improve the standard of production in Spain and to reach a popular audience, although he saw that his presence in the credits as director would hazard the films' popular success. Also, this was during the *bienio negro,* the two-year period of right-wing government, that included the revolution in Asturias in October 1935, by Lerroux and the C.E.D.A. (the Catholic party), with whom Buñuel was *persona non grata;* he may have feared censorship problems if his named appeared as director. (Roger Mortimore, "Buñuel, Sáenz de Heredia and Filmófono," *Sight and Sound* 44, no. 3 [Summer 1975]: 180)

With the exception of Aranda, Mortimer provides the most detailed coverage of this period in Buñuel's career.

28. Quoted by Aranda, 110.

29. As quoted by Roger Mortimore, 181.

30. As Hopewell points out, its flamenco music was quite memorable and was used again by Berlanga in his great 1985 box office success *La vaquilla* (The Heifer). *Out of the Past,* 5.

31. Aranda, 109. He also reports that Sobrevila was originally hired to direct the film but fell behind schedule and then resentfully resigned once Buñuel was hired, yet his extravagant decors were left behind.

32. "The differences that once existed between native Mexicans and *gachupines* (Spanish immigrants) have now largely disappeared" (*My Last Sigh,* 211). Lorca also observed that in "the popular triumph of Spanish death"— particularly as expressed through the combined rites of Good Friday and the bullfight—"in all the world, only Mexico may take my country's hand" ("Teoría y juego del duende," 69).

33. For example, the prologue to *Los olvidados* explicitly states that this film could take place in any major city, and in the adaptation of the Galdós novel *Nazarin,* the hero is a priest who was born in Spain and who hears the drums of Calanda.

34. In an essay that was originally written as an introduction to the Spanish edition of the memoirs of Buñuel's widow, Jeanne Rucar (published in 1991), Borau writes, "The book's definitive contribution is the discovery that Buñuel was, in reality, a creature worthy of his own imagination, . . . just as authoritarian, as macho, as paranoid—or—almost—as some of his unforgettable characters, precisely those with whom he was most merciless." "A Woman without a Piano," 13.

35. For a fuller treatment of this dimension of the two films, see the discussion of *Land without Bread* in Marsha Kinder and Beverle Houston's *Close-up: A Critical Perspective on Film* (New York: Harcourt Brace Jovanovich, 1972): 106–110; and of *Exterminating Angel* in my essay, "The Disastrous Escape," in *Contemporary Literary Scene,* II, ed. Frank N. Magill (Englewood Cliffs: Salem Press, 1976): 173–180.

36. *My Last Sigh,* 195.

37. Robert Stam, *Subversive Pleasures: Bakhtin, Cultural Criticism and Film* (Baltimore and London: Johns Hopkins University Press, 1989): 175–176.

38. *The Acoustic Mirror,* 22.

39. Although his book on Buñuel focuses on narrative experimentation (including films made in Mexico), Paul Sandro curiously claims, "Nor does the progressive mental derangement of Don Francisco in *This Strange Passion* affect the orderly telling of his tale" (*Diversions of Pleasure: Luis Buñuel and the Crises of Desire* [Columbus: Ohio State University Press, 1987]: 89). Apparently, once a spectator is sutured into the plot, the narrative pull toward secondary revision is so strong that one can ignore even the most extreme surrealistic jolts.

40. As Charles Eidsvik reports in "Dark Laughter: Buñuel's *Tristana* (1970)" (in *Modern European Filmmakers and the Art of Adaptation,* ed. Andrew Horton and John Magretta [New York: Frederick Ungar, 1981]),

> *Tristana* slipped by Spanish censors, international audiences, and even by critics as a somber, almost humorless study of the decline of two people—a film that is the most classically structured, accessible, and readily comprehensible of his recent works. A quietly gloved social critique of Spanish mores . . . that contains "no social criticism or condemnation of this or that." (174)

Of the discussions of the film I have read, only Eidsvik's seems to emphasize its deeply subversive nature, which leads him to conclude, "Beneath its somber surface, *Tristana,* like Buñuel's other films, shouts for rebellion and may even be, like *Un chien andalou* (1928), a desperate, passionate appeal to murder" (174). Still, he does not pay much attention to its narrative subversion but focuses primarily on the changes from the original novel by Galdós.

41. *The Acoustic Mirror,* 27.

42. In fact, Linda Williams's *Figures of Desire* is entirely structured around the close parallels she perceives between *Un chien andalou* and *That Obscure Object of Desire* as metaphoric works and between *L'age d'or* and *The Phantom of Liberty* as metonymical narratives.

43. Although one could argue that this dialectic is already present in *L'age d'or,* which features the arrival of Majorcans in the second episode and ends with the Duke of Blangis and his fellow sadists leaving a castle after 120 days of debauchery, the intervening episodes supposedly take place in Rome, making it decidedly international (or at least European).

44. Other examples include *Un chien andalou* (1928), where the hair from the woman's armpit is displaced onto the man's mouth; *Ensayo de un crimen* (1955), where protagonist Archibaldo de la Cruz cuts himself while shaving and the blood triggers the erotic memory of his first murderous impulse toward a woman, which has shaped his life of imaginary crime; *Exterminating Angel* (1962), where an effeminate young man compulsively shaves his legs with an electric razor and then viciously attacks a woman who combs her hair with a similar compulsiveness, breaking the comb in half with a castrating gesture that underlines the gendering of these symbolic activities; and *Simon of the Desert* (1965), where the saint tells a young monk to return after he has grown a beard because his youth makes him vulnerable to temptation and where Satan is apparently listening, for he reappears as a wolf in sheep's clothing (i.e., as a bearded Sylvia Pinal holding a lamb, or as a devil impersonating a woman impersonating a man).

45. The Marquis de Sade also appears in *The Milky Way*—speaking against God as he tortures a young woman and thereby demonstrating Stam's point that Buñuel uses sexuality "not gratuitously but . . . for its primordial power of scandal" (176).

46. Like *Weekend,* which paid homage to Breton and Buñuel, *The Milky Way* pays tribute to Godard; it is a two-way road over the cultural abyss. As Kolker put in his discussion of *Belle de jour,* "The references to *Breathless* in Buñuel's film are more than an homage by an old filmmaker to a younger one. They are a sign of rejuvenation, an indication that the old man who taught so much could still learn" (*The Altering Eye,* 215).

47. Roland Barthes, *Writing Degree Zero and Elements of Semiology,* trans. Annette Lavers and Colin Smith (Boston: Beacon Press, 1970): 86.

48. Luis Buñuel, *El fantasma de la libertad* (Barcelona: Aymá, S.A. Editora, 1974): 18.

49. Mary Ann Doane, "The Voice in the Cinema: The Articulation of Body and Space," *Cinema/Sound, Yale French Studies* 60 (1980): 33–50. Kaja Silverman, *The Acoustic Mirror,* chap. 2.

50. Jane Gallop observes, "The family never was, in any of Freud's texts, completely closed off from questions of economic class. And the most insistent intrusion into the family circle . . . is the maid/governess/nurse. As Cixous says, 'she is the hole in the social cell.'" *The Daughter's Seduction: Feminism and Psychoanalysis* (Ithaca: Cornell University Press, 1982): 144.

51. Susan Suleiman, "Freedom and Necessity: Narrative Structure in 'The Phantom of Liberty,'" *Quarterly Review of Film Studies,* special issue, "The Practical Application of Structuralism and Semiotics to Film Criticism," ed. Marsha Kinder, vol. 3 (Summer 1978): 289.

52. For a fuller discussion of this scene, see my essay, "The Tyranny of Convention in *The Phantom of Liberty,*" *Film Quarterly* (Summer 1975): 20–25.

53. The Republic actually banned Von Sternberg's *The Devil Is a Woman* because this foreign españolada presented a negative image of Spain. For an excellent comparison of Buñuel's adaptation with the original novel, see Katherine Singer Kovács's essay, "Luis Buñuel and Pierre Louys: Two Visions of Obscure Objects," *Cinema Journal* 19, no. 1 (Fall 1979): 86–98.

7: THE ECONOMICS OF EXILE

1. Borau, "Without Weapons," 89.

2. Quoted by Marsha Kinder in "José Luis Borau *On the Line* of the National/International Interface in the Post-Franco Cinema," *Film Quarterly* (Winter 1986/87): 36. This essay is an earlier version of this chapter.

3. *Río abajo* is, next to *Furtivos,* the film by José Luis that I like best. To my way of seeing, it marks the culmination of a long and conscientious apprenticeship and, at the same time, the totalization of an experience. After its realization, Borau entered in contact with a reality profoundly marked at all levels by the phenomenon of the frontier. Although perhaps chance may have intervened, it doesn't seem to me a casual matter, but rather the logical result of a search which was already being presented in some of his previous works. . . . The avatars of its difficulty and uneven shoot appear deeply embedded in the final result, endowing it with a special spirit: that which

breathes a truth severely conquered. Therefore it is a shame that it received such a reticent reception from the public and from some of the critics. . . . *Río abajo* . . . was, in general terms, a misunderstood work. (Victor Erice, as quoted by Agustín Sánchez Vidal, *Borau* [Zaragoza: Caja de Ahorros de la Inmaculada, 1990]: 164)

In an essay in which he lists "the ten best Spanish cinematic creations, made between 1981 and 1991," Spanish critic Antonio Lara includes *Río abajo* in this select group, describing it as follows:

With *Río abajo,* a film on two cultures, the Hispanic and the American, José Luis Borau succeeded in doing an old project, bristling with difficulties, on the relations between the borders. In this story the law and the illegals are locked in a desperate combat, from which there is no exit, nor ever will be, because the two cities, divided by the great river, are also separated, by the riches and power of the great American friend. The story is bilingual—as it was in *La Sabina*—pervaded by the secret yearning for an impossible harmony. Borau is one of the Spanish directors at present who is most inspired by the narrative told directly and with simplicity, and his great familiarity with the major American and European cinema has helped him develop a very personal and vital style in which actions and characters are expressed on screen with a splendid rhythm, without any dead spots, and with a thrilling conviction. (Antonio Lara, "Diez años de cine español," *Revista de occidente,* no. 122–123 [Julio-Agosto 1991]: 224–225)

The source for Fernando Méndez-Leite's statement that "*Río Abajo* is Borau's best film" is an informal conversation I had with him in Madrid in 1987.

4. Javier Castro, "20 años de mercado cinematográfico español," *Cineinforme,* Edicion Especial, no. 494 (Septiembre 1986): 70–71. Peter Besas, "Global Report Spain," *Variety* (September 24, 1990): 45.

5. Pilar Miró, "Ten Years of Spanish Cinema," trans. Alma Amell, in *Literature, the Arts, and Democracy: Spain in the Eighties,* ed. Samuel Amell (Rutherford: Fairleigh Dickinson University Press, 1990): p. 40.

6. John Hopewell, "'Art and a Lack of Money': The Crises of the Spanish Film Industry, 1977–1990," *Quarterly Review of Film and Video,* special issue, "Remapping the Post-Franco Cinema," edited by Marsha Kinder, vol. 13, no. 4, 117.

7. "Art and a Lack of Money," 117.

8. For example, even Hopewell (who is generally favorable toward Miró) writes,

> Filmmakers could now make the film they wanted to make while ignoring its marketability, as they were sometimes rather disarmingly ready to admit. "I've become so independent or so strange . . . that I don't really care if my film connects with large audiences," Basilio Martín Patino told Juan Antonio Bardem in 1985, talking about *Los paraísos perdidos* (Lost Paradises). "But you haven't risked any of your own money," Bardem replied. "Too, right," said Patino. "Otherwise I wouldn't have made the film. You're mad if you spend 80 million on a little toy (*jueguecito*) like that." ("Art and a Lack of Money," 119)

9. Hopewell claims that this "tradition of liberal filmmaking" is characterized by "their distinctive story-line (the hero rebelling against a backward society), their concept of character (weak, doubting protagonists), their narrative (a growing-up story featuring a moral adolescent), their audience (liberals who identify with their heroes), their point (humanistic entertainment), their ideology (film is art, culture, national patrimony, and inspired individual creation), their idealism (Spain enjoys ever greater freedoms), and even their larger subject (the artist director struggling against the Censor or residual restrictions to freedom in post-Franco Spain" ("Art and a Lack of Money," 119).

10. "Art and a Lack of Money," 117.

11. According to Hopewell, "In 1988 Spain's theatrical market even for U.S. movies was only 6.6% of overseas theatrical film rentals for American major studios, lower than comparable figures for Italy (7.2%), Britain (8.9%), France (9.7%), West Germany (9.9%), Canada (12.3%), and Japan (13.9%). Despite the spiralling budget costs of Spanish films in the mid 80s (which in 1987 reached an average of 126 million pesetas for a movie with an ICAA advance subsidy), from the European end of the telescope, Spanish production still looks piddling. The E.F.D.O. (European Film Distribution Office) definition of a European (non-UK) low-budget film for 1988 was any under 2.7 million U.S. dollars. Only around three Spanish films pass that budget mark every year" ("Art and a Lack of Money," 116).

12. Katherine Singer Kovács, "Berlanga Life Size: An Interview with Luis García Berlanga," *ORFS* (Spring 1983): 10.

13. Quoted by Georges Sadoul in *Dictionary of Film Makers,* trans., ed., and updated by Peter Morris (Berkeley and Los Angeles: University of California Press, 1972): 213–214.

14. The action could not unfold in just any social context, historically neutral, partly abstract like the setting of a tragedy, as so frequently happens to varying degrees with the American, French, or English cinema. As a result, the Italian films have an exceptionally documentary quality that could not be removed from the script without thereby eliminating the whole social setting into which its roots are so deeply sunk. . . . What is a ceaseless source of wonder, ensuring the Italian cinema a wide moral audience among the Western nations, is the significance it gives to the portrayal of actuality. (Andre Bazin, "An Aesthetic of Reality: Neorealism," in *What Is Cinema* II, ed. Hugh Gray [Berkeley and Los Angeles: University of California Press, 1971]: 20)

15. Acknowledging both Renoir and DeSica as primary models, Satyajit Ray claimed that neorealism led to a new appreciation for his own cultural specificity.

> Before I made my first film—*Pather Panchali*—I had only a superficial knowledge of what life in a Bengal village was like. Now I know a great deal about it. I know its soil, its seasons, its trees and forests and flowers; I know how the man in the field works and how the women at the well gossip; and I know the children out in the sun and the rain, behaving as all children in all parts of the world do. My own city of Calcutta, too, I know much better now I've made a film about it. (Quoted by Roy Armes in *Third World Film Making and the West* [Berkeley, Los Angeles, and London: University of California Press, 1987]: 84)

16. Although Ford is usually considered the prototypical American director, his roots in Ireland are apparently of great interest to Spaniards—not only to Borau but also more recently to Catalan filmmaker José Luis Guerin, whose fascinating feature-length documentary *Innisfree* (1990) explores the traces left on this small Irish village where Ford was born and where he returned in 1952 to shoot *The Quiet Man.* Guerin's film also examines the theme of economic exile, the way it was forced on the young Irish as a mode of survival and the way it has enriched North American culture.

17. Quoted by Sánchez Vidal, *Borau,* 164.

18. "Art and a Lack of Money," 120.

19. Ibid., 119.

20. This chapter in no way pretends to offer a complete auteurist coverage of Borau. The two best and most comprehensive works of this kind are Agustín

Sánchez Vidal's *Borau* (Zaragoza: Caja de Ahorros de la Inmaculada, 1990) and Carlos F. Heredero's *José Luis Borau: Teoría y práctica de un cineasta* (Madrid: Filmoteca Española, 1990).

21. This chapter does not treat *Furtivos* or *Camada negra* in detail since these films have already been discussed in chapters 4 and 5.

22. Quoted by Manuel Hidalgo in *Carlos Saura* (Madrid: Ediciones JC, 1981): 81.

23. Quoted from a lecture Borau gave at the University of Southern California on April 14, 1982. I previously cited this quote in an article entitled "The Children of Franco in the New Spanish Cinema," *Quarterly Review of Film Studies* (Spring 1983): 58–59.

24. From an unpublished interview that I conducted with Borau in spring of 1987.

25. Hopewell, *Out of the Past,* 98–99.

26. Hopewell, *Out of the Past,* 95.

27. Ironically, during the shooting of this sequence, the ocelot (which Pal was supposedly hunting) was also accidentally killed. According to cinematographer Luis Cuadrado,

> I remember that when we were shooting *Hay que matar á B,* José Luis Borau, who is Aragonese, had miraculously managed to get an ocelot for the film, a South American animal that looks like a cat but is bigger. We treated it like gold in the pan, but it died on us. Finally we got another one and the day of the shoot in one of the scenes we had to tie it up with a cord around its neck so that it wouldn't move. But by an error in one of the effects, the animal was strangled by one of its movements. When the chief of production, Alburne, told Borau, instead of reacting violently, after remaining stunned for a few seconds (thinking, where was the next ocelot to come from?), the guy came out singing an Aragonese *jota* whose lyrics were: "They killed the ocelot, they killed the ocelot . . ." (Quoted in "Luis Cuadrado, después del homenaje," *El Alcazar* [Diciembre 9, 1977]: 18)

28. Hopewell, *Out of the Past,* 99.

29. Robin W. Fiddian, "The Role and Representation of Women in Two Films by José Luis Borau," *Essays on Hispanic Themes,* ed. Jennifer Lowe and Philip Swanson (Edinburgh: Dept. of Hispanic Studies, University of Edinburgh, 1989): 290.

30. Roger Mortimore, "Reporting from Madrid," *Sight and Sound* (August 1980).

31. Quoted by José Vicente G. Santamaría, "José Luis Borau: El síndrome de 'Furtivos,'" *Contracampo,* no. 8 (Enero 1980): 6–7.

32. Katherine Singer Kovács, "José Luis Borau Retrospective," *The Spectator* 3, no. 2 (Spring 1984): 2.

33. Although Fiddian acknowledges this homosexual dimension in one fleeting reference, he merely catalogs it (along with Monica's "aggressive" sexuality and "Daisy's abuse of Manolito") as one of the many "perversions" or "foreign idiosyncrasies" that are to be contrasted with the "local standards of morality" imposed on Pepa (308).

34. Vicente Molina-Foix, *Fotogramas,* no. 1, 703 (December 1984): 82; and Agustín Sanchez Vidal, "Una meditación sobre las patrias ('Hay que matar á B', de José Luis Borau)," *Artigrama,* no. 1 (1984): 359.

35. Author of *From Enchantment to Rage: The Story of Surrealist Cinema* (London and Toronto: Associated University Presses, 1980), Steven Kovács subsequently wrote, directed, and coproduced an independent feature entitled *Sixty-eight* (1988). Currently he is the chairman of the film department at California State University, San Francisco.

36. You got a bad case of pussy fever, kid. [Pause.] I understand 'cause she's got somethin' special. You can't keep it for yourself. So why not share it with a friend? It's got a nice kind of a ring to it. Like two buddies having a drink together. [Pause] . . . We're not gonna get laid, we might as well get drunk. To Engracia. [Lifting his glass for a toast] To us. [Pause. Mitch stands up, goes over to Chuck and puts his arm around him and continues the monologue as the lights in the bar grow dimmer.] You know what I like about her? She doesn't like to do it. But she's a real pro. You know how she starts out by faking it, and she just gets caught up in it and she starts to likin' it and likin' it and lovin' it. At least that's the way she is with me. [Pause.] What's she like with you, kid? [Pause. Chuck removes Mitch's arm from his shoulder.] What's the matter? You don't wanna talk about it? Well, you're wrong. That's the best part of it, talking about it afterward.

37. Quoted by Sanchez Vidal, *Borau,* 164.

38. Unpublished interview I conducted with Steven Kovács in summer 1986.

39. After *Río abajo,* Borau turned to projects that focus on totally Spanish material. *Tata mía* (1987) stars Carmen Maura as a nun who, after having spent seventeen years in a convent, returns to her family home in Madrid where she confronts the dramatic cultural changes that have occurred in the

post-Franco period. The film evokes an allegorical reading of Spanish film history through its reflexive casting: with Imperio Argentina (as Tata), who represents the 1930s when she was the most popular star in Spain and who was reputed to be a supporter of Franco; Alfredo Landa (as Teo), who represents the comedies of the 1960s, which frequently disguised their political content through a discourse on sexual repression; and Carmen Maura (as the nun), who is associated with the flagrantly liberated 1980s, when she became the star of Almodóvar's outrageous comedies and played one of the zany sacrilegious nuns in his *Entre tinieblas* (Dark Habits, 1983). As of this writing, Borau's most recent project is *Celia* (1992), a six-part series for Spanish television (TVE), which is based on a series of Spanish children's stories from the pre–Civil War period by Elena Fortún (the pen name for Encarnación Aragoneses, 1886–1952) and which, despite its immersion in Spanish specificity, has already been purchased by Britain's Channel 4 as well as by other European networks.

40. This quotation from Pilar Miró and all that follow are taken from an unpublished letter to Mr. D. Moritz DeHadeln, dated November 7, 1984, a copy of which was made available to me by Borau. The translation is mine.

41. Carlos Fuentes, "A Glory Seldom Seen: *Spain,* a Nation Recovers Its Open, Democratic Tradition," *Los Angeles Times* (August 3, 1986), V 1. Fuentes is apparently very fond of this trope, for when he was receiving the Menéndez Pelago Prize for literary achievement in Madrid in June 1992, he presented a slightly different version: "The miserable, dominating Spain, La Celestina seated in a church, foul-smelling and intrusive, has been converted into a Marilyn Monroe and now everyone wants to go to bed with her." Quoted in *El país* (12 Junio 1992): 41.

42. Quoted by Sanchez Vidal, *Borau*, 164.

43. If we bear in mind that in those first "talkies" Lubitsch was devoting all his talents to operetta, Capra was still searching for his bearings, McCary and LaCava were sticking to the tried formulas of comic films which had been so successful in the past, Hawks was devoting his artistic energy to portraying the seamy side of life, Cukor and Mamoulian were still just assistant dialog directors, and Preston Sturges was launching his career as a scriptwriter, it isn't difficult to understand why a film like *Laughter,* d'Arrast's first sound film, was so important, and just what it meant for the debut and development of a genre, which defied imitation and would soon become a feature of American motion pictures: the screwball comedy. A well-qualified New York critic of the times, Herman G. Weinberg . . . declared that d'Arrast was the

creator of the most perfect seven comedies—his entire American production—filmed up to that moment, an opinion Fritz Lang did not hesitate to support. And even Chaplin himself, in spite of the falling out of his former assistant, when asked . . . which films, besides his own, did he consider worth saving, he immediately replied: "Just one, d'Arrast's *Le Tricorne*." (Borau, *El Caballero D'Arrast,* 85)

8: MICRO- AND MACROREGIONALISM IN CATALAN CINEMA, EUROPEAN COPRODUCTIONS, AND GLOBAL TELEVISION

1. Ed Buscombe, "Film History and the Idea of a National Cinema," *The Australian Journal of Screen Theory* 9/10 (1981).

2. John Hartley, "Invisible Fictions: Television Audiences, Paedocracy, Pleasure," in *Television Studies: Textual Analysis,* ed. Gary Burns and Robert J. Thompson (New York: Praeger, 1989): 225–226.

3. These concepts of micro- and macroregionalism and of defining the terms "regional" and "center" as linguistic shifters were developed while I was chairing the doctoral committee of Denise Brooke Jacobson, who wrote an excellent dissertation, *Regional Film in the United States: Resistance to Cultural Dominance* (University of Southern California, 1989). While focusing primarily on regional film in the United States, her study also contained an introductory chapter, "Regionalism in the Global Marketplace," which uses a concept of micro-/macroregionalism similar to the one I had theorized for this Spanish project. In a sense, we collaborated on the development of some of these ideas, and thus my own essay was influenced by her dissertation.

4. Quoted by Jane Hall, in "Network News: An Endangered Species?" *Los Angeles Times* (February 16, 1991): F1.

5. At a conference on Spanish cinema held in Los Angeles at the University of Southern California on April 8, 1991, Pedro J. Ramirez, the editor of the Spanish newspaper *El Mundo,* informed me that when his journalists covering the Persian Gulf War from Baghdad asked CNN to transmit their stories, they were refused.

6. William Boddy, "The New Geopolitical Landscape of Television: Rethinking Program Flows and Cultural Sovereignty," an unpublished paper presented at the Society for Cinema Studies Annual Conference, Los Angeles, May 25, 1991.

7. David Morley and Kevin Robins, "Spaces of Identity," *Screen* 30, no. 4 (Autumn 1989): 22.

8. Jesus Arilla Perez, "Los retos de las RTV publicas regionales en la Europa de las regiones," in *Las radiotelevisiones en el espacio Europeo,* ed. Enrique Linde Paniagua (Valencia: Ente Público RTVV, 1990): 247.

9. Benedict Anderson, *Imagined Communities: Reflections on the Origin and Spread of Nationalism* (London: Verso, 1983): 12, 15. Anderson claims that nationalism constructs an imagined, bounded community that is "always conceived as a deep horizontal comradeship" but its "style" varies from culture to culture (15–16).

10. Peter Zimmermann, "Las TV regionales en Europa," in *Las radiotelevisiones en el espacio Europeo,* 148.

11. Pedro Orive Riva, "Rasgos diferenciales de los comportamientos de las audiencas de las TV regionales," in *Las radiotelevisiones en el espacio europeo,* 167.

12. Peter Besas, "Olé Showbiz! It's Boomtime," in "Global Report Spain," *Variety* (September 24, 1990): 45.

13. Peter Besas, "TV Ad Sales Grow 7-fold in 10 Years," *Variety* (September 24, 1990): 58.

14. "Olé Showbiz! It's Boomtime," 45.

15. For example, in July 1991, Javier Arenas (general vice secretary of the Partido Popular and his party's representative on the Commission of Parliamentary Control of RTVE) charged that "exclusive responsibility" for RTVE's dramatic financial losses between 1990 and 1992 (which he claims will be over 147,000 million pesetas, some 145 million daily) should be attributed to Gonzalez's Socialist party (PSOE) since they have the majority control over the network and have appointed all of the general directors, including Pilar Miró. Challenging these projected figures and denying these charges, RTVE accused Arenas of merely playing politics. For more details, see José Sámano, "RTVE niega perder 145 millones diarios desde 1990, como asegura el PP," *El país* (27 Julio 1991).

16. After having read this paper at the Conference on Spanish Cine-Lit in Oregon (February 27–March 3, 1991), I heard Rick Maxwell present an excellent unpublished paper at the Society for Cinema Studies Annual Conference in Los Angeles (May 25, 1991) entitled "Spatial Eruptions, Global Grids: The Dialectic of Multiculturalism in International Image Markets." Maxwell similarly argued that Spanish television was the ideal case study for analyzing the globalization of European television in the 1990s, particularly with its paradoxical combination of political regionalism and international consumerism.

17. One could cite the notorious case of Pilar Miró, who, despite being a close friend of Felipe Gonzalez, was forced by her political enemies to resign from her post as general director of Spanish television on the grounds that she had charged the cost of expensive clothes worn at official functions to her

expense account. Miró countered that this issue was merely a red herring, since she had openly declared these expenses to demonstrate the different demands placed on a woman in a ministerial position as opposed to a man, who could wear the same tuxedo to all official events.

18. Pedro Fernaud Casais, "Reflexiones sobre la reforma del estatuto de las radiotelevisiones públicas," in *Las radiotelevisiones en el espacio europeo,* 81.

19. P. M. Canavarro, "Las televisiones regionales en el marco de la 'Television sin fronteras,'" in *Las radiotelevisiones en el espacio europeo,* 243.

20. For example, Victor Erice is working primarily in advertising, and other highly acclaimed auteurs have been recruited by the state-run television network, RTVE, to do ambitious literary series: e.g., Manuel Gutiérrez Aragón (*Half of Heaven, Demons in the Garden, Black Brood*) and Mario Camus (*The Holy Innocents, The Beehive, The House of Bernarda Alba*) have each directed half of the two-part, twelve-hour, $24 million adaptation of *Don Quixote;* Oscar winner José Luis Garci (*To Begin Again*) has directed a seven-part dramatic series called *Stories from the Other Side;* and José Luis Borau has co-written (with award-winning novelist Carmen Martín Gaite), produced, and directed *Celia,* a six-part series based on the well-known Spanish children's stories by Elena Fortún.

21. Marvin D'Lugo, "Catalan Cinema: Historical Experience and Cinematic Practice," *Quarterly Review of Film and Video* 13, nos. 1–3: 144.

22. Mikhail Bakhtin, "Discourse in the Novel" (1934–35), in *The Dialogic Imagination,* trans. Caryl Emerson and Michael Holquist (Austin: University of Texas Press, 1981): 369–370. It is no accident that Bakhtin, who conceived of regionalism as a valuable resource for a subversive form of hybridization, came from what was formerly the Soviet Union, a nation where the interaction between micro- and macroregionalism has always been apparent. In fact, this interaction helped destroy the cold war paradigm and the macrostructure of Eastern Europe and helped trigger the explosive liberation movements in microregions like Lithuania, Estonia, and Latvia and the brutal civil war in Yugoslavia—violent conflicts that helped to dissolve the Soviet Union and that still threaten the utopian vision of a totally unified Europe. More specifically, the turmoil in Yugoslavia (which is now being compared with the Spanish Civil War) is reported to have sparked new demonstrations for independence in Cataluña.

Interestingly, among the twelve members of the European Community (who quickly established diplomatic relations with the Baltic states after the failure of the 1991 coup in the Soviet Union), only Spain and the Netherlands had previously "officially" recognized these Baltic regions as part of the Soviet Union. In the case of Spain, this action was probably related to Franco's resistance to the political drive toward regional autonomy within his own monolithic state.

23. David Gilmour, "Homage to Catalonia," *New York Review of Books* XXXIX, no. 11 (June 11, 1992): 3.

24. Peter Besas, "Catalan Filmmaking, an Industry Apart," in "Global Report: Spain," *Variety* (September 24, 1990): 78.

25. "Ten Years of Spanish Cinema," 45. This provincial emphasis on the exclusive use of Catalan extends far beyond the cinema. During the Olympics, many tourists complained about the labels in Barcelona's Picasso Museum being solely in Catalan. Far more disturbing to Spaniards because of the long-range consequences, Catalan is currently the sole language of instruction in half of the schools in the region, while the other half uses both Catalan and Castilian Spanish.

26. José María Unsain, *El cine y los Vascos* (San Sebastián: Filmoteca Vasca, 1985). Also see two works by Alberto López Echevarrieta: *Cine vasco: ¿Realidad o ficción?* (Bilbao: Mensajero, 1982) and *Cine vasco: De ayer a hoy* (Bilbao: Mensajero, 1984).

27. José Luis Ibáñez, "Estado actual de la programación de las televisiones públicas y privadas españoles," in *Las radiotelevisiones en el espacio europeo,* 196.

28. Inma Tubella, "Television regional: La confusión de un termino," in *Las radiotelevisiones en el espacio europeo,* p. 149.

29. These competitive dynamics concerning regional and national identity and televisual culture are not restricted to Spain, though Spain may be one of the most dramatic examples. Arguing that "*television*—over other pre-war cultural forms, such as literature, theater or cinema—has become the central metaphor *and* the central site for defining cultural rupture and continuity," James Hay perceives a similar pattern in the competition between private and public television networks in Italy.

> In the late 70s, the private networks do not necessarily resist their image as regional programmers in order to avoid being constructed as at odds with RAI's image as mediator of national culture, and . . . find themselves in the 80s with an image that is at once regional *and* cosmopolitan.

Hay concludes that in the 1980s and 1990s, "the question of a national television or national television audience in Italy has more to do, than it did in the 1960s and 1970s, with situating national identity or national subjects within positions that are both local and global" (19–20).

30. Emilio Pérez de Rozas, "En vivo y en casa," *El país* (25 Julio 1991). As Stanley Meisler put it, "Most *Barceloneses* believe that their wondrous Mediterranean port of sophisticated style and beauty will soon reassert itself as a grand city of Europe and push the thriving Spanish capital of Madrid back into the shadows, back where it belongs, at least for a summer, perhaps much longer" ("Barcelona Blossoms for Games," *Los Angeles Times* [October 13, 1991]: A1).

31. For example, between 1989 and 1991, Spanish television (RTVE) made a substantial contribution to what is now being called the New Mexican cinema—helping to fund some of the most interesting works like María Novaro's *Danzón* (1991), Nicolás Echevarría's *Cabeza de vaca* (1991), and Paul Leduc's *Latino Bar* (1991). When he appeared in Los Angeles with his film, Echevarría told me that *Cabeza de vaca* could not have been made without the participation of Spanish television, which provided 40% of the budget. He expressed deep concern that now in 1991, since Spanish television was in financial difficulty, this source of funding was drying up.

32. Román Gubern, "El nuevo reto audiovisual," *El mundo* (3 Abril 1991).

33. Miquel de Moragas, head of an Olympic studies center at Barcelona's Autonomous University, as quoted by William D. Montalbano in "Catalonia: A Nation Within a Country," *Los Angeles Times* (July 14, 1992): 6.

34. Hopewell, *Out of the Past,* 40.

35. Produced by the Filmoteca Española in 1984, both the documentary film and the monograph were entitled *Bajo el signo de las sombras* (Beneath the Sign of Shadows), the original title of Llobet Gràcia's screenplay. Alberich's film includes interviews with his widow, Beatriz Sanz, and with Delmiro Caralt and Carlos Serrano de Osma, as well as excerpts from Llobet Gràcia's films.

36. Ramiro Cristobal, "*Vida en sombras:* Recuperada un película 'maldita,'" *Tele radio* (11–17 Marzo 1985): 17. According to Alberich, Llobet Gràcia remained in Barcelona during the war; he was rejected from the army because of his myopia.

37. Drawing on other sources, my earlier commentaries on *Vida en sombras* erroneously state that Llobet Gràcia committed suicide. But according to Alberich, he died of an asthma crisis.

38. Indeed, Alberich's documentary contains several excerpts from Llobet Gràcia's home movies of his own family, suggesting that he conceived this to

be primary material for the medium. Yet the untimely deaths of his father and son must have deprived him of the regenerative function of the family, leading him to fetishize their surviving representations in photographs and film footage.

39. Jesús González Requena, "Vida en sombras," *Revista de occidente,* no. 53 (October 1985): 76–91.

40. This sequence prefigures a similar chain of images in Gutiérrez Aragón's allusive *La mitad del cielo* (Half of Heaven, 1986).

41. For an overview of Chomón, (1871–1929), see Agustín Sánchez Vidal's "Segundo de Chomón: Compás de espera para un turolense universal," in *Artigrama,* no. 2 (1985): 265–278; and *El cine de Chomón* (Zaragoza: Caja de Ahorros de la Immaculada, 1992).

42. Borau, "Without Weapons," 86.

43. Augusto M. Torres, "1896–1929," in *Spanish Cinema,* 26–27.

44. André Lange and Jean-Luc Renaud, *The Future of the European Audiovisual Industry* (Manchester, England: The European Institute for the Media, 1989): 253.

45. Lange and Renaud, 322. Also see table 67, p. 287.

46. Hybrids rather than mere coproductions, both Bigas Luna films present intriguing cross-cultural studies—of violence (*Anguish*) and power (*Reborn*)—yet neither was commercially successful in the U.S. market. Though supposedly set in Los Angeles, *Angustia* was shot in Barcelona. It stars Zelda Rubenstein as a manipulative "Mommy" (fresh from her success in *Poltergeist*) and Michael Lerner as her Norman Bates–type murderous son in an inset Eastern European horror film, which is supposedly being screened in a movie theater in Hollywood, where it inspires another sexually repressed serial killer who must be subdued by a Los Angeles SWAT team.

   Reborn (1981) was actually made in the United States. Like a cross between Huston's *Wiseblood* and Rossellini's *Miracle* (with parallels to Godard's *Hail Mary*), *Reborn* pits American postmodernist evangelism against European re-creations of the holy birth. Dennis Hopper plays a phony television evangelist from Houston who is joined on his "Miracle Tour across the heart and soul of America" by "Big Mary" (Antonella Murgia), an Italian vestal virgin with authentic stigmata who has been bought from the Vatican by an Italian mobster (Francisco Rabal), who knows "the real thing." Inspired by the luminous light of a holy helicopter, which periodically hovers overhead, Mary reaches religious and erotic ecstasy with the American messenger Mark (Michael Moriarty) and soon gives birth to a holy child in a Gulf gas station.

47. The only Spanish actor in a major role is the highly accomplished José Luis Gómez as "poor" Polidori, who is interpreted here as an inferior masochistic attendant to the aristocratic, narcissistic Byron (played by British actor Hugh Grant)—a relation that perhaps evokes the historical subordination of Spain to Anglo culture within the global economic and political context. Interestingly, Polidori is the first to identify with Mary's "creature," who functions as the latent horror or death drive (the internalized source of the Black Legend) responsible for all of their deaths and who looks suspiciously like Goya's *Colossus.* While the film's painterly visuals are brilliant, the characterizations are silly, for they reduce these historic figures to mere caricatures—especially William Godwin (who is merely a bad, materialistic father) and Percy Shelley (who is terribly weak), and even Mary Shelley (whose artistic creation of the Frankenstein monster is highly dependent on her collaboration with Byron, inspiration from her husband Shelley, and the suicidal madness that runs in her family). Her famous mother, pioneering feminist Mary Wollstonecraft, is mentioned only briefly as a victim of Mary Shelley's birth. Thus, traces of her maternal heritage and their feminist implications are totally effaced; in fact, all women in the film other than Mary are stupid, and even she is incapable of creating important works of art on her own. The film lacks any sense of the important historical and political dimensions of these figures or of the mythic power of the monster.

48. These figures are drawn from *Cine español 1988* (Madrid: Ministerio de Cultura, 1989) and *Cine español 1990* (Madrid: Ministerio de Cultura, 1991).

49. As the daughter of a powerful publisher, Rosa Vergés is hardly marginal in terms of class. In fact, she is frequently described in the popular press as an "ex-debutante." Yet, as in every other nation and culture, female directors are quite rare in Spain—the two best known being Pilar Miró and Josefina Molina—which makes Vergés, as a 35-year-old woman making her directorial debut, quite marginal in terms of gender.

50. Fernando Trueba, as quoted by Diego Muñoz, "Trueba produce una serie de TVE y espera a Ryan O'Neal para su próxima película," *La vanguardia* (6 Mayo 1988).

51. The film won Goya awards for Trueba's direction, for José Luis Alcaine's cinematography, for Trueba's and Manolo Matji's screenplay adaptation, and for best production and best picture.

52. Antonio Lara, "Pesadilla Parisiense: Fernando Trueba ha realizado su filme más ambicioso," *El país* (12 Enero 1990). José Luis Guarner also noted that

El mono loco is "the first Spanish production made in English to represent us at an international festival" ("Trueba presenta *El mono loco,* un 'thriller' de engaños e incesto protagonizado por Jeff Goldblum," *La Vanguardia* (7 September 1989)—a privilege denied to Borau's *Río abajo.* Javier Perez Pellon observed, "In Italy, at Venice, Fernando Trueba is considered, after Pedro Almodóvar, the most genuine image of the New Spanish cinema" ("*El mono loco,* de Trueba, no respondió a la espectación creada," *El independiente* [8 Setiembre 1989]). Indeed, Trueba is one of the few Spanish directors, besides Almodóvar, Saura, Bigas Luna, and Borau, who have even tried reaching an international market—an attempt that was made possible by his previous success with comedies like *Opera prima* (First Work/Opera Cousin, 1980) and *El año de las luces* (The Year of the Lights, 1986), which won a Silver Bear at the 1987 Berlin Film Festival.

53. Javier Maqua, "*El sueño del mono loco,* la mejor película española," 5 *Cinco Días* (8 Febrero 1990).

54. Lluís Bonet Mojica, "La insoportable perversidad de Peter Pan," *La vanguardia* (25 Enero 1990).

55. Teresa Rubio, "Trueba estrena su filme más internacional," *El periódico* (20 Enero 1990).

56. "Las Sorpesas de *El mono loco,*" *Faro de vigo* (8 Setiembre 1989).

57. "I never thought of working with Spanish actors, nor did I want the film to focus on the stereotypical European intellectual. For this reason I changed the protagonist to an American. People may think I am compromising in order to reach a larger audience, but in reality I have been concerned with making a better film." Trueba, as quoted by Diego Muñoz, "Lo importante es la pasión: *El sueño del mono loco,*" *Cine,* La guia de *El Mundo* (26 Enero 1990): 7.

58. Ahmad Rafat, "Mi próxima película la rodare en Estados Unidos," *Tiempo* (18 Setiembre 1989): 126. Also see Manuela Montero, "Goldblum: 'El filme de Trueba me parece misterioso y erótico,'" *El periódico* (14 Enero 1989).

59. "Art and a Lack of Money," 120.

60. Trueba has described his next film as "a completely North American story," a comedy called *Two Much,* which he plans to shoot in the United States. Teresa Rubio, "Trueba estrena su filme."

61. Trueba claims that his protagonist's immaturity was intensified by changing his nationality, for in contrast to the "intellectual European," "the American writer [is] more vital and innocent, more of a big child"—qualities that are

also readily apparent in the childlike Hollywood blockbusters that have dominated world markets ever since 1977 with the phenomenal success of *Star Wars*. As quoted by Félix Flores, in "Fernando Trueba, riesgo cuerdo en *El sueño del mono loco*," *La vanguardia* (20 Enero 1990).

62. Trueba, as quoted by Javier Perez Pellor.

63. Quoted by C.D. in "*Boom boom de Amor*," *El país* (15 Junio 1990).

64. Jordi Beltrán, who co-wrote the screenplay with Vergés, claims the film was "inspired by the cinema of the great Billy Wilder." Quoted by Mercè Ibarz, "Una comèdia del cor que fa 'Boom Boom,'" *Diario de Barcelona* (24 Agosto 1989).

65. José Luis Guarner, "Locos corazones," *La vanguardia* (13 Junio 1990).

66. Rosa Vergés, as quoted by Teresa Rubio, "*Boom Boom*, filme Catalan realizado por dos mujeres," *El periódico* (10 Marzo 1989).

67. For a detailed analysis of *Toute une nuit*, see my essay, "The Subversive Potential of the Pseudo-Iterative," 2–16.

68. Diego Muñoz, "El bumerán de *Boom Boom*, La película consigue reestrenarse en Madrid tras triunfar en los festivales de cine de Venecia y Montreal," *El mundo* (14 Junio 1990).

69. Quoted by C. D. in "*Boom Boom de Amor*."

70. Quoted by Teresa Rubio.

71. Ibid.

72. Quoted by Diego Muñoz, "El bumerán de *Boom Boom*." Here is Angel Fernández Santos's version of the story, told with greater sarcasm.

> The film opened in Madrid one bad day in the bad month of June, the same day on which either the Rosary or . . . the broadcast of the World Soccer Championship vacated the streets of the city and emptied the cinemas, theaters, discotheques, taverns, and, amazingly, even the bingo parlors. . . . In almost all Spanish cities, *Boom Boom* opened on the same date, thus its death was not only madrileña, but also barcelonesa, abulense, bilbaína . . . and whatever other geographical names you know. . . . *Boom Boom* lasted long enough in Barcelona to survive the end of the football epidemic, and this saved it from total death. ("Resurrección de un bello filme," *El país* [27 Octubre 1990])

73. Quoted by Diego Muñoz.

74. Quoted by Marsha Kinder, in "Pleasure and the New Spanish Mentality: A Conversation with Pedro Almodóvar," 34, 36–37.

75. "Cine Español: De lo particular a lo universal," *Fotogramas y Video* (Abril 1987): 7.
76. As D'Lugo puts it,

> This new moral matrix serves to center a group of characters who, within the culture of the dictatorship and in the immediate post-Franco period, were viewed as marginal types. . . . [Moreover] the dramatized audience and presumably the authenticators of that new demarginalization are the police, the enforcers of those repressive social and moral codes. (Marvin D'Lugo, "Almodóvar's City of Desire," in *Quarterly Review of Film and Video,* special issue on "Remapping the Post-Franco Cinema," 63)

77. Lawrence Cohen, "More National Bests in the U.S.," *Variety* (January 5, 1991): 87.
78. David Garland, "A Ms-take in the Making? Transsexualism Post-Franco, Post-Modern, Post-Haste," *Quarterly Review of Film and Video* 13, no. 4 (1991): 96. For a more comprehensive discussion of the representation of homosexuality in Spanish cinema, see Paul Julian Smith, *Laws of Desire: Questions of Homosexuality in Spanish Writing and Film 1960–1990* (Oxford: Clarendon Press, 1992).
79. Jenny Livingston appeared in a documentary directing course at the USC School of Cinema–Television. When describing her next comedy, she also said it was in "the early mode of Woody Allen," the American director whom former Almodóvar star Carmen Maura claims she would most like to work with in the United States.
80. "Cultural rectifica y apoya el filme 'El amante bilingüe' con 65 millones," *El país* (11 Junio 1992): 30.

EPILOGUE: EL SOL ALSO RISES

1. Diego Muñoz, "Las multinacionales proponen que el cine español sólo se exhiba por televisión," *El país* (3 Junio 1992): 29.
2. Diego Muñoz, "Audiovisual Español 93 trata de buscar soluciones al declive del cine español," *El país* (2 Junio 1992): 37.
3. Angel Fernández Santos, "Ante un genocidio cultural?" *El país* (4 Junio 1992): 30.
4. Paula Ponga, "Entrevista: Carmen Maura," *Fotogramas y video* XLV, no. 1,786 (Junio 1992): 49.

5. Diego Muñoz, "Los cineastas españoles piden al Gobierno la creación de una ley del audiovisual," *El país* (4 Junio 1992): 30.

6. "A Survey of Spain: After the Fiesta," *The Economist* 323, no. 7756 (April 25–May 1, 1992): 1.

7. S. Belausteguigotia, "Luis García Berlanga propone el sistema vigente en Francia como modelo para el futuro cine español," *El país* (7 Junio 1992): 29.

8. Carlos F. Heredero, "*El sol del membrillo,* reinventar la mirada," *Dirigido,* no. 202 (Mayo 1992): 26.

9. Michel Foucault, *The Order of Things: An Archaeology of the Human Sciences,* trans. of *Les mots et les choses* (New York: Random House, 1970), chap. 1.

Aguilar-Jaume Genover, Carlos. *El cine español en sus interpretes.* Madrid: Verdoux, 1992.

Aguirre, Begoña, "'Madrid aún puede evitar los guetos de immigrantes,' dicen los expertos," *El país* (11 Junio 1992): 4.

Alas, Leopoldo. *La Regenta,* trans. John Rutherford. Middlesex, England, and New York: Penguin Books, 1984.

Alberich, Ferrán. *Bajo el signo de las sombras.* Madrid: Filmoteca Española, 1984.

Alonso, Maximiliano. "Entrevista con Carlos Saura." *Joven crítica cinematográfica* 13 (Junio 1968): 7–8.

Althusser, Louis. "Ideology and Ideological State Apparatuses (Notes Towards an Investigation)." In *Lenin and Philosophy and Other Essays,* trans. Ben Brewster. New York and London: Monthly Review Press, 1971. Pp. 127–186.

Alvares, Rosa, and Belen Frias. *El cine como pasión.* Valladolid: Semana Internacional de Cine de Valladolid, 1991.

Amell, Samuel, ed. *Literature, the Arts, and Democracy: Spain in the Eighties.* London and Tortonto: Associated University Presses, 1990.

Anderson, Benedict. *Imagined Communities: Reflections on the Origin and Spread of Nationalism.* London: Verso, 1983.

Aranda, Francisco. *Luis Buñuel: A Critical Biography,* trans. David Robinson. New York: DaCapo Press, 1976.

Arenas, Miguel Angel, Paco Navarro, and Mimmo Cattarenich. "Interview with Pedro Almodóvar." *Ronda Iberia* (September 1990): 62–71.

Arilla Perez, Jesus. "Los retos de las RTV publicas regionales en la Europa de las regiones." In *Las radiotelevisiones en el espacio europeo,* ed. Enrique Linde Paniagua. Valencia: Ente Público RTVV, 1990. Pp. 247–255.

Armes, Roy. *Third World Filmmaking and the West.* Berkeley, Los Angeles, London: University of California Press, 1987.

Azcona, Rafael. *Otra vuelta en El cochecito.* Logroño: Biblioteca Riojana, 1991.

Baena, Juan Julio. *Temas de cine,* no. 6, "Numero especial dedicado a la pelicula *El cochecito* invitada al Festival de Venecia, 1960," 13–14.

Baker, Peter. "El cochecito." *Films and Filming* (November 1960): 9.

Bakhtin, M. M. *The Dialogic Imagination,* ed. Michael Holquist. Austin: University of Texas Press, 1981.

Balagué, Carlos. "Entrevista con Ricardo Franco." *Dirigido por . . . ,* no. 37 (Octubre 1976): 12–15.

Balmary, Marie. *Psychoanalyzing Psychoanalysis: Freud and the Hidden Fault of the Father.* Baltimore and London: Johns Hopkins University Press, 1982.

Bardem, Juan Antonio. "Informe sobre la situación actual de nuestra cinematografía." *Objetivo,* no. 6 (Junio 1955): 7–8.

Barthes, Roland. "The Rhetoric of the Image." In *Image, Music, Text,* trans. Stephen Heath. New York: The Noonday Press, 1977. Pp. 32–51.

———. *Writing Degree Zero and Elements of Semiology,* trans. Annette Lavers and Colin Smith. Boston: Beacon Press, 1970.

Bartholomew, Gail. "The Development of Carlos Saura." *Journal of the University Film and Video Association* 35, no. 3 (Summer 1983): 15–33.

Bataille, Georges. *Erotism: Death and Sensuality* (1957), trans. Mary Dalwood. San Francisco: City Lights Books, 1986.

———. "Sade." In *Literature and Evil,* trans. Alastair Hamilton. New York and London: Marion Boyars, 1985.

———. *The Trial of Gilles de Rais,* trans. Richard Robinson. Los Angeles: Amok, 1991.

Bazin, André. "An Aesthetic of Reality: Neorealism." In *What Is Cinema?* II, ed. Hugh Gray. Berkeley, Los Angeles, and London: University of California Press, 1972.

———. *El cine de la crueldad de Buñuel a Hitchcock,* trans. into Spanish by Béatrice Meunier de Galipienso. Bilbao: Ediciones Mensajero, 1977.

Belausteguigotias, S. "Luis García Berlanga propone el sistema vigente en Francia como modelo para el futuro cine español." *El país* (7 Junio 1992): 29.

Bernaola, Carmelo. *Evolución de la banda sonora en España*. Madrid: Festival de Cine de Alcalá de Henares, 1986.

Besas, Peter. *Behind the Spanish Lens: Spanish Cinema under Fascism and Democracy*. Denver: Arden Press, 1985.

———. "Catalan Filmmaking, an Industry Apart." *Variety* (September 24, 1990): 78.

———. "Global Report: Spain." *Variety* (September 24, 1990): 45–80.

———. "Olé Showbiz! It's Boomtime." *Variety* (September 24, 1990): 45.

———. "TV Ad Sales Grow 7-fold in 10 Years." *Variety* (September 24, 1990): 58.

Bhabha, Homi K., ed. *Nation and Narration*. London and New York: Routledge, 1990.

Boddy, William. "The New Geopolitical Landscape of Television: Rethinking Program Flows and Cultural Sovereignty." Unpublished paper presented at the Society for Cinema Studies, 1991.

Bondanella, Peter. *Italian Cinema: From Neorealism to the Present*. New York: Ungar, 1983.

Bonet Mojica, Lluís. "La insoportable perversidad de Peter Pan." *La Vanguardia* (25 Enero 1990).

Borau, José Luis. *El caballero d'Arrast*. San Sebastián: Festival Internacional de Cine de San Sebastián, 1990.

———. "A Woman without a Piano, a Book without a Mark." *Quarterly Review of Film and Video* 13, no. 4 (1991): 9–16.

———. "Without Weapons." *Quarterly Review of Film Studies* 8, no. 2 (Spring 1983): 85–90.

Brasó, Enrique. *Carlos Saura: Introdución incompleta*. Madrid: Taller de Ediciones Josefina Betanto, 1974.

Brooks, Peter. *The Melodramatic Imagination: Balzac, Henry James, Melodrama, and the Mode of Excess*. New Haven: Yale University Press, 1976.

Bruno, Giuliana. "Dora Film: Street-walking Around Plato's Cave." Unpublished paper read at the conference, "Feminist Theory and the Question of the Subject," UCLA, Los Angeles, May 17, 1990.

Buñuel, Luis. *El fantasma de la libertad*. Barcelona: Aymá, S.A. Editora, 1974.

———. *My Last Sigh*, trans. Abigail Israel. New York: Vintage Books, 1984.

Burch, Noel. *To the Distant Observer: Form and Meaning in Japanese Cinema*. Berkeley, Los Angeles, and London: University of California Press, 1979.

Buscombe, Ed. "Film History and the Idea of a National Cinema." *Australian Journal of Screen Theory*, 9/10 (1981): 141–153.

Calendoli, Giovanni. "Neorealismo: 1955." *Objetivo,* no. 9 (Septiembre–Octubre 1955): 18–24.

Canavarro, P. M. "Las televisiones regionales en el marco de la 'Television sin fronteras.'" In *Las radiotelevisiones en el espacio europeo,* ed. Enrique Linde Paniagua. Valencia: Ente Público RTVV, 1990. Pp. 239–245.

Cano, José Luis. "Valle-Inclán and Contemporary Spain," trans. José Sánchez. In *Valle-Inclán: Centennial Studies,* ed. Ricardo Gullón. Austin: University of Texas, 1968. Pp. 97–122.

Caparrós-Lera, J. M. *El cine español bajo el regimen de Franco (1936–1975).* Barcelona: Ediciones de la Universitat de Barcelona, 1983.

Caparrós-Lera, J. M., and Rafael de España. *The Spanish Cinema: An Historical Approach.* Madrid: Film Historia, 1987. Published in conjunction with the retrospective on Spanish cinema held at the University of New Mexico, September 1987.

Carr, Raymond. *Modern Spain, 1875–1980.* New York: Oxford University Press, 1980.

Casais, Pedro Fernaud. "Reflexiones sobre la reforma del estatuto de las radiotelevisiones públicas." In *Las radiotelevisiones en el espacio europeo,* ed. Enrique Linde Paniagua. Valencia: Ente Público RTVV, 1990. Pp. 67–81.

Castro, Javier. "20 años de mercado cinematográfico español." *Cineinforme,* special ed., no. 494 (Septiembre 1986): 70–71.

Cela, Camilo José. *The Family of Pascual Duarte,* trans. Anthony Kerrigan. New York: Avon Books, 1966.

"Cine español: De lo particular a lo universal," *Fotogramas y video* (April 1987): 7.

Cine español (1896–1988). Madrid: Ministerio de Cultura, 1989.

Cine español 1988. Madrid: Ministerio de Cultura, 1989.

Cine español 1990. Madrid: Ministerio de Cultura, 1991.

Cobos, Juan. "Spanish Heroism." *Films and Feeling* (November 1960): 9, 41.

Cohen, Lawrence. "More National Bests in the U.S." *Variety* (January 5, 1991): 87.

Cohn, Bernard. "Entretien avec Carlos Saura." *Positif* 110 (Noviembre 1969): 27–33.

"Coloquios internacionales de Venecia sobre el nuevo cine y la 'nouvelle vague'" (originally published in *Schermi*). *Temas de cine,* no. 2 (Marzo–Abril 1960): 22–37.

Cook, David. *A History of Narrative Film.* New York and London: W. W. Norton, 1981; 2d ed., 1990.

Cristobal, Ramiro. "*Vida en sombras:* Recuperada un película 'maldita.'" *Tele Radio* (11–17 Marzo 1985): 17.

"Cultural rectifica y apoya el filme 'El amante bilingüe' con 65 millones," *El país* (11 Junio 1992): 30.

DeLauretis, Teresa. *Alice Doesn't.* Bloomington: Indiana University Press, 1987.

Deleuze, Gilles. *Masochism: An Interpretation of Coldness and Cruelty,* trans. Jean McNeil. New York: George Braziller, 1971.

Deveny, Thomas. "In Search of the Past: The Return of the Exile in Spanish Cinema." Unpublished paper read at a conference, "Politics and Sexuality in New Spanish Cinema," at Clark University, April 1990.

Devereux, George. "Why Oedipus Killed Laius." *International Journal of Psycho-Analysis* 34 (1953): 132–141.

Dickinson, Robert. "The Unbearable Weight of Winning: Garci's Trilogy of Melancholy and the Foreign Language Oscar." *Spectator* 11, no. 2 (Spring 1991): 6–15.

D'Lugo, Marvin. *Carlos Saura: The Practice of Seeing.* Princeton: Princeton University Press, 1991.

———. "Catalán Cinema: Historical Experience and Cinematic Practice." *Quarterly Review of Film and Video* 13, nos. 1–3 (1991): 131–147.

———. "Almodóvar's City of Desire." *Quarterly Review of Film and Video* 13, no. 4 (1991): 47–66.

Doane, Mary Ann. "Film and the Masquerade: Theorising the Female Spectator." *Screen* 23, nos. 3–4 (September–October 1982): 74–87.

———. "The Voice in the Cinema: The Articulation of Body and Space." *Cinema/Sound, Yale French Studies* 60 (1980): 33–50.

Eidsvik, Charles. "Dark Laughter: Buñuel's *Tristana* (1970)." In *Modern European Filmmakers and the Art of Adaptation,* ed. Andrew Horton and Joan Magretta. New York: Frederick Ungar, 1981.

Elsaesser, Thomas. *New German Cinema: A History.* New Brunswick, N.J.: Rutgers University Press, 1989.

———. "Tales of Sound and Fury: Observations on the Family Melodrama." In *Movies and Methods,* II, ed. Bill Nichols. Berkeley, Los Angeles, and London: University of California Press, 1985. Pp. 165–189.

Fernández Santos, Angel. "¿Ante un genocidio cultural?" *El país* (4 Junio 1992): 30.

———. "Resurrección de un bello filme." *El país* (27 Octubre 1990).

Fiddian, Robin W. "The Role and Representation of Women in Two Films by José Luis Borau." In *Essays on Hispanic Themes,* ed. Jennifer Lowe and Philip Swanson. Edinburgh: Dept. of Hispanic Studies, University of Edinburgh, 1989.

Fiddian, Robin W., and Peter W. Evans. *Challenges to Authority: Fiction and Film in Contemporary Spain.* London: Tamesis Books, 1988.

Flores, Félix. "Férnando Trueba, riesgo cuerdo en *El sueño del mono loco.*" *La vanguardia* (20 Enero 1990).

Foucault, Michel. *The Order of Things: An Archaeology of the Human Sciences,* trans. of *Les mots et les choses.* New York: Random House, 1970.

Freud, Sigmund. *The Interpretation of Dreams* (1900). Vols. 4 and 5, *The Standard Edition of the Complete Psychological Works of Sigmund Freud,* ed. James Strachey. London: Hogarth Press and the Institute of Psychoanalysis, 1962.

Frugone, Juan Carlos. *Rafael Azcona: Atrapados por la vida.* Valladolid: International Cinema Week at Valladolid, 1987.

Fuentes, Carlos. "A Glory Seldom Seen: *Spain,* A Nation Recovers Its Open, Democratic Tradition." *Los Angeles Times* (August 3, 1986): V 1.

Galán, Diego. "1950–1961." In *Spanish Cinema, 1896–1983.* Madrid: Ministerio de Cultura, 1986. Pp. 146–167.

Galdós, Benito Pérez. *Doña Perfecta,* trans. Harriet De Onís. Woodbury, N.Y.: Barron's Educational Series, Inc., 1960.

———. *Fortunata and Jacinta: Two Stories of Married Women,* trans. Agnes Moncy Gullón. London and New York: Penguin Books, 1988.

Gallop, Jane. *The Daughter's Seduction: Feminism and Psychoanalysis.* Ithaca: Cornell University Press, 1982.

García Escudero, José María. "Pacifism in the Contemporary Cinema." *Temas de cine,* no. 2 (Marzo y Abril, 1960).

———. *Temas de cine,* nos. 8–9 (Octubre–Noviembre, 1960): 24.

García Lorca, Federico. "Teoría y juego del duende" (Theory and Play of the Duende, 1928). In *From the Havana Lectures,* trans. Stella Rodriguez. Kanathos, 1981. Pp. 59–73.

Garland, David. "A Ms-take in the Making? Transsexualism Post-Franco, Post-Modern, Post-Haste," *Quarterly Review of Film and Video* 13, no. 4 (1991): 95–102.

Genette, Gerard. *Narrative Discourse: An Essay in Method,* trans. Jane E. Lewin. Ithaca: Cornell University Press, 1980.

Giannetti, Louis, and Scott Eyman. *Flashback: A Brief History of Film.* Englewood Cliffs, N.J.: Prentice Hall, 1986.

Gil, Manuel. "'Innocent Victims' in the Works of Valle-Inclán," trans. Douglas Rogers. In *Valle-Inclán: Centennial Studies,* ed. Ricardo Gullón. Austin: University of Texas Press, 1968. Pp. 43–62.

Gilmour, David. "Homage to Catalonia." *New York Review of Books* XXXIX, no. 11 (June 11, 1992): 3–6.

Girard, René. *Violence and the Sacred,* trans. Patrick Gregory. Baltimore and London: Johns Hopkins University Press, 1977.

Gledhill, Christine, ed. *Home Is Where the Heart Is: Studies in Melodrama and the Woman's Film.* London: British Film Institute, 1988.

Gledhill, Christine. "The Melodramatic Field: An Investigation." In *Home Is Where the Heart Is: Studies in Melodrama and the Woman's Film.* London: British Film Institute, 1988. Pp. 5–39.

González Requena, Jesús. "Vida en sombras." *Revista de occidente,* no. 53 (Octubre 1985): 76–91.

Graham, Robert. *Spain: A Nation Coming of Age.* New York: St. Martin's Press, 1984.

Gray, Rockwell. "Spanish Diaspora: A Culture in Exile." *Salmagundi,* nos. 76–77 (Fall 1987–Winter 1988): 53–83.

Guarner, José Luis. "Locos corazones." *La vanguardia* (13 Junio 1990).

———. 30 años de cine en español. Barcelona: Kairos, 1971.

———. "Trueba presenta *El mono loco,* un 'thriller' de engaños e incesto protagonizado por Jeff Goldblum." *La vanguardia* (7 Septiembre 1989).

Gubern, Román. *Cine español en el exilio,* 1936–1939. Barcelona: Editorial Lumen, 1976.

———. "The Civil War: Inquest or Exorcism?" *Quarterly Review of Film and Video* 13, no. 4 (1991): 103–112.

———. *La imagen pornográfica y otras perversiones ópticas.* Madrid: AKAL/ Comunicación, 1989.

———. *Melodrama en el cine español (1930–1960).* Barcelona, 1991.

———. "1930–1936: II Republic." In *Spanish Cinema, 1896–1983.* Madrid: Ministerio de Cultura, 1986. Pp. 32–45.

———. *1936–1939: La guerra de España en la pantalla.* Madrid: Filmoteca Española, 1986.

———. "El nuevo reto audiovisual." *El mundo* (3 Abril 1991).

———. "Teoría del melodrama." In *Mensajes icónicos en la cultura de masas.* Barcelona: Editorial Lumen, 1974.

Gullón, Ricardo. "Reality of the *esperpento*," trans. Miguel González-Guth. In *Valle-Inclán: Centennial Studies,* ed. Ricardo Gullón. Austin: University of Texas Press, 1968. Pp. 125–131.

Hall, Jane. "Network News: An Endangered Species?" *Los Angeles Times* (February 16, 1991): F1.

Hartley, John. "Invisible Fictions: Television Audiences, Paedocracy, Pleasure." In *Television Studies: Textual Analysis,* ed. Gary Burns and Robert J. Thompson. New York: Praeger, 1989. Pp. 223–243.

Hay, James. *Popular Film Culture in Fascist Italy: The Passing of the Rex.* Bloomington: Indiana University Press, 1987.

———. "'Neo-TV' and the Cultural Politics of National Identity," forthcoming in *Channels of Discourse,* 2d ed., ed. Robert Allen.

Heredero, Carlos F. *José Luis Borau: Teoría y práctica de un cineasta.* Madrid: Filmoteca Española, 1990.

———. "*El sol del membrillo,* reinventar la mirada." *Dirigido,* no. 202 (Mayo 1992): 24–27.

Hernández Les, Juan. *El cine de Elías Querejeta, un productor singular.* Bilbao: Ediciones Mensajero, 1986.

Hidalgo, Manuel. *Carlos Saura.* Madrid: Ediciones J.C., 1981.

Higginbotham, Virginia. *Spanish Film under Franco.* Austin: University of Texas Press, 1988.

———. "Spanish Film under Franco: Do not Disturb." In *World Cinema Since 1945,* ed. William Luhr. New York: Ungar, 1987. Pp. 499–513.

Hivnor, Mary. "The Baroque Equation in Spanish Films." *Partisan Review* 17, no. 4 (1990): 616–620.

Hollier, Denis, ed. *The College of Sociology: 1937–1939.* Minneapolis: University of Minnesota Press, 1988.

Hopewell, John. "Art and a Lack of Money": The Crises of the Spanish Film Industry, 1977–1990." *Quarterly Review of Film and Video* 13, no. 4 (1991): 113–122.

———. *Out of the Past: Spanish Cinema after Franco.* London: British Film Institute, 1986.

Ibáñez, José Luis. "Estado actual de la programación de las televisiones públicas y privadas españoles." In *Las radiotelevisiones en el espacio europeo,* ed. Enrique Linde Paniagua. Valencia: Ente Público RTVV, 1990. Pp. 181–217.

Ibarz, Mercè. "Una comèdia del cor que fa 'Boom boom.'" *Diario de Barcelona* (24 Agosto 1989).

Ilie, Paul. *Literature and Inner Exile.* Baltimore: Johns Hopkins University Press, 1980.

Jacobson, Denise Brooks. *Regional Film in the United States: Resistance to Cultural Dominance.* Ph.D. dissertation, University of Southern California, 1989.

Kinder, Marsha. "Carlos Saura: The Political Development of Individual Consciousness." *Film Quarterly* (Spring 1979): 14–25.

———. "The Children of Franco in the New Spanish Cinema," *Quarterly Review of Film Studies* 8, no. 2 (Spring 1983): 57–76.

———. "The Disastrous Escape." In *Contemporary Literary Scene,* II, ed. Frank N. Magill. Englewood Cliffs: Salem Press, 1976.

———. "José Luis Borau *On the Line* of the National/International Interface in the Post-Franco Cinema." *Film Quarterly* (Winter 1986–87): 35–48.

———. "*El Nido.*" *Film Quarterly* 35, no. 1 (Fall 1981): 34–41.

———. "Pleasure and the New Spanish Mentality: A Conversation with Pedro Almodóvar." *Film Quarterly* (Fall 1987): 33–44.

———. "Review of John Hopewell's *Out of the Past: Spanish Cinema after Franco.*" *Film Quarterly* (Spring 1988): 49–51.

———. "Review of Peter Besas' *Behind the Spanish Lens: Spanish Cinema Under Fascism and Democracy.*" *Film Quarterly* (Fall 1986): 30–36.

———. *Spanish Cinema: The Politics of Family and Gender.* Los Angeles: The Spanish Ministry of Culture and the USC School of Cinema-Television, 1989. A catalog for a film series that was organized by Katherine Singer Kovács and Marsha Kinder.

———. "The Subversive Potential of the Pseudo-Iterative." *Film Quarterly* 43, no. 2 (Winter 1989–90): 2–16.

———. "The Tyranny of Convention in *The Phantom of Liberty.*" *Film Quarterly* (Summer 1975): 20–25.

Kinder, Marsha, ed. Special Issue, "Remapping the Post-Franco Cinema." *Quarterly Review of Film and Video* 13, no. 4 (1991).

Kinder, Marsha, and Beverle Houston. *Close-up: A Critical Perspective on Film.* New York: Harcourt Brace Jovanovich, 1972.

Kolker, Robert. *The Altering Eye: Contemporary International Cinema.* New York: Oxford University Press, 1983.

Kovács, Katherine S. "Berlanga Life Size: An Interview with Luis García Berlanga." *Quarterly Review of Film Studies* (Spring 1983): 7–13.

———. "Berlanga Retrospective at U.S.C." *The Spectator* 3, no. 1 (Fall 1983): 1, 9.

———. "Introduction: Background on the New Spanish Cinema." *Quarterly Review of Film Studies* 8, no. 2 (Spring 1983): 1–6.

———. "José Luis Borau Retrospective." *The Spectator* 3, no. 2 (Spring 1984): 1–2.

———. "Pierre Louys and Luis Buñuel: Two Visions of Obscure Objects." *Cinema Journal* XIX, no. 1 (Fall 1979): 86–98; reprinted in *Cinema Examined,* ed. Richard Dyer MacCann and Jack C. Ellis. New York: E. P. Dutton, 1982. Pp. 282–233.

———. "The Plain in Spain: Geography and National Identity in Spanish Cinema." *Quarterly Review of Film and Video* 13, no. 4 (1991): 17–46.

Kovács, Katherine S., ed. Special Issue, "The New Spanish Cinema," *Quarterly Review of Film Studies* 8, no. 2 (Spring 1983).

Kovács, Steven. *From Enchantment to Rage: The Story of Surrealist Cinema.* London and Toronto: Associated University Presses, 1980.

Laclau, Ernesto. *Politics and Ideology in Marxist Theory: Capitalism-Fascism-Populism.* London: Verso Editions, 1979.

Landy, Marcia. *Fascism in Film: The Italian Commercial Cinema, 1931–1943.* Princeton: Princeton University Press, 1986.

Lange, André, and Jean-Luc Renaud. *The Future of the European Audiovisual Industry.* Media Monograph No. 10. Manchester, England: European Institute for the Media, 1989.

Lara, Antonio. "Diez años de cine español." *Revista de occidente,* no. 122–123 (Julio–Agosto 1991): 211–229.

———. "Pesadilla Parisiense: Fernando Trueba ha realizado su filme más ambicioso." *El país* (12 Enero 1990).

Larraz, Emmanuel. *El cine español.* Paris: Masson et Cie, 1973.

———. *Le cinéma espagnol des origenes à nos jours.* Paris: Editions du Cerf, 1986.

Lawrence, Amy. *Echo and Narcissus: Women's Voices in Classical Hollywood Cinema.* Berkeley, Los Angeles, and Oxford: University of California Press, 1991.

Liehm, Mira. *Passion and Defiance: Film in Italy from 1942 to the Present.* Berkeley, Los Angeles, and London: University of California Press, 1984.

Light, Fred. "El moralismo del arte de Goya en el contexto de su época." *Goya y el espíritu de la ilustración.* Madrid: Museo del Prado, 1988. Pp. 89–98.

Linde Paniagua, Enrique, ed. *Las radiotelevisiones en el espacio europeo.* Valencia: Ente Público RTVV, 1990.

Llinás, Francisco. *Directores de fotografía del cine español.* Madrid: Filmoteca Española, 1989.

Llorens, Antonio. *El cine negro español.* Valladolid: Semana de Cine de Valladolid, 1988.

López Echevarrieta, Alberto. *Cine vasco: De ayer a hoy.* Bilbao: Mensajero, 1984.

———. *Cine vasco: ¿Realidad o ficción?* Bilbao: Mensajero, 1982.

Luhr, William, ed. *World Cinema Since 1945.* New York: Ungar, 1987.

"Luis Cuadrado, después del homenaje." *El alcazar* (9 Diciembre 1977): 18.

Maqua, Javier. "*El sueño del mono loco,* la mejor película española." 5 *Cinco Días* (8 Febrero 1990).

Mast, Gerald. *A Short History of the Movies,* 4th ed. New York: Macmillan, 1985; 5th ed., revised by Bruce F. Kawin. New York: Macmillan, 1992.

Maxwell, Rick. "Spatial Eruptions, Global Grids: The Dialectic of Multiculturalism in International Image Markets." Unpublished paper presented at the Society for Cinema Studies, 1991.

McClelland, I. L. *Spanish Drama of Pathos, 1750–1808,* II. Toronto: University of Toronto Press, 1970.

Medialdea, Sara. "Sánchez Silva: 'Escribí el cuento para que los padres lo contasen a sus hijos.'" *Ya* (25 Agosto 1989).

Meisler, Stanley. "Barcelona Blossoms for Games." *Los Angeles Times* (October 13, 1991): A1.

Metz, Christian. *The Imaginary Signifier: Psychoanalysis and the Cinema.* Trans. Ceclia Britton, Annwyl Williams, Ben Brewster, and Alfred Guzzetti. Bloomington: Indiana University Press, 1982.

Miró, Pilar. "Ten Years of Spanish Cinema." In *Literature, the Arts, and Democracy: Spain in the Eighties,* ed. Samuel Amell, trans. Alma Amell. Rutherford, Madison, and Teaneck: Fairleigh Dickinson University Press, 1990. Pp. 38–46.

Molina-Foix, Vicente. *Fotogramas,* no. 1, 703 (December 1984): 82.

———. *New Cinema in Spain.* London: British Film Institute, 1977.

Montalbano, William D, "Catalonia: A Nation within a Country." *Los Angeles Times* (July 14, 1992): 6.

Montero, Manuela. "Goldblum: 'El filme de Trueba me parece misterioso y erótico.'" *El periódico* (14 Enero 1989).

Mora, Carl. *The Mexican Cinema: Reflections of a Society, 1896–1980.* Berkeley, Los Angeles, and London: University of California Press, 1982.

Morley, David, and Kevin Robins. "Spaces of Identity." *Screen* 30, no. 4 (Autumn 1989): 10–34.

Morris, Cyril Brian. *This Loving Darkness.* Oxford, 1980.

Mortimore, Roger. "Buñuel, Sáenz de Heredia, and Filmófono." *Sight and Sound* 44 (Summer 1975): 180–182.

———. "Reporting from Madrid." *Sight and Sound* 49, no. 3 (Summer 1980): 156–158, 188.

Mosse, George L. *Nationalism and Sexuality: Middle-Class Morality and Sexual Norms in Modern Europe.* Madison: University of Wisconsin Press, 1985.

Mulvey, Laura. "The Oedipus Myth: Beyond the Riddles of the Sphinx." In *Visual and Other Pleasures.* Bloomington: Indiana University Press, 1989.

———. "Visual Pleasure and Narrative Cinema." *Screen* 16, no. 3 (1975): 8–18.

Muñoz, Diego. "Audiovisual Español 93 trata de buscar soluciones al declive del cine español." *El país* (2 Junio 1992): 37.

———. "El bumerán de *Boom Boom,* la película consigue reestrenarse en Madrid tras triunfar en los festivales de cine de Venecia y Montreal." *El mundo* (14 Junio 1990).

———. "Los cineastas españoles piden al Gobierno la creación de una ley del audiovisual." *El país* (4 Junio 1992): 30.

———. "Lo importante es la pasión: *El sueño del mono loco.*" *Cine,* La guia de *El mundo* (26 Enero 1990): 7.

———. "Las multinacionales proponen que el cine español sólo se exhiba por televisión." *El país* (3 Junio 1992): 29.

———. "Trueba produce una serie de TVE y espera a Ryan O'Neal para su próxima película." *La vanguardia* (6 Mayo 1988).

Naficy, Hamid. "Cross-cultural Syncretism and Hybridity in Exile." Unpublished paper presented at the Society for Cinema Studies, 1990.

———. "Culture in Exile: Fetishized Iranian TV in the U.S." Unpublished paper presented at the Society for Cinema Studies, 1988.

———. *The Making of Exile Cultures: Iranian Television in Los Angeles.* Minneapolis: University of Minnesota Press, 1993.

Nowell-Smith, Geoffrey. "Minnelli and Melodrama." In *Movies and Methods,* II, ed. Bill Nichols. Berkeley, Los Angeles, and London: University of California Press, 1985. Pp. 190–194.

Orive Riva, Pedro. "Rasgos diferenciales de los comportamientos de las audiencas de las TV regionales." In *Las radiotelevisiones en el espacio europeo,* ed. Enrique Linde Paniagua. Valencia: Ente Público RTVV, 1990. Pp. 165–171.

———. *Europa: Guerra "Audiovisual."* Madrid: Eudema, 1990.

Ortega y Gasset, José. "Sobre el Fascismo" (1927). In *Obras completas,* II. Madrid, Revista de Occidente, 1954.

———. "The Dehumanization of Art." In *Velázquez, Goya and the Dehumanization of Art,* trans. Alexis Brown. New York: W. W. Norton, 1953.

———. "Teoría de Andalucia" (1927). In *Obras Completas,* II. Madrid: Revista de Occidente, 1961.

Packer, Peter. "I.F.G. Dossier: Spanish Cinema Now." *Variety International Film Guide* (1990): 29–65.

Parker, Andrew, Mary Russo, Doris Sommer, and Patricia Yaeger. *Nationalisms and Sexualities,* New York and London: Routledge, 1992.

Payne, Stanley G. *Fascism: Comparison and Definition.* Madison: University of Wisconsin Press, 1980.

———. "Spanish Fascism." *Salmagundi,* nos. 76–77 (Fall 1987–Winter 1988): 101–112.

Pérez Sánchez, Alfonso E. "Introduction." In *Ribera, 1591–1652,* ed. Alfonso E. Pérez Sánchez and Nicola Spinosa. Madrid: Museo del Prado, 1992. Pp. 15–17.

Pérez de Rozas, Emilio. "En vivo y en casa." *El país* (25 Julio 1991).

Pérez Pellon, Javier. "*El mono loco,* de Trueba, no respondió a la espectación creada." *El independiente* (8 Septiembre 1989).

Pineda Novo, Daniel. *Las folklóricos y el cine.* Huelva: Festival de Cine Iberoamericano, 1991.

Ponga, Paula. "Entrevista: Carmen Maura." *Fotogramas y video* XLV, no. 1,786 (Junio 1992): 46–54.

Pozo, Santiago. *La industria del cine en España.* Barcelona: Publicacions i Edicions de la Universitat de Barcelona, 1984.

Puig, Manuel. *Betrayed by Rita Hayworth,* trans. Suzanne Jill Levine. New York: E. P. Dutton, 1971.

Rafat, Ahmad. "Mi próxima película la rodaré en Estados Unidos." *Tiempo* (18 Septiembre 1989): 126.

Reik, Theodor. *Masochism in Modern Man,* trans. Margaret H. Beigel and Gertrud M. Kurth. New York: Farrar & Rinehart, 1941.

Rigol, Antoni, and Jordi Sebastián. "España aislada: *Los últimos de Filipinas* (1945) de Antonio Román." *Film historia* 1, no. 3 (1991): 171–184.

Robinson, David. *History of World Cinema.* New York: Stein and Day, 1981.

Rubio, Teresa. "*Boom boom,* filme Catalan realizado por dos mujeres." *El periódico* (10 Marzo 1989).

———. "Trueba estrena su filme más internacional." *El periódico* (20 Enero 1990).

Sadoul, Georges. *Dictionary of Film Makers,* trans., ed., and updated Peter Morris. Berkeley and Los Angeles: University of California Press, 1972.

Sámano, José. "RTVE niega perder 145 millones diarios desde 1990, como asegura el PP." *El país* (27 Julio 1991).

Sánchez Vidal, Agustín. *Borau.* Zaragoza: Caja de Ahorros de la Inmaculada, 1990.

———. *El cine de Carlos Saura.* Zaragoza: Caja de Ahorros de la Inmaculada, 1988.

———. *El cine de Segundo de Chomón.* Zaragoza: Caja de Ahorras de la Inmaculada, 1992.

———. "Florián Rey y las dos versiones de *La aldea maldita.*" *Artigrama,* no. 4 (1987): 309–324.

———. *José Luis Borau: Una panoramica.* Teruel: Instituto de Estudios Turolenses, 1987.

———. *Lorca, Buñuel y Dali: El enigma sin fin.* Barcelona: Editorial Planeta, 1988.

———. *Luis Buñuel: Obra cinematográfica.* Madrid: Ediciones J.C., 1984.

———. "Una meditación sobre las patrias ('Hay que matar á B,' de José Luis Borau)." *Artigrama,* no. 1 (1984): 359–366.

———. "Segundo de Chomón: Compás de espera para un turolense universal." *Artigrama,* no. 2 (1985): 265–278.

———. *Tres aventuras americanas.* Zaragoza: Diputación General de Aragon, 1990.

Sandro, Paul. *Diversions of Pleasure: Luis Buñuel and the Crises of Desire.* Columbus: Ohio State University Press, 1987.

San Migel, Santiago. "Cuatro notas a *Los golfos.*" *Nuestro cine,* no. 13 (Octubre 1962): 8.

Santos Fontela, César. "1962–1967." In *Spanish Cinema, 1896–1983.* Madrid: Ministerio de Cultura, 1986. Pp. 172–199.

Sanz deSoto, Emilio. "1940–1950." In *Spanish Cinema, 1896–1983.* Madrid: Ministerio de Cultura, 1986. Pp. 102–141.

Saura, Carlos. *Temas de cine,* "Numero especial dedicado al film de Carlos Saura, *Los golfos,*" nos. 8–9 (Octubre–Noviembre, 1960): 6.

Schaffer, Kay. *Women and the Bush: Forces of Desire in the Australian Cultural Tradition.* Cambridge: Cambridge University Press, 1988.

Schwartz, Ronald. *The Great Spanish Films: 1950–1990.* Metuchen, N.J., and London: Scarecrow Press, 1991.

———. *Spanish Film Directors, 1950–1985: 21 Profiles.* Metuchen, N.J.: Scarecrow Press, 1986.

Sergeant, Bernard. *Homosexuality in Greek Myth.* Boston: Beacon Press, 1986.

Shipman, David. *The Story of Cinema: A Complete Narrative History from the Beginnings to the Present.* New York: St. Martin's Press, 1982.

Silverman, Kaja. *The Acoustic Mirror: The Female Voice in Psychoanalysis and Cinema.* Bloomington: Indiana University Press, 1988.

Smith, Paul Julian. *Laws of Desire: Questions of Homosexuality in Spanish Writing and Film 1960–1990.* Oxford: Clarendon Press, 1992.

Sophocles. *Oedipus the King.* In *Greek Tragedies,* I, ed. David Grene and Richmond Lattimore. Chicago and London: University of Chicago Press, 1942.

Spanish Cinema, 1896–1983. Madrid: Ministerio de Cultura, 1986.

Stam, Robert. *Subversive Pleasures: Bakhtin, Cultural Criticism and Film.* Baltimore and London: Johns Hopkins University Press, 1989.

Stoekl, Allan. *Politics, Writing, Mutilation: The Case of Bataille, Blanchot, Roussel, Leiris, and Ponge.* Minneapolis: University of Minnesota Press, 1985.

Studlar, Gaylyn. "Masochism and the Perverse Pleasures of the Cinema." In *Movies and Methods,* II, ed. Bill Nichols. Berkeley, Los Angeles, and London: University of California Press, 1985. Pp. 602–621.

Suleiman, Susan. "Freedom and Necessity: Narrative Structure in 'The Phantom of Liberty.'" *Quarterly Review of Film Studies* 3 (Summer 1978): 277–295.

———. *Subversive Intent: Gender, Politics, and the Avant-Garde.* Cambridge: Harvard University Press, 1990.

"A Survey of Spain: After the Fiesta." *The Economist* 323, no. 7756 (April 25–May 1, 1992): 1–24.

Theweleit, Klaus. *Male Fantasies,* Vol. 1: *women floods bodies history,* trans. Stephen Conway. Minneapolis: University of Minnesota Press, 1987.

Todorov, Tzvetan. *The Conquest of America: The Question of the Other,* trans. Richard Howard. New York: Harper & Row, 1984.

Torres, Augusto M. "1896–1929." In *Spanish Cinema, 1896–1983,* ed. Augusto M. Torres. Madrid: Ministerio de Cultura, 1986. Pp. 16–27.

Torres, Augusto M., ed. *Spanish Cinema, 1896–1983.* Madrid: Ministerio de Cultura, 1986.

Tubau, Iván. *Crítica cinematográfica española: Bazin contra Aristarco, la gran controversia de los años sesenta.* Barcelona: Publications Edicions Universitat de Barcelona, 1983.

Tubella, Inma. "Televisión regional: La confusión de un término." In *Las radiotelevisiones en el espacio europeo,* ed. Enrique Linde Paniagua. Valencia: Ente Público RTVV, 1990. Pp. 149–155.

Unamuno, Miguel de. "Agony." In *The Agony of Christianity and Essays on Faith,* trans. Anthony Kerrigan. Princeton: Princeton University Press, 1974.

———. "The Spanish Christ." In *Perplexities and Paradoxes,* trans. Stuart Gross. New York: Greenwood Press, 1968.

———. "The Virility of Faith." In *The Agony of Christianity and Essays on Faith,* trans. Anthony Kerrigan. Princeton: Princeton University Press, 1974.

Unsain, José María. *El cine y los vascos.* San Sebastián: Filmoteca Vasca, 1985.

Valleau, Marjorie A. *The Spanish Civil War in American and European Films.* Ann Arbor: UMI Research Press, 1982.

Vernon, Kathleen M. "La politique des auteurs: Narrative Point of View in *Pascual Duarte,* Novel and Film." *Hispania* 72, no. 1 (March 1989): 87–96.

———. "Re-viewing the Spanish Civil War: Franco's Film *Raza.*" *Film and History* 16, no. 2 (1986): 26–34.

———. "Melodrama Against Itself: Pedro Almodóvar's *What Have I Done to Deserve This?*" *Film Quarterly* 46, no. 3 (Spring 1993): 28–40.

Vicente G. Santamaría, José. "José Luis Borau: El síndrome de 'Furtivos.'" *Contracampo,* no. 8 (Enero 1980): 6–7.

Vidal, Nuria. *The Films of Pedro Almodóvar.* Madrid: Ministerio de Cultura, 1988.

Villegas Lopez, Manuel. "En la ruta del humor español." *Temas de cine,* "Numero especial dedicado a la película *El cochecito* invitada al Festival de Venecia, 1960," no. 6.

Wagner, Jon. "The Mother as Spectacle: Cinema under the Sign of Erasure." *The Spectator* 8, no. 1 (Winter 1987): 12–17.

Williams, Linda. *Figures of Desire: A Theory and Analysis of Surrealist Film.* Champaign/Urbana: University of Illinois, 1981.

Woodward, Kenneth L. "Saint Isabella? Not so Fast." *Newsweek* (April 15, 1991): 67.

Zimmermann, Peter. "Las TV regionales en Europa." In *Las radiotelevisiones en el espacio europeo,* ed. Enrique Linde Paniagua. Valencia: Ente Público RTVV, 1990. Pp. 139–147.

Designer:	Steve Renick
Compositor:	Braun-Brumfield, Inc.
Text:	Garamond
Display:	M. Gill Sans
Printer:	Braun-Brumfield, Inc.
Binder:	Braun-Brumfield, Inc.